American Society of Interior Designers

PROFESSIONAL PRACTICE MANUAL

ASID

American Society of Interior Designers

PROFESSIONAL PRACTICE MANUAL

EDITED BY JO ANN ASHER THOMPSON
for the American Society of Interior Designers

WHITNEY LIBRARY OF DESIGN
an imprint of Watson-Guptill Publications/New York

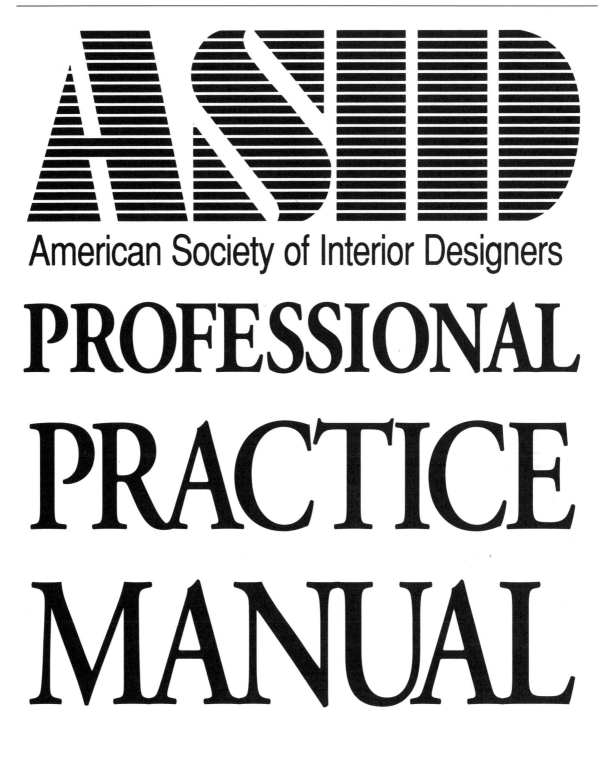

First published in 1992 in the United States by
Whitney Library of Design,
an imprint of Watson-Guptill Publications,
a division of BPI Communications, Inc.,
1515 Broadway, New York, N.Y. 10036.

ASID professional practice manual / edited by Jo Ann Asher
Thompson for the American Society of Interior Designers.
p. cm.
Includes bibliographical references and index.
ISBN 0-8230-0371-X
1. Interior decoration firms—United States—
Management—Handbooks, manuals, etc. I. Thompson,
Jo Ann Asher, 1948-
II. American Society of Interior Designers.
NK2116.A85 1992
729'.068—dc20 92-4917
CIP

Distributed in Europe, the Far East, Southeast and Central
Asia, and South America by RotoVision S.A., 9 Route
Suisse, CH-1295 Mies, Switzerland.

Manufactured in the United States of America
First printing, 1992

2 3 4 5 6 7 8 9 10/96 95 94 93

For my husband, Bruce, and my children, Jessica and Tyler, whose support, patience, and understanding made the completion of this project possible;

with thanks to all the authors who selflessly contributed their time and expertise toward the continued understanding and advancement of the interior design profession;

and with special thanks to the American Society of Interior Designers, whose administration provided the vision and financial support necessary to bring this project to fruition.

Contents

PREFACE AND ACKNOWLEDGMENTS 8

I. THE PROFESSION **9**

PHILOSOPHICAL FRAMEWORK Kerwin Kettler 10

PHILOSOPHICAL FRAMEWORK Norman DeHaan 12

PHILOSOPHICAL FRAMEWORK Arnold Friedmann 14

DESIGN AND HUMAN ECOLOGY Ronald Beckman 17

SPACE, MEMORY, AND VISUALIZATION Catherine Bicknell 19

THE PAST AS PROLOGUE: ASID FROM 1931 TO 1981, AND THE PROFESSION NOW Olga Gueft 21

RELATIONSHIP TO ALLIED PROFESSIONS Stanley Abercrombie 26

EDUCATION Ronald M. Veitch 27

PROFESSIONAL INTERNSHIP Dianne R. Jackman 30

TESTING Louis Tregre 35

NCIDQ INFORMATION HANDOUTS National Council for Interior Design Qualification 37

LICENSING Elizabeth Castleman 44

CONTINUING EDUCATION Odette Lueck and Daniel Webster 45

DESIGN RESEARCH Jo Ann Asher Thompson 47

II. THE PRACTICE **51**

PROFESSIONAL ETHICS Carl E. Clark and Roger L. Greenlaw 52

PROFESSIONAL PRACTICE CHOICES: OVERVIEW OF THE PROFESSION Joyce Burke-Jones 55

GUIDELINES FOR STARTING A PRACTICE Diane B. Worth 59

STRATEGIC PLANNING AND MANAGEMENT Martha G. Rayle and Sandra H. Sober 73

BUSINESS MANAGEMENT Charles Gandy 85

FINANCIAL MANAGEMENT Harry Siegel and Steven L. Sacks 87

LEGAL MANAGEMENT Alan M. Siegel and Jerrold M. Sonet 92

INSURANCE Patricia V. Conley 99

INFORMATION MANAGEMENT: RESOURCES Catherine von der Hude 101

INFORMATION MANAGEMENT: COMPUTERS David H. Swain 103

INDUSTRY RELATIONS Norman Polsky 106

III. THE PROJECT **109**
PROJECT CONTROL BOOK Sheila Danko 110

IV. SPECIALTY DESIGN AREAS **167**
RESIDENTIAL DESIGN Jack Lowery 168
OFFICE DESIGN Peter B. Brandt 172
HEALTH CARE DESIGN Jain Malkin 176
HEALTH CARE DESIGN Jim Seeks 178
HOSPITALITY DESIGN Trisha Wilson 185
HISTORIC PRESERVATION AND REHABILITATION Josette Rabun and Robert Meden 189
RETAIL STORE DESIGN Charlene Nelson-Penski 199
RETAIL STORE DESIGN Barbara Ebstein 203
GOVERNMENT DESIGN Mary Knopf 205
FACILITIES MANAGEMENT Robert Lee Wolf 213
SPORTS FACILITY DESIGN Doug Stead 215

NOTES AND BIBLIOGRAPHY 219
AUTHORS' BIOGRAPHICAL SKETCHES 222
INDEX 223

Preface and Acknowledgments

The purpose of the *ASID Professional Practice Manual* is twofold. First, the overarching goal of this manual is to elevate the profession of interior design by providing a comprehensive framework that will improve the knowledge base of the discipline. A second goal is to provide a "user-friendly" guide that will enhance the competencies of practitioners, educators, and students of interior design.

The *ASID Professional Practice Manual* has been designed to knit together identities, definitions, and supporting information in a concise package. Specifically, the manual identifies areas of practice within the interior design profession, specifies the skills and abilities required for competency in the provision of professional services to clients, and provides core information that will expand the knowledge base of the profession. Through the contributions of articles from many authors with interior design backgrounds as diverse as practitioners, educators, historians, and publishers, the manual provides a focal point for defining the what, when, where, why, and how of interior design as a profession. In total, the manual serves to reconfirm and validate interior design as a separate, emerging profession.

Support and guidance for the preparation of this book came from many sources. The idea for such a manual began with ASID in 1979, and the concept has evolved and changed as the profession has grown and matured. The continued support of Mr. Robert H. Angle, Executive Director, ASID, has been instrumental to the completion of the manual. Mr. Bill Fellenberg, former Director of Communications, ASID, provided guidance and stability as the manual progressed. Charles D. Gandy, Sheila Danko, Kerwin Kettler, and Alan M. Siegel, members of the Advisory Committee for the manual, willingly contributed their time and expertise to developing the topical outline—in addition to writing strategic sections of the manual.

It is important to recognize and thank once again each of the authors who contributed a section to this manual. In every instance the author or authors voluntarily contributed their expertise. When approached with a request to write a specific piece, all the authors enthusiastically accepted the responsibility and expressed pleasure in the opportunity to contribute to the growth and recognition of the profession of interior design.

Last but not not least, I thank Kathleen Rei for her assistance in the final preparations of the manuscripts for submittal to the publisher. Without her efficient and professional assistance, the editorial process would have been much more difficult to complete.

JO ANN ASHER THOMPSON

I. THE PROFESSION

Philosophical Framework

KERWIN KETTLER

Over the past nineteen decades, and throughout the industrialized areas of our world, the activity known as work has been revolutionized. Compared with ancient, medieval, and early modern industrial systems of sustaining life such as hunting, fishing, gathering, and working the land, the shift to the modern concept of "profession" is a radical one.

THE MODERN CONCEPT OF A PROFESSION

The late twentieth-century definition of a profession, which includes occupations such as doctors, lawyers, architects, accountants, interior designers, nurses, and dentists, has been centuries in the making. This concept of a profession has developed around the idea of exchanging knowledge, experience, and expertise for money—the universal currency in open markets. According to sociologists, this system of professions is characterized by the following important features:

1. Education

New members are socialized through a formal educational process to ensure that they are capable of performing quality work and that they behave according to the ethical standards of the group. Admissions requirements in professional schools, examinations, grades, and evaluations create standards for entry into the profession.

2. Legal Recognition

Through state licensing, registration procedures, and national certification programs, formal recognition can be attained by an occupational group. Skills required to perform the service must be complex enough for entry requirements to be met. Although important, legal recognition is usually last in a long process. Sociologists who focus on the development of professions emphasize that professions today receive their strength and power through a long process of negotiation with the society. Throughout this process, occupational groups seek to capitalize on social needs, organize knowledge relevant to those needs, develop clearly marketable solutions, identify markets for their work, and—in rare and highly successful cases—capture *exclusive* rights to service those markets.

An occupational group moving toward professional status must be grounded in a strong knowledge base that focuses on a specialized expertise. For this reason, it is impossible to separate knowledge and educational institutions from the modern concept of profession. Viewed from this orientation, the institutions expand, protect, and support the knowledge associated with each profession.

COMMONALITIES IN THE MATURATION OF A PROFESSION

Since the development of the modern concept of profession there are few that have been untouched by formal study. Studies have shown certain commonalities in the professions' growth and maturation process. These commonalities include the following:

1. Social Organizations Develop

Strong national organizations develop to govern the members and seek social control of the domain of knowledge and work activity.

2. The Core Task of the Occupation Is Redefined

In the process of redefining the occupational activity, work is often adjusted to avoid overlapping with other current occupations. For example, a comparison between the professions of architecture and civil engineers revealed a similarity of function that confused the public. This confusion led each group to move in strong, independent directions, with the architects emphasizing the visual and humanistic aspects of building and civil engineers focusing on the mechanical arts.

3. Restriction of Membership Is Sought

By restricting membership, the organization protects its clients from incompetent practices while maintaining its professional values and standards. Although membership restriction in professional societies does not prevent nonmembers from practicing, the public and clientele are made aware of competency levels of practitioners. For example, the NCIDQ exam has been accepted as a prerequisite to professional membership in many interior design organizations. Although this exam is not yet a universal legal requirement to practice interior design, it is a clear signal to the public of competency standards for the profession.

4. Conflicts Develop with Old-timers

Any attempts to upgrade the nature of the work in a profession, through education and/or membership restriction, leave some practitioners feeling as though they're being defined out of the system, or in other words, redefined as incompetent.

5. Conflict with Neighboring Occupations Arises

It is common for charges of encroachment to be brought against the new specialization, especially if its domain of knowledge, expertise, and service overlaps—even partially—with older, more developed occupational groups. Numerous examples of such conflict exist, including doctors/chiropractors, doctors/psychologists/ sociologists, architects/engineers, and architects/landscape architects—to name only a few.

6. A Code of Ethics is Developed

Members devise social rules for governing those who use the professional title and perform the professional service. There is an attempt to keep providers "in line" so that clients can count on consistent behavior from one professional to another, and to disassociate from poor providers who can destroy client/professional trust.

7. Legal Recognition Is Sought

As mentioned earlier, one of the last steps in the maturation process of a profession is an attempt to make the organizational membership restriction part of the law.

INTERIOR DESIGN AS A PROFESSION

All of design has been molded and woven into the fabric of this complex and highly structured world of professions and business enterprises. There are legal codes and other legal requirements through federal and state intervention; there are professional codes and responsibilities dictating certain forms of appropriate professional behavior; and there are ethical business practices. All these are required to survive within this system. These *local conditions* are formidable and must be understood. These are important—yet recent—issues in our world, having occurred only within the last two centuries as the modern concept of profession has developed and interfaced with our capitalistic structures. Further, the local conditions that are most relative to interior design have developed only since World War II. This essential focus on legal requirements and codes makes designing in today's world workable.

It is easy to become distracted from the essential purpose of our work by the complex business context in which the designer functions. Daily demands involving budgets, suppressed economic conditions, intricate discount rates, union contracts, work schedules, critical material specifications, construction details, client relations, contracts, fees, education, and the ultimate need for advanced knowledge dominate each day for most practitioners. It must always be kept in mind that while the mechanics are critical, the product of our work is the essential source of inspiration.

CONCLUSION

Stand and look about you. Go out, look around, up, down. Grasp the full dimension of the physical world. It is indeed important to us, the inhabitants. When we search back in time for some contrast to our current physical world, we find tree houses, caves, and huts. This basic need for shelter is still at work. In the essence of building, little has changed since ancient times. We only *think* change has occurred in a new age; and a new frame of mind; with a dramatically different language; fueled by new, conceptual, energetic ideas.

This essential purpose of design, when unencumbered by the distractions of our late-twentieth-century world, is embodied in the ASID philosophy: Interior design is dedicated to "advancing the quality of life through meaningful inhabitation." This principle endures when stripped of the current problems that are locally defined by time, economics, the social institutions of professions, legal constraints, and legal recognition. Stranded on an island, without the materials, construction systems, and symbolic and visual trappings of a sophisticated "society," people simply *inhabit*. It is not a discretionary act of life. Designers minister to this primary need and serve an essential function.

Philosophical Framework

NORMAN DEHAAN

My philosophy of design involves my philosophy of life. Because I believe it is a result of the personal interplay of ideas, agents, and cultural context, some personal background is essential.

My thoughts are the result of several readings of Bertrand Russell's *A History of Western Philosophy* during World War II, honed by *The Great Ideas of Western Man* series of Container Corporation of America advertisements, followed by fitful attacks on The Great Books and some of Mortimer Adler's writings. In addition to Mies Van der Rohe's teachings, (which also included his reading list of books starting with the *Iliad* and the *Odyssey*), there was the inspired teaching of our English professor S. I. Hayakawa, who wrote *Language in Action.* To this must be added an education in the 1940-1950 decade when schools of architecture instilled the idealistic belief that design should, and would, bring about a social change for the better. Illinois Institute of Technology (ITT) conditioned its students to be of service to society and to believe in what I've dubbed "the hairshirt school of design," that is, if you went out and made a lot of money you were not doing anything good for society.

The belief that one's role in society and within the profession is one of utility leaves many of us on the far side of an undeniably popular shift in our culture. This is what Russell Lewis, in discussing the growth of our consumer society, calls "the shift from the Protestant ethos of salvation through self-denial to gospel of the therapeutic release stressing self-realization in this world."

World War II and the Korean conflict fortuitously tempered my idealism, and left me with a fear of absolutism in any form and a great respect for relativism. Politically this was abetted by the writings of Alexander Herzen in *From the Other Shore*, and my friend Richard Hertz's *Man on a Rock.* Spiritually the latter book also deals with how an individual can grow although surrounded by circumstantial obstacles. Here and in his later book *Chance and Symbol*, he explores creativity and "exposition of the process by which inanimate nature transcends itself and rises from the world of chance, where the law of statistical average rules, to that of art, where spiritual intention is sovereign."

Philosophically this obviously places me in the school of critical impulse, for what philosophy I have is analytic. I start with the whole, and then divide and concentrate on the parts of the whole for clarity and precision. Ironically, in practice, I believe my clients perceive my work as the exact opposite: one of speculative impulse wherein one starts with the parts to embrace the whole for unity and completeness.

My design philosophy is conditioned by my firm conviction that interior design is a profession of service to the public, as are architecture and industrial design. This excludes design that is undertaken as a personal creative effort without regard for the suitability of materials and use. The interior design, architecture, and industrial design professions are defined by the fact that they solve a client's problem. Without the problem, even a hypothetical one, there is no creative impetus. I believe that, unlike the fine arts, interior design, architecture, and industrial design have pragmatic problem solving as an objective base. And, unlike architecture and industrial design, interior design has a further constraint: It occurs inside a building shell that normally has been created by others.

Interior design may be a utility as well as a commodity—but this is not always a popular position. It means that once the objective goal, the problem, has been solved, the solution becomes subjectively appraised. Any pleasure derived as a result of this subjective creativity is what lends an interior its distinctive identity. And whether the two phases, objective and subjective, occur sequentially or simultaneously is not as important as the recognition of the fact that both exist.

An appreciation of interior design is very much dependent on the level of design awareness of the viewer, which varies widely in our society. Ralph Caplan, in *Postwar America Design and Its Cultural Ramifications*, correctly perceives: "The efforts of increased design awareness have generally been concentrated on something perceived as *good design* rather than on the awareness of design as a process that acts for better or worse through all our lives. Design begins with a need, and what makes it appropriate to an art museum is that it uses the resources of art in responding to that need. But museums as a rule view design as consisting of those artifacts—sometimes classified as decorative arts—that are not unlike the ones museums have always collected and displayed."

This is not to say that an individual work of art, as an abstract art object, cannot also be a successful design, be it an interior, a building, or a product. That success is happenstance, however, for it supplements an entirely different goal arrived at through a different creative process.

What art and design have in common is imagination, an indispensable gift. W. Duff, in his 1769 *An Essay on Original Genius and its Various Modes of Exertion in Philosophy and the Fine Arts*,[1] defines it as: "Imagination—that faculty whereby the mind not only reflects on its own operations, but which assembles the various ideas conveyed to the understanding by the canal of sensation, and treasured up in the repository of the memory, compounding and disjoining them at pleasure; and which by its plastic power of inventing new associations of ideas and of combining them with infinite variety is enabled to present a creation of its own, and to exhibit scenes and objects which never existed in nature."

This conviction that design is relative and inductive—and that it defers to history and experience—eliminates all color systems and golden means as rules and reinstates them as mere tools in the design process. Design by the rules is not creative; it is a stale, rote, two-dimensional process. One must have an intuitive sense of design and visualize in three dimensions.

I also believe it is handy to have a sense of humor. To paraphrase Cornelia Congor, the dowager designer of Chicago, humor is essential. Without it, ill will flourishes, and there is already enough unpleasant design in the world. Most clients would agree. To this I would add the necessity for a modicum of stoicism, as noted in *Encyclopedia Britannica, Macropaedia 14*, "to give consolation, composure, and fortitude in times of trouble" to a proud man living a virtuous life.

Philosophical Framework

ARNOLD FRIEDMANN

A philosophical framework for interior design starts with a definition that sets the profession within the context of our culture. There are many who define this field as a business—and indeed parts of the field are just that. There are those who define the field as a form of art, and as an integral part of the built environment. Others define it as a part of other fields that are concerned with the shaping of the human environment. Clearly, the best definition is that interior design is a profession. If one wishes to attach further labels, the term of social art is appropriate—particularly in an age when laws, rules and regulations, and indeed professional liability have brought the field beyond its origins of interior decoration, where it was until the middle of the twentieth century.

Interior design is a significant aspect of our culture, a culture that embodies changing conventions and constraints. It is within this ever-changing domain that the profession of interior design functions. Designers acquire a background and a perspective that involves not only the liberal arts and humanities, but the history of art, architecture, and design—a wide perspective that requires an understanding of the history of ideas and major themes of philosophy, and an understanding of criticism as it pertains to design. Whether young graduates are aware of it or not, much of what pertains to the design field is connected to thought processes developed by early thinkers such as Plato and Aristotle. Chances are that interior designers routinely draw upon the thinking of Giedion, Norberg-Schulz, and Christopher Alexander. It is not the specific acquaintance with these and other thinkers that matters. Rather, what matters is that interior designers conceptually understand design and architecture in a broader sense as they relate to interior environments.

Like its allied profession of architecture, interior design most often forces the practitioner to be concerned with "nuts and bolts" and "the bottom line." Such a profession must look from time to time at its basic goals and ideas. A thorough study and discussion of history, theory, and philosophy is not required or expected. However, an awareness of issues that go beyond the daily office routine is one of the underlying requirements for serious professional interior design.

THEORY OF PRACTICE

A philosophical framework for interior design must be predicated upon a theory of design. Such a theory consists of several sequential factors that result in the design process and ultimately in the completed space or project. Ideally, this sequence starts with the gathering of data, research, and the development of a program; one can call this phase *intelligence*. The next step is *design*, which consists of sketching alternate solutions. The designer, with the client, then makes the *choice* by selecting the best alternative. The next step is *implementation*, consisting of the production of working drawings, details, specifications, contracting, and construction. The final step is one that is rarely done in a formal or organized manner, yet is an essential nevertheless. This step, *evaluation*, involves a structured appraisal of the design process and a close look at the building or space as it is being used by the occupants.

These five steps result in a theory of design for the future, which in simple terms might be the next project. Evaluation should result in corrections and modifications of completed projects. The completion of this process creates a closed loop, where the theory of design and the correction and modification of errors feeds back into research and development for future projects. This circular process can be looked at as a creative phase for the first three steps (intelligence, design, choice), followed by supervision or implementation and, lastly, evaluation. This theory of design might more appropriately be called a theory of practice since it is a paradigm leading to an actual project.

Theory of Practice Case Study

Some of the concepts just discussed are best illustrated through an example from my professional and personal experiences. I have purposely chosen an unusual example. In this project, my role was one of researcher, which made it possible for me to observe the process and impact of design in an objective way.

I served as a principal investigator for a major research study sponsored by the Department of Health, Education and Welfare to observe and evaluate the effect of the living environment on the institutionalized mentally retarded. My role was to gather data. The study was done in a major Massachusetts State institution that was mandated by a court action to improve the residents' environment. The observational study was designed to monitor groups of residents before and after renovations in the same environments. Precise methods of observation were utilized to establish valid results. I and the other designers involved in the project were confident that providing a better interior environment would, by itself, have beneficial results upon the behavior of residents.

To simplify a four-year study in a few words—it turned out not to be true. During the process of observation, design changes, and experimentation with the designed environment, it was found that although the environment can support behavior, it cannot cause it. Institutional programs, the attitude of staff members, and a variety of other factors have as much influence upon the behavior of the participants as newly created spaces. The summary findings of the study conclude that the *opportunity for control* is the most significant factor in changing the residents' behavior. This includes such elements as locks on doors, privacy, the ability to turn light switches on and off, and doors on bathroom stalls. What we (designers and behavioral scientists who were a part of the team) had assumed as significant factors—private rooms, double or triple rooms instead of wards—turned out to be of less importance.

One would expect that this important research study would positively impact the project by providing significant information; that is, the intelligence component in a theory of design practice. One would further expect to be able to move with relative ease to the next phase in this theory of practice to design and choice. Unfortunately, the real world can create havoc in a logical process. In this case, because deadlines were set by the State Court to provide "home-like environments," a local architectural firm was commissioned to make changes without being given time for the research to be completed or for a proper program to be developed. Subsequently, when federal regulations mandated even more changes, research and thoughtful design were deemed wasteful by administrators of the institution. As a result, there were cases when new construction was going on while another firm was already engaged in the preparation of working drawings for the demolition of construction.

Good design and thoughtful, creative solutions were limited because these were considered by the institutional administrators to be an unnecessary luxury and too time-consuming an investment. As a result, the spaces provided and the interior components specified were not only nonfunctional, but ugly. An additional complication in this project was that throughout the four-year study, we were not permitted to consult our clients: the residents. For a number of reasons—some legal, some simply based on history, and some on absurdity—residents were not asked about their needs and expectations. This essential component—the designer/client interaction and choice phase—was missing from the process.

In the implementation phase of this project another problem resulted. Contracts were given out on the basis of speed and expediency. Incredibly costly mistakes were made because state building codes were the paramount, and only, guidelines.

The fact that a multimillion-dollar interior renovation project was undertaken without attention to the appropriate phases in a theory for interior design practice caused costly mistakes and an interior environment that still does not meet the physical and psychological needs of the residents.

FORMAL THEORY OF INTERIOR DESIGN

A more formal, less applied, theory of interior design is represented by the following elements:

- History
- Environment/behavior issues
- Function (solving problems)
- Criticism
- Aesthetics

History in this connection needs to be historiography and must concern itself with analysis that leads to theoretical constructs and not simply an amassing of facts and dates. Environment/behavior, a field of study that started in the early 1960s, has become an accepted and recognized branch of psychology through the use of research methodologies developed by psychologists, combined with naturalistic observations used by sociologists.

Many designers look to the *environment/ behavior* field of study to provide answers to questions of design; however, answers are not necessarily the goal or the result of scientific inquires. Scientists, including behavior scientists, are concerned with analysis, that is, taking apart a problem. Designers, on the other hand, are concerned with synthesis—with putting things together, with solutions. What has resulted from the field of environmental psychology is an awareness of the needs of the ultimate consumer of design. For designers, it means a way of asking questions and attempting to create spaces or designs that satisfy the needs of the users, rather than those of the editors of glossy design publications.

Although *function* has become a somewhat dated term (since it was the backbone of modernism, and modernism is no longer the prevailing dogma in interior design and architecture), it is still important to recognize that design is concerned with the solution of problems. Any space created by interior designers, from a residence to a complex retail store or corporate facility, must "work." Unless a space is created as a purely symbolic statement or as a display, it always must solve a problem for a specified purpose. This can be referred to as the teleology inherent in the process of design. Added to this is the ongoing development of technological innovations of which practitioners must be constantly aware.

Traditionally, *criticism* is a major component in a formal theory of design, but in the field of interior design it is the component most sadly neglected and frequently missing. Creative fields such as literature, art, theater, architecture, and dance include extensive criticism, but not so interior design. There are at this time approximately twenty newspapers in the United States employing full-time architectural critics, yet not one has a staff member writing interior design criticism. Occasionally an architectural critic will discuss some important interior aspects; or certain design periodicals will offer criticism. However, most of the time magazines publish articles with extensive descriptions, implying enthusiastic editorial approval, but not a critical word.

Criticism need not be negative, but even negative criticism presented on an objective level is important to serious interior designers. It is even more important to the public. Some newspapers feature interiors on their real estate, home, or women's pages, but all too often these featured interiors are an embarrassment to the profession. Hence the introduction of more interior design criticism as a regular feature in newspapers, as well as periodicals, will do much towards the enhancement of the profession and foster a better understanding of the field by the public. Criticism helps shape an ongoing theory and philosophy of Interior design.

Aesthetics also play an in important role in interior design. If all the elements fall into place logically, the project in question should be a satisfying one aesthetically. In recent years, aesthetics and beauty have become somewhat suspect terms. For a number of years, architects—more so than interior designers—have almost consciously avoided the creation of "beautiful" buildings or spaces. They were concerned solely with creating buildings that work, that are contextual, and that satisfy the needs of the users.

Interior design must be concerned with beauty. It is incumbent upon designers to incorporate aesthetics into a formal theory of design and to create spaces that are aesthetically satisfying. Function alone does not constitute interior design. The concept of beauty must incorporate the appropriate cultural and social climate, the ever-changing fashion trends, and the historic perspective from which one views design.

PROFESSIONALISM AND INTERIOR DESIGN

By its very nature, professionalism implies a superior knowledge of a particular human endeavor. For interior design this superior knowledge often is not acknowledged for two basic reasons: (1) most untrained individuals have an opinion and feel a degree of expertise that would be pretentious in any other specialized profession, and (2) the articulation of such superior knowledge implies a degree of elitism, which is not looked upon favorably in today's society. However, it appears certain that once all requisite research has been done, clients consulted, and alternate solutions and ideas considered, someone must make the final decisions. If that constitutes elitism, so be it.

FUTURE PROJECTIONS FOR INTERIOR DESIGN

On the basis of observations made over the past four decades, there is no doubt that interior design will continue to grow and mature. It has, in the span of one and a half generations, become a respected profession—a far cry from the often amateurish practice of interior decoration in years past.

Our current society is often referred to as the information society, or the postindustrial society. Many fields and professions had to adapt to this new set of needs and expectations. Interior design did not have to make serious adjustments. In fact, it was in some ways a profession at the cutting edge of the postindustrial society; it consisted of offering services rather than products, and the need for the services of interior designers grew rapidly in the years following World War II. One might recognize that postmodernism—one of the fashionable directions in architecture and design of recent years—came more easily and naturally to interior design. Practitioners of interior design have always used historic adaptations and classical design, a direction newly discovered by architects starting in the 1970s.

In practical terms, the role of the interior designer has expanded. Today the subspecialties of interior design have developed into separate professional activities, offering numerous employment opportunities in a period of just a few years. It appears clear that the American public has become more discriminating in its expectations. The level of client sophistication, the quality of shelter publications, and the products manufactured all point toward an increased need for interior design services.

CONCLUSION

In this outline of an interior design philosophical framework, there remains one more question that must be considered. What constitutes success? Here we are talking not just about the success of a particular space or project, but the success (real or imagined) achieved by the practitioner, or more often than not, the success that professionals try to achieve. Is success measured by financial rewards? Is a successful designer one whose work is frequently published? If so, is it more successful to be published in popular shelter magazines or fashionable periodicals, or is publication in professional design periodicals more significant? Is success the acknowledgment by colleagues of superior work and ability, or is it the adulation of the public at large? Success is probably a little of all of these things, but clearly it depends upon each designer to set standards and goals. Critical acclaim, recognition from peers, and a degree of financial reward should constitute universal recognition for the successful interior designer.

Finally, one may note that no distinction was made in this brief discussion between residential and contract interior design. Additionally, specific trends in interior design—be they traditional, modern, neoclassical, or new wave design—were not dwelt upon. In a broad, philosophical sense there is no place for these specific considerations. If the ideas suggested here can be accepted, it follows clearly that the focus of professional interior designers must be the creation of satisfactory and beautiful environments carried out in a professional manner for the benefit of the public.

Design and Human Ecology

RONALD BECKMAN

Interior design is far from an egalitarian art form. Reviews, trade journals, and home design magazines contain articles depicting historically eclectic and overbearingly geometric environments, interspersed with advertisements for the expensive materials and products featured on the editorial pages. As in the fashion apparel magazines, an index lists sources for the purchase of showcased goods, because advertising subsidizes these costly publications. Glossy color photographs show giant corporations where people work in deeply carpeted, deftly furnished offices whose parent companies incorporate fine art programs for tax shelter investments. In some cases, soundless automatic robots deliver the mail to each department by gliding along electronic control tapes in the floor. Private hospitals win design awards for their brightly colored interiors. Stylish shops and malls, schools, museums, government centers, and factories are showcased monthly as paradigms of progress.

Meanwhile, county hospitals, inner-city housing, public schools, railway stations, highway facilities, and the rural and urban places most people inhabit deteriorate and invite crime, disease, and social disorder. Many design professionals shun working in this public domain, seeking instead the freedom to "do their own thing" in the private sector. This freedom of expression requires that the public must tolerate whatever stylistic trends or fads a patron wants and is willing to fund.

The majority of interior design output and a good deal of interior design education is dedicated to the traditional patron/artist arrangement. However, designers can accomplish much that embodies social conscience and public responsibility. It is possible for designers to express the dignity of free individuals existing in tension with a body politic.

As noted by Joseph Esherick, a recognized design educator and professional designer, some buildings seem to be designed to hide the presence of human beings or to divert attention from them. Esherick further notes that the most successful design schools are founded on a humanistic approach and are antielitist. According to Esherick, "Our goal should be work that is liberating, that makes the quality of life better for all."[1]

A design statement of social responsibility should have aesthetic characteristics different from those of customized interior design. Unfortunately, the expression of a collective social conscience has been largely ignored by most interior design professionals and rarely discussed by design critics.

THE CREATION OF WANT

More than 30 years ago, economist John Kenneth Galbraith in his landmark book *The Affluent Society* identified the symptoms of neglect in the American public domain. He claimed that the three persistent social problems threatening the quality of life in the United States are the process of want creation, the adverse effect of economic growth on the environment, and an imbalance between public and private consumption that adversely affects public services. Galbraith called want creation a result of modern advertising. With the production of goods, he said, came the creation of the demand for goods.

Evidence of Galbraith's thesis is abundant. The concern for conservation of natural and human resources is losing the battle with global warming; fouled water, air, and soil; and resource depletion. The "conventional wisdom" (another of Galbraith's terms) defines interior design as a decorative visual art and evaluates its excellence within the bounds of that definition. But an alternative to this practice of formalism is human ecology, which trains interior design students to create with the basic social and psychological needs of people in mind.

This education maintains the balance between private and public requirements, with an appreciation for ecological consideration in the selection of methods and materials, and the evaluation of human needs beyond the singular goal of commercial gain. Design from the viewpoint of human ecology originates from a holistic study of the needs and aspirations of people: individual and collective, social and spiritual, physical and psychological. It addresses the homeless, the elderly, and the disabled as readily as it addresses housing developers.

Students of human ecology are learning that medical spaces can be designed to enhance the individual esteem of patients subjected to the dehumanizing stress of clinical procedures. Students understand that cooperative housing for the elderly will become a major priority of the aging American citizenry. Economically these designs foster patient cooperation and improved health, lowering hospital costs and insurance rates. To create these facilities, designers rely upon the body of information available from the fields of sociology, cultural anthropology, and applied psychology. The practice of facility management continues to grow as design and psychology are used together to improve the quality of life and the productivity of working people.

The social role of interior designers is expanding, and attitudes and values are changing. Historically, practicing artists who were under patronage were obligated to delight and satisfy their solitary sponsors. Dependent painters, actors, musicians, or designers regarded themselves as the "humble servants" of their patrons. Going directly to the public for support was a risky venture.

Today interior designers play a different role, if they will take the initiative to do so. Designers not only serve as advocates for their clients, but can contribute to the preservation of resources and the enhancement of the social consciousness.

Without condemning that which has gone before, designers can direct the profession on a path other than the creation of conspicuous consumption. The challenge is for designers to instill an ecological awareness, making consumers sensitive to the issues of health, safety, ergonomics, and psychological security—an awareness that will generate a fresh and original aesthetic expression. In this way designers can contribute to a balance between private consumption and the public welfare.

Space, Memory, and Visualization

CATHERINE BICKNELL

If designers are to be more than professionals who can carry through a design program with efficiency, they must respond to the challenge of building a personal design philosophy and theory. My own theory of design is based on a concern for the experiencing of space with all the senses, the use of memory and how it is triggered and provoked by the mnemonics of our environment as we perceive it, and the alternative legacies of visual communication of the East and the West.

THE EXPERIENCING OF SPACE

The first visit to a French Gothic cathedral involves the observer in much more than walking into a surprisingly high interior. The articulation of space through the structural elements is extraordinary to view, but it is not the structure and spatial quality alone that make the experience so rich. The iconography in stone, glass, and other materials represents many layers of symbolism that proclaim the cathedral's significance. The acoustics are astounding; voice and music can be heard as if resounding within a stone umbrella in the sky. The natural light can play guide through the day as it moves round the stained-glass windows, picking out significant biblical scenes. If, in addition, the visitor understands the cathedral as a biblical encyclopedia for medieval pilgrims, the experience is even richer.

On a completely different scale, moving through a contemporary space such as the Kimbell Art Museum by Louis Khan in Fort Worth can be equally involving. The horizontally expanding space is strong in character and expression; the detailing is crisp and clean; the materials are carefully chosen and juxtaposed; both daylighting and electric light are handled with imagination and expertise. All the elements of the interior combine to make a richly satisfying spatial experience on a human scale. The interior effectively houses artifacts that engage the mind, and it heightens the observers' interest in their content and meaning.

An element of surprise can also be effective in arousing our senses. To go from the plain brick exterior of the Mausoleum of Galla Placidia in Ravenna to its interior is a revelation to anyone. It appears dark upon entering. It is only as the eyes adjust to the mellow light of the alabaster windows that one becomes aware of being surrounded by the impressive spatial qualities of a barrel-vaulted Greek cross with a dome, whose surfaces are alive with some of the richest mosaics in the world. As in this example, the finished work of an interior designer can evoke, stimulate, involve, and manipulate an observer. It is a marvel that this type of experience can continue even when one is revisiting familiar interiors. Because of human responses to space, we as designers are challenged to broaden our understanding of human perception.

The baroque designers of seventeenth-century Italy and eighteenth-century Germany had the amazing ability to touch all our senses simultaneously. The designs of Borromini, Bernini, and later the Asam brothers were intentionally dramatic and unashamedly manipulative; they integrated structural elements, sculpture, and painting with natural light and acoustics to involve the participant in a theatrical setting. To hear a Bach fugue played in the church of St. John Nepomuk in Munich is to enjoy a sensual feast. But whether it be the interior of a baroque masterpiece or a contemporary interior of your own discovery, the chances are that your experience transcends accurate explanation; words seem inadequate to describe it.

In order to explain the experience of space, twentieth-century authors have tried to extend the five senses identified by Aristotle: sight, sound, smell, touch, and taste. For instance J. J. Gibson in the role of environmental psychologist added the haptic sense as the sense of touch combined with memory. Unlike Aristotle, Gibson defines the senses as perceptual systems capable of obtaining information about objects in the world, in a combination and not just as the original five senses in isolation. Frances Yates, the knowledge historian, in her book *The Art of Memory*[1], speaks about the three-dimensional environment as an intrinsic aid to our intellectual memory. Yates explains this by showing the way in which the ancients in Greece and Rome actually built special proximate environments that were specifically designed to be visually articulate in order to aid orators. These environments were used to memorize verbal ideas. Orators were trained to attach the separate elements of their speeches' ideas to a sequence of visual cues like architraves, doorways, ledges, alcoves, and other details, while walking through an interior. The memory of details would then aid an orator by leading him through the same sequence in his mind.

The art of memory as first used by the Greeks, and later adopted by the Roman orators, is an art that people no longer even practice. There seems no apparent twentieth-century equivalent. Society seems far more reliant on the immediate verbal content of writers, especially those who express society's experiential perceptions.

The twentieth-century philosopher Merleau Ponty in his *Phenomenology of Perception*[2] continued to redefine the original Greek concept of the basic five senses. The expression he gives to all senses is as perceptual systems that rely on the body's own spatiality. By body spatiality he no longer adheres to the geometrical ratios of the Italian Renaissance but rather to a person's own space, orientation, and situation in the world or in an environment. He examined the "body image" as he saw it and explains how any of us can bring only our own perceptual responses, our own history, to anything that we see or do. Through the writings of Merleau Ponty one can understood the individuality that all of us bring to any visual field. The perceptual differences between us give us confidence in our own design ideas. The need to pursue every possible avenue of visual knowledge in order to enrich perceptions then becomes all the more important. If designers have to rely, in the terms of Merleau Ponty, on what we can bring to any given situation, it is their responsibility as individual designers to make that as rich as possible.

USE OF MEMORY

There are certain characteristics of really imaginative designers that I take for granted. These include their endless visual curiosity, their love of reading from sources of inspiration from Vitruvius to *Vogue*, and their capacity to keep memories of environments they admire.

To work with design skills alone without a rich mental tapestry of images and ideas is a sadly dull and empty process that can culminate in an interior design without character and atmosphere. Images are an invaluable part of any designer's vocabulary. The number of times that one needs to make visual comparisons is endless. How can a client tell how rich a designer's visual memory is unless there is an effective way to communicate it? Frequently the designer's challenge is to communicate numerous visual ideas to nonvisual people. For this reason alone, the images have to be strong and clear to us so that the communication shares the same clarity.

Sketching, taking photographs, and many other methods help designers to build a visual bank. A jazz musician once told me that if you are going to keep working, you have to know all the songs; after all, if there's a request that you cannot play, you lose your credibility. Similarly if a client begins describing a museum in Italy by Carlo Scarpa as a design approach that is inspirational, it is disappointing if the designer must scramble for books and cannot respond spontaneously from mental pictures.

OUR WESTERN VISUAL ORIENTATION

In the fifteenth century in Italy, when the illusion of realism was emphasized and perfected through the art of perspective, a tradition was born. It is impressive how strongly Westerners still adhere to this way of seeing and visualizing environments. The perspective method typically shows a scene that only illustrates one event from one point of view. It has clear conventions, demanding that designers see and draw from a strictly frontal viewpoint. The height of eye level is fixed; we know what is up, what is down; there is no ambiguity between foreground, middle distance, and the furthest plane.

In contrast, the Eastern visual examples show multiple events happening at different times and viewpoints. For example, on the Chinese willow pattern plate, the whole story is shown simultaneously. The observers are able to see every part simultaneously, or focus on one part at a time. There are no red arrows showing where to start and where to finish; the separate elements of the story are shown from above, in elevation or in quasi-perspective, all together. The observer is given many choices of interpretation, and time has to be understood as a visual continuum.

To a Western observer this approach is very unfamiliar; Westerners are far more accustomed to visual images that show just one moment, or follow a very clear sequential order. Westerners are so conditioned by the fifteenth century illusion of realism through perspective that when viewing the work of other cultures, they find it hard to assimilate the juxtaposition of time and place. Images with no apparent baseline, no particular orientation, but with superimposition and simultaneity are confusing. It is almost as though Westerners have locked themselves into a way of seeing that precludes easy comprehension of other visual conventions. Eastern examples simply do not look so real to them. Alternative means of representation have become for me one of the richest sources of expression. Awareness of them has assisted me in the process of finding new solutions and to becoming more flexible in visualizing and communicating ideas.

CONCLUSION

Expression of space, use of memory, and visual orientation are three intertwined areas that contribute to the consciousness of the designer; they form a foundation of knowledge and experience from which memorable work can spring. Armed with a personal design philosophy, interior designers can develop solutions to functional problems and in so doing, enrich the lives of their clients.

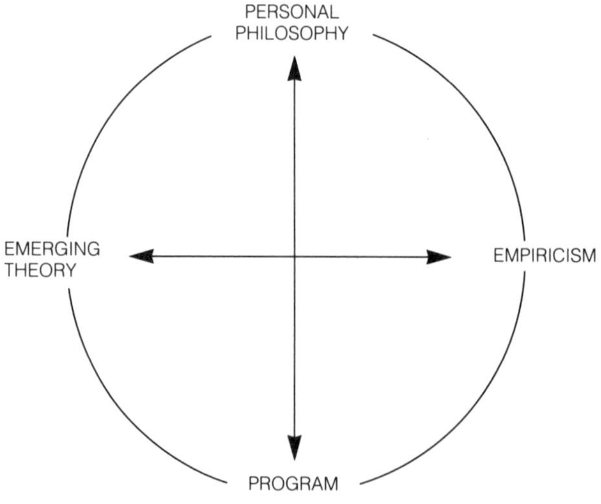

Figure 1. This diagram shows all the elements that need to be considered equally in the design process.

The Past As Prologue: ASID from 1931 to 1981, and the Profession Now

OLGA GUEFT

ASID was founded in Grand Rapids, Michigan, in July 1931 and celebrated its 50th anniversary in the same city. The following article consists of two excerpts: (1) from "The Past as Prologue," a historic overview written for ASID's 1981 Conference, and (2) from the manuscript (copyright © 1985 and 1991, Olga Gueft) of the author's forthcoming history of interior design as a profession.

As a human activity, interior design is older than architecture. As a coherent profession identified by the label *interior design*, it was born yesterday. At the 1931 conference that produced the American Institute of Interior Decorators (AIID), its future first president, William R. Moore, drafted a definition of the profession which, though simpler than the one ASID now uses, is absolutely consistent with it. But because the term interior *designer* was not current at that time, he labeled the interior designer an interior *decorator* and named the society accordingly. He also called *himself* an interior decorator.

Does this matter? Admired interiors have been designed by people who called themselves architects, painters, sculptors, decorators, carpenters, builders, cabinetmakers, antiquarians, stage designers, industrial designers—anything and everything except interior designers. For example, think of Michelangelo, the Brothers Adam, Thomas Jefferson, Charles Le Brun, Dominikus Zimmermann, John Nash, Hector Guimard, Antonio Gaudi, Louis Comfort Tiffany, William Morris, Eugene Emanuel Viollet-le-Duc, J.E. Ruhlmann, Charles Rennie Mackintosh, Frank Lloyd Wright, Le Corbusier, Marcel Breuer, Isamu Noguchi, Alvar Aalto, Syrie Maugham, Norman Bel Geddes, and Elsie de Wolfe.

Does it matter? Is it necessary to perceive interior design as a distinct professional discipline?

An interior—the proximate environment—is not only space to shape, enclose, plan, organize, light, and ventilate, but to furnish and adorn, providing an arena for arts without number. Over time, many of these arts have preempted attention, especially where the shaping and organization of the space were fixed by tradition. That is why there are more histories of the decorative arts than of interior design.

Interior design is the total creative solution for a programmed interior. The totality encompasses the conceptual planning, technical, and artistic solution of the client's program under any number of building conditions ranging from a fixed and unalterable architectural shell through a shell that may be altered more or less, and finally to an unbuilt shell that will be custom-designed to suit the interior solution.

Interior decoration, the earlier, more limited term, is the decorative completion and furnishing of an already planned interior. It is not only a perfectly valid function but an art which can reach into glory. The skills and talents it recruits range from those of a drapery workroom to the *tromp l'oeil* murals and ceilings of Palladio's Villa Maser.

Interior design encompasses interior decoration, but the reverse is not true. *Interior architecture* is synonymous with interior design, and the term is preferred by some architects. In practice, what people label themselves need not describe what they do in general or on particular projects.

By 1931, the evolving profession was already an immensely powerful cultural and economic force in the United States. But its *economic* effectiveness was what brought the AIID into being in a time of economic stress—the Great Depression.

The profession—by whatever name—had from the beginning served as *the* focus for myriad arts, crafts, and interiors industries. Over time, the small, essentially craft-oriented operators typical of the industry which served (or supplied) our profession were joined by highly mechanized mass producers of textiles, flooring, and residential and office furniture. To the residential furniture manufacturers, retail stores were a primary distribution outlet, closed showrooms secondary. In the Great Depression, however, the stores failed the furniture industry, while the interior design profession saved it. Basically, the furniture industry's efforts to enlist the profession's aid was responsible for the creation of AIID.

Only the people directly involved seemed to be aware of the most important fact about interior design in the United States—that it is not only an art and a profession but the control center of a huge industry. Today's specialized market centers testify to the phenomenon clearly enough, but the Department of Commerce does not yet differentiate between such products as furniture specified by interior designers and that sold in retail stores. However, as long ago as 1931, the Grand Rapids furniture manufacturers paid attention to the distinction because their survival depended on it.

THE ATELIERS

In building, the explosive growth of industrialized America favored speculative development and the delivery of raw, unfinished, anonymous space rather than of finished interiors. Except for a few forceful total designers like Wright, LeCorbusier, Hoffmann, and Horta, few architects were interested in taking on the responsibility for interiors except in such specialized major buildings as churches or civic capitols.

Who, then, was designing interiors if not architects or builders? As early as the mid-nineteenth century, the gap began to be filled by commercial establishments staffed with designers, draftsmen, artists, sculptors, and craftsmen of all kinds, and equipped with cabinetmaking shops and workrooms. Typical were Emil Galle in France, Davis & Mewes in England; and in the United States, A. Kimbel & Sons (founded in 1851), Hoffstatter, Louis Comfort Tiffany's Studios, and the Rambusch Company, founded in 1898 and run by the Rambusch family till 1991.

The last third of the nineteenth century and the first third of the twentieth witnessed a plethora of contradictory vogues in decor. Victorian clutter and a kind of stuffy traditional conspicuous consumption reigned in the great New York mansions created by the commercial ateliers, even while Art Nouveau, De Stijl, Bauhaus, and the Paris Moderne of 1925—with its Art Deco spinoff—were ushering in a new era. It was not until after World War I that the prevailing ponderousness promoted by the ateliers ceased to dominate American interiors.

ELSIE DE WOLFE

The hand that let in the fresh air belonged to an adventuress with no credentials whatsoever—a spinster and ex-actress born in an era which regarded both actresses and career women with a raised eyebrow. Elsie de Wolfe (1870-1950), eventually Lady Mendl, parlayed her intelligence, taste, and aplomb into an international career as the first interior decorator, more particularly the first "society" decorator—no mere tradesperson. Opening a decorating shop in New York in 1904, she designed the first club for women, the Colony Club, and in the next year the ground floor of the Frick Mansion, later the Frick Museum. Venetian mirrors, French antiques, crystal chandeliers, and chintz were her stock-in-trade. Her interiors were noted not only for glamour and showmanship but suitability, intimacy, lightness, comfort, and common sense about maintenance. Seized by the set decorators of Hollywood's burgeoning movie industry, and devoured by millions of moviegoers, her livable, elegant style had a more lasting effect on American taste than the avant-gardes of France and Germany or even the white wave from England—Syrie Maugham's work.

Elsie de Wolfe's success inspired imitators galore—gifted and ungifted, and highly varied in experience and training. Ateliers, the decorating departments of big stores, and unaffiliated individuals swelled the ranks of the new decorating profession, while Parsons School of Design in New York City was the outstanding school producing graduates with proper training to practice it.

No doubt the members of this growing profession would have organized themselves into a national organization sooner or later. By 1931 New York had a Society of Interior Decorators (for men only) and a Decorators Club (for women only); Chicago had a Women Decorators' Association; Philadelphia had the Interior Decorators' Club of Philadelphia. Abroad there were several organizations including a British Institute of Interior Decorators which had some specially invited foreign members. One of them was the designer William R. Moore of Chicago, who had designed the interiors of the Lake Shore Drive and Belmont Hotels in Chicago, and refurbished the Civic Auditorium in Grand Rapids. He knew Grand Rapids well.

Moore believed that the American decorators needed a national organization of their own, and talked about the idea for years. His chance to do something about it came sooner than he expected.

Grand Rapids, Michigan, called itself "the furniture capital of the world" and in the 1920s deserved that title because its manufacturers had gradually refined the design and craftsmanship of their furniture from "borax" to first class—far beyond the competence of the Southern manufacturers of the time. Hollis S. Baker of the Baker Furniture Company had pioneered in buying English and French antiques in Europe and manufacturing meticulous reproductions. There were early stirrings toward sophisticated contemporary design as well. Grand Rapids had its own semiannual furniture markets immediately after the ones in Chicago, its own exhibitors' building, and a huge hotel for buyers from the fine stores and decorators from all over the country.

GRAND RAPIDS, JULY 1931

On October 29, 1929—"Black Tuesday"—the New York stock market crashed, and the biggest boom in U.S. history was followed by a worldwide Depression that did not reveal its deadly staying power until hitting rock bottom in 1931. The laissez-faire government, insurance, and banking systems of the time provided no safety nets for the speculators and stockbrokers, who committed suicide in record numbers; for depositors in the more than 500 banks that failed; and for the nine million unemployed—25 percent of the work force then.

In the chain reaction that followed, Grand Rapids' furniture industry faced imminent demise as furniture sales in stores plummeted. What could the city do with its factories, its exhibition building, and its gargantuan Pantlind Hotel if the department store furniture buyers did not come?

Among the industry's leaders pondering the question in 1931 were Frank W. Mueller, President of the Grand Rapids Furniture Manufacturing Association and owner of his own factory; Joseph H. Brewer, President of the Grand Rapids Convention Bureau, Inc., and owner of his own factory; and Eric W. Dahl, Manager of the Grand Rapids Convention Bureau, Inc. All of them knew Moore.

Which of them first proposed the ideas of inviting the interior decorators of the land to attend a conference in Grand Rapids for the purpose of forming a national organization we do not know, nor who originated the premise on which the proposal was based. Perhaps all three of them had made the same interesting observation.

This observation had to do with the staying power of the decorators' clients. Whether because they were Super Rich rather than merely rich, or because some were corporations rather than individuals, they appeared relatively immune to the effects of the Depression, and continued to behave as though nothing much—or not *that* much—had happened to their incomes. The best of the decorators were weathering hard times surprisingly well. All Grand Rapids needed to do to win more of the decorators' business was to show them what it had to offer in craftsmanship, design, and service.

The Grand Rapids furniture industry put that plan into effect. The man in charge, the Convention Bureau's Eric W. Dahl, was both thorough and persuasive. As attendees, participants, and speakers, he bagged not only leading decorators but such architects as Frank Lloyd Wright and Harvey Wiley Corbett (two years later Architectural Chairman of the 1933 World's Fair in Chicago), such museum curators as the New York Metropolitan Museum's Richard F. Bach, and such editors as *House & Garden's* Richardson Wright. Others: Cleveland decorator Louis Rorimer, father of future New York Metropolitan Museum Director James Rorimer; Nancy V. McClelland, who wore three different professional hats—as a scholar of the decorative arts, as a merchant selling wallpapers and fabrics (chiefly documentary) to the trade, and as an interior decorator; Frank W. Richardson, president of the Society of Interior Decorators of New York.

The Grand Rapids furniture manufacturers footed all the bills and paid the invited decorators to furnish 28 rooms and five gardens in a model town house and country house designed by William R. Moore for the Waters-Klingman Furniture Exhibition Building. The Association scrubbed, beflagged, and relandscaped the entire center of town.

By the close of the conference, the new American Institute of Interior Decorators—AIID—had 342 members. Its first president was William R. Moore, its first vice president Frank W. Richardson, its first executive director Eric W. Dahl, and its headquarters were in Chicago until 1933, when they were moved to New York. In 1936 its name and initials were changed to American Institute of Decorators—AID.

And the Grand Rapids furniture industry weathered the Depression, though its wood furniture factories were destined to be dwarfed by the increasingly mechanized furniture factories of the South, and by its own burgeoning steel office furniture factories.

GROWTH AND CONFLICT

From the organization's start, AID's membership requirements covered both education and experience, with explicit trade-offs possible between the two. In general, the requirements were made higher over the years. There was, however, no objective test of the candidates' basic professional competence until the 1960s.

From the start, programs for the membership included ongoing education and the development of a code of ethics and practice guidelines. Outreach to the public through such projects as showhouses, outreach to students with scholarships, and outreach to related professionals through affiliate memberships were other continuing efforts.

From the start, obviously, the organization was on the right track. But after World War II it became apparent that the profession was growing and changing faster than AID. Nonresidential design—offices, hotels, small and large retail establishments—grew more important, mitigating against the prevailing retail mark-up system. The "society" decorator role model was challenged by the space planner and other alien types. Office and school design, among others, were revolutionized by new furniture component systems and the "open plan."

The very dynamism of the profession exacerbated the disagreements inevitable in any organization. Among the thorny issues were the acceptance and rejections of specific candidates for admission, the word *decorator* versus *designer* in AID's name, and the single-slate system for the election of officers.

The last item was probably the direct cause of the schism of 1957, in which a faction of the AID's New York Chapter refused to accept the results of the election and formed the rival National Society of Interior Designers (NSID). As a result, there were two national professional organizations for interior designers in the United States from 1958 until their reconciliation and consolidation on January 1, 1975.

The experience, though painful, was not without benefits. The rival organizations goaded each other forward. Simply by naming itself the National Society of Interior *Designers*, NSID had taken the bull by the horns on the designer versus decorator issue. By 1961, three years after the founding of NSID, AID followed suit.

IDEC AND FIDER

As the interior design community grew in number, so did its educational establishment. Some teachers of interior design practiced interior design themselves, but many were wholly in academia. To alleviate their isolation and ally themselves with the profession in the field, design educators formed IDEC, the Interior Design Educators Council, in 1962. IDEC participates energetically in many ASID programs, but particularly in those pertaining to education.

Another program related to qualification—the accrediting of educational programs (not of schools per se but of particular programs aimed at training prospective interior designers)—was also launched as the two rival organizations drew closer together. In 1967 AID, NSID, and IDEC asked Professor Arnold Friedmann, then Co-Chairman of Pratt Institute's Department of Interior Design (in Brooklyn, New York) to drop his regular schedule and make a survey of schools teaching professional-level programs in interior design. The resulting report was the launching pad for an ongoing effort for which a new foundation was created: FIDER—the Foundation for Interior Design Education Research. Funded primarily by the ASID membership and chapters, industry, students, and fees paid by the schools, FIDER sends teams to educational institutions requesting evaluation of their interior design programs, and periodically publishes the results of these evaluations as a nationwide guide.

STRUGGLING FOR LEGAL STATUS*

In the early sixties, AID and NSID campaigned vigorously for statutory licensing of interior designers—variously title or practice acts. AID focused on California, NSID on New York. They were completely frustrated. Retailers blocked such laws as restraint of trade. Legislators pointed out that the only justification for the licensing of professions was the protection of the public's health, safety, and welfare. Architects, taking the opposite tack, insisted that interior designers were so ignorant of building codes that they posed a potential danger to their clients whenever they attempted anything but the most superficial decorating without the oversight of a licensed architect or engineer. As the lucrative potential of interior design became obvious, the architectural establishment wanted to elbow aside the interior design community.

And the interior design community was burdened with the legacy of the "society decorators," some talented and some not, some with proper studios, and some who, without even learning to draw or read a blueprint, relied on craftsmen and contractors to cope with the technical challenges of achieving the effects they wanted. The least qualified of these decorators tainted the image of the entire profession.

It was obviously imperative for the interior design community to develop an unchallengeable qualification system to: (1) *define the profession*; (2) *describe the skills and knowledge it requires*; and (3) *identify individuals competent to practice accountably so as to protect the health, safety, and welfare of the public.*

Such systems are notoriously difficult to develop. Governments scrutinize them, asking whether it is the public or the annointed pros who are protected. Candidates fear them, complaining that they are unfair, invalid, and inconsistent. Rejected candidates, excluded from the professions of their choice, may sue the agencies involved.

Despite these odds, the interior design community has succeeded in developing and perfecting such a system through the National Council for Interior Design Qualification, NCIDQ, which, despite its name, covers Canada as well as the United States. Like FIDER, it is independent of all the interior design societies. Most of them, however, are members of NCIDQ as *societies*, and participate in its work.

LOUIS TREGRE AND NCIDQ

There is an accurate account of NCIDQ's history and examination system on pages 35-36. We discuss it here only because the author omitted certain information worth recording. To begin, he failed to identify himself as the father of NCIDQ—the AID member who talked up the campaign to create a credible NCIDQ prototype for AID in the early sixties, who chaired the original AID Voluntary Accreditation Committee, who saw it through to the development of its examination, and who, when NCIDQ was spun off as an independent body, served as its president until 1981, monitoring it through computerization and change until his death at the age of 66 on May 17, 1991.

Like some of the most interesting architects in ASID, Louis Severin Tregre asserted that an architectural degree does not in itself assure competency in interior design. In his own case, he said, the critical factor was long association in excellent interior design firms. Born in Baton Rouge, Louisiana, Tregre collected a Bronze Star for wartime service in Asia and went on to earn a degree in architecture at Texas A&M University. He worked first on the Oak Ridge Atomic Plant and department store interiors before moving to New York and doing posh residences, hotels, and night clubs for stylish William Pahlmann Associates and Valerian Rybar Inc. On his own after 1961, he specialized in facilities for the elderly and health care, though NCIDQ's affairs were obviously his first priority.

It is important for us to make an evaluation of his contribution, since he did not. Simply:

> *The success story of NCIDQ is the crucial component in the long campaign to win legal recognition for interior design as a bona fide profession. Without it, licensing or certification efforts would be as futile today as they were thirty years ago, and the interior design community would still be denied the rights, respect, and autonomy accorded to architects, engineers, physicians, and all others whose professional status is affirmed by law.*

Not that Tregre accomplished the feat single-handedly. From the outset he worked with collaborators as dedicated as they were distinguished. Like him, some had degrees in architecture: Irving D. Schwartz, AIA, FASID, in the sixties a Professor at Illinois Institute of Technology, later an ASID National President; Norman DeHaan, AIA, FASID, of Chicago, another future ASID National President; Ruth Lynford, FASID, who since 1981 has spearheaded the grueling, triumphant IDLNY (Interior Designers for Licensing in New York State) campaign for the Interior Design Certification Law signed in 1990. Tregre's first AID Accreditation Committee included Marjorie Helsel, now designing Fiat autos in Italy; Lloyd Bell, FASID; and Rita St. Clair, FASID, another activist later elected ASID National President. St. Clair, whose brilliantly managed Baltimore firm was one of the first to go on computer and whose staff includes two full-time architects, was the original instigator of Harry Siegel's *Guide to Business Principles and Practices for Interior Designers*.

A full list of directors and consultants who contributed to NCIDQ would require another book, but one other addendum to Tregre's chapter in this manual belongs here:

At last count, fourteen states of the Union and all of Canada's provinces had practice acts, title acts, or certification acts in effect. What all these statutes have in common despite their considerable diversity is the NCIDQ exam "or

*From this point on, the text is excerpted from the manuscript (copyright © 1985 & 1991, Olga Gueft) of the author's forthcoming history of interior design as a profession.

equivalent" required. No "equivalent" has been attempted. The NCIDQ investment in care, research, and money has been prodigious.

Nationwide professional design organizations have come and gone since the early days of AIID/AID/ASID. NCIDQ is the thread of continuity that binds them together, in Canada as well as in the United States. It is a living thread that keeps up with ongoing changes in actual practice. The current list of NCIDQ member organizations includes an organization created by designers who intended *not* to take the NCIDQ examination. It, too, has recanted and joined the family. Licensing (or registration or certification) of interior designers never excludes architects from practicing interior design, since the national architectural board exams (the NCARB in the United States) are accepted as alternatives to NCIDQ. Nevertheless, architects are encouraged to take the NCIDQ exam. Some do.

ABOUT PROFESSIONAL DISCIPLINES

Propelled by explosive growth in population, in affluence, and in industry, interior design has evolved into a recognized profession with such speed that not even its most knowledgeable clients are fully aware of the scope of expertise it demands of its practitioners; nor of its impact on the public's health, safety, and welfare; nor of its economic reach.

In certain fields of great economic and social importance, there may be symbiotic interactions between a profession and an indispensable attendant industry. Eisenhower alerted us to the military-industrial complex. To understand the medical profession we must take into account the hospital and pharmaceutical industries. Architects are constrained by builders, developers, land-use legislators, and realtors. As for the industry that initiated the organization of ASID, it is so varied and complex that we tend to forget its size and influence.

Vitruvius' *Ten Books of Architecture* cover not only the design and construction of buildings but of fortifications, harbors, aqueducts, and cities. In the ancient world, architecture encompassed what we now call civil and construction engineering and city planning. When the growing complexity of technology made that impossible, engineering had to be spun off as a separate profession—with subprofessions too. The same process has spun off interior design. Despite the fact that some people qualify in more than one of them, architecture, engineering, and interior design are now three separate professions, each existing as a core discipline in its own right, with its own knowledge base, skills, and technologies. Interior design, the newest, has undeniably reached that status. As an art, as a scientific response to our stressed environment, it is gaining momentum.

Relationship to Allied Professions

STANLEY ABERCROMBIE

Interior design and architecture are sister arts that grew up together a long time ago. It is possible that interior design is the elder of these siblings. After all, humans had furnished their caves with animal pelts and painted cave walls long before they constructed freestanding buildings. But, once such construction began, people practiced interior design and architecture simultaneously, along with structural engineering.

Specialization has now established the separation of architecture, engineering, and interior design. In fact, educational requirements of each field have become so specific that it is rare for a single person to practice more than one. But more so than many professions, interior design is one that never can be practiced in isolation. Its successful practice requires the coordination of work in a large number of allied fields. For example, further specialization has fragmented interior design into fields such as residential, health care, hospitality, retail, and office design. Designers also may be classified as space planners, color and materials experts, and technical adepts. In a design firm of considerable size, there also are related professionals who ensure that everything runs smoothly: who keep the payroll and personnel records, who market the firm's services, and who administer the overall operation.

In addition to these aspects, interior design, like architecture, is a marriage of art and technology. Its successful practice requires the exercise of artistic talent, which may be intuitive, and also the application of scientific knowledge, which can be acquired only by conscious effort. It is because of the latter that an interior design practice materially affects the health, safety, and welfare of its users. Architecture affects these as well, but, as currently practiced, interior design is potentially the more dangerous of the two. (Cases in point are a number of recent hotel fire disasters, in which the basic masonry structures emerged intact, but life was threatened seriously by toxic fumes from the burning of designer-specified materials.)

Because of interior design's artistic element, the profession is allied closely with a number of arts and crafts such as furniture design, fabric and carpet design, and mural painting and decorative plasterwork, to name a few. These alliances are not proper relationships among equal partners, for the coherence of the final result will depend upon all factors being submitted to a single concept, and this concept must come from the interior designer who guides all phases of the work. Also, it must be recognized that the interior designer is greatly dependent on suppliers of merchandise that can be specified. Key as the designer's general concept may be, it must be translated into material goods.

The independence of interior design from architecture is a natural consequence of specialization, although not necessarily a desirable one. The architect and the interior designer (and the landscape architect and urban designer as well) still have as their common goal the creation of a satisfactory habitation for mankind, one in which the design of the exterior and the interior are in consonance.

Specialized as the practice of interior design has become, this does not give designers a monopoly to create interior effects. Some of the greatest and most celebrated interiors have been the work of architects; some, particularly in Renaissance times, have been the work of those we think of primarily as painters or sculptors. The spectacular interior of London's 1851 Crystal Palace was the work of a landscape architect; many interiors have resulted from the work of engineers; and others from the hands of amateurs.

Finally, we may note that the interior design profession is not practiced free of influence from any major aspect of our culture. In subtle ways it is touched by economics, by religion and politics and concepts of social justice, by educational and moral standards, just as surely as it is touched by the other arts. Interior design is concerned with nothing less important than the ways in which people live and work, and these ways are inextricably connected with who we are and who we aspire to be.

Education

RONALD M. VEITCH

Interior design education in North America is a twentieth-century phenomenon. While fine arts, decorative arts, and architecture programs of study began in the 1800s, it was not until after the turn of the century that interior decoration, as it was then called, was identified as a separate program. From interior decorating, which mainly involved the furnishing and decorating of existing spaces, programs of interior design evolved to encompass the study of complex design processes, various behavioral theories, and the creation of new spaces.

Curricula for interior design education developed from three primary academic areas: (1) as an outgrowth of the fine and decorative arts, (2) as a component of home economics, and (3) as a specialized focus in architecture. The majority of interior design programs today are still administered through fine arts, architecture, or home economics/human ecology. Each provides a slightly different focus, yet contains the necessary elements required for a professional interior design program.

HISTORIC PERSPECTIVE OF INTERIOR DESIGN EDUCATION

Historically, one of the most significant events in the evolution of interior design education occurred in 1963, when a group of educators and practitioners met to discuss mutual concerns regarding educational programs. This benchmark meeting resulted in the creation of the Interior Design Educators Council (IDEC) in 1964. Subsequently, IDEC organized and commissioned a study of interior design education, which was funded by the then-existing professional organizations of AID and NSID. The study revealed strengths and weaknesses in interior design education, suggesting that a system of program assessment was advisable.

In 1969, a Joint Commission on Interior Design Accreditation came to the conclusion that an independent accrediting agency was necessary to establish an unbiased mechanism for researching educational needs and setting standards for maintaining quality. As a result, the first meeting of the Foundation for Interior Design Education Research (FIDER) was held in 1971. The stated purpose of this organization was to establish and administer a voluntary plan for the special accreditation of programs of interior design education offered at institutions of higher learning located throughout the United States, its possessions, and Canada. Such a voluntary plan would use accreditation procedures to ensure that programs of interior design education would meet the needs of society, interior design students, and the interior design profession, and would serve as a means of protecting the public against professional incompetence. As part of this plan, FIDER established a program of continuing research and investigation to ensure that accreditation criteria would continue to reflect current practice in education and professional interior design.

During the next two and a half years, FIDER developed a set of standards and guidelines to assess the quality of interior design programs, using a basic set of criteria initially formulated by a group of design educators. FIDER accreditation site teams, using these standards and guidelines, began visiting educational programs in January 1973. Those standards and guidelines for accreditation included the following program types:

- Paraprofessional (terminal education) (2 years)
- Preprofessional (preparatory) (2 years)
- Professional school (3 years)
- Baccalaureate (4-5 years)
- Graduate (4-5 years)

The efficacy of the standards and guidelines was tested prior to use and the results of site visits were monitored. This monitoring provided evidence that the accreditation section on educational content needed closer examination. Using matrixes developed in the mid-1970s by four interior design educators as a base, two research projects were conducted in 1979; the purpose of which was to review the accreditation standards and guidelines and evaluate the process. These research projects culminated in the publication of revised standards and guidelines in 1980 and a major two year project which examined the context of educational programs across the United States and Canada.

At approximately the same time that FIDER was organized, the professional interior design societies and IDEC concluded that a qualifying examination for entrance into the profession was needed. The National Council for Interior Design Qualification (NCIDQ), an autonomous body for testing the knowledge of individuals entering the practice of interior design, was created to serve this purpose. Written and design examinations of applicants began in the mid-1970s. Concurrent FIDER and NCIDQ research projects showed an amazing correlation between educators' and practitioners' views on the necessary knowledge and skill levels required to produce qualified professional interior designers. These studies provided the basis for what is now referred to as "the common body of knowledge of interior design."

As a result of research and investigation by FIDER and NCIDQ through interviews, questionnaires, and analysis, it is now possible to give substance to the knowledge and skills held in common by competent practitioners of the profession of interior design. This common body of knowledge has been defined in a manner that may be communicated to others.

THE COMMON BODY OF KNOWLEDGE OF INTERIOR DESIGN

Each interior designer may have unique qualities and possess highly specialized abilities in certain areas; but all interior designers will hold knowledge of:

- The basic elements of design and composition that form the foundation for creative design, and the visual arts that assist in understanding the universality of these fundamentals.
- Theories of design, color, proxemics, behavior, visual perception, and spatial composition, which lead to an understanding of the interrelationship between human beings and the built environment.
- The design process—that is, programming, conceptualization, problem solving, and evaluation—firmly grounded on a base of anthropometrics, ergonomics, and other human factors.
- Space planning, and furniture planning and selection, developed in application to projects including all types of habitation (for work or leisure, new or old) and for a variety of populations (young or old, disabled, low or high income).
- Design attributes of materials, lighting, furniture, textiles, color, and so on, viewed in conjunction with physical, sociological, and psychological factors to reflect concern for the aesthetic qualities of the various parts of the built environment.
- The technical aspects of structure, construction, and building systems—such as HVAC, lighting, electrical, plumbing, and acoustics—sufficient to enable discourse and cooperation with related disciplines.
- Technical aspects of surface and structural materials, soft goods, textiles, and detailing of furniture, cabinetry, and interiors.
- The application of laws, building codes, regulations, and standards that affect design solutions in order to protect the health, safety, and welfare of the public.
- Oral, written, and visual communication skills for the presentation of design concepts, the production of working drawings, and the conduct of business.
- The history and organization of the profession, the methods and practices of the business of interior design, and an appreciation of a code of ethics.
- Styles of architecture, furniture, textiles, art, and accessories in relation to the economics, social, and religious influences on cultures.
- Methods necessary to conduct research and analyze the data in order to develop design concepts and solutions on a sound basis.

CLASSIFICATIONS OF INTERIOR DESIGN EDUCATIONAL PROGRAMS

Through a survey conducted in 1984 of institutions with educational programs of interior design, it became apparent that a great variety of interior design programs were in existence—ranging from two to seven years and from paraprofessional to postprofessional degrees. This resulted in difficulty in assessing the educational backgrounds of entering professionals. In an effort to clarify the situation, an intensive study of FIDER categories and the redevelopment of standards was begun. The study led to the proposal of new classifications for FIDER accreditation, including a postprofessional master's degree program, a first professional degree-level program, and a preprofessional assistant-level program. The original "preprofessional" (preparatory) classification was discontinued.

Concurrent with the research study of FIDER categories and standards, other studies were being conducted. Those studies provided guidance in the mission and foci of interior design educational programs across the United States and Canada. A distinct difference between two-year programs and other longer programs was readily apparent. The majority of the two-year programs educated students as merchandisers, delineators, or design assistants, while the three- to five-year programs educated students for entry-level professional positions. As a result the new category of preprofessional assistant was defined, and a new set of standards and guidelines was designed specifically for two-year programs.

Three-to seven-year programs were examined holistically from the perspective of the necessary knowledge and skills for a student to be formally educated as a practicing professional interior designer. It was concluded that a formal education that would fulfill FIDER's first professional degree requirements must combine specific studies in interior design with a sound base of general studies in liberal arts, sciences, and humanities. The number of years of study was deemed irrelevant, providing that opportunities for exposure existed and a minimum level of achievement was reached. Thus the focus of accreditation became the student's achievement level rather than the length of the program.

In addition to a variety of baccalaureate degree programs, several master's programs were found to exist, which required a university degree as an admission requirement and offered essentially the common body of knowledge of interior design offered in a baccalaureate program. Because this educational experience equated to the defined entry-level education requirements for an interior designer, this type of program was assigned to the first professional degree category, so that graduate programs remain true postbaccalaureate degrees. In keeping with this, the graduate degree category was renamed as postprofessional master's degree.

Today, the first professional degree level of accreditation is defined as those programs that provide academic preparation for the professional interior designer. The goal of this level is to prepare professional interior designers who are qualified by education, experience, and examination to enhance the function and quality of interior spaces for the purpose of improving the quality of life; increasing productivity; and protecting the health, safety, and welfare of the public. In addition, programs at this level prepare entry-level interior designers who can analyze clients' needs, goals, and life/safety requirements; integrate findings with knowledge of interior design; formulate preliminary design concepts; develop and present final design recommendations; prepare design development drawings and specifications; coordinate the services of other professionals; prepare and administer bid/contract documents as the client's agent; and review and evaluate design solutions.

Programs of education in interior design that are devoted to providing a first professional degree of education must meet the standards and guidelines for that level. This means that the program must include methods of information retention, skill building, and intellectual development that prepare individuals to cope with the complexity of the profession.

INTERIOR DESIGN EDUCATION TODAY

Dedicated educators, in conjunction with practitioners, have continued the evolution of interior design education. Just as there is more than one solution to a design problem, there is more than one solution to the development of educational programs of interior design. Clearly, the satisfaction of complex user needs requires a breadth of specialized knowledge, plus an education sufficient in its scope to enable the designer to be conversant with many aspects of life. Designing for people requires knowledge of people. It is this marriage of specialized knowledge and general education that comprises the common body of knowledge necessary for interior design education. Flexibility, creativity, and innovation in teaching methodology and curriculum development based on the solid foundation of the common body of knowledge has kept the process fresh and alive.

The profession of interior design can be likened to a fabric with threads represented by education, IDEC, FIDER, accreditation, internship, NCIDQ, professional examination, professional organizations, and licensing, with each thread supported by and supporting the others—inextricably bound together. As the profession matures, licensing will become more of an issue and more widespread. Interior design education must be prepared to meet these new challenges in the future.

With the enthusiasm and dedication that have been shown in the last three decades, the profession will continue to evolve and prepare students to seek knowledge. Formal education at an institution of learning is the first step. The profession today demands continual updating and refreshing of knowledge, plus a search for new knowledge in specialized areas. Educators and practitioners working in harmony with one another will mean that interior design education and the profession will continue to evolve, grow, and fill a leadership role in the design of human habitation.

Professional Internship

DIANNE R. JACKMAN

Formal education can only prepare students for the entry level of the interior design profession. Learning must continue through experience. An internship system or training program that expands the opportunities for the new graduate to become versed in issues related to the safety and welfare of the public can address this need. Such a program should assist in the preparation of candidates for the qualification examination and enhance the opportunity for a new graduate to enter the profession at a higher level of competence. Internship can contribute to the development of qualified interior designers who are a credit to the profession and increase the value of junior designers at an accelerated rate.

STUDENT INTERNSHIP

A student internship should not be confused with a professional internship that follows graduation at the first professional degree level. The professional internship is, by necessity, more rigorous. A student internship is considered to be cooperative education—a partnership between the educational institution and the employer. Student internships are designed to provide qualified students with preparation for future classroom activities. Extension of classroom and studio teaching by practice in the profession adds a unique dimension to this learning process.

Individual growth is enhanced by the realization that, in addition to demonstrating theoretical knowledge, the student intern also is learning to become an integral part of the interior design working community and developing an awareness of the interrelationship between the academic and professional worlds. Thus, during the college years, the student intern obtains firsthand knowledge of interior design practices, expectations, and opportunities. At the same time, a student is offered a realistic test of career interest and aptitude.

PROFESSIONAL INTERNSHIP

A comprehensive professional internship system can reinforce the education, discipline, integrity, judgment, skills, knowledge, and quest for learning that serves the interior designer for a lifetime. Such experience can provide direction, order, and support and offer the opportunity for growth under the guidance of a design practitioner.

For a professional internship to be valuable, it must have structure. A professional internship system should include exposure to practical skills that relate to the design and development of the built environment. Such a system has several objectives, which include opportunities to:

- Provide information and advice on entry-level experience, and on professional issues and opportunities, relative to previous education.
- Define and encourage activity in critical areas of interior design practice where entry-level designers are expected to apply the knowledge gained through education and acquire basic skills and knowledge.
- Encourage additional activities in the broad aspects of interior design practice.
- Provide a uniform system for evaluation and documentation of individual training activity.
- Provide access to supplementary education opportunities that augment formal education.

In order to meet these objectives and ensure broad exposure to the practice of interior design, the structure of a professional internship must include:

- A description of the training.
- An accommodation for the differences in level of experience of the intern and identification of the minimum-level requirements for an internship experience.
- A review of program costs and compensation.
- A placement process and an advisory system.
- An administrative unit that includes delivery, record keeping, evaluation/supervision, and communication systems.

Recent modifications to the professional qualification examination focus on performance testing and place an emphasis on practical experience. A structured internship system that provides on-the-job training for recent graduates provides an opportunity for individuals to build upon their formal education and apply it in such a way that they are better prepared for the qualifying examination.

CONTENT OF A PROFESSIONAL INTERNSHIP PROGRAM

Research conducted by FIDER and NCIDQ led to the delineation of a common body of knowledge for interior design. A strong correlation exists between the requirements of formal education and the needs of the profession for practice. This common body of knowledge is defined by the following categories:

Interior Design
- Programming
- Conceptual design
- Design development
- Contract documents
- Contract administration
- Evaluation

Business Management
- Office and financial management
- Client relations and legal considerations
- Public relations and marketing

Profession
- Professional associations
- Community service
- Regulatory bodies

The content of a professional internship should be based on (1) an educational foundation and (2) the needs of the qualification examination. Such an internship system necessarily includes exposure in the areas of programming, conceptual design, design development, contract documentation and administration, evaluation, code research, specification writing, and bids processing. Additionally, it should include business and financial management, client relationships, legal considerations, public relations, and marketing. Exposure to the profession through professional associations, community service, and regulatory bodies would also be part of the internship system.

To clarify each of the categories and the appropriate level of involvement for an intern, a detailed review of each area follows.

INTERIOR DESIGN

The following areas fall under the heading of interior design itself. Here are several key aspects of the interior designer's job and ways that the professional intern can learn related skills.

Programming

Programming is the process of setting forth, in written form, clients' and users' requirements for a given project. To offer this as a professional service, a designer must identify and analyze the clients' and users' needs and goals. This includes the evaluation of existing premises, the assessment of project resources and limitations, identification of life safety and code requirements, consideration of site issues, the preparation of the project schedule, budget development, analysis of design objectives and spatial requirements, and the development of preliminary space planning and furniture layouts. Further, the need for and coordination of consultants must be determined and an investigation of the requirements for regulatory approval made. All this information must be organized, discussed, and approved by the client.

To build programming skills, an intern should:

- Participate in interviews and conferences with clients and users.
- Assist in preparing minutes or reports.
- Help gather and evaluate pertinent data on existing premises.
- Assist with presentations for regulatory approval.
- Participate in office conferences regarding scheduling and the development of a budget, visit existing projects.
- Participate in interviews with project owners and consultants.
- Assist the designer or design team in an analysis of spatial requirements, space planning, and furniture and fixture layouts.
- Research current literature pertaining to interior design.
- Help prepare documents.
- Evaluate data and requirements obtained from various sources.

Conceptual Design

From the programming approved by the owner or user, the interior designer explores and develops solutions to satisfy aesthetic, functional, and behavioral requirements. Interior design professionals formulate preliminary space plans and three-dimensional design concepts that are appropriate to the program budget and describe the character, function, and aesthetics of the project. Image boards and preliminary cost estimates are prepared, and conceptual designs are presented to clients and users for discussion and approval.

To build conceptual design skills, an intern should:

- Participate in the development and preparation of preliminary design concepts to determine the spatial relationships that best satisfy the project program.
- Observe the development and coordination of program requirements with consultants.
- Assist in the preparation of presentation materials.
- Observe design reviews and approval meetings with client and user groups.

Design Development

Based on the conceptual design approved by the owner or user, the interior designer develops for the owner's further approval the character of the project, space planning, furniture plans, selection of materials, fixtures, and furnishings. The professional is responsible for the development and refinement of the approved conceptual design; the research and consultation with jurisdictional authorities regarding building and life safety codes; communication with necessary specialists and consultants; the development of art, accessory, and graphic/signage programs; final design recommendations for space planning, furnishings, fixtures, millwork, and all interior surfaces including lighting, electrical, and communication requirements; and the preparation of drawings.

To build design development skills, an intern should:

- Participate in the preparation of detailed development drawings from conceptual documents.
- Observe design review and approval meetings with clients and user groups.
- Assist in the selection of materials and furnishings for appropriateness, durability, aesthetic quality, cost, and life cycle cost.

Building inspectors and other officials in zoning, environment, health, liquor control, and in fields relating to the health, welfare, and safety of the public, oversee the enforcement of federal, state, and local regulations related to building and interior construction. The codes enforced by these officials have a direct bearing on the total design process, and the professional interior designer understands that a thorough knowledge of all requirements is essential to the satisfactory completion of any project.

To learn these aspects of design development, interns should help professionals:

- Search and document codes, regulations, ordinances, and so on.
- Study procedures necessary to obtain a variance.
- Calculate variables such as numbers and sizes of exits, stair dimensions, public washrooms, and barrier-free requirements to satisfy code requirements.

Contract Documents

Working drawings, related schedules, interior construction specifications, and furnishing specifications are very important in the design office, and much time and effort are spent preparing them. The drawings describe in graphic form all the essentials of the work to be done; the related schedules and the specifications describe quality in written form. It is extremely important that the documents be clear, accurate, consistent, and complete. This requires thorough quality control, including constant review and cross-checking of all documents. In addition, effective coordination of the drawings, schedules, and the specifications of the consultants is essential to avoid conflicts among the various trades.

To publish documents, interior design practitioners must first prepare working drawings and related schedules for interior construction, materials, and finishes; coordinate professional services of specialty consultants and licensed practitioners in the technical areas of mechanical, electrical, and load bearing; identify bid documents, interior construction specifications, and furnishings specifications; issue addenda as necessary; collect and review bids; and assist the client in awarding contracts.

To gain skills in working with contract documents, the intern should:

- Assist in preparation of working drawings.
- Develop technical skills in drafting and/or computer-aided drafting, with accuracy, completeness, and clarity.
- Prepare all schedules: color and finish, door and window, and lighting.

Well-grounded knowledge of specification writing principles and procedures for both interior construction and furnishings specifications is essential. The interior design practitioner knows that unless these skills are developed properly, expert knowledge of materials, contracts, and construction procedures and furnishings installation cannot be communicated successfully. A cardinal principle of specification writing requires the interior designer to understand clearly the relationship between drawings and related schedules/specifications, and to be able to logically communicate the requirements of the construction and installation process.

To learn specification writing skills, interns can:

- Review the organization, purpose, and format of specifications.
- Review and analyze bidding forms, insurance aspects, bonding requirements, liens, and special conditions.
- Research and evaluate data for materials and furnishings to be specified, including information regarding availability, cost, code acceptability, and manufacturer's reliability.
- Attend sales presentations in connection with this research.
- Check drawings prepared by other draftpersons or design assistants for accuracy of dimension notes, abbreviations, and indicators.
- Assist in development of a schedule for proper coordination with other disciplines.
- Check consultants' drawings.
- Assist in the final project review for compliance with applicable codes, regulations, and so on.

The professional interior designer establishes and administers bidding procedures, issues addenda, evaluates proposed alternates, reviews the qualifications of bidders, analyzes bids on negotiated contracts, and makes recommendations for the selection of the successful contractors. The construction and furnishing contracts are the formal instruments that bind the major parties. These detail the desired product and the services to be provided.

To learn skills related to contract bidding and awards, interns should:

- Review carefully the bidding/award stages of previous projects to develop an understanding of problems and solutions.

- Assist in the preparation of sample bids.
- Help in the prequalification of bidders.
- Review bids as they are received and examine alternates.
- Learn more about the process required prior to issuance of notice to proceed.

Contract Administration

During the contract administration phase, some tasks are handled in the office while others demand site observation. Office tasks include paying contractors; processing change orders, shop drawings, and samples; and adjudicating disputes. The manner in which these matters are handled affects the smooth functioning of work on the site. Items such as shop drawings and samples submitted for the designer's review should be processed promptly to expedite the construction process. Changes in the work that may affect the time of construction or installation, or modify the cost, are accomplished by proposed change notices and change orders.

In administering the contracts, the designer determines whether the contractor's work generally conforms to the requirements of the contract documents. In order to evaluate the quality of materials and workmanship, the designer must be familiar with all the provisions of the construction or furnishings contracts. Periodic reports on the stage of completion of scheduled activities are collected and compared to the overall project schedule at project meetings. These meetings facilitate communication between the contract parties and produce a detailed progress record. The designer determines, through observation, the completion of the project and receives all data, warranties, and releases required by the contract documents prior to final inspection and final payment. In addition to these project-related functions, the designer interprets contract documents when disagreements occur, judging the dispute impartially.

To learn contract administration skills, interns can:

- Help process applications for payment and prepare certificates for payment.
- Check shop drawings.
- Evaluate samples submitted.
- Maintain records.
- Evaluate requests for changes.
- Interpret documents.
- Prepare proposed change notices, change orders, and certificates for payment.
- Participate in the resolution of disputes and interpretation of conflicts relating to the contract documents.
- Participate in the preparation of record documents at project completion.

At the site, the intern can:

- Observe the work, storage, and installation of materials and furnishings.
- Prepare field reports of routine inspections.
- Revise and analyze time schedules of construction and furnishings installation.
- Develop an awareness of contractual obligations.
- Assist in recording and documenting all actions taken and agreed upon.
- Participate in periodic inspections.
- Assist in listing deficiencies.
- Observe final inspection.

Evaluation

Postoccupancy evaluation is a rigorous process aimed at measuring project performance. It is a deliberate means of obtaining relevant data to assist in achieving and maintaining a quality standard. The data gathered in the postoccupancy evaluation process allows suitable action to be taken to correct recognizable problems in that project, but more importantly, to avert their recurrence in future projects.

To learn postoccupancy evaluation skills, the intern should help:

- Develop questionnaires and personal satisfaction scales.
- Provide assistance in the appraisal of the project.
- Evaluate the facility's performance by probing the users to solicit responses that address client/user satisfaction, fitness for purpose, technical performance, and value for cost.

BUSINESS MANAGEMENT

Interior design is a creative profession, but techniques of practice require that the interior design office operate in the same manner as any other commercial enterprise. For this reason interns should also learn business management skills in the following areas.

Office and Financial Management

In an interior design office, as in any other, steady income must be generated and expenses must be carefully budgeted and monitored so that economic stability, essential to successful practice, can be maintained. Accurate records must be kept for tax purposes and for use in future projects. Established office requirements and regulations are essential to maintaining a successful operation; office manuals are a typical tool for dissemination of this information. Profitable use of human resources requires budgeting of time and the development of schedules that are adhered to rigidly.

An intern's role in office and financial management should be to:

- Review the process of internal accounting and cost-control systems for the operation of the interior design office.

- Participate in allocation of time to all elements involved in a total project, from programming through postoccupancy evaluation.

Client Relations and Legal Considerations

The interior designer's relationship to the owner is established by contractual agreement. For a contract to be enforceable, the practitioner knows that there must be mutual agreement between competent parties and acceptable monetary consideration. The agreement also must be for a lawful purpose and accomplishable within an established time frame.

To build skills for client relations and legal negotiations, an intern should:

- Review professional interior design service contracts for format, content, responsibility (determination), and enforcement procedures.
- Review the compensation structure.
- Understand contractual relationships with consultants.
- Look at the firm's professional liability insurance policy.
- Develop an awareness of professional practices and procedures that cannot be taught elsewhere.

Public Relations and Marketing

Effective public relations plays an essential role in the creation of the interior designer's image. Good public relations is important for bringing new clients and work into the office, as well as for attracting qualified designers to the professional staff. The professional interior designer must participate in marketing activities for the practice to succeed, but these activities may be subject to certain professional constraints. The intern must learn marketing techniques that are effective while remaining within the rules of professional conduct.

PROFESSION

The interior designer supports the development of the profession by working with others involved in the built environment and by participating in public service programs. Various professional associations and other public service opportunities offer a means of serving the profession and the community.

To support the development of the interior design profession, interns can:

- Participate in the work of the professional associations through committee activity.
- Provide service to the public by contributing expertise toward community affairs.
- Become familiar with the regulatory bodies of the profession.

BENEFITS OF THE INTERNSHIP SYSTEM

The primary beneficiary of an internship system is the intern. To acquire the greatest value from the program, the intern must plan carefully and be self-motivated. At this time it is the responsibility of new graduates to apply for and to organize their own professional internships. The interns should be aware that differences among firms and organizations may result in various exposure opportunities. The intern needs to take the initiative. An internship should not be narrow or restrictive, but bring into proper perspective the broad aspects of practice. It should offer a flexible system that responds to each intern's personal initiative and career goals.

An internship system provides the intern with an organized means of preparing for chosen careers through broad exposure to the interior design profession, thus making selection of a career direction easier. Through an internship, a network of participants and advisors is established that would otherwise be difficult to establish without many years in the business. Acquiring the necessary exposure and ensuring a meaningful preparation for the qualification examination (NCIDQ) establishes confidence and increases the self-esteem of an intern.

The secondary beneficiary of an internship system is the interior design office. Design employees are more knowledgeable and highly motivated as a result of working with interns. Those firms that participate directly in the program have the opportunity to evaluate potential future employees without long-term commitment. Those who serve as advisors within the design office find that they have to be on their toes in order to "teach" the intern. Interns, on the other hand, begin to appreciate the problems of running an office and, therefore, become better employees, as well as knowledgeable designers. The profession encourages this attitude and facilitates the quest for knowledge, thus raising the general caliber of all interior designers. Well-prepared interior designers enhance the public image of the profession of interior design.

Testing

LOUIS TREGRE

The National Council for Interior Design Qualification (NCIDQ) has become internationally recognized as the organization chartered to formulate and administer a qualifying examination that tests minimal competency of interior designers. This examination is used by the various states and Canadian provinces that have registration or certification statutes governing the practice or title of an interior designer.

HISTORICAL PERSPECTIVE

The NCIDQ examination was created to provide a vehicle for testing the professional qualifications of interior designers for government licensure or certification. In the mid-1960s, there were no examinations or academic or professional criteria that set minimum standards for those wishing to be interior design practitioners. The closest criterion was professional membership in one of the interior design organizations—with each organization having its own set of membership requirements. At the same time, interior design schools offered various curricula, and there were no uniform standards by which to achieve accreditation. Interior design, at this time, was considered by many a vocation, not a profession. In a society accustomed to government-regulated professions, the identification of qualified interior designers was a confusing issue to potential clients and the general public.

Recognizing the public confusion and lack of adequate guidelines, the American Institute of Interior Designers (AID) inaugurated the Voluntary Accreditation Program, which consisted of a three-part examination: written, design, and oral. It was first given to designers identified as members of the professional organization who were willing to be pretesters. As of July 1, 1970, AID required the test for all individuals wishing to become professional members. During this time, AID's counterpart professional organization, The National Society of Interior Designers (NSID), formulated and administered its own examination. This continued to add to the confusion in the public's mind because there were two large design organizations, each administering a different examination.

In 1972, AID and NSID met under the banner of the Joint Council for Interior Design Qualification and agreed to administer one exam. To enhance acceptance of the new examination, one representative from each national design organization that had professional interior design members was invited to sit on the Joint Council. Thus an organization representing the interior design profession with no vested interest was created, and through this the Joint Council was able to incorporate the thinking, knowledge, and expertise of practicing designers and trained interior design educators into the exam.

In 1973, AID and NSID turned their examinations over to the Educational Testing Services, one of the nation's most highly respected testing agencies, to create a single examination. Additions and deletions were made and approved by the Joint Council. The first official NCIDQ examination was given in October of 1974.

In May of 1974, NCIDQ was incorporated in the state of Delaware. The first members were the American Institute of Interior Designers (AID), the Interior Design Educators Council (IDEC), the Industrial Designers Society of America (IDSA), the Institute of Store Planners (ISP), the National Home Fashion League (now the IFDA), and the National Society of Interior Designers (NSID). The incorporation papers stipulated that only national design organizations, not individuals, could be members of NCIDQ.

NCIDQ TODAY

NCIDQ has continued, since its inception, to evaluate, update, and improve its examination. It has not remained static, but instead strives to remain current. In 1975 the examination underwent a thorough evaluation through the support of a matching grant from the National Endowment for the Arts. Five years later it underwent a year-long study to determine the requirements for practicing interior designers.

In 1987 NCIDQ began—with a matching grant from the American Society of Interior Designers—a job analysis, item writers' workshops, and a cut score study under the expert guidance of the Educational Testing Services and Hale Associates, performance testing specialists. These exercises verified the examination to be both credible and valid. Revisions made as a result of this exercise represent a shift from standardized testing (which relies on academic recall) to performance testing (which places a greater emphasis on practical experience).

The job analysis, conducted in collaboration with Educational Testing Services as part of the continuing evaluation of the examination, identified the following categories and percentages as requirements for interior design practitioners:

Theory: ....9 percent
Programming, planning and predesign: ......16 percent
Contract documents: ....16 percent
Furniture, fixtures, equipment, and finishes: ...4 percent
Building and interior systems: ....21 percent
Communication methods: ....4 percent
Codes/standards knowledge: ....13 percent
Business and professional practices: ....7 percent
Project coordination: ....7 percent
History: ....3 percent

With assistance from performance testing specialists, NCIDQ then evaluated and categorized questions into appropriate requirement sections at one of three levels—recall, application, and development. The examination was made as candidate-friendly as possible.

The current examination format is divided into the following sections and time allocations:

Building and barrier-free codes: ....2 hours
Two sections on identification
and applications: ....2 hours each
Problem-solving: ....2 hours
Practicum: .... 5 hours

The practicum section of the examination tests a designer's ability to interpret information and communicate solutions in a graphic form. Although in the practicum candidates are permitted to select one of five specialities (office, residential, retail, institutional, or hospitality), the knowledge testing is identical in each. The assumption is made that the basic body of knowledge necessary to practice as a professional interior designer remains the same regardless of the specialty area of practice.

A final step in the testing process is the establishment by NCIDQ of an annual certificate renewal program. Such a program will provide administrative support for legal recognition and supply state and provincial regulatory agencies with up-to-date NCIDQ certification status reports. It will also act as a clearinghouse for licensing reciprocity and will monitor continuing education units where applicable.

NCIDQ Information Handouts

NATIONAL COUNCIL FOR INTERIOR DESIGN QUALIFICATION

Conceived in the late 1960s by Louis Tregre and other key individuals working together, the National Council for Interior Design Qualification became a reality in 1972. The purpose of NCIDQ is to identify, for the benefit of the public, those interior designers who have met the minimum standards for professional practice. This is achieved by jurying the NCIDQ examination in locations throughout North America. At the present time fourteen states and all of Canada's provinces have practice acts, title acts, or certification acts serving as the measurement tool for each.

NCIDQ was incorporated in 1974 as a not-for-profit organization. The founder organizations were the American Institute of Design (AID) and the National Society of Interior Designers (NSID), which have since merged into the American Society of Interior Designers (ASID). The founding organizations recommended a separate council in order to better focus efforts upon the development of a qualifying exam for interior design practitioners, as well as to devote special attention to critical related issues such as exam administration, certification, and licensing.

The following information forms were prepared by The National Council for Interior Design Qualification in an attempt to answer questions that might arise regarding NCIDQ and the examination. For further information, contact:

National Council for Interior Design Qualification
118 East 25th Street
New York, NY 10010

GENERAL INFORMATION

Purpose: The National Council for Interior Design Qualification serves to identify to the public those interior designers who have met the minimum standards for professional practice by passing the NCIDQ examination.

The Council endeavors to maintain the most advanced examining procedures, and to update continually the examination to reflect expanding professional knowledge and design development techniques. It seeks the acceptance of the NCIDQ examination as a universal standard by which to measure the competency of interior designers to practice as professionals.

History: Conceived in the late 1960's to serve as a basis for issuing credentials to today's professional interior design practitioner, the Council has been in effect since 1972. It was formalized as a not-for-profit organization when it was incorporated in 1974.

NCIDQ's founders were the American Institute of Interior Designers (AID) and the National Society of Interior Designers (NSID), the two national organizations who were then preparing to merge into what became the American Society of Interior Designers (ASID). All national design organizations, whose membership was made up in total or in part of interior designers, were asked to join.

The parent organizations felt that a separate council was needed to (1) develop, administer and certify, through a qualifying examination, the interior design practitioner competent to practice; and (2) study and present plans, programs and guidelines for the statutory licensing of interior design practitioners.

Membership: The incorporation charter of the Council provides membership for professional design organizations and licensing boards only; it offers no provisions for membership to individuals. National organizations whose membership is made up in total or in part of interior designers may apply for membership.

Acceptance: The NCIDQ examination must be passed by every interior designer applying for professional membership in NCIDQ's constituent member organizations: American Society of Interior Designers (ASID), Council of Federal Interior Designers (CFID), Institute of Business Designers (IBD), Institute of Store Planners (ISP), Interior Design Educators Council (IDEC), Interior Designers of Canada (IDC), and International Society of Interior Designers (ISID). It must also be passed by applicants for a license in states of the United States and provinces of Canada which have licensing or registration statutes governing the profession. NCIDQ is a member of the International Federation of Interior Architects/Interior Designers.

Administration: Representatives of the member organizations (which consist of the seven national interior design organizations in the United States and Canada mentioned above) are appointed to serve as directors on the Council for three-year terms. The number of representatives is determined by the number of professional members actively engaged in the practice and/or teaching of interior design in each organization. Regulatory agencies are invited to appoint one representative each (for a three-year term) to the Council's Board of Directors.

The activities and affairs of the Council are managed by its Board of Directors which has the right and authority to manage its affairs, property, funds and policies.

Beyond the Council's responsibilities for conducting and jurying the examination in locations throughout North America, it is charged with defining, researching and updating bodies of knowledge, conducting field surveys, analyzing candidate performance, evaluating subject areas and item validity, developing and pre-testing questions and problems, improving scoring, implementing grading and jurying procedures, reviewing education and practice requirements, and identifying public health, safety and welfare issues.

NCIDQ

NATIONAL COUNCIL FOR INTERIOR DESIGN QUALIFICATION

DEFINITION

SHORT DEFINITION The Professional Interior Designer is qualified by education, experience, and examination to enhance the function and quality of interior spaces.

For the purpose of improving the quality of life, increasing productivity, and protecting the health, safety, and welfare of the public, the Professional Interior Designer:

* analyzes the client's needs, goals, and life and safety requirements;
* integrates findings with knowledge of interior design;
* formulates preliminary design concepts that are appropriate, functional, and aesthetic;
* develops and presents final design recommendations through appropriate presentation media;
* prepares working drawings and specifications for non-load bearing interior construction, materials, finishes, space planning, furnishings, fixtures, and equipment;
* collaborates with professional services of other licensed practitioners in the technical areas of mechanical, electrical, and load-bearing design as required for regulatory approval;
* prepares and administers bids and contract documents as the client's agent;
* reviews and evaluates design solutions during implementation and upon completion.

LONG DEFINITION (SCOPE OF SERVICES) The interior design profession provides services encompassing research, development, and implementation of plans and designs of interior environments to improve the quality of life, increase productivity, and protect the health, safety, and welfare of the public. The interior design process follows a systematic and coordinated methodology. Research, analysis, and integration of information into the creative process result in an appropriate interior environment. Practitioners may perform any or all of the following services:

Programming. Identify and analyze the client's needs and goals. Evaluate existing documentation and conditions. Assess project resources and limitations. Identify life, safety, and code requirements. Develop project schedules, work plans, and budgets. Analyze design objectives and spatial requirements. Integrate findings with their experience and knowledge of interior design. Determine the need, make recommendations, and coordinate with consultants and other specialists when required by professional practice or regulatory approval.

Conceptual Design. Formulate for client discussion and approval preliminary plans and design concepts that are appropriate and describe the character, function, and aesthetic of a project.

Design Development. Develop and present for client review and approval final design recommendations for: space planning and furnishings arrangements; wall, window, floor, and ceiling treatments; furnishings, fixtures, and millwork; color, finishes, and hardware; and lighting, electrical, and communications requirements. Develop art, accessory, and graphic/signage programs. Develop budgets. Presentation media can include drawings, sketches, perspectives, renderings, color and material boards, photographs, and models.

Contract Documents. Prepare working drawings and specifications for non-load bearing interior construction, materials, finishes, furnishings, fixtures, and equipment for client's approval. Collaborate with professional services of specialty consultants and licensed practitioners in the technical areas of mechanical, electrical, and load-bearing design as required by professional practice or regulatory approval. Identify qualified vendors. Prepare bid documentation. Collect and review bids. Assist clients in awarding contracts.

Contract Administration. Administer contract documents as the client's agent. Confirm required permits are obtained. Review and approve shop drawings and samples to assure they are consistent with design concepts. Conduct on-site visits and field inspections. Monitor contractors' and suppliers progress. Oversee on their clients' behalf the installation of furnishings, fixtures, and equipment. Prepare lists of deficiencies for the client's use.

Evaluation. Review and evaluate the implementation of projects while in progress and upon completion as representative of and on behalf of the client.

NCIDQ

NATIONAL COUNCIL FOR INTERIOR DESIGN QUALIFICATION

CERTIFICATION

NCIDQ certification recognizes that an individual has met minimum competency standards for the practice of interior design. NCIDQ's role in the certification process includes the establishment of standards for education and experience and the administration of a minimum competency examination. The examination tests the candidate's performance within the profession.

Certification by NCIDQ gives the interior designer a sense of personal achievement and contributes not only to the individual's professional recognition but to the recognition of the profession as a whole. NCIDQ certification serves as a qualifier for professional membership within interior design organizations and, for non-affiliates, represents a voluntary individual accomplishment.

The most significant aspect or by-product of the examination is the certificate candidates receive when they successfully complete the examination cycle. A certificate identifies the qualified practitioner, ensures recognition of expertise and assists in development and self-improvement through the individual's understanding of a body of knowledge and a set of professional standards.

Certification is generally defined as a voluntary form of recognition of an individual, granted by an organization or agency which is non-governmental. However, minimum competency in any profession is usually a baseline standard accepted by state and provincial governments for purposes of legal recognition. At the present time, NCIDQ certification is included among the license eligibility criteria in all American states and Canadian provinces with enacted statutes.

As a part of NCIDQ's ongoing effort to provide administrative support to facilitate legal recognition for interior design practitioners, the Council's board of directors approved a certificate renewal requirement to be effected in 1990. The $25 (U.S.) per individual, annual fee for renewing certificates enables NCIDQ to

(1) maintain an accurate mailing list of certificate holders for ongoing notifications pertaining to NCIDQ's certification program;

(2) update state and provincial regulatory agencies with current certification data for residents within a given jurisdiction;

(3) confirm NCIDQ certification status for initial licensing purposes in states and provinces; and

(4) act as a clearinghouse for purposes of licensing reciprocity.

In order to ensure the continued acceptance of NCIDQ certification in existing and proposed licensing statutes, the NCIDQ examination must continue to evaluate minimum competencies for the profession. However, as minimum competencies in any profession may change or evolve with the development of the profession and with the demands of the public, the examination and other certification standards must be continually reviewed and modified accordingly.

NCIDQ encourages current certificate holders to periodically keep current with the profession through re-examination. At the present time, this is a voluntary action, and existing certificates are not jeopardized if a certificate holder elects to take a subsequent examination. NCIDQ will issue renewal acknowledgments to those individuals, already certified, who are successfully re-examined in 1990 or thereafter. As the profession evolves, however, recertification may be a necessity, and NCIDQ is investigating such a program.

NCIDQ certification, therefore, provides interior designers with peer recognition, allows reciprocity to practice in licensed jurisdictions, and promotes public acceptance through awareness of a profession with certified practitioners.

NCIDQ encourages the use of the designation "NCIDQ Certified", along with the issued certificate number, on qualified practitioners' business forms, letterheads and business cards.

NCIDQ

NATIONAL COUNCIL FOR INTERIOR DESIGN QUALIFICATION

TERMINOLOGY

Professional certification is often confused with similar terms, such as accreditation and licensing. Certification itself may take many forms. The following will clarify the various terms.

Certification: Although a few state and provincial governments refer to the term "certification" as a level of legal recognition for individual practitioners within that state or province, certification is generally defined as a voluntary form of recognition of an individual, granted by an organization or agency which is non-governmental. This organizational certification recognizes that an individual has met predetermined requirements established by the organization. Certification may recognize only minimum competency levels, or may recognize advanced levels of accomplishment or proficiency within a profession.

Recertification: Some organizations require certificate holders to keep certificates current through periodic re-examination and/or the recording of continuing education units (CEU's). New certificates, or dated stickers affixed to certificates, are issued upon successful completion of each examination. This may be a condition for certificate renewal. In some cases, states or provinces may require periodic re-examination of specialized areas of knowledge, such as codes.

Advanced Certification: In professions where practice has become specialized, certifying organizations have expanded their scope to issue special certificates for highly developed disciplines. In the interior design profession, this could include, for example, the areas of commercial design, health care, retail or store planning, hospitality, historic preservation, and so forth.

Certificate Renewal: The annual recording of a certificate, by the certificate holder, to keep the certificate current for legislative and professional purposes is certificate renewal.

Accreditation: Accreditation applies to programs within institutions, rather than to individuals. Generally, accreditation is a voluntary form of recognition and is granted by an agency or association to programs or organizations that meet established qualification and education standards, as determined through initial and periodic evaluations. The Foundation for Interior Design Education Research (FIDER) accredits interior design programs.

Licensing: The specific terminology for licensing (or legal recognition) of a profession varies among jurisdictions. Licensing regulates individuals within a profession, such as interior design. The sole basis for licensing individuals is the protection of the health, safety and welfare of the public. Licenses are granted by a state or provincial government to individuals who have met predetermined qualifications, generally including education and experience requirements, and who have successfully completed an examination for minimum competency within a profession. Licensing may limit the use of a title associated with the profession, as in the case of title act legislation, or, in the case of practice act legislation, may restrict the practice of a profession to those individuals who have become licensed under the legislation.

Grandfathering: A regulating jurisdiction may, at its discretion, issue licenses to long-term practitioners, or others, who may not meet all license eligibility criteria as set forth in a licensing statute. For example, licensing requires examination, and grandfathering provisions may (but do not always) waive the examination criterion. This general acceptance, often offered only during a specified period of time, is called grandfathering. Practitioners in allied professions may also be grandfathered if the regulatory agency determines that professional and educational backgrounds of the allied practitioners conform to the practice or title criteria established for the licensed practitioner.

NCIDQ

NATIONAL COUNCIL FOR INTERIOR DESIGN QUALIFICATION

EXAMINATION

The NCIDQ examination is the most effective vehicle known for measuring minimum competency in the practice of interior design. It is the only interior design exam developed and administered in the United States and Canada by an agency that is independent from other interior design organizations.

After two years of extensive research and development, NCIDQ recently modified its two-part format to a six-part examination format. The changes to the examination are, in part, the result of the *NCIDQ Report of the Job Analysis of Interior Design*. The modifications that were made to the examination should not diminish nor undermine the importance and credibility of the old format. Revisions represent a shift from standarized testing, which relies on academic recall, to performance testing which places a greater emphasis on practical experience. Furthermore, it is important to remember that while the format and structure changed, the common body of knowledge being tested did not.

NCIDQ evaluated and categorized questions into three levels:

LEVEL A (recall) requires the candidate to name, identify or remember the correct term or concept from a list. Basically, the question requires the candidate to recall or recognize. The ability to discriminate can fall into this category.

LEVEL B (application) requires the candidate to apply a principle, concept or skill. Comparison and contrast can be tested at this level.

LEVEL C (developmental) requires the candidate to make a judgment, solve a problem or apply a skill, principle or concept to a difficult, complex situation. The candidate could be asked to integrate many principles or concepts to answer a question or problem in an acceptable way.

The six-part examination (all six parts of which must be passed within a five-year time frame) are described, administered and priced as follows:

Friday 8:30 a.m. to 12:00 p.m.
Identification and Application ($150) Multiple choice questions (up to 70 in each sub-section); A and B levels; computer scored. Two parts lasting one-and-one-half hours each with a half-hour break in between.

Saturday 8:30 a.m. to 10:00 a.m.
Problem Solving ($75) Multiple choice questions (24); C level; computer scored. One-and-one-half hours. Asks the candidate to review a designer's drawings, to understand them and to answer questions about a hypothetical situation. All the answers may be correct solutions, however only one will be appropriate to the particular drawing or situation.

Saturday 10:30 a.m. to 12:00 p.m.
Building and Barrier Free Codes ($75) Multiple choice questions (up to 64); A and B levels; computer scored. One-and-one-half hours. Generally, the codes questions test concepts rather than specifics (which vary from jurisdiction to jurisdiction). An understanding of building and barrier free codes in current printed editions of codes books is necessary. Candidates will be tested on the application of codes and the results and impact on public health, safety and welfare.

Manual Development sections are offered on both Friday and Saturday. C level; jury scored. Short succinct exercises demonstrate a designer's ability to interpret information and communicate solutions in a graphic form (by either drawing or drafting) which emphasize programming, space planning, lighting and three-dimensional development. These sections are scheduled as follows:

Friday 1:00 p.m. to 3:00 p.m.
Programming ($50) Evaluates the candidate's ability to gather, assimilate and interpret programmatic information into exercises. One exercise involves how a designer conducts a client interview. The second exercise asks the candidate to produce a bubble diagram/schematic from given program information.

NCIDQ

NATIONAL COUNCIL FOR INTERIOR DESIGN QUALIFICATION

Friday 3:30 p.m. to 5:00 p.m.
Three-Dimensional Exercise ($50)
Evaluates the candidate's ability to apply the principles and elements of the theory of interior design within a three-dimensional volume of space. Candidates must understand spatial volume, rather than just surfaces and planes. The integration of a lighting solution is required.

Saturday 1:00 p.m. to 3:30 p.m.
Project Scenario ($50) Evaluates the candidate's ability to analyze and interpret a written program of a chosen scenario into a space plan with furniture arrangement. A reflected ceiling plan is required.

With the project scenario section, it is important to realize that although candidates are permitted to select one of five scenarios to work with (office, residential, retail, institutional or hospitality), the knowledge being tested is identical in each. The flexibilty of choice simply allows the candidate to work in a familiar area.

All six examination sections must be passed within five years to receive certification by NCIDQ. Candidates have the option to take as many or as few of the sections as they deem necessary or desirable. Candidates may perform better if the Building and Barrier Free Codes and Identification and Application sections are taken during one administration and the manual development and Problem Solving sections are taken at a subsequent administration. During 1990 only, candidates who take all six parts of the examination during one administration, in either the spring or fall, may do so for a total price of $300.

Examination Eligibility: Spring and fall examinations are given in approximately fifty-five locations throughout the United States and Canada to those candidates who have achieved one of the following combinations of interior design education (or allied field) and professional experience:

* Four or five year degree in interior design or equivalent educational credits, plus two years practical professional experience.

* Three year certificate in interior design or equivalent educational credits, plus three years practical professional experience.

* Two year certificate in interior design or equivalent educational credits, plus four years practical professional experience.

NCIDQ proposes to establish an educational equivalency evaluation service for candidates not meeting the above criteria. This "window" may provide access to the examination for those candidates not meeting the above standards. A review process, for a fee, will be provided in such instances. The revised criteria are a means for incorporating FIDER standards into NCIDQ eligibility criteria.

Statement on Examination Equivalency: The first NCIDQ examination was administered in 1974. The AID and NSID exams in use at that time formed a preliminary basis for the 1974 NCIDQ exam. Records indicate that these exams were part of the process of developing the first NCIDQ exam. However, equivalency to other examinations was not considered when NCIDQ was formed, and there is no objective basis for determining if the AID and NSID exams were equivalent to the 1974 NCIDQ exam. NCIDQ has no means nor methodology for evaluating equivalency of examinations utilized prior to the formation of NCIDQ.

Examination Guide: A complete Examination Guide, with binder, is available for $35 from the NCIDQ office.

NCIDQ
NATIONAL COUNCIL FOR INTERIOR DESIGN QUALIFICATION

Licensing

ELIZABETH CASTLEMAN

As pointed out in previous sections of this manual, over the past years interior design organizations—recognizing the need to establish credibility and standards for the profession—joined together to support the creation of The Foundation for Interior Design Education Research (FIDER) and National Council for Interior Design Qualification (NCIDQ). Through these two organizations, educational standards and a professional qualification examination were established. Although these were important steps toward establishing professional standards and guidelines, the fact remains that these programs continue to be voluntary and are *not* a prerequisite for practicing interior design in most states.

At the present time, an individual who passes the NCIDQ examination qualifies as a professional member of certain interior design organizations such as ASID, IBD, ISID, and ISP. However, only 10 percent of the people who call themselves interior designers are members of these organizations. This leaves the public uninformed regarding the qualifications of 90 percent of the "interior designers" in the country. Such gaps in quality control reinforce the need for licensing. The public deserves the assurance that interior designers are qualified to practice, just as they are in other professional fields such as architecture, engineering, and medicine. The only viable means for this is state licensing.

LICENSING TODAY

Licensing for interior designers has been a concern for a number of years. As early as 1950 there were attempts to pass such legislation on a state level. However, at that time there was no organized national effort and these attempts were unsuccessful. The need for regulation and a guarantee of competency becomes apparent when one realizes that the only member of the building team not licensed is the interior designer. Yet, in most cases, the designer may be directing the work of other licensed practitioners.

As a first step toward licensing, title registration for interior designers was endorsed in the early 1980s by ASID. Title registration records the title "interior designer," and means that only those interior designers who have met minimum standards may use the title. Although this does not restrict the practice of interior design, it provides the public with a measure for determining qualifications. In the mid-1980s, ASID formed the Government Affairs Department to assist its professional members in the introduction and passage of licensing legislation in their states.

Efforts to secure licensing legislation are ongoing with 23 active state coalitions. Because this is a dynamic and ever-changing process, the statistics vary. At this time, Alabama, Connecticut, Louisiana, Florida, New Mexico, New York, California, Virginia, Illinois, the District of Columbia, and Puerto Rico have licensing acts. Of these, only the District of Columbia and Puerto Rico have a practice act that restricts the practice of interior design. The others have title acts. Each act has a form of a "grandfather" clause whereby designers with specific levels of experience and education are exempted from taking a licensing exam for a short window of time after the law becomes effective.

Opposition to licensing of interior designers comes from several different points of view. Some fear that licensing will limit their flexibility to offer decorating services in furniture stores. Others, such as the architectural community, feel that licensing of interior designers is an invasion of turf that has historically been designated to them. In addition to these concerns, the legislative climate of recent years has leaned more toward deregulation rather than regulation.

Regardless of these issues, the move toward licensing continues. Of particular significance in addressing the areas of conflict was the 1988 Accord document, which was developed and signed by the presidents of American Society of Interior Designers, the Institute of Business Designers, the International Society of Interior Design, and the American Institute of Architects. The Accord lists several points of common agreement that allow further discussion to continue between the two professions of interior design and architecture.

THE FUTURE OF LICENSING

The future looks bright. Several states are very close to achieving licensing or certification, and most states are becoming more legislatively active. The need to be aware of legislation affecting the profession is critical. By becoming more aware, designers can contribute to the public welfare by supporting legislation that will improve the built environment. It is the designers' responsibility to help shape the world, and legislation can make this happen.

Continuing Education

ODETTE LUECK AND DANIEL WEBSTER

The time has long passed when education was considered complete with the earning of a degree. Today the changes taking place in the world and the environment are staggering. In order to keep pace with the demands these changes place upon design professionals, continued education and professional development activities are a necessity.

The social and demographic changes emerging in society have a profound effect on interior design as a profession. Dual-career households, women in the workforce, the graying of America, and the growth of minority populations—all affect interior environmental decisions. Technology, too, is developing rapidly. Computers, communication aids, voice activation, smart houses, computer-aided design, VCR, FAX, and electronic mail are but a few examples. Economic considerations such as global markets and the growing merger and acquisition business, combined with political changes associated with regulation and deregulation, also have an impact on design decisions. A disciplined program of continuing education is critical for designers to be able to keep pace with these social, technical, economic, and political changes.

DEFINITION OF CONTINUING EDUCATION

Continuing education is a structured form of adult education, while professional development describes the broad spectrum of postcollege educational activities. Continuing education courses are, therefore, a form of professional development and represent only one vehicle for professional advancement. Continuing education courses that offer CEU's are recognized as noncredit courses with measurable hour units. Typically, one CEU (continuing education unit) is awarded for ten contact hours of participation in an organized continuing-education experience under responsible sponsorship, capable direction, and qualified instruction. However, a minimum of five hours may be acceptable depending upon the content and rigor of the course.

Independent organizations, such as the American College Testing (ACT) registry in Iowa, record the hours earned by professionals taking such courses. This registration is a verifiable record for participants to use on resumes for career advancement, or simply to document professional growth. As an incentive for pursuing professional development activities, ASID has established the Honors Program, which recognizes members who have attained seven CEU's (70 hours) within a three-year period.

Professional development activities and experiential learning situations appropriate for professional designers include conferences, seminars, lectures, tours, and networking. Management and business courses offered by the professional design community are also appropriate activities and may be, in some instances, the practitioner's only avenue for strengthening these skills.

Requirements for CEU's

Most state licensing acts require that the professional be attentive to continuing-education needs. State requirements vary, but a typical bill requires one CEU per year as a requirement for license renewal. One state proposes a mandatory course in life, fire, and safety before a license can be renewed. As more states approve licensing and title acts, legislators will come to expect evidence of the design professional's commitment to the health, safety, and welfare of the public.

THE CONTINUING EDUCATION PROGRAM

In 1977 the Council on the Continuing Education Unit (CCEU) was created to establish standards in the field of continuing education and training. The CCEU was established as a nonprofit federation of educational and training organizations and individuals devoted to the constructive and consistent use of the CEU. In 1984, after three years of research, the council published *Principals of Good Practice in Continuing Education*. This publication provides the sponsoring organizations' guidance in learning needs, learning outcomes, learning experiences, assessment of learning outcomes, and administration. It is available to organizations interested in sponsoring a continuing education course.

Recently the CCEU changed its name to the International Association for Continuing Education and Training. Because the need to emphasize certification and training in the business world has expanded, this title better represents the work of the Council.

CONTENT OF CONTINUING-EDUCATION COURSES

ASID, AIA, NHFL, IBD, IDC, and IDEC formed the Designer's Forum on Continuing Education to ensure that content and instruction of continuing education courses is applicable to the design profession. Under the direction of Interior Design Educator's Council (IDEC), the forum meets twice each year to review, monitor, and evaluate continuing-education activities in the design profession.

Typical courses relating to the design profession cover lighting, health and life safety issues, barrier-free design, historic preservation, legal issues, design-related business skills, and personal development such as communication, time management, and creativity.

The Forum has established standard forms for use by all sponsoring organizations. Course instructors and reviewers use these forms when submitting new courses for review. An evaluation form is also used by the participants at the completion of the course. As a minimum requirement for CEU approval, each course must be design-related and last a minimum of five hours on a specific subject. The courses must be taught by qualified instructors and can address technical, business, or personal skills applicable to design.

Each of the current members of the Forum (ASID, IBD, IDC, and IDEC), with the exception of IDEC, has a Course Review Committee composed of the professional development chair, design practitioners, and a member of IDEC. Each committee member, using the established forms as a guide, receives courses submitted for approval of CEU. Specific chapters submit and approve courses for local use at conferences, or for publication in the professional development manual, making them available for use by any chapter. In addition, the professional associations have worked with independent consultants who develop, promote, and conduct courses that are available to design professionals. These courses also must go through the review process.

SOURCES OF CONTINUING EDUCATION

Valid sources of continuing education, which initially were limited to schools and universities, now include professional associations, independent continuing education firms, association conferences, consultants, museums, art institutions, civic organizations, and travel study courses. Some of these carry CEU's and some do not. The value of the educational experience must be measured against the time devoted. A workshop or seminar is typically one to four hours, whereas a CEU course will be a minimum of five hours.

CONCLUSION

The importance of providing education as a part of membership services has been recognized by ASID, as well as other professional associations. In 1989 ASID established the Education Research and Development Committee. This committee was charged with researching and developing all areas of professional development. In addition to developing CEU courses at the intermediate and advanced levels, the committee has expanded its charge to include courses that address specific areas of various design specialities. The committee also studies differences in learning situations, including content, instructor qualification, delivery, and evaluation.

The increasing competitive market for design services requires constant attention to business. This demand places a strain on available time for research and study. However, never has it been more critical that the professional stay abreast of technical and business developments. Dedication to a personal program of continuing education is a professional's assurance of keeping competitive.

Design Research

JO ANN ASHER THOMPSON

In the busy world of interior design, it is difficult for practicing designers to understand and appreciate the importance of design research to their job. Most practitioners are too caught up in the daily routine of running the office, meeting the demands of clients, keeping abreast of new product and technological advances, and exploring design ideas to realize that design research is fundamental to each of these activities.

What is design research and why is it important to the interior design community? What are the primary objectives of design research? Who or what is affected by design research? Who should do design research? These important questions need addressing.

WHAT IS DESIGN RESEARCH AND WHY IS IT IMPORTANT?

Design research provides the fundamental theoretical underpinnings for interior design as a profession. It is through design research that the profession achieves academic credibility among other disciplines. Because of the applied nature of interior design, the linkages between design research and the professional community are necessarily strong.

Design research in its broadest context touches on every aspect of the interior design profession. It encompasses topics as different as history, human behavior, and technology. It provides designers with answers to complex questions about how and why people and groups with different needs and purposes behave in certain ways in different settings. The design researcher may choose to explore the theoretical nature of basic design constructs such as color, creativity, and visual perception, or try to measure the behavioral, psychological, and physiological responses of human beings to physical space. The focus of a research project may be on how people of different cultures define privacy and utilize physical space; or perhaps the researcher will choose to look at primary and secondary historical documentation to further our understanding and theoretical base for interior design. The list of possible research activities that contribute to our understanding of how better to design interior space to meet the physical, psychological, and utilitarian needs of human beings is unending.

Simply stated, design research is the identification of important design questions and the development and use of organized problem-solving methods. It is a process for seeking and finding answers. Many times the answers found are not straightforward and lead to even more questions. In this sense, design research is an ongoing process with one question leading to another. According to John Zeisel, in his book *Inquiry by Design*,

> *Research can provide deeper insight into a topic, better understanding of a problem, more clearly defined opportunities for and constraints on possible action, measurement of regularities, and ordered descriptions. . . . It is more than just searching (which can be haphazard) or just solving problems (which can be pragmatic). What researchers want to do is systematically use their experience to learn something to identify and help solve new problems. Presented with a problem, researchers draw on theory, training, accumulated knowledge, and experience to generate tentative ideas about how to solve it.*[1]

The objectives of design research are many and varied, but primary among these are (1) to predict behavior, (2) to verify patterns, and (3) to validate decisions. Design research impacts the profession by predicting behavior of individuals and families in the home, the workplace, and other public spaces; it verifies patterns through observations and experimental testing; and it validates decisions through theoretical design constructs and postoccupancy evaluation. The results of design research can justify design decisions, clarify ambiguities, and provide answers to problems.

THE RELATIONSHIP BETWEEN PRACTICE AND RESEARCH

At this point, it is important to examine more closely the relationship between the practice of interior design and design research. Remember, interior design is an applied science. What does this mean? According to *Webster's New World Dictionary*, the word "applied" is an adjective that means "used in practice or to work out practical problems." Given this definition, one can assume that the practicing interior designer applies the knowledge he or she has gained through education and life experiences in making design decisions.

One might ask, "How does this relate to design research?" The relationship is clear because the overarching goal of any research endeavor is to contribute to the profession's body of knowledge—and, in the specific case of interior design, to provide information to the design community that contributes to the advancement of the quality of life through meaningful inhabitation. The practice of interior design and design research are interdependent. The knowledge base from which the practicing interior designer draws is based upon research—both theoretical and experimental. This point is crystallized by Stanley Abercrombie in his book *A Philosphy of Interior Design* when he states,

> *Just as the success of any design will be limited by the wisdom of the concept it follows, the wisdom of any concept is limited by the vision and knowledge of the designer who conceives it. Before we presume to furnish our clients' rooms...we must furnish our minds. The amount of knowledge needed by a designer continues to proliferate.*[2]

Design research defines and expands the knowledge base and theoretical framework for the profession of interior design. Issues and problems that the practicing interior designer faces often become the design researcher's area of study and investigation. It is the practicing interior design community that calls upon design researchers to address arising needs and areas of concern. As the profession of interior design grows and matures, the relationship between the practicing design community and the research design community is dynamic and ever-changing. Cooperation between the practicing interior design community and the design research community serves to strengthen the profession as a whole and is a critical component in the future development of the profession. To quote John Zeisel once again,

> *People look to cooperate with others when they want to do more than they can do alone. . . . Research and design cooperation grows out of the variability of social reality: boundaries of problems change, situations differ, viewpoints are flexible, and people grow. The solutions that designers or researchers provide to their own problems have side effects in the other discipline. Cooperation is fostered when designers or researchers decide they want to use the other discipline as a tool to improve their control over side effects—that is, to solve more broadly defined problems than they can solve alone.*[3]

DESIGN RESEARCH AND THE DESIGN PROCESS

Research models utilized in design research are multidisciplinary, drawn from areas such as sociology, psychology, and anthropology. The research technique used in seeking answers varies depending upon the nature of the question being explored and might include techniques such as survey instruments, experimentation, historical documentation, behavioral observation, or combinations of these and other established means of gathering information.

Given these complexities, it is no wonder that design research is often misunderstood and a rather foreboding concept—particularly to the entry-level interior design instructor just entering the world of academia. At the same time, it is understandable that the practicing interior designer might simply dismiss the concept of design research as irrelevant and unrelated to his or her work. After all, the educational background of interior designers—both those who choose to go into practice and those who choose to teach—is focused upon creative problem solving, visual imaging, and presentation of ideas. In this context, design research is often perceived as uncreative and even foreign to the design process.

It is time to do away with the stereotype that design research is not creative and that it forces designers to perform in an arena where they have little expertise or training. Granted, the primary focus of undergraduate design programs is visual, and the concept of research seems contrary to this training. However, design training also provides a basis for critical thinking, order, and organization in design problem solving. The perception that someone trained in design cannot do or would not enjoy research is exacerbated by the fact that research terminology is different from that commonly used by the design practitioner.

With this comes the understandable perception that the design process and design research are so different that they are incompatible. However, design research—when approached without barriers—should be seen as a creative activity integral to the design process. At the same time, it is an area in which anyone trained in design is well prepared to engage. According to John Zeisel,

> *Design is difficult to describe because it includes so many intangible elements such as intuition, imagination, and creativity—which are essential to research as well. . . . Physical design inventively mixes together ideas, drawings, information, and a good many other ingredients to create something where nothing was before. Design can also be seen as an ordered process in which specific activities are loosely organized to make decisions about changing the physical world to achieve identifiable goals. . . . Anyone can become a researcher by doing normal, everyday things in an orderly way and for interesting, generalizable purposes. The orderly way to do research can be learned rationally and impersonally. The ability to develop interesting concepts—to go beyond the information given—can also be learned. But it is a creative ability, to be learned as one learns a skill.*[4]

A COMPARISON BETWEEN THE RESEARCH MODEL AND THE DESIGN MODEL

One way to alleviate misconceptions about the differences between design research and design practice is to compare the processes and terminologies used by the design researcher and the design practitioner and look at commonalities between the two. Usually the first step in the process for both the design practitioner and the design researcher is identification of the problem. The problem is often multidimensional with many different aspects, so the design practitioner and the design researcher must focus the problem, identify the key elements, and organize them in an orderly and manageable fashion.

Graphically comparing the design model and the research model clearly shows similarities between the design practitioner's approach to a design problem and the design researcher's approach in addressing a research hypothesis. Figure 1 shows that once the design problem is identified, the design process begins. The process usually includes some sort of literature review—even though it may be informal—which helps to focus the designer's ideas, provides examples of other similar design problems and solutions, and provides the designer with insights on possible technical considerations that must be made to best solve the problem. The literature review in the research model is used for the same purposes, but the focus is usually on other research activities and/or academic journal publications that might shed light on the hypothesis being tested.

Often at the same time that the literature is being reviewed, the design practitioner begins the process of collecting and analyzing data. This process is usually referred to by the practicing interior designer as programming, while the researcher refers to this process as data collection and analysis. Both are essentially the same in the sense that each process involves gathering important background and supportive information relevant to solving a problem or answering a question.

In the design model the client and/or the users of the space provide program information to the design practitioner. From a research perspective, the client and/or the users of the space in the programming process would be defined as the sample group from which information is drawn to answer a question or questions.

A close-up of the design model and the research model clearly illustrates that the biggest difference between the two models occurs in the area of data collection and analysis.

As can be seen in Figure 2, many times the tools and techniques the design practitioner uses to help focus the information gathered in the programming process is graphically or visually oriented, while the tools and techniques a design researcher uses may take the form of surveys, inter-

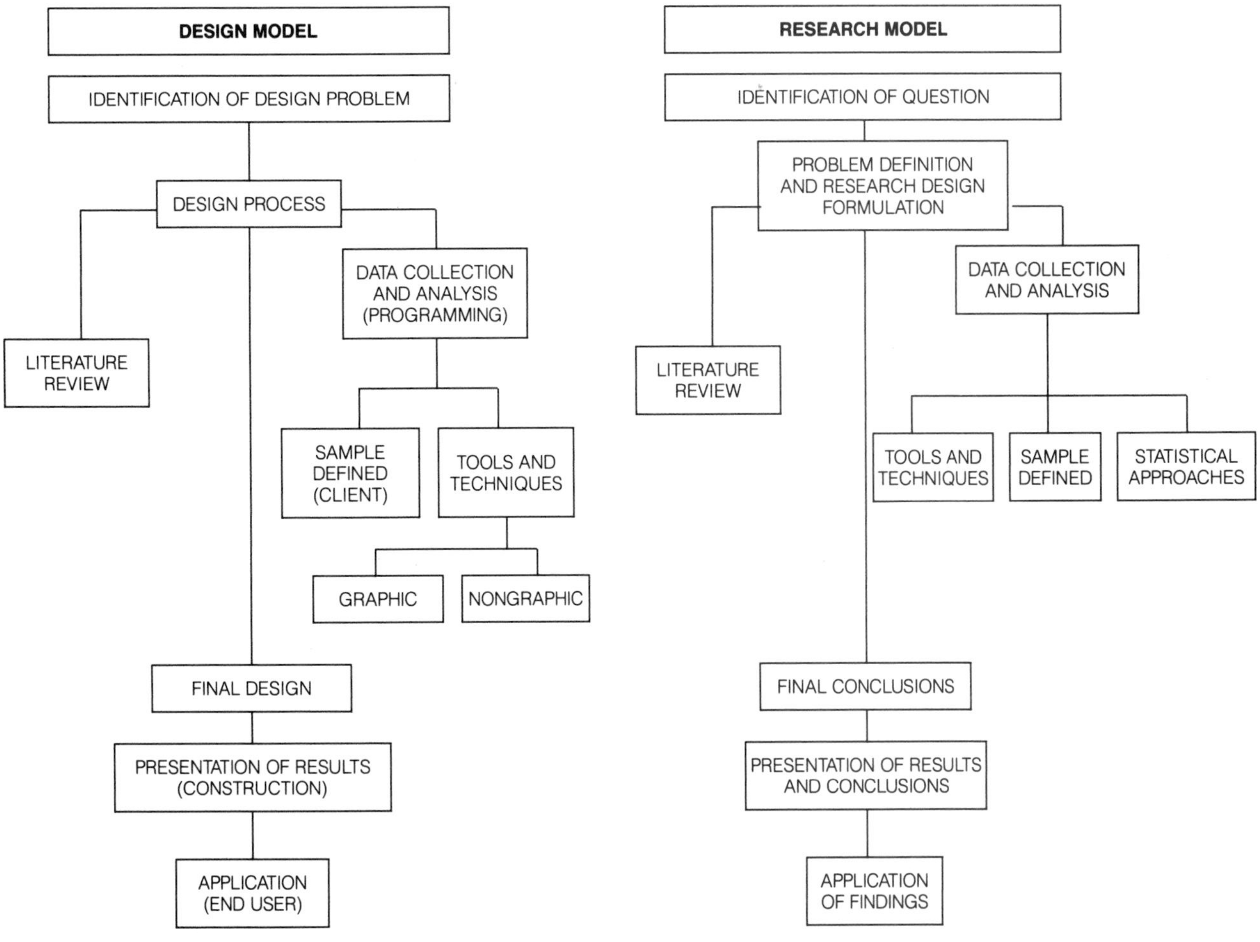

Figure 1. Comparative charts of design model and research model.

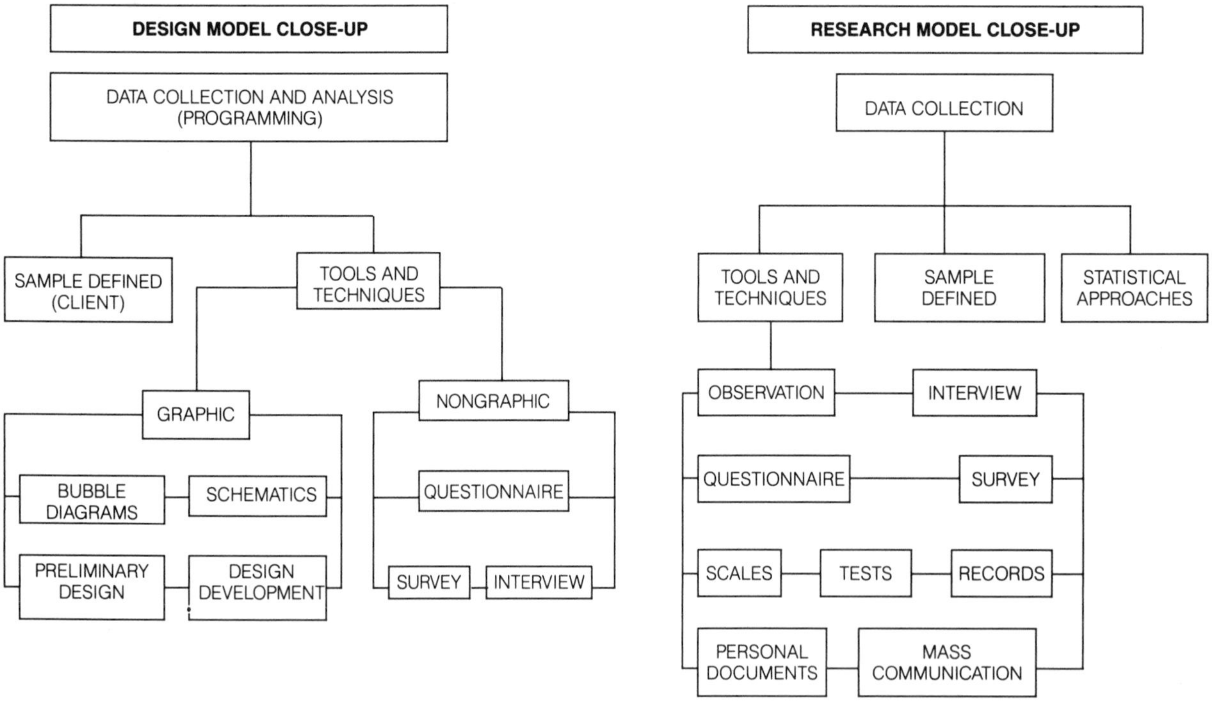

Figure 2. Close-up charts of data collection and analysis.

views, or statistical analysis. After completing the design phase and utilizing the appropriate visual and nonvisual tools and techniques in the design process, the design practitioner moves to a final design solution. Similarly, the design researcher—at this stage of the research project—draws final conclusions.

In each model, presentation of the results is a key part of the process. The design practitioner's results take the form of construction, while the design researcher's results are in a written and published form. The final step in both models is the application of the findings. In the case of the design model, the application is evaluated by the end user and other designers. In the case of the design researcher, the application of the results is evaluated by both the design community at large and by various other researchers and academicians.

CONCLUSION

Why is it important to compare the design practitioner model and the research model? Such an examination emphasizes the fact that both the design practitioner and the design researcher are involved in a creative process of problem solving. Although the tools and techniques used to solve problems are different—and although the end product takes different forms—there are many similarities. Research should not be intimidating to those who are trained as design practitioners. Research activities should not be viewed as foreign or foreboding, since—when the two processes are compared in this context—they are quite similar.

An educational background in design provides the fundamental underpinnings necessary to pursue design research activities. In many ways the procedures that a design practitioner follows on any given project echo those done by the design researcher. Perhaps through the recognition of these similarities, a better understanding between the design practitioner and the design researcher will emerge. Through this type of recognition and mutual support the interior design profession as a whole benefits and grows.

II. THE PRACTICE

Professional Ethics

CARL E. CLARK AND ROGER L. GREENLAW

Ethics is the study and philosophy of human conduct with emphasis on the determination of right and wrong. Organizations such as the American Society of Interior Designers (ASID) and other professional organizations are governed internally by bylaws and externally by a code of ethics. Membership in ASID therefore signifies an agreement to a set of moral principles and transcends the mere transaction of business.

RESPONSIBILITY TO THE PUBLIC

The designer's responsibility to the public comprises following building codes and permits, and not using unethical advertising and promotion.

Building Permits and Codes

The designer's responsibility to the public is to obey the laws—just as with any business endeavor. The designer, however, also must be cognizant of the codes and regulations of construction and understand how these laws apply to the practice of interior design. This is critical since the building code ensures the safety, health, and welfare of the people who occupy the interior built environment.

Certain projects an interior designer becomes involved with need not be submitted for a building permit, such as a project that only calls for wallcovering, paint, and reupholstery. When such a project occurs, is it necessary to design to codes regarding flammability, egress to exit, toxicity, and handicap access? The answer is yes. The designer is the enforcer and as such must provide furniture layouts and products that will minimize the hazards of the interior built environment.

Where else might this ethical principle apply? Let us take the example where a client of an interior designer wishes to remodel a kitchen. The designer accepts the commission, prepares the necessary design documents and specifications, and has the project bid by a licensed contractor. The bid is awarded. The client, however, asks that the drawings not be submitted for a building permit. Should the designer comply with the client's request?

If the designer complies with this request, the designer and the client are breaking the law. The proper inspections from the department of building and safety will not be made to ensure that the construction is in compliance with the safety laws. Ethically, the designer must convince the client that it is necessary to comply with the building code, or the designer must resign from the project, keeping the drawings and specifications so that they cannot be used by a contractor.

In this same arena, it is the interior design professional's obligation to prevent any attempt to influence the judgment of a public official regarding any project. Whether from the owner or an employee, such action cannot be tolerated and must be reported to the proper authorities.

Advertising and Promotion

Advertising and promotion is as old as the country itself. Over the years, advertising has become more sophisticated. Although many members of ASID feel that interior designers should not advertise their services, the professional code of ethics does not prevent designers from informing the public of such services.

To protect the public, fraudulent or misleading advertising is against the ethical guidelines of ASID. ASID prevents firms from giving the impression that all designers employed have met professional qualifications unless the appropriate credentials are held by each member of the company. Therefore, ASID appellations cannot be used after a company name, but rather only after each person's name. In addition, a professional designer should not seal or sign drawings or specifications of another designer unless those documents have been prepared by that person's firm. Signing on design documents means that person assumes the liability of said documents. Lastly, a designer should claim only that work for which he or she was responsible. It truly is unethical to present another's work as your own, whether through advertisement, slide presentations, or brochures.

RESPONSIBILITY TO THE CLIENT

The designer's responsibility to the client comprises clear communication about compensation and about liability for consultants, as well as confidentiality.

Compensation

The contract for design services between a client and the designer must clearly state a description of the project, where it is located, the name of the client, how the work will be accomplished, and the compensation to the designer. The client has a right to understand all aspects of the contract. The designer's obligation to the client is paramount and must not be compromised.

Take, for example, the situation where a designer has always used a particular cabinetmaker for projects. The cabinetmaker quotes a price to the designer's client. The client accepts the price as legitimate, but asks the designer, "Is this the best price?" The designer affirms the quotation. The contract is awarded. Several days later, the cabinetmaker sends a "finder's check" amounting to 10 percent of the quoted price to the designer. What are the ethical ramifications? Should this have been reported or mentioned to the designer's client? In essence, the designer lied to the client. The price quoted from the cabinetmaker was not the "best price." If the client should find out about the "finder's check," the client would be suspicious about other financial arrangements made with the designer. This is a fraudulent practice, and the reputation of the designer is seriously jeopardized.

All remuneration should be reported or understood by the client, leaving no reason for questioning the designer's integrity regarding the project. There are many ways for a designer to charge for services as long as the charges are completely understood by the client and the client has approved the compensation section of the contract. A designer has the right to change the compensation section when the client has requested additional services not stated in the contract, when the project has been delayed or postponed, or when conditions that were not previously evident are found after the project has commenced.

A designer must fully disclose all compensation. Although this appears to be a straightforward obligation, it can become a complicated issue. Take the instance where a manufacturer that the designer has been using for a long time is having a contest and will award so many points for each specification over a certain dollar amount. The prize is a trip to a vacation resort. Does the designer have to disclose that if he or she specifies this product on the client's project, the designer has a chance to win this contest? Yes, this is a form of compensation. If the client should find out about the contest, it would raise the issue of prejudicial selection, possibly not in the best interest of the client. The designer should always be the client's advocate, and there should not be the slightest hint of collusion.

Consultants

A designer must be truthful and confident that the work to be performed can be accomplished. However, most projects will require consultants, and the client should be informed about such conditions.

It is the best policy that consultant contracts be between the client and the consultant, with the designer coordinating the design documents for construction purposes. This avoids the problem of assumed liability of consultants by the designer. For example, a client has requested that a room be divided into two spaces. This project does not involve any structural changes, but a mechanical engineer is required to provide the necessary design documents for heating, ventilating, and air conditioning. If the contract for the consultant's design documents is a part of the interior designer's contract, then the interior designer is required to review this work. Since the designer's knowledge in this area is limited, the assumption would have to be made that the consultant's work is correct. By including the consultant as part of the interior designer's contract, the designer assumes liability for the consultant's work.

Confidentiality and Business Relationships

In the course of doing business, the designer will have knowledge of the client's business that requires confidentiality. It is the duty of the designer to maintain this confidentiality with the same trust agreement as between an attorney and a client.

All business relationships must eventually deal with payment transactions. All businesspeople are obligated to honor their indebtedness and pay invoices on time. There are times when business goes into recession. At times such as these, it behooves the designer/businessperson to inform suppliers of his or her condition and develop the means of eventual payment.

RESPONSIBILITY TO OTHER INTERIOR DESIGNERS AND COLLEAGUES

An interior designer establishes and maintains a clientele by the use of good business practices, professional ethics, and an astute sense of design and aesthetics. Successful interior designers acknowledge and respect the needs and desires of each client. This same designer/client respect must be present in designer-to-designer relationships. Acknowledgment of the rights, privileges, and obligations of fellow professionals is essential.

A client under contract with one designer should never knowingly be approached or solicited for business by another designer. Marketing strategies may include random solicitations. However, coercion, planned influence, repeated attempts, criticism of a fellow designer, and the assumption of credit for another designer's work are unethical approaches for developing clientele. To maintain a respected practice in interior design, one must work within the established standards of the interior design community. It is more rewarding to work together than to work against our design colleagues.

For example, take the following situation. A prominent interior designer charges another with unethical procedures when Designer A hires a local colleague, Designer B, to oversee the installation of Designer A's specifications for an out-of-town client. Designer B was accused of changing specifications and making new decisions during meetings with the client without Designer A's knowledge. Because both the client and Designer B were under contract to Designer A, each was contractually obligated to be loyal to Designer A. Ethically, Designer B could work with the client and change Designer A's specifications only upon proof of the termination of the contract between the client and Designer A, and only after the contract had been terminated between Designers A and B.

RESPONSIBILITY TO THE PROFESSION

The interior design profession is in the process of gaining legal recognition in the states, provinces, and jurisdictions throughout the United States and Canada. Legal recognition allows the public to recognize those who have specific qualifications and who practice within established ethical procedures.

All interior designers have a professional duty to maintain high ethical standards by conducting themselves and their practices in a responsible manner; to continually upgrade their professional knowledge and competency; and to encourage and contribute to the sharing of knowledge and information with other designers, allied professional disciplines, the industry, and the public.

A designer needs to remain current in order to guarantee that the best interests of clients are consistently maintained. Public speaking, community service, teaching, and of course the design of functional and pleasing environments are avenues for sharing professional knowledge with allied disciplines and the public. The greater our individual aspirations as professionals, the healthier the profession of interior design as a whole.

Professional Practice Choices: Overview of the Profession

JOYCE BURKE-JONES

Whether small, medium, or large, interior design firms have diversity as a common denominator. The interior design profession includes a multitude of service- and product-related specialities—individually, in multiples, and in totality. Moreover, the choices management or design principals make determine the size, organization, service, and client mix of firms. Although these choices may have little to do with the decision to bill for services, these choices have major ramifications relative to the management of staff, financial resources, and physical facilities. To better understand how and why decisions are made that determine the size of an interior design firm, the type of service offered, and its clientele, a close examination of organizational models for small, medium, and large firms is helpful.

SMALL INTERIOR DESIGN FIRMS

The small interior design firm of six or fewer owners and employees is the most prevalent interior design practice if retail product sale firms are excluded. A firm of this size allows its owners maximum flexibility and personal freedom.

A small firm's ownership can vary from a sole proprietorship to a partnership or a business corporation—depending upon the number of principals, specific services provided, and risk aversion. Circumstances will dictate the appropriate type of structural organization; however, it should be kept in mind that even when a firm is legally incorporated, the owners may still have personal financial liability. The liability of a small corporation is limited to some extent, but it is taxed on profit. As an employee of a corporation, the employee-president is also taxed on income or wages earned. Hence, a dual taxing situation is a consequence. For this reason many owners choose to remain small as proprietorships or partnerships.

Regardless of the size of the firm, a business plan is important. In many small firms this may be only a future projection of past costs and revenues with relatively non-specific identification of target markets, analysis of competition, and definition of the service/product to be sold. This type of flexible plan is adequate in most cases because of relatively low revenues and costs, and the opportunistic nature of small firms. However, the better organized the firm's business plan, the higher the probability of success.

In a small firm, a flexible business plan usually means a flexible business development and marketing plan, primarily because of the opportunistic nature of this size firm. For example, it is not unusual for each professional principal in a two-principal firm to be responsible for securing his or her own clientele and producing his or her own design services, while both principals will take responsibility for marketing the firm.

In a small firm clients are obtained through personal contacts and referrals. Target clients are usually price-sensitive and follow a simple selection process such as references and/or price quotes. The small interior design firm frequently sustains itself on a number of small projects with quick turnovers and quick payment. Some small firms specialize in an area such as residential or historic renovations. This focus on a speciality keeps marketing procedures simple and turnovers and referrals high.

Low overhead costs are crucial to a small firm's profitability. Although this is the goal of any size firm, it is essential to the small design firm. In order to be competitive, a small firm must be flexible enough to remain stable during economic highs and lows. Although there are always exceptions to this profile, the primary advantage of a small interior design firm is that it allows its owners the most flexibility and the most personal freedom of any size firm.

MEDIUM-SIZE FIRMS

Most medium-size firms feel that theirs is the ideal situation because they are autonomous, flexible, and profitable with less overhead and less management structure than a large firm. In some cases, the medium-size firm of approximately 7 to 20 owners and employees may conduct business similarly to a small interior design firm. However, to enhance efficiency and profitability, the medium-size firm usually has slightly different characteristics from those of a small firm.

Organizationally a medium-size firm can be a sole proprietorship, a partnership, or a legal corporation. Many medium-size firms began as small firms; therefore, it is important that small firms periodically review their organizational structure to verify their growth relative to their original size.

A business plan is a key to the successful transition from a small to medium-size firm. As a firm grows, the resources required and the revenues generated are larger and must sustain a larger staff and cash flow. Communication and the implementation of formal methods of internal information sharing are primary differences between small and medium firms. Partner or principal meetings evolve as a forum for consensus decision making. Frequently the office-wide meeting and interoffice memo serve to disseminate information and key decisions to the rest of the firm.

Business development practices also become more structured in the medium-size firm where one or two principals are responsible for obtaining commissions for the remainder of the staff to design and produce. Marketing efforts become more demanding and time-consuming, often requiring a firm to have a marketing coordinator and perhaps a principal who focuses directly on marketing and administrative requirements. Some firms also hire consultant lead finders as a supplement to the firm's own in-house efforts. Usually the firm implements some form of marketing plan that identifies revenue goals, market penetration objectives and strategies, and developmental tactics.

The medium-size firm often focuses on larger projects requiring specialized expertise. Frequently design firms for these projects are selected through a formalized procedure involving numerous client representatives, board members, or staff. Often these projects are generated through a request for proposals (RFP). The client, along with other professionals seeking the commission, may be part of a selection committee in order ultimately to provide a full-service package. Because the up-front costs required from these types of projects can be high, and unsuccessful attempts at getting projects through lengthy selection processes can be quite costly and time-consuming, medium-size design firms must be cautious in pursuing them in order to remain solvent and profitable as a firm. Again, a business plan is helpful to the firm when making these decisions.

With availability and affordability, computers have become an asset to a medium-size firm. When used properly, the computer can become almost like an additional staff member: It increases design efficiency and financial management, including the ability to track billable and nonbillable hours, reimbursable and nonreimbursable costs, and office overhead expenses.

LARGE INTERIOR DESIGN FIRMS

The large interior design firm of more than 20 owners and employees represents a small percentage of the design firms in the United States and Canada. The general characteristics of large firms are as diverse as are the size variations. Many of these firms are architecturally or corporately oriented.

As with small and medium-size firms, the business organization may be a partnership or a corporation. Sole proprietorship in large firms is less frequent because of the financial risk, taxes, and liability. With title legislation and licensing for interior designers, the requirements for employment within all sizes of firms may have to change in some ways. However, with large firms these changes will be less noticeable because most employees must be professionally trained upon hiring in order to be competitive within the firm and therefore have met a significant portion of the state requirements for registration.

Large interior design firms have typically been in business longer than small and medium-size firms. Most large interior design firms have multiple owners and have the most formalized business system of the three groups. The largest firms are most likely to have formal and lengthy business plans documenting long- and short-range business goals and analyzing past achievements.

In a large firm, business development follows a formalized marketing plan that states goals, objectives, strategies, and tactics. These are usually an expansion of the firm's business plan and directed by a marketing director. This director, who may be a principal, is responsible for marketing, strategic planning, and coordination. Frequently, one or more of the firm's principals are involved in the marketing effort, each responsible for specific clientele. Another marketing approach may be an in-house and/or consultant lead-finding marketing coordinator with supporting staff for preparing proposals and producing marketing materials.

Large firms will have the largest variety of clientele, with a number of associated professional selection processes. These may range from referrals generating a contract to elaborately formed professional teams submitting qualification statements, request for proposal submittals (RFP), and presentations. The cost of marketing and preparing for the selection process for the larger-volume projects is offset by the establishment of a firm's reputation for specialized projects. In uncertain economic times this becomes a strong stabilizing factor for large firms.

Business management in large interior design firms can be hierarchic or matrix, depending on firm ownership and size. The large firm, even with several branch offices, will usually centralize management and operations for cost efficiency. However, when the centralized management and staff become too unwieldy, the firm may decentralize into a number of separately operating regional offices that keep central management apprised of their activities.

When a firm reaches approximately 20 employees and its business structure becomes more formalized, it may be necessary for one principal to focus on administration, or become totally separated from design production. Formal documentation of office standards, quality control procedures, project management procedures, and human resources standards becomes important. This trend toward formalization can extend to in-house training/development programs and employee performance reviews. Additionally, large firms generally develop a continuation plan to ensure the firm's survival after the original founders leave.

Design management in larger firms operates differently from that in smaller firms, and project managers become more important than in medium-size firms. As pointed out previously, it is not uncommon for principals to be totally removed from the design process. Additionally, a variety of professionals such as architects, engineers, and other specialists may be employed by the firm to provide a full scope of design services in-house. These teams of professionals may be organized by design disciplines, used for specific projects, and disbanded when the project is complete. Another organizational pattern is to have specialized design discipline departments that work on projects across the board supported by a large centralized computer-aided design (CAD) and/or manual drafting department. Both scenarios are used successfully by large design firms.

Financial management in large firms, as with business and design management, is usually highly specialized and structured with automated systems for efficient billing and cost data information systems. These sophisticated methods enhance productivity and efficiency, thus providing owners and employees of large firms the highest compensation and benefit packages in the profession.

COMPARISON CHART

Figure 1 (below and on the next page) has been developed to provide a simplified reference guide to the essential similarities and differences of small, medium-size, and large interior design firms.

CONCLUSION

The key to a profitable interior design firm is not size. Conscious planning and management can make any size firm a success. A successful firm is judged by its achievements, and by meeting its goals and objectives, both professionally and financially.

Operation Categories	Small Firms	Medium-Size Firms	Large Firms
Business Structure	• Sold proprietorship • Partnership • Corporation (less frequently) • Approx. firm size 1–6	• Sole proprietorship • Partnership • Corporation • Approx. firm size 7–20	• Sole proprietorship (less frequently) • Partnership • Corporation • Approx. firm size 21–up
Business Plans	• Usually unstated "shoot from hip" approach; follow opportunities	• Verbal consensus of direction among principals shared with associates. Sometimes loosely documented.	• Formal long- and short-range statement of goals, objectives, and strategies at various stages of elaboration.
Business Development (Approach)	• No marketing plan. • Proprietor responsible for getting clients through personal contacts for staff. • Each professional firm member is responsible for getting own work through personal contacts.	• Verbal marketing plan based on general consensus, following opportunities, and occasionally targeting new markets. • One principal allocates majority of time to marketing while others produce. • Majority of principals responsible for marketing. • Frequently in both cases staff includes a part-time marketing coordinator to assist principals in management effort. • May have consultant lead finder.	• Formal marketing plan. • Director of business development responsible for market strategic planning and coordination (may be principal). One or more principals participate heavily in marketing effort. Each responsible for definite client types. In-house and/or consultant lead-finding program. Full-time marketing coordinator(s) and staff responsible for proposal preparation and marketing material production.
Business Development (Client Types)	• End users with informal selection process, i.e., referrals, repeat business, or short qualification proposals.	• Team with other professionals for clients in comprehensive and formalized selection procedures.	• Team with other professionals for clients in comprehensive and formalized selection procedure.

Figure 1. Comparison chart for interior design firms of different sizes.

Operation Categories	Small Firms	Medium-Size Firms	Large Firms
Business Development (Client Types)	• Team with other professionals for clients in comprehensive and formalized selection procedure (less frequently).	• End users with comprehensive and formalized selection procedures.	• End users with comprehensive and formalized selection procedures.
Business Management	• Size gives ability for loosely structured management. • Informal communications. • Decision-making process either autocratic or democratic depending on sole ownership or partnership. • Decision-making process for design and business problems are responsibility of same person.	• More structured management (matrix). • Combined informal and formal lines of communication. • Decision-making process more commonly is either autocratic or consultive. • Business decision maker may be different from design decision maker(s). • Need for documented office standards. • Need for workload forecasting and progress reporting. • Automated progress reporting.	• Highly structured management hierarchical or matrix. • Decision process tends to be bureaucratic or consultive. • One principal responsibility solely lies in administration of firm. • One principal responsible for office production. • Formal documentation of office standards, quantity control, and project management procedures. • In-house training and development programs. • Formal performance review. • Formalized firm continuation plans. • Automated progress reporting.
Design Management	• Design is usually controlled by client more than by professional. • Ability to produce as one design team for unusually large projects or short time frames. • Flexibility to break down to single-person teams for typically smaller projects. • CAD use improbable.	• Project managers begin to take the place of principals managing projects. • Designs are executed by teams appropriate to size of task. • Principals may delegate design authority and become more responsible for quality control. • Possible CAD use.	• Project managers control project with minimal principal involvement. • Designs are executed by teams appropriate to size and duration of project or through departments with separate production staff. • CAD use.
Financial Management	• Automated accounting probable. • May be somewhat unstructured and flexible in accounting for time spent on projects and associated reimbursable costs. • Usually has low overhead cost ratio.	• Automated financial management. • Structured billing system for professional hours spent and reimbursable costs. • May have less efficient overhead cost ratio than smaller or larger firms because of physical plant or technology.	• Highly structured automatic financial system. • Efficient billing systems and procedures for gathering cost data. • Efficient overhead ratio.

Guidelines for Starting a Practice

DIANE B. WORTH

No designer can set up a practice without first setting up a business organization. It shouldn't be necessary to make such a ridiculously obvious statement, but it is. Many designers commit themselves to the dream of making beautiful interiors happen without stopping to make the decisions and go through the formalities that must be attended to before they have the legal right to do business. These decisions and formalities cannot be evaded even if the designer wants to start small—as small as a one-person office. For not even the one-person office can function until a business vehicle has been provided to roll it along.[1]

Harry Siegel, *A Guide to Business Principles and Practices for Interior Designers*

These words were written in 1968, when the impact of practicing designers and their contributions to the national economy was still to be realized. Yet these words are as true today as they were in 1968. Since that time a great many changes have occurred in the profession and in the economic and business structures within which the profession functions. Interior design has changed and matured; today's designers are seen as technically skilled, creative professionals with several years of college education and training. In today's world, interior designers provide solutions to interior spaces that are creative and cost-effective, and that provide for the health, safety, and welfare of fellow humans, both at home and in the workplace.

These changes in the profession have been supported by the furniture manufacturing industry, whose goods and services are an integral part of interior design. In the late 1950s and 1960s, interior designers became an important vehicle for bringing quality furnishings to the marketplace through the development of regional design centers created for designers to research and analyze furnishings. At this time most interior designers depended on product markup to provide income. Today, a large segment of the design community continues to do business based on this method of service and supply. The basic business structure for this type of organization is monitored by the Uniform Commercial Code and is commonly found in retail operations.

As technology has advanced and interest in creating healthful, productive, and safe interior environments has increased, the public has demanded that design professionals be trained beyond basic arts, crafts, and home furnishings. In response, institutes of higher education have expanded curricula to include specialized courses in lighting, acoustics, and climate control. In addition, most university programs place an emphasis on accessibility for the handicapped and on fire and life safety codes.

At the same time that institutes of higher education began refining curricula to reflect the maturation of the interior design profession, the furniture manufacturing industry was addressing these same problems by introducing flame-retardant upholstery and producing ergonomically sensitive furnishings for the work environment. In addition, the dealer showroom concept was developed to better address bringing the product to the market.

During this period of transition, the commercial interior designer practiced in business formats much like architects, specifying the appropriate finishes and products and leaving the purchase and delivery of furnishings to purchasing agents, dealers, or the end user. These designers prepared contracts and charged fees for the service of designing, specifying, and overseeing the project for the client. This new generation of designers was trained to specify the best product for the project, as well as to prepare specifications for the most functionally desirable solution.

During this time many established and well-known designers whose emphasis had been on residential design began offering design services for a fee on small commercial projects. This expansion from residential work into commercial work was often seen as a success pattern. Many design firms that continued to purchase products for their clients, in addition to charging a design service fee, still maintained a markup on the purchase and resale of products as a part of their profit margin.

The purchase of products was, and still is, accomplished in several different ways. One of the most common purchasing methods is cost-plus with the plus as a purchasing fee or an agreed markup. Another method is percentage-off-retail. As the designer deals with increasingly larger projects, this latter method is fraught with problems. Without a clear definition of what retail pricing means, clients often expect sizable discounts on furnishings from interior design firms using this method.

The trend to continue to sell products at a markup, as well as charge a design service fee, continues today. This is clearly a combination of two basic business operations. When a design firm is trying to determine an appropriate business structure, design service fees and product sales should be evaluated independently for financial performance, income projections, and capital risk.

TIME

The service a designer provides for a fee is represented by time. A clear definition of the service to be provided is imperative when starting a practice. Written communications and accurate, consistent financial records are essential to protect both the professional and the client.

PRODUCT SALES

Product sales by interior designers have never had clearly defined rules and regulations. The standards applied have evolved from practices borrowed from wholesalers, dealers, custom manufacturers, and retailers. Each has established, although not uniformly, certain guidelines accepted by the public. Many designers involved in product sales are defined as merchants— buying at wholesale and selling products at retail, and legal matters rely on "business custom" rather than specific accounting or legal guidelines.

Retail business procedures are based on sales volume of differently priced products. Designers who choose to adopt a policy of discount-off-retail for less than high-volume purchasing may find clients whose final purchase price may be more than "retail" once all the costs of freight, handling, and delivery are included. These clients may demand full cost disclosure. Today most large projects that include the purchase of products are controlled by knowledgeable facilities managers. Such managers usually insist upon full disclosure of net costs. They also recognize that the payment of a purchasing fee, established as a percentage of the product sales, is a more efficient procedure than tracking and managing in-house a large project with product purchases. Designers who price products on the basis of "what the traffic will bear" are following an outdated practice.

The legal issues applying to product sales by merchants are outlined in the Uniform Commercial Code; however, certain aspects of the code in the case of designers may be supplanted by general contract law. The responsibilities of the designer are similar for both product sales under the UCC and fee-for-service under general contract law, but the remedies may be different. These differences can create financial chaos for the designer who is unaware. Traditionally, product sale remedies involve replacement or repair of products, while fee-for-service remedies involve the repayment of money.

In both product sales and fee-for-service, it is important to define the designer's role clearly. While fee-for-service is publicly accepted as a business practice in most professions, the interior designer's variable of product sales confuses the issue for the public because of the lack of clearly defined guidelines and standards. The need for clear and consistent guidelines for product sales is emphasized by Magili Larson, a sociologist concentrating on the development of professions in our current social system. He states that the future growth of a profession depends upon the producers of special services constructing and expanding a market for their expertise. He elaborates by pointing out:

> *As a part of this stage, successful "selling" depends on some degree of standardization of both "commodity" and "provider." This is achieved through establishing practices, procedures, and common educational paths. In any large-scale marketing endeavor, clients will seek products and/or services only if they can depend on consistency of behaviors and procedures from the large number of professionals who claim to be providing similar services. Inconsistency breeds mistrust and confusion on the part of the client.*[2]

TYPES OF BUSINESS STRUCTURES

To establish a private practice, the designer must determine a specific business organization structure. For a business structure that charges a fee-for-service, Andrew Loebelson, author of *How to Profit in Contract Design*, states:

> *Each form varies in its characteristics in terms of organization, the personal liability of the owners, the continuity and transferability of the firm, the latitude management is allowed in running the firm, the ease of raising capital, and the taxation of profits.*[3]

The addition of product sales under any business entity changes the risk and liability factors, as well as the legal means for recovery.

Regardless of the type of business structure chosen, several decisions must be made if product sales are to be a part of the practice. Consultation with an attorney and accountant will clarify some of the issues involved when product sales are incorporated as part of the practice. These professional consultants will assist the designer in making the final decision.

Figure 1 has been developed for quick reference to help readers evaluate the pros and cons of various organization structures and to provide guidance for appropriate procedures to follow when setting up a practice. Note that each of the business structures outlined in the reference guide uses the same basic accounting principles, but varies in terms of equity where liability and ownership are concerned. Whether a sole proprietorship or a major corporation, each combines the same principles of planning—the numbers and the risks just get larger.

Other Business Types

The business designation of associate has been used by designers for many years. It does not, however, constitute a formal business relationship and is referred to by the Internal Revenue Service as having independent contractor status. This status designates a person in a separate business

I. THE SOLE PROPRIETORSHIP

DEFINITION: Individual Ownership

Organizational Requirements	**Essential Things to Consider for Inclusion of Product Sales**
• Selection of location.	• Retail or wholesale?
• Registration of company name with county and city.	• Resale license? Bond requirements? Zoning?
• Application for federal I.D. number.	• Declaration of service or supply.
• Attainment of appropriate licenses.	• Specialty or contractor license if required for floorcovering, window covering, wallcovering, painting, carpentry, cabinetwork and millwork, plumbing, electrical, etc.
• Establishment of a commercial bank account.	• Establishment of a line of credit for product purchasing and financial statement.
Capital Requirements and Liability	
• Owner's assets only.	• Must have a substantial credit history.
• Unlimited liability.	
Management and Taxation	
• Complete control of management by owner.	
• Profit and loss as personal income.	• Accounting system must address large projects in progress at end of fiscal year.
	• Larger retained earnings for handling jobs in work and on warranties.
Profits and Assets	
• Owner's discretion.	• Profit on fees-for-service and product sales clearly delineated.
Salability of Firm	
• Freedom to sell or transfer.	• Gross dollar volume may be distorted if service fee versus product sales are not clearly identified.
• Company terminates with death of sole proprietor.	

Figure 1. Quick reference guide to the pros and cons of business organizational structures.

II. GENERAL PARTNERSHIP

DEFINITION: Two or more persons engaged in the same business enterprise and sharing its profits and risks.

Organizational Requirements

- Written agreements based on business plan: capital needs, management of the firm, distribution of money and profit, and concepts of ownership defined.
- Selection of location.
- Registration of company name with county and city.
- Application for federal ID.
- Attainment of appropriate licenses.
- Establishment of a commercial bank account.

Capital Requirements and Liability

Capital:

- Small initially; partners' assets combined but no protection of interest in partnership.
- Ample insurance recommended.
- Credit history; all partners considered.

Liability:

- Unlimited; personal bankruptcy insurance is one form of protection.

Management and Taxation

Management:

- Majority of management duties with a specified general partner.

Taxation:

- Personal income for each partner.

Profits and Assets

- As agreed by partners' majority.

Salability

- Death dissolves partnership unless otherwise agreed. Transferred by consent of all partners or other signed agreements.

Essential Things to Consider for Inclusion of Product Sales

- Retail or wholesale?
- Resale license? Bond requirements? Zoning?
- Declaration of service or supply.
- Specialty or contractor license if required for floorcovering, window covering, wallcovering, painting, carpentry, cabinetwork and millwork, plumbing, electrical, etc.
- Establishment of a line of credit for product purchasing and financial statement.
- General partner's name must appear on all documents.
- Must have a substantial credit history.
- Accounting system must address large projects in progress at end of fiscal year.
- Larger retained earnings for handling jobs in work and on warranties.
- Profit on fees-for-service and product sales clearly delineated.
- Gross dollar volume may be distorted if service fee versus product sales are not clearly identified.

III. LIMITED PARTNERSHIP

DEFINITION: A limited association of two or more partners in a business enterprise; a structure not often seen in a service business.

Organizational Requirements	Essential Things to Consider for Inclusion of Product Sales
• Written agreements same as for general partnership; general partner must have limited partner.	
• Selection of location.	• Retail or wholesale?
• Registration of company name with county and city.	• Resale license? Bond requirements? Zoning?
• Application for federal ID.	• Declaration of service or supply.
• Attainment of appropriate licenses.	• Specialty or contractor license if required for floorcovering, window covering, wallcovering, painting, carpentry, cabinetwork and millwork, plumbing, electrical, etc.
• Establishment of a commercial bank account.	• Establishment of a line of credit for product purchasing and financial statement.
Capital Requirements and Liability	
Capital:	
• Slightly higher than general partnership; this structure makes it easier for general partner to raise capital.	
• Combined assets of all partners.	• Must have a substantial credit history.
Liability:	
• General partner in firm has unlimited liability; limited partners have only to the extent of investment or as agreed.	
Management and Taxation	
Management:	
• General partner is manager; majority required; some legal regulation.	
Taxation:	
• Profit and loss as personal income.	• Accounting system must address large projects in progress at end of fiscal year.
Profits and Assets	
• As structured by the general partners; majority rules.	• Larger retained earnings for handling jobs in work and on warranties.
	• Profit on fees-for-service and product sales clearly delineated.
Salability of Firm	
• Same as general partnership except limited partners have right to sell; transfer by consent of general partners.	• Gross dollar volume may be distorted if service fee versus product sales are not clearly identified.

IV. CORPORATIONS

DEFINITION: Business organization structure treated as individuals by law; corporation continues regardless of the death or withdrawal of any managing stockholder.

Organizational Requirements

- Legal requirements for articles of incorporation, filing fees, issuing stock, statutory agent.
- Written agreements prepared similarly to partnership to be incorporated in procedures for corporation.
- Selection of location.
- Registration of company name with county and city.
- Application for federal ID.
- Attainment of appropriate licenses.
- Establishment of a commercial bank account.

Capital Requirements

Capital:

- Most expensive form for setup as well as maintenance.
- Easiest to raise capital.

Liability:

- Limited to the amount invested except for officers and board in the event of criminal actions.

Management and Taxation

Management:

- Board of Directors elected, influenced by stockholders.
- Strict legal regulations.

Taxation:

- Taxed at corporate level and again when distributed to stockholders; depends on tax bracket of stockholder, whether good or bad.

Profits and Assets

- Special stock issues are taxed at personal income level rather than capital losses.

Salability of Firm

- Continues regardless of death, sale, or withdrawal of any managing stockholder.
- Transferred by stock, assets, assigned income, etc.

Essential Things to Consider for Inclusion of Product Sales

- Retail or wholesale?
- Resale license? Bond requirements? Zoning?
- Declaration of service or supply.
- Specialty or contractor license if required for floorcovering, window covering, wallcovering, painting, carpentry, cabinetwork and millwork, plumbing, electrical, etc.
- Establishment of a line of credit for product purchasing and financial statement.
- Must have a substantial credit history.
- Accounting system must address large projects in progress at end of fiscal year.
- Larger retained earnings for handling jobs in work and on warranties.
- Profit on fees-for-service and product sales clearly delineated.
- Gross dollar volume may be distorted if service fee versus product sales are not clearly identified.

who is contracting for work from another business entity. The independent contractor must perform specific services for more than one business entity; therefore, associates must clearly be employees, partners, or stockholders, and the method of payment must identify commission on sales, or other contractual arrangements for specific projects or jobs.

Another commonly seen business organization structure is the joint venture. Though sometimes assumed to be a business entity, joint ventures are really two or more firms working together under the same contract to accomplish a single objective.

Yet another type of business enterprise, which is similar to a joint venture and is often mistaken for a separate business entity, is an association. Actually associations are a collaboration of independent business entities working together under a specifically prepared set of rules and regulations for the initiation, preparation, and/or operation of a common goal or entity.

STARTING A PRACTICE

The profession of interior design is currently listed in the Standard Industrial Classification (SIC) codes of financial institutions as 7389-20, which is the category for businesses not elsewhere listed. Such businesses are usually considered high risk by bankers and insurance carriers. Given this tentative national financial recognition for the interior design profession, it is imperative for the fledgling firm to develop a financial plan or feasibility study as a first priority. This plan should include carefully thought out answers to the following detailed list of questions:

The Goals and Objectives of the Principal or Principals

Why are you starting this business?

What are your financial and professional expectations?

What background, in terms of education and training, is needed?

The Business Statement

What is the purpose of the business?

What needs does the business fulfill?

What operations are defined to fulfill those needs?

What will be produced?

Who will be involved in that production?

The Starting Position

With whom, when, and where will the business begin?

Will it be an existing practice, merger, or buy-out?

What are the existing relationships with clients, suppliers, lessors, and so on?

What are the financial needs for start-up funds and working capital?

The Market Description

Who are the clients and what are the services of the practice?

Why is the service needed and by whom?

What are the characteristics of the market?

What types of contracts, fees, and terms are to be used?

The Competition Description

What is the competitive environment of the market?

How well are others in the field doing?

How will this firm improve upon what exists in the marketplace?

The Financial Pro Formas

What will the business operation be in three to five years?

What are the anticipated cash flows, working capital requirements, profits and losses, and loan repayment schedules?

Additional information required will include:

a. Why is the money needed?
b. When will it be repaid?
c. How much money is needed?
d. Where is the money available?

Once these issues have been addressed, it is important to be specific regarding financing. Consider two kinds of financing: equity and debt. With equity financing, the source of funds to invest is usually from personal resources, friends, or relatives. Some banks and investment companies will entertain investing, but usually a person is on his or her own to find initial funds. In a corporation, when start-up funds are invested, dividends/profits result and these are shared among stockholders. In debt financing, funds are usually borrowed from a bank or other lending agency; therefore, debt is incurred. A repayment schedule that lowers profit margins for a few years is necessary. Short-term loans, trade credit, and lines of credit are forms of debt financing.

When only one person supplies all the money or capital required, the firm is legally designated as a sole proprietorship. If more than one investor is involved, a partnership may be developed. Sometimes limited partners contribute money or capital only. These individuals do not have the right to manage or direct the business. Management is the responsibility of the general partner.

A corporation is the most efficient method of handling equity investment, and a small corporation may be privately held and controlled by family, friends, and business associates. Publicly held corporations are viewed as the ultimate investment. Stockholders have very limited liability and are generally not held for any business debts. The goals of the owners and how much of the responsibility and control they maintain dictates the size and amount of available resources.

SOURCES OF CAPITAL

In 1958 the federal government authorized Small Business Investment Companies (SBIC's) to assist small business development. These are privately owned venture capital firms that are eligible for federal support and financing to help increase the funds available for small businesses. The federal government controls, licenses, and regulates these venture firms and requires a minimum private capitalization of $150,000. Once approved, these firms are eligible for matching amounts of $3 to $4 in federal funds for every $1 in private funds. These funds are then available to firms that meet the Small Business Administration (SBA) standards—assets less than $9 million, net worth less than $4 million, and net income after taxes less than $450,000.

Though more conservative than the federal government, many state governments have passed legislation for State Businesses and Industrial Development Corporations (SBIDC's). These are generally companies such as utility, oil, insurance, and major retail chains that provide equity funds for investment.

No matter what form of business a new practice elects to take, the use of personal funds and savings to launch the enterprise must be carefully considered and evaluated. A designer's education and expertise often does not include business or finance, so it is important to utilize professional counsel. In order to be prepared for meeting and discussing business plans with financial advisors, it is wise to consider the following things:

Financial goals for at least five years
Short-term goals
Net worth - financial statement
Existing financial obligations, business and family
Personal income needs
Projected cash flow needs for business
one to five years

When a designer sets up a business, working capital is a necessity and is generally provided through short-term debt financing to establish inventories, payroll, and accounts receivable as needed. Capital expenditures are also necessary. This is nearly always long-term debt that also provides for expansion and remodeling. When used for starting a business, capital expenditure is also available for extra fixtures and equipment. Sources from which to secure capital include banks, venture capitalists, the SBA, life insurance companies, vendors, and mortgage lenders.

Because banks are conservative lenders, they are primarily interested in short-term loans and working capital loans, not capital expenditure loans. Personal signature loans for lines of credit can be arranged, even though this is considered only "secondary support." Whatever the type of loan, the lender will consider first the four "C's" of credit:

The *character* of the borrower.
The *collateral* pledged to secure the loan.
The *capital* provided by the borrower.
The *capacity* of the borrower to repay the loan.

In addition to the four "C's," the lending agency will look at the financial statement, which is prepared from the income statement (profit and loss statement), the balance sheet, and the cash flow statement.

BASIC ACCOUNTING PRINCIPLES FOR STARTING A DESIGN PRACTICE

Without getting into a short course in accounting, there are some basics essential for starting a design practice. According to John Myer in his book *Accounting for Non-Accountants*:

> *Accounting is a technique whereby financial transactions are recorded, classified, and summarized. Financial transactions are those that are measured in terms of money. They comprise such events as the making of investments in a business, sales of merchandise or services, collections of money from debtors, and payments for purchases and for services received. In addition to the three phases of accounting technique, there is a fourth, which is concerned with the interpretation of the final summaries or financial statements as they are called.*
>
> *The interpretation of financial statements is not necessarily performed by those who prepare them (bookkeepers, assistants) but whoever interprets them (principal or accountant) needs to have thorough familiarity with the nature of the data contained therein.*[4]

All the data generated by financial transactions must be delegated to categories that will provide guidance for a business. The generally accepted format for the order of all these accounts is known as the chart of accounts.

As shown in Figure 2, the chart of accounts includes two separate categories: the balance sheet and the operating statement. The balance sheet category includes current assets, fixed assets, other assets, current liabilities, long-term liabilities, and stockholders' equity. The operating statement category includes income primary, income secondary, cost of sales primary, administrative expense, and administrative expense other.

The category of customer deposit/merchandise under the current liabilities section of the balance sheet lists the customer's or client's deposits on merchandise. This is a liability and is not earned income until the merchandise or service is delivered. A separate subaccount keeps track of this liability and should be monitored on a regular basis. This also applies to the sales taxes payable category. This is money that has been collected from clients and must be paid to the local tax authority.

The operating statement used in the sample chart of accounts was created for a design firm with both product sales and design service fees. To better track the two income sources, separate sections titled income primary

Balance Sheet

Account Number		Category Code
	CURRENT ASSETS	
00-1010-00	Petty Cash	1
00-1020-00	Checking Account #1	1
00-1030-00	Money Mgmt. Account	1
00-1110-01	Accts. Rec. Clients	1
00-1150-00	Deposits w/Vendors	1
00-1160-00	Allowance for Bad Debts	1
00-1200-00	Inventory	1
	FIXED ASSETS	
00-1420-01	Office Furniture	2
00-1420-02	Office Equipment	2
00-1450-00	Accum. Depreciation	2
	OTHER ASSETS	
00-1699-01	Lease Deposits	3
00-1600-02	Rental Deposits	3
00-1600-03	Utility Deposits	3
00-1610-00	Unearned Income	3
	CURRENT LIABILITIES	
00-2010-00	Cost of Sales Payable	4
00-2020-00	General Admin. Payable	4
00-2030-00	Customer Deps./Mdse.	4
00-2050-00	Sales Tax Payable	4
	LONG-TERM LIABILITIES	
00-2400-01	Long-Term Loans	5
	STOCKHOLDERS' EQUITY	
00-3002-00	Addl. Contributed Capital	5
00-3003-00	Retained Earnings	5

Operating Statement

Account Number		Category Code
	INCOME PRIMARY	
01-4000-01	Taxable Sales	6
01-4000-02	Nontaxable Sales, Labor	6
01-4010-05	Deposits Earned	6
01-4010-07	Freight & Handling	6
01-4010-00	Sales from Inventory	6
	INCOME SECONDARY	
01-5000-00	Fees Earned	7
01-5010-02	Commission from Vendors	7
01-5010-05	Discounts Taken	7
	COSTS OF SALES PRIMARY	
01-6000-01	Labor Only	8
01-6000-02	Materials Only	8
01-6000-03	Resale Merchandise	8
01-6010-00	Freight & Handling	8
01-6500-05	Telephone/Travel	9
01-6500-06	Commissions	9
01-6500-07	Pro. Services/Fees	9
01-6500-08	Deposits to Vendors	9
	ADMINISTRATIVE EXPENSE	
01-7000-01	Rent	10
01-7000-02	Telephone	10
01-7000-03	Utilities	10
01-7000-04	Repairs & Maintenance	10
01-7000-05	Taxes	10
01-7000-06	Office Supplies	10
01-7000-07	Labor	10
01-7000-08	Employ. Payroll Tax	10
01-7000-09	Pro. Dues/Books/Subs	10
01-7000-10	Promotion/Advertising	10
01-7000-11	Cont. Educ./Conferences	10
01-7000-12	Travel	10
01-7000-13	Samples/Catalogs/Inventory	10
01-7000-14	Pro. Services Expense	10
01-7000-15	Auto Expense	10
01-7000-16	Bank Charges/Interest	10
01-7000-17	Insurance	10
01-7000-18	Transfer Account	10
	ADMINISTRATIVE EXPENSE OTHER	
01-7200-01	State Sales Tax	11
01-7210-00	Depreciation	11
01-7220-00	Bad Debts	11
01-7230-00	Amortization	11

Figure 2. Sample chart of accounts.

and income secondary are used. In this manner, income from product sales versus income for design service fees can be easily identified.

The category of cost of sales primary is for product sales expenses and design service fee expenses with separate subheadings to track income and expense separately. Note that the category of deposit to vendors is under a separate subheading. It is imperative that a design firm keep track of outstanding deposits to vendors because these are assets to the company.

The category of administrative expense is self-explanatory and simply delineates all fixed costs and overhead. The category of administrative expense other is used primarily by accountants to calculate annual financial data for tax reporting.

PHYSICAL AND HUMAN RESOURCES

The evaluation of physical and human resources should start with the designer/owner. A necessary asset of a successful designer is a broad base of knowledge. In today's demanding market, the interior designer cannot be a "jack of all trades" but indeed must be "master of several." Recognition of a distinct talent for tackling complex design projects is the first step in assessing the necessary human resources for starting a practice.

In addition to honestly evaluating one's own ability to execute complex projects, of equal importance is the pleasure one derives from the design process. Skill in developing a project and presenting it to a client may have a different personal value for one person than for another who prefers preparing sketches, drawings, and specifications. Traditionally, most designers place accounting and bookkeeping low on the scale of favorite elements of work, yet these are undeniably a necessity. Designers who do not recognize and prioritize these essential elements can spend hours on paperwork or other activities that could well be done better or more efficiently by others.

The principal should evaluate the staff needs of a design practice and hire appropriate individuals to perform certain specific tasks. Another important consideration when evaluating human resources is the talent and compatibility of potential partners or associates. Successful professional partnerships are founded on the basis that each partner assumes specific areas of responsibility. Each should have a distinctive competence, balanced by the other to form a single working unit or team.

In the early development stages of a practice, the office labor should be identified by line item. The knowledgeable financial planner knows that to experience growth and profit, a professional service requires staff backup that will maximize time spent on functions that result in the greatest return on salary dollars. A job description for each function should be prepared to reflect the estimated hours per day, week, and month. A clear business plan results from attaching a salary scale to these functions and adding this to the operating budget.

A job description for the principal or principals of the firm is a good starting point. In the beginning of a practice, the principals are often the prime design talent and also assume other duties including marketing, bookkeeping, and even receptionist's duties. A well-prepared principal's job description should describe that person's distinctive competence and explain how it will be utilized.

A fast-growing design office needs to spin off additional duties promptly and efficiently to minimize downtime on projects. Growth should dictate the need for new positions, particularly in areas such as drafting, computer and CAD operation, library management, specification writing, additional secretarial support, and graphics. This process can be most efficient through the use of job and duty descriptions. For example:

Receptionist/Switchboard Operator: provide information on office hours, availability of staff, message delivery and tracking, solicitations, vendors, appointment schedules, and classified information.

Secretary: manage and handle all written communication, including contracts, letters of agreement, proposals, and so on.

Bookkeeper: record all financial transactions, prepare purchase proposals and work orders, and prepare checks for signing, including payroll. (As volume increases the bookkeeper may become office manager and the functions split between additional personnel; specifically, proposals and work orders prepared by one employee and checks and accounts payable by another.)

Design Assistant: handle drafting, specification preparation, and color boards.

Fast-growing practices handling large-scale projects will quickly develop the need for project managers and marketing personnel. These are key positions for a large office, and job descriptions should describe performance objectives and target marketing directions as set out by the principals. To round out the office staffing, consultants should be given written agreements describing their role as independent contractors.

The identification of the target market is critical. The job description and time allocation varies considerably depending upon this decision. The residential design office that traditionally deals in product sales may have a smaller volume of transactions and often deals directly with clients. The residential back-up staff may need a stronger education in fine arts; spend more time evaluating products on a custom basis; and need experience in the purchase, delivery, and installation of products. On the other hand, the commercial design staff must be prepared to complete complicated proposals, specify products in larger quantities for their clients, and deal with complex interior spaces.

Team building is an essential element in any human resource plan. Depending on the location and the business community choice, the pool of employees can be drawn from local educational institutions. Many colleges and universities incorporate a student internship as part of the curriculum. This is an ideal time to try out a new member for the team. Architects and other consultants with special skills related to interior design—and with clear-cut job descriptions—can provide project orientation and experience.

SOCIAL AND ECONOMIC DEMOGRAPHICS

The practice of interior design varies from area to area and state to state. Climate, social and historic background, and economic differences will influence the type of design work that will be successful. Ethnic origins, age group distribution, and history of an area are essential to understanding a marketplace and its design orientation.

With the arrival of the sandwich generation, where families are faced with caring for aging parents as well as becoming grandparents themselves, it is increasingly apparent that the disposable income once available to the 1950s through 1980s is being devoted to the elderly and children—the two fastest-growing segments of our population. As designers, we must keep in mind that these two populations must be served differently, with their space needs identified appropriately.

Designers must evaluate their own talent as it relates to the community they serve and live in. An examination of local economics and population trends will provide valuable information for starting a practice. Professional organizations can also provide valuable data for evaluation of the business opportunities in a community. The local banker may be the best source of information in this regard.

COMPETITION

Competition is usually good for business and is imperative in a retail business. Another imperative for interior designers is the compatibility of the service to be offered with the needs of the community. A chat with the owner of a design shop and a tour of the sales floors of office and home furnishings dealers can provide data on styles, price ranges, and the general design quality demands of a community. A quick check in the yellow pages will provide insight into the level of competition in an area. It is important to remember to check the architectural offices that provide interior design services. The sheer numbers involved in the profession relative to the population to be served reveal a great deal.

Interviews with established professionals and an examination of the general economic health of the community can provide information on the direction of the design climate. Notice should be taken of the match between the design expertise to be offered and these indicators.

An office glut on the real estate market may indicate a growing need for space planning in a competitive marketplace. Competitive prices for rent may invite business clients to move, whereas businesses choosing to stay could need renovation of old spaces. Home sales and building starts in each community will provide information about competition, particularly regarding the availability of finish craftspeople.

A new practice needs at least six months to get started. Capital to carry the practice for that length of time is critical. Two to three years in business should be the point where a true profit is seen. At five years a firm should be established, barring any unforeseen economic crisis in the community.

Is competition good for business? Indeed. The presence of already successful professionals in a community indicates that the community at large understands the service and has expressed a willingness to engage interior design services. In fact, many large companies and corporations, aware of their need to maintain an image and provide functional interior environments for their employees, are rounding out their management teams with interior designers.

Once established, a design firm must market its expertise. The competitive edge will not always be talent, but will be based on the true value of the service. Educated clients demand value received for dollars spent. The designers' biggest competition should be their own office, where the staff constantly strive to improve not only the design quality, but the value-added service provided.

OFFICE AND STUDIO SITE

Once the competition has been evaluated and the service identified, the client base must be identified. If the practice is to be heavily dependent on product sales, access to these products is important. Thus, it is imperative to have a setting where foot traffic is heavy, parking is ample, the square footage is large enough for display, and a merchandise receivable area is accessible. Striving to be unique in the location selected, yet compatible with other retail operations in the immediate proximity, is also important. The selection of location should reflect the price range and style of the products that will be offered as a part of your practice. (A point of consideration is that shopping centers usually control hours and ask for percentage of the gross sales as a part of the lease agreement.)

If a design firm is considering buying a building, all of the above criteria should apply. It is also important to evaluate the ability to carry the debt, tax advantages or disadvantages, initial improvements necessary, maintenance costs, and zoning regulations, as well as future plans for the area by local government jurisdictions.

THE STUDIO

As with many other professions, the home office may be a good starting place for a designer. However, this environment also has to be considered carefully. If the practice is to be dedicated to seeing clients in their own setting rather than in the office, then the staff requirements are minimal, and a work area can be set aside in the home. A permit for a home office should be secured to meet zoning requirements of the jurisdiction. Some criticize this arrangement as unprofessional and claim that it can create traffic problems in residential areas. The key questions to be addressed are whether the location provides access for and to clients, and whether the location meets with the goals of the business plan.

A relatively new concept for designers is the executive suite, where a group of related businesses share space, employees, library, and equipment. Compatibility of the businesses may be an issue, but if handled sensitively these arrangements can be very successful.

THE BUSINESS OFFICE

As the profession has grown, the public has found the business office the most acceptable image for professional services and has responded to the business image in a positive way. Sometimes a business office location is less costly than a retail location; however, care must be taken to achieve an appropriate look for the office. If too ostentatious it may make clients feel uncomfortable. Again, reliance on a business plan is important in developing the proper atmosphere for the targeted clientele. Proximity to a market center for product information is desirable for both residential and commercial design firms.

Residential design firms usually must purchase most samples and catalogs, while contract firms are usually supplied with samples and catalogs by vendors. Easily retrievable and accessible storage for these items is always an important space consideration for a design firm. As a company grows and design projects become more complex, drafting space and presentation facilities become an additional space concern. It is wise to project for future growth and analyze the potential for space expansion when selecting the location.

Architectural offices that offer interior design services recognize the extra space this service requires. It is not uncommon for an architectural office to have a subsidiary firm, perhaps in a separate location, that not only specifies the finishes and products for a project but will secure them for the client with purchasing services. It may be wise for the growing interior design firm to consider marketing its services to major architectural firms for this purpose and even choose a location proximate to them.

SOURCES OF SUPPLY

Not only are interior designers creative, they are experts at combining available technologies into productive, healthy, and aesthetically satisfying environments. Although not inventors in the true sense of the word, designers are combiners and coordinators of existing elements, providing new and unusual solutions to design problems.

The sources of supply are only as limited as the imagination, yet for each project the designer must decide which product will best solve the problem. In nearly every case, designers rely on representatives of product lines, hired by the manufacturer, to keep them informed about the market availability of product lines. Because of regional marketing and service from the manufacturer, the type of trade sources used most frequently by a design firm may be influenced by geographic proximity.

The sales representative of any product line is usually paid on a commission basis. Therefore, a representative will evaluate the design firm on the basis of personal financial return on sales generated. The representative services a specific territory on the basis of population and previous sales performance from that area. Product samples and catalogs are usually the representative's financial responsibility and are either sold or provided to a design firm. A quota for distribution of their samples and catalogs is not uncommon. As increased sales in an area generate more business, this representative may hire a "sub rep" to service a specific area or city more effectively. The sales representative usually handles purchase orders; however, an "open account status" must first be established with the manufacturer.

The manufacturer's representative is usually salaried and is assigned a specific area of the market to service. Even though salaried, in most cases, there are bonuses to be earned for volume sales. These employees usually service the architectural and design specification community with catalogs and samples provided at no cost to designers. Manufacturer's reps will assist in the preparation of purchase orders, but the design firm is responsible for expediting and credit arrangements.

Architectural and design representatives serve many commercial product lines. These salaried employees call on and service the architectural and design community that specifies product only. These representatives are specifically provided by the manufacturer or dealer to assist in technical data information and in many cases preparation of drawings, specifications, and pricing for specific product lines. They generally are not involved in purchasing other than to provide information on dealers or sales representatives for a particular line.

Dealers represent a specific product line, usually through the purchase of a sample collection of the product. Dealers contract to meet a sales quota within a specified period of time. For this investment and commitment, the dealers are usually guaranteed larger discounts for all products ordered during the time of their dealer agreement with the manufacturer. A dealer may be a small office or a large showroom operation. It is not uncommon for large companies to be dealers for several products, but generally these products are not in competition with one another.

Contracts for dealerships may be renegotiated or awarded to another business if the manufacturer does not feel that his or her product line is being represented in accordance with the signed agreements. Dealers may sell the represented products at suggested retail, or at a discount to qualified buyers, at their discretion. These discounts will vary depending upon the size of the order, the performance record, and the creditworthiness of the purchaser.

The sign "showroom" usually indicates that the products represented are available only to qualified buyers who have conformed with the state laws for buying products at a discounted price, sometimes referred to as wholesale. Such establishments usually do not service the general public. Buyers must sign an agreement or resale tax card pledging to collect the appropriate taxes due to government agencies. The buyers must be prepared to provide their business cards and license numbers to the showroom staff.

Each buyer in these showrooms must establish his or her own accounts and discounts. These accounts may be with the showroom itself or may be directly with the manufacturer. Each place of business establishes its own policies, and the design firm must fully understand and comply with all the terms and conditions of sale as well as the Uniform Commercial Code, which controls all product sales in excess of $500.

As with dealers, the owner of a showroom may carry many different product lines, usually all related to the same product category. Manufacturers' showrooms are generally operated the same as the traditional showroom, except they are owned by a specific manufacturer and will display only products from that one source.

With the advent of the showroom concept, regional design centers have become common. Large manufacturers provide the marketing money and research necessary to evaluate markets and serve as anchor tenants for design centers. Based on specific criteria for display and product promotion, design centers are usually found in large population centers and are composed of a collection of showrooms all in close proximity to one another. In recent years, controversy has resulted from the fact that some centers have changed their policy from "trade only" to "open to public." Whatever policy has been adopted by a particular center is a direct result of the economic climate and requirements of both the showrooms and the purchasing clientele.

An important source of labor supply is the area contractors, subcontractors, artisans/ craftspeople, and guilds. These are usually independent businesspersons with their own set of procedures. It is important to determine legal business requirements for licensing of these groups, since many states prohibit contracting of any kind without a license for particular occupations. Whatever the legal requirements may be, these must be incorporated into day-to-day operations. The key factor is to clearly define the liability and responsibility factors regardless of whether a contract is with the design firm or directly with the client.

SOURCES OF INFORMATION

Sources of information for starting an interior design practice are many and varied. Some of these sources have been identified previously. It is important to remember that all information gathered will need to be interpreted in the light of a designer's particular expertise; the economic climate; and the potential for the service to fill a need and, of course, make a profit.

One of the simplest methods for evaluating the information gathered is to start by making a list of sources to explore for information. This list might include banks and loaning institutions, the local Better Business Bureau, the Chamber of Commerce, local and regional institutes of higher education, libraries, and professional organizations. Additional sources of information include product representatives, major trade magazines, design centers, and other industry and trade sources.

PROFESSIONAL EXPERTISE AND CONSULTANTS

Professionals with special expertise and consultants are a necessity for any design firm. A designer starting a firm should develop a list of consultants and supplemental expertise, and put it in priority order. The highest priority should be a banker or comparable financial advisor. This person provides guidance for management of business funds and could be a valuable reference when establishing lines of credit.

Second on the list should be an accountant. An accountant provides advice on the elements of risk in a new enterprise and helps secure the Federal Employer Number, register the name of the business with the proper agencies, and prepare a chart of accounts for business transactions. Taxes—federal, state, and local—can be processed by an accountant who will also provide periodic consultations on the progress of the business.

Of equal importance is the establishment of a working relationship with an attorney. The legal structure a design firm takes may be the direct result of a consultation with a lawyer. Once this structure has been established, an attorney should review any correspondence, letters of agreement, contracts, or documents used in day-to-day business to assure continuity and maximum protection under the law.

Another important advisor/consultant is the insurance counselor. An insurance counselor can evaluate long-term plans and business risks. The most important insurance policies to consider are:

Property insurance
Liability insurance
Personal injury protection
Professional liability, including errors and omissions
Automobile insurance
Umbrella insurance
Workmen's compensation

The insurance industry has recognized the needs of small business by packaging business insurance to allow the selection of coverage amounts, while keeping the package comprehensive and within budget. An insurance agent should be kept abreast of business ventures and any changes that take place in the firm. As the company grows, the insurance agent will be able to provide protection and safe growing plans such as business life, group health, business interruption, valuable papers, burglary, and accounts receivable insurance.

People with special expertise or talents are often needed to enhance a design practice. In this age of fast-changing technology and complex projects, special expertise is often a necessity in order to keep pace. The following list provides an overview of special expertise that may be necessary to incorporate into design projects:

Architects
Landscape architects
Structural engineers
Electrical engineers
General contractors
Communication consultants
(telecommunication, computer, and so on)
Hazardous waste removal experts
Specialized groups (handicapped, elderly, and so on)
Kitchen specialists
Toxic materials experts
Space planning and productivity analysts

Health care specialists
Freight, delivery, and handling specialists
Transportation specialists
Real estate experts

Internally, to ensure that a design firm runs smoothly, the following expertise may be needed:

Employee benefits consultants
Import-export brokers
Recruitment specialists
Software and computer specialists
Marketing or advertising consultants
Record or information managers
Mergers and acquisitions consultants

CONCLUSION

Starting an interior design practice is a complex and involved process. It can also mean the fulfillment of a dream. The key to success is confidence that the service to be offered meets a need and can be competitive within the chosen marketplace. Once this is established and thoughtful consideration is given to the issues presented in this chapter, the chances for success in this challenging but rewarding field are increased.

Strategic Planning and Management

MARTHA G. RAYLE AND SANDRA H. SOBER

Strategic planning and strategic management sound like business school jargon, but they are really no mystery. Designers use strategic planning and management each day in project work. Strategic planning is a thinking and decision-making process that results in an action plan. The action plan specifies what is to be done, how it will be done, when it will be done, and how much it will cost.

When a designer completes a project for a client, each of the following processes occurs:

Programming: The client's existing situation is defined.

Analysis: The existing situation and future goals are evaluated.

Schematic design: Alternative plans are developed for the client in view of the future expectations and conditions.

Design development: Design decisions are focused on the basis of the alternatives developed.

Final design: The final design and specifications are implemented.

Bids, negotiations, and construction bids: Contractors and vendors are selected, and construction starts.

Postconstruction and project closeout: When construction is finished, the designer completes a punch list and final inspection with the client. Necessary modifications are made to the project on the basis of this final review.

To start strategically planning and managing a practice, the designer should think in terms of the larger context, using the same thought processes as when dealing with individual projects. There's only one big difference. Strategic planning and management of a business are never complete—they are ongoing processes. Management consultant Harrison Coerver[1] presents strategic planning and management in a clear and efficient way. He outlines the following necessary steps:

Define the situation
Analyze the situation
Develop alternatives
Make decisions
Take action
Follow up and control
Identify deviations

Here's how to start the process and jump into the circle. (See Figure 1).

The best way to understand the overall process of strategic planning and management is to examine each of these steps in turn.

DEFINE THE SITUATION

The first step is to define the situation. To do so, the designer must answer several questions. Here are pertinent questions and examples of possible answers.

What is the company profile? Ours is an independent interior design and space planning firm in a rapidly growing city of 750,000. While we presently lack strong financial resources, we have three designers (each with at least eight years of experience) and four recent graduates of interior design programs.

What is the ideal profile for the company? A health care and hospitality design firm with four principals, ten staff designers, a business manager, and clerical support, generating income for the principals exceeding $60,000 a year each. It is important to be perceived as serious members of the business community. For that reason each of the principals will seek active roles in community leadership in areas such as economic development, work with industrial authorities, or community long-range planning. (Caution: Avoid the "decorator" stereotype. Avoid volunteer work where you are expected to be in charge of decorations.)

What have been the company's successes?

- Won 1990 design competition.
- Completed highly visible public service project that resulted in public recognition.
- Successfully completed award-winning 100-bed addition to city hospital.
- Conducts seminars for hospital administrators on the color psychology of health care facilities design.

Why does the company exist? The principals in the firm are entrepreneurial in spirit, wanting design and financial control of their work environment.

How many competitors are there? There are only two other firms of a similar size and nature that would be considered competitors.

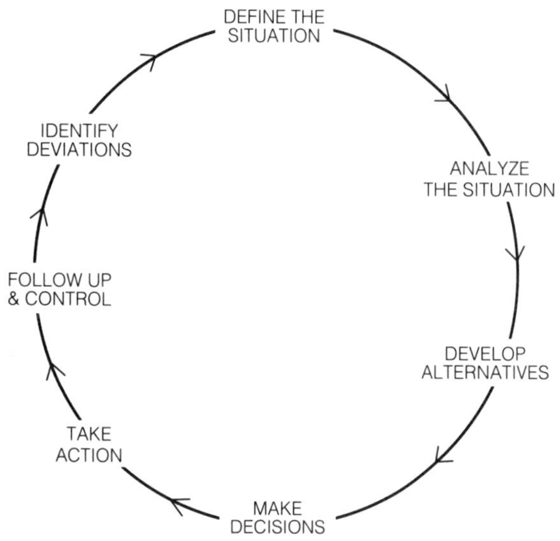

Figure 1. The steps in the strategic planning process.

What is known about each competitor?

- Acme Interiors has six employees and provides consulting for health care equipment vendors.
- Interiors division of "Architects R Us" is well connected politically and has a strong marketing staff that aggressively pursues all nonresidential work in the community.

Who are existing clients? (List current clients. Project their needs for design services in the next year, and in the next three years. Consider what might happen to threaten the company's ability to do this work, such as competition, problems with in-house facilities design staff, and so on.)

ANALYZE THE SITUATION

Following this strategy for planning and management, the second important step is to analyze the situation. An analysis of the company internally and externally is important. An internal analysis evaluates three key elements: (1) the financial situation, (2) the human resources, and (3) the traditions and beliefs.

Financial Analysis

Financial analysis requires asking where the money comes from and where it goes. In this phase, income and expense projections are prepared.

- Income includes fees, product sales, and other sources such as interest collected.

- Expenses, fixed and variable. Fixed expenses are things that must be paid—no matter what—such as rent, utilities, and taxes. Variable expenses are items that have discretionary control, such as additional employees, consultants, sales tax, marketing brochures, and client entertainment.

Human Resource Analysis

Human resource analysis requires a long, hard look at the staff and principals. It is necessary to be painfully honest about strengths and weaknesses. In a partnership, this is done in conjunction with the partners and/or the key staff members. Although painful, it can provide all the participants with a clearer understanding of their value to the organization and team.

One method of human resource evaluation begins with a staffing analysis. Start by making a sheet for each staff member. Separate the sheet into two categories: strengths and weaknesses. List all the skills and qualities that a staff member possesses. In many cases, for each strength, there will be a corresponding weakness. A staffing analysis for the principal of the firm might look like this:

Name: Jane Doe
Title: Principal

Strengths

Good client relationship building skills.
Sees the big picture of the firm's goals.
Works well in a team.
Trains junior employees well—shares knowledge.
Delegates clearly and concisely.
Good pressure worker—works well under stress—maintains cool.
Creative design concepts development.
Has completed 15 skilled nursing facilities with good understanding of client needs and current technology.

Weaknesses

Poor writing skills for marketing—proposals sound like a specification.
Poor attention to detail—doesn't want to be bothered—"let someone else handle it."
Waits until the last minute—does not schedule and pace the work.
Doesn't always understand the technical aspects of the problem and really doesn't care to understand.
Out of date with technology and with care delivery philosophy in acute care hospital environment.

Once the resource analysis for each member of the staff is completed, the principals can take a look at how the skills of each staff member complement one another, where weaknesses can be supplemented; what needs to be developed; and what staff additions or deletions are called for. This becomes a basis for the following management decisions:

Assignment of people to projects to create supportive, complementary teams.
Assignment of short-term and long-term responsibilities.
Determination of responsibilities not adequately handled by the staff.
Development of an internal training program.
Development of an external professional and technical training program, in conjunction with what is affordable.
Development of the salary and performance review process.

In any systematic human resource plan, it is a good idea to have an organized salary and performance review. Whether part of a two-person firm or a two hundred person firm, the salary and performance review system can be a means by which individual and collective progress is measured.

Employees want to know what is expected of them, what they are doing right, what they are doing wrong, what is in their future, and what they need to do and know to get there. A regular salary and performance review process helps the principals and the employees maintain an organized communication, providing at least one opportunity each year to hear how the employees feel about their work and the firm.

An example of a successful salary and performance review system is one developed by Stetson-Harza Architects, Engineers, and Planners in Utica, New York. In this approach all employees are annually reviewed on the anniversary date of their employment. This process provides each employee with an opportunity to voice his or her achievements and disappointments, expectations, and suggestions in a direct and equitable way. The review process is initiated by the employee's completion of a self-evaluation form. (See Figure 2.)

The self-evaluation form is given to the supervisor, or in the case of a small firm, the principal or partners. This self-evaluation becomes the outline for the prereview discussion. This discussion occurs in neutral territory such as a conference room. The prereview is intended to be the employee's opportunity to say what is on his or her mind, good or bad, and to talk about the past and future. The employee may choose whether or not to have the self-evaluation form included and retained in the personnel file.

At the same time, the employee is asked to develop personal objectives and goals for the coming year. (See Figure 3) These objectives should be achievable and controllable by the employee without relying on the firm's workload or financial resources, such as a goal to develop better writing skills. After the prereview, the supervisor has a clear understanding of how the employee feels about the firm and what the firm should do to support this employee's goals and expectations.

The supervisor then asks all the key people (supervisors, peers, and subordinates) with whom the employee has worked during the past year about the employee's performance. This provides the supervisor with a balanced picture of the employee's creative and technical work, as well as his or her team and interpersonal communications skills.

With this knowledge, the supervisor presents the findings and salary and performance recommendations to a committee (this could be a management team or the principals of a firm) to make the final salary determination. This prevents one supervisor from singularly and unfairly determining the employee's future salary. The committee then supports, adds to, or amends the employee's objectives and goals for the coming year.

After the committee has made its determination, the supervisor meets with the employee in a postreview meeting to communicate the firm's support, goals, and improvement expectations along with suggestions for individual objectives. All steps in the process are documented on the employee's evaluation form and retained in the personnel file. (See Figure 4.)

The employee emerges from this process with a clear understanding of what he or she is doing right, where improvement is needed, and what the short- and long-range future looks like. The employee also knows that the review is not the result of one person's opinion. At the same time, the firm has the same information about the employee and knows what must be done to develop this employee. If the employee is not doing well, or just is not working out, the process provides documentation against unfair dismissal claims in the future.

Analysis of Traditions and Beliefs

Analysis of traditions and beliefs can be harder to define, but is no less important. These are the common values that the partners agree upon and around which all decisions are made. Important issues such as client relationships, supplier relationships, and ethics must be addressed.

Client relationships: How are clients to be treated? Will "The customer is always right" be one of the company mottoes? Does the staff meet with clients in the evenings or weekends if schedules require it? Is it all right, or even expected, to socialize with clients?

Supplier relationships: How are sales representatives, manufacturers' representatives, and contractors to be treated? Although sales and manufacturers' representatives can be one of a firm's greatest assets, discretion about client and project information can be crucial. How is confidentiality maintained when working with suppliers?

Ethics: The ASID Code of Ethics and Professional Conduct should be the principles by which a firm operates. The entire staff of an office should be familiar with and apply this code. (See Figure 5.)

Of particular concern relative to the question of ethics is point 3.4 of the ASID Code of Ethics, which states that members "shall fully disclose to a client all compensation which the Member shall receive in connection with the project and shall not accept any form of undisclosed compensation from any person or firm with whom the member deals in connection with the project." Adherence to this principle is essential in order for an interior design firm to maintain a solid reputation with clients and other professional colleagues.

Community relations: The relationship of an interior design firm with the community can be very important to the viability of a practice. The chamber of commerce, United Way agencies, or the local community leadership organization are possible avenues for involvement. The firm may even want to become involved, either directly or through an ASID project, in pro bono (free) work for a worthwhile nonprofit agency that would benefit from the firm's expertise. An example of this could be a homeless shelter or jury waiting area needing assistance with space planning, finishes, and color selection. In these instances it is in the firm's best inter-

PERFORMANCE SELF-EVALUATION NOTES

☐ Please incorporate in my personnel folder.

By ______________________

☐ Please use for our discussion, return to me, and do not file.

Date ______________________

1. **Responsibilities**—Please list briefly your major responsibilities, noting any changes since your last evaluation.

2. **Professional Development & Outside Activities**—Please list seminars, courses, formal training, changes in registration, etc., since your last evaluation; and note professional, community, or other outside activities that you consider relevant to your work.

3. **Performance Evaluation**—Please look back and note your evaluations in light of the responsibilities listed above and your work objectives and career goals outlined during your last review.

    a. What have been the major achievements (objectives achieved, successful projects, improved work methods and results, etc.)?

    b. Refer to your last "Memo on Objectives" form and comment on progress made toward each of these objectives.

    c. Have there been any important setbacks, disappointments, or areas where you feel you need to improve (objectives not achieved, not-so-successful projects or tasks, etc.? What do you plan to do about these?—and can the firm help?

    d. Overall evaluation.

4. **Future Goals & Objectives**

    a. What would you like to establish as your major work objectives for the coming year?

    b. What about long-term?

5. **Firm's Role**—Any ideas on things the firm might do to help (or stop hampering!) your performance? Any other suggestions?

/brw

Rev. 2/8/89

Figure 2. Sample self-evaluation form that employees fill out to evaluate their own performance.

PERFORMANCE REVIEW

Name ______________________ Date ______________________

Reviewed in Category ____________ Category Change Y or N

INCLUDE IN YOUR EVALUATION COMMENTS ON THESE FACTORS:

- **For All Personnel:** Achievement of past period's objectives; motivation and attitude; technical/professional growth; responsiveness to company needs

- Performance measures for Project Managers or Team Leaders, based on project results and input from Project Directors and Project Managers:

  For a Project Manager: Client satisfaction; on-time/on-budget results; team leadership, organization/planning; performance measures, creative problem solving, teamwork/coordination, communication

  For a Team Leader: Technical quality; on-time/on-budget results; responsiveness to Project Manager; department team leadership; cooperation and coordination; creative problem solving; staff development, communication

- **Areas of good or outstanding performance:**

- **Areas where improvement is needed:**

- **Objectives** (Record on attached Memo on Objectives. In setting objectives, consider the objectives noted on the Self-Evaluation as well as work areas needing improvement.)

  Proposed Development Program:

  Remarks:

REV 6/90 (See back of page for interview notes.) Form 1470

Figure 3. Memo on objectives for the coming year.

Review of ______________________

Comments on Performance Prior to Review

Interviewer:

____

Discuss the Self-Evaluation, make general notes below, and use the separate Memo on Objectives to list objectives agreed upon. *Note:* This discussion should not anticipate the final Salary Review action.

Notes of Prereview Discussion

By ______________

Date ______________

Discussion During Salary Review

Date ______________

Record general notes here, and make any necessary modifications to the objectives on the separate memo sheet.

Notes of Postreview Discussion

By ______________

Date ______________

Figure 4. Performance review form for salaried employees.

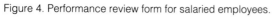

Memo on Objectives

Name ______________________________ Date ______________

1. Progress on objectives established during last evaluation:

2. Objectives established during prereview discussions:

3. Any modification of the above objectives based on salary/performance review and postreview discussion?

By: ______________________________

cc: Staff Member ______________________ (date)

ASID CODE OF ETHICS AND PROFESSIONAL CONDUCT

Revised March 1989

1.0 **PREAMBLE**

Members of the American Society of Interior Designers are required to conduct their professional practice in a manner that will command the respect of clients, suppliers of goods and services to the profession, and fellow professional designers, as well as the general public. It is the individual responsibility of every member of the Society to uphold this Code and the Bylaws of the Society.

2.0 **RESPONSIBILITY TO THE PUBLIC**

2.1 Members shall comply with all existing laws, regulations and codes governing business procedures and the practice of interior design as established by the state or other jurisdiction in which they practice.

2.2 Members shall not seal or sign drawings, specifications, or other interior design documents except where the member or the member's firm has prepared, supervised or professionally reviewed and approved such documents.

2.3 Members shall at all times consider the health, safety, and welfare of the public in spaces they design. Members agree, whenever possible, to notify property managers, landlords, and/or public officials of conditions within a built environment that endanger the health, safety and/or welfare of occupants.

2.4 Members shall not engage in any form of false or misleading advertising or promotional activities and shall not imply through advertising or other means that staff members or employees of their firm are qualified interior designers unless such be the fact.

2.5 Members shall not take any action intended to influence the judgment of a public official for the purposes of any project.

2.6 Members shall not assist or abet improper or illegal conduct of anyone in connection with a project.

3.0 **RESPONSIBILITY TO THE CLIENT**

3.1 Members' contracts with a client shall clearly set forth the scope and nature of the project involved, the services to be performed, and the method of compensation for those services.

3.2 Members may offer professional services to a client for any form of legal compensation.

3.3 Members shall not undertake any professional responsibility unless they are, by training and experience, competent to adequately perform the work required.

3.4 Members shall fully disclose to a client all compensation which the Member shall receive in connection with the project and shall not accept any form of undisclosed compensation from any person or firm with whom the member deals in connection with the project.

3.5 Members shall not divulge any confidential information about the client or the client's project, or utilize photographs or specifications of the project, without the express permission of the client, with an exception for those specifications or drawings over which the designer retains proprietary rights.

Figure 5. ASID Code of Ethics and Professional Conduct, revised March 1989.

3.6 Members shall be candid and truthful in all their professional communications.

3.7 Members shall act with fiscal responsibility in the best interest of their clients and shall maintain sound business relationships with suppliers, industry and trades to insure the best service possible to the public.

4.0 RESPONSIBILITY TO OTHER INTERIOR DESIGNERS AND COLLEAGUES

4.1 Members shall not interfere with the performance of another interior designer's contractual or professional relationship with a client.

4.2 Members shall not initiate, or participate in, any discussion or activity which might result in an unjust injury to another interior designer's reputation or business relationships.

4.3 Members may enter into the design work on a project upon being personally satisfied that the client has severed contractual relationships with a previous designer.

4.4 Members may, when requested and it does not present a conflict of interest, render a second opinion to a client, or serve as an expert witness in a judicial or arbitration proceeding.

4.5 Members shall not endorse the application for ASID membership and/or certification, registration or licensing of an individual known to be unqualified with respect to education, training, experience or character, nor shall a Member knowingly misrepresent the experience, professional expertise, or moral character of that individual.

4.6 Members shall only take credit for work that has actually been created by that Member or the Member's firm, and under the Member's supervision.

5.0 RESPONSIBILITY TO THE PROFESSION

5.1 Members agree to maintain standards of professional and personal conduct that will reflect in a responsible manner on the Society and the profession.

5.2 Members shall seek to continually upgrade their professional knowledge and competency with respect to the interior design profession.

5.3 Members agree, whenever possible, to encourage and contribute to the sharing of knowledge and information between interior designers and other allied professional disciplines, industry and the public.

6.0 ENFORCEMENT

6.1 The Society shall follow standard procedures for the enforcement of the Code as approved by the Society's Board of Directors.

6.2 Members having a reasonable belief, based upon substantial information, that another member has acted in violation of this Code, shall report such information in accordance with accepted procedures.

6.3 Any deviation from this Code, or any action taken by a Member which is detrimental to the Society and the profession as a whole, shall be deemed unprofessional conduct subject to discipline by the Society's Board of Directors.

est to use its professional skills and talent, as opposed to directing traffic or other less substantive activities.

Image: What is the firm's image? Is it high-tech and sleek, or traditional with wainscot paneling and brass detailing? Is it important to have an image at all? If the firm decides to pursue any and all work, would certain images be a hindrance to receiving some projects? The image of the firm is expressed not only in the physical environment in the office, but also in its stationery, promotional pieces, and the format of letters and presentation boards.

Commitment to professionalism, career path, and CEU's: Does the firm support NCIDQ qualification, legal registration and licensing, and participation in professional associations? Will the firm pay NCIDQ exam fees, state license registration fees, and ASID membership fees and expenses? Or is it each staff member's responsibility? Will the firm pay for continuing education (CEU's) and postgraduate coursework? Will the firm allow office time for professional association volunteer work? Supporting these activities helps attract and maintain quality employees, as well as advancing the practice of interior design.

External Analysis

External analysis is a review of the conditions and situations external to the firm. This process helps develop an awareness of conditions that may exist now or in the future that cannot be controlled internally. It also provides a picture of the opportunities these external factors present. Indeed, in many instances success may lie in the ability to recognize these opportunities and create a niche for the design practice.

Demographic and social analysis: An analysis of the demographic and social conditions in the area in which the firm intends to practice is essential. What is the population of the area? What are the statistical breakdowns by age, type of employment, race, gender, religion, and political preferences? Which individuals and groups are most important in the social, political, and business environments? Does the area appear to have enough people with discretionary money to avail themselves of interior design services? Are the companies really divisions of companies with headquarters elsewhere?

All the answers to these questions may not be available, but the better the community is known, the better a firm can target its services.

Economic and market analysis: Economic and market analysis calls for research and study. It is important that a firm learn which external conditions can provide opportunities and which can create problems. Nothing substitutes for reading everything possible about the local, regional, and national economy.

Economic analysis: Read! Read! Read! The *Wall Street Journal* and the *Kiplinger Report* can provide daily and weekly information about interest rates, taxes, energy, politics, and legislation. Let's examine what these things have to do with an interior design practice.

Interest rates have a serious impact on residential and commercial construction. If interest rates are going up, this can mean a significant slowdown in new construction projects. Increased or reduced taxes in certain sectors can result in problems or opportunities. For example, new tax credits for rehabilitation or restoration projects can provide signals for opportunities in renovation, or a tax on interior design services can affect the way a practice is internally structured. If energy prices are going up, there may be new energy conservation incentives, requiring more knowledge in energy-saving lighting systems. Politics affect legislation that can negatively or positively affect the practice. New federal accessibility legislation may require more knowledge in barrier-free design, or it may provide an opportunity to offer barrier-free audit services to past clients.

The beginning interior design firm should think about the external economic factors that may affect the practice in the next year, two years, five years, and beyond.

Technological analysis: What new technology will affect the way clients do business? Will bar code and optical disk technology affect the library facilities of educational clients? What existing technologies should clients adopt, and can this firm help? For example, have all clients developed and computerized their facilities' data base? If not, perhaps this is an opportunity to propose that this firm help them computerize their facilities.

Do residential clients have personal computers, security systems, and media centers? Is the firm's staff prepared for the clients who have them or want them? Will special expertise in security systems attract new clients in vulnerable locations?

What new technologies will affect the practice? Should bar code technology for existing furnishings inventories be adopted? Should the specification system be automated to remain competitive? How will computer voice recognition influence the acoustical design of work space in the future?

Market analysis means an examination of the firm's local external environment. If practice is limited to a local geographic area, research on a particular region may be sufficient. If the practice is nationally based, the focus may be on certain business or client types.

When focus is on a particular local geographic area, it is necessary to know the business base of the community. This may already be known, but it might be worth checking with the local chamber of commerce or community development agency for statistics on the following:

1. The largest employers in the area and the number of employees in each, along with the primary business of each employer.

2. How many manufacturing-sector businesses, and jobs, are in the city?

3. How many service-sector businesses, and jobs, are in the city?

4. Does the chamber of commerce, and/or the community itself, have a community development plan? What businesses are being attracted to the community? What will

those businesses mean to the practice? How is the development plan working?

5. What is the projected population and economic growth over the next few years? (Many chambers of commerce can even provide information on which neighborhoods and suburbs will experience the most growth.)

6. What are the average housing costs and availability in the area?

7. What is the available office and retail space?

With this information certain problems or opportunities emerge. For example, if the area's economy is based upon oil, it can be predicted that the local economic health will rise or fall with oil prices. If the locale has a large dependence upon defense-related business, it can be predicted that local economic health will rise or fall depending upon events in the world. If these can't be predicted, a firm can still plan for good and bad times.

This information allows for the identification of opportunities. For example, if an area has a shortage of office space, marketing of services directed toward companies needing to reorganize space is a likely strategy. To organize a plan of action, first make a list of what is known about an area. Then itemize what is known, what can be predicted, what opportunities exist, and what problems or market conditions could make the practice vulnerable.

Banking Relationships

As mentioned in other sections of this manual, a close working relationship with a bank is essential. Sometimes the first contact is to obtain a loan for starting the business. Keep in mind that the primary thing that the loan officer is looking for is the ability to pay back the loan. A realistic business plan outlining cash flow projections is necessary, along with evidence of collateral. It is a good idea to keep the loan officer advised of the firm's financial status regularly so that a line of credit can be established. A line of credit provides for available funds up to a certain limit. Having this availability is certainly advantageous to a new enterprise since it provides additional funds without requiring continually returning to the bank. The firm should provide the bank with quarterly reports showing the comparison of the firm's actual expenses to the budgeted amounts, as well as an updated personal financial report. This will require discipline for a new firm; however, if the firm faces economic downturns, the bank being well acquainted with the firm's financial picture will be an advantage.

Trade Relationships

The designer's relationship with suppliers, vendors, distributors, and sales representatives is critically important to the success of a practice. All too often the trade is treated as a necessary evil. Designers complain that the sales representatives spend too much time in the designer's office, thereby reducing the billable hours, or that they don't come often enough to keep their product information complete and up to date. Manufacturers are accused of making life difficult by employing unpleasant credit managers and of not shipping when promised. Although every designer can recite a horror story about dealing with the trade, it is essential that members of the trade be treated as colleagues and as valuable resources. When treated this way they can become an asset to the firm, smoothing out problems and helping with product solutions.

Legal Issues

Political, governmental, and environmental issues; professional liability; codes; product liability; taxes; audits; and interior design licensing are all legal issues that must be addressed by a design firm. Things such as a new sales tax can affect the internal financial structure of a design firm; a changed building code may affect the interior finish materials specified for a project; and an audit by the Department of Labor can affect the staffing organization and employee compensation practices of a firm. Latex adhesives, volatile organic compounds, and "out-gassing" formaldehyde are just a few of the environmental issues affecting the practice of interior design in the next decade.

Participation in professional associations like ASID is one of the best ways to maintain current information on legal issues. Continuous exploration and sensitivity to these and other related issues is important to the success of a design firm.

Critical Exposures

Critical exposures means asking questions that address difficult circumstances and providing potential solutions for such circumstances if these develop in a design practice. By going through a process of listing things, the design firm can critically evaluate emergency needs and situations. For example, what happens if the key senior designer, responsible for the top three revenue-producing clients, decides to leave and open his or her own design firm? Or what happens if the number one client, accounting for 50 percent of the practice's work, goes out of business?

This process identifies vulnerable areas and provides an opportunity to develop contingency plans. A possible solution to the examples given above might be to offer the senior designer an equity position in the business or to plan to add two new clients equal to the revenues received from the current 50 percent client.

DEVELOP ALTERNATIVES

Step three in the process of strategic planning and management is to develop alternatives. Having completed a difficult process like identifying the critical exposures, a more invigorating and positive one, such as developing alternatives, should follow. This is the brainstorming phase. This entails going through each area of the practice and developing possible plans. As with any brainstorming process, thinking creatively—without limitations—is important.

Set aside time with partners and key staff members to develop alternatives. An evening or a Saturday session, without telephone interruptions, is usually best for a creative thinking environment. The use of a flip chart to record everyone's ideas is a valuable technique. When brainstorming, write every idea down without evaluation. Evaluation comes in the next phase.

MAKE DECISIONS

The fourth step in the process of strategic planning and management is to make decisions. Say, for example, that the staffing analysis indicated that the firm was unable to keep good employees and that for the most part after two years of employment, good staff members would leave to work for the competition. A brainstorming session developed two alternatives: (1) increase staff salaries and (2) implement a training program. Since the existing staff salaries are already competitive, the decision is to implement a training program. Once this decision is made, an action plan is necessary that specifies what to do, who should do it, when it should be done, and how much it will cost. In this example, this means the development of a training program by the managing partner by the end of the calendar year at a cost of $1,000 per employee. This process provides a blueprint for accomplishing results.

TAKE ACTION

Step five is to take action. In the example just provided, a training program was the resulting plan of action to help retain good employees. As was inferred through the example, most people do not switch jobs for increased salary alone, but rather because they are not learning and growing. With the completion of the staff analysis, a firm should have a good idea of the staff's collective and individual training needs and should move forward to implement such a program. Training programs do not have to be expensive. A training program can be as simple as a commitment from the senior staff to share knowledge with the junior staff. Some techniques for internal training are to:

- Assign an entry-level staff member to a junior staff member to develop good verbal and graphic presentation skills.
- Ask a senior staff member to spend six months coaching a junior staff member on good written communications skills for projects and clients.
- Spend one lunch hour per week with a sales representative to learn technical information about products or services.

External training allows the development of skills and knowledge that do not exist within the organization. Because there are usually fees associated with external training, the firm should carefully select the training vehicle and determine how much can be spent on each staff member. Consider some of the following training sources:

- The local university or junior college can provide general training programs in many business skills, such as finance, accounting, real estate, and computer applications.
- One-day low-cost programs offer seminars on self-improvement topics such as time management, team building, leadership, and speed reading. Many offer targeted seminars on telemarketing, collections, business, and technical writing.
- ASID, other professional organizations, and many design centers offer low-cost, one-day technical seminars on design and business topics targeted for the interior designer.

FOLLOW UP AND CONTROL

The next-to-last step in a strategic planning and management process is to follow up and control. The best way to be certain that this is actually done is to set periodic dates to review the documentation on the existing conditions, the decisions made, and the action steps taken. If the strategic plan was well thought out, the actions necessary for implementation should be in priority order. To check the progress, tasks should be in manageable sizes so that every day some portion of the objective is accomplished.

IDENTIFY DEVIATIONS

The final step in organizing a strategic planning and management plan is to identify deviations. Pay particular attention in this phase to how time and energy are spent. If the time sheet reflects major categories of time expenditure that weren't listed in the strategic plan, perhaps the plan is not being followed closely enough or the plan is not complete. Periodic examination of the plan will ensure that it remains dynamic and responsive to change.

CONCLUSION

Strategic planning and strategic management are harmonious with the design process used for interior design projects. Application of this process to the business side of an interior design firm requires a more global perspective.

Remember the steps.
Define the situation
Analyze the situation
Develop alternatives
Make decisions
Take action
Follow-up and control
Identify deviations

And then start all over.

Business Management

CHARLES GANDY

Managing the internal and external facets of any business is a difficult job at best. Many argue that creative people are not businesspeople. However, the interior designer who is a good businessperson is usually in a better position to be creative. One should be as creative with business structure and implementation as with an interior design project. There are certain givens and standard ways of conducting business. Following these time-proven methods is far from boring and can even be creative. Good business management should be thought of as establishing a solid business image by paying attention to internal and external concerns.

INTERNAL CONCERNS

Internally, the designer must be concerned with two issues: the physical plant and employee relations.

The Physical Plant

The first major question in any design firm is where it should be located. Just what type of business does the designer have? Is it necessary for the designer to be close to a decorative center or a certain business district? Is it advisable for the designer to locate the business where the public has easy access? How much space is necessary? Is expansion a possibility? How many employees are there, or will there be? What type of image must be created?

All these questions, and more, are essential in determining the correct location or place of business. This decision will, of course, determine the amount of money needed to secure the proper facility. This overhead expense must be weighed against the total cash flow necessary to keep the business operating.

The location is only part of the physical plant. Once the designer chooses the office's location, the next major decision is the kind of look the office should have. Often, designers go overboard in their own offices, making them showcases of their work. Is such an expenditure necessary? The answer depends, of course, on exactly how the office will function. Will clients come to the office? Will presentations occur in the office or away from the office? Sometimes, however, designers neglect their own offices, rationalizing that "the cobbler never has shoes." A compromise between an elaborately overdone office environment and one of neglect is usually the best approach.

Equipping the office is also an important consideration. What type of computer system will be used, if any? Is CAD essential? And what about the telephone system, copy machines, adding machines, and other office equipment? These questions will vary from firm to firm, but they certainly must be considered in the overall planning of a successful office. What about things such as stationery, portfolios, coffee service, and maintenance of flowers and plants? All of these, although somewhat minor in nature, contribute to the overall image of the business and affect the bottom-line management philosophy of the firm.

Timing is essential when planning an office. It may be advisable to develop a master plan for growth and opportunity that affects the office. Remember, it is advisable to plan cautiously.

Employee Relations

Without question, the biggest operating expense of a business is its employees. How many people should a designer hire? What level of expertise is needed? How many clerical staff members versus designers are necessary? These questions, like those about location, depend upon the type and amount of work. It is advisable to understaff rather than overstaff. Nothing is worse than having a large staff with nothing to do and then being forced to let them go. Invariably when that happens, new work will arrive and new staffing will have to be done. This "yo-yo" image is detrimental to the productivity of the firm and its reputation among designers.

Many firms are finding that the use of freelance or independent employees is a good management technique. It allows the employer to staff up or down as the workload demands and also provides a workforce that may be specifically trained and experienced in a speciality area. Although the hourly rates for freelance employees may be higher, the overall costs to the company are minimized because FICA taxes and fringe benefits such as holidays, vacations, insurance, and retirement plans are not usually picked up by the business for such employees. It is important to note that there are very strict federal guidelines regarding the employment of such consultants, and these guidelines should be understood fully before they are hired.

Dealing with employees once they have been hired offers even greater challenges. Most people who work for, and with, someone do so because they want to succeed in their chosen endeavor. They need to feel they contribute and that there is opportunity to advance financially. Design staff members are no exception. Designers tend to work best under conditions that allow for personal expression and constant reinforcement for work well done.

Unfortunately, most designers who become principals in their own firms are not trained to be people managers. They learn the hard way—through trial and error. Usually, the most successful managers are those who outline specifically what is expected of employees and then provide enough freedom for them to learn and grow. At the same time, these managers work with the employees—directing, guiding, and challenging them to improve. An important rule of thumb is that employees need to be respected, trusted, and allowed to do what they were hired to do. Deviations from these principles will usually create problems between employees and management.

Rules and guidelines for the smooth operation of a business need to be established and followed. How strictly these are followed, of course, depends on the firm. Usually larger firms require a somewhat stricter enforcement of the rules. The secret to success is creating an atmosphere where employees *want* to work and to avoid an office where employees *have* to work. Employee manuals are helpful. Many potential problems can be eliminating by specifically outlining such essential items as job descriptions; fringe benefits, including sick days, holidays, "personal" days, vacations, and maternity leaves; and general expectations, including hours and office policies and procedures.

No matter how specific the rules or how lenient or understanding an employer, a situation invariably will occur where an employee is simply not contributing to the firm as expected. In such a case, the best and most effective method for handling the situation is to terminate that person's employment. Do so clearly and decisively. Chances are, if the disgruntled employee is not doing the job, it means that person is not happy.

The hiring and management of consultants such as insurance consultants, accountants, lawyers, and financial consultants, is another important concern. These people are essential to the successful operation and maintenance of any design practice. More specific information regarding these specialists is found elsewhere in this manual, but it should always be kept in mind that as employees, these people must be treated with respect and courtesy. As trite as it may sound, successful employee relations happen if one follows the adage: "Do unto others as you would have them do unto you."

The person managing a design office also needs to remember that a good manager must be a good leader—even a good cheerleader. By following the rules, giving employees strokes for work well done, and disciplining when necessary, a good manager creates an environment that encourages success.

EXTERNAL CONCERNS

Although the internal workings of any office are essential, without proper external management, the business will not succeed. Considerations such as relationships with vendors, manufacturers, and manufacturing representatives—as well as professional associations—all play a major role in successful business management.

Professionalism in Management

The best way to establish a solid reputation and create a good image is to develop the business internally and externally in a professional manner. Professionalism means accurate, clear, and honest communication; it means proper financial management, good recordkeeping, and prompt payment of bills; and it means staying abreast of each situation.

Dealing with clients on a straightforward basis is essential to the success of a business. Again, the more direct and honest the communication, the better the results will be. Clients, be they individuals or corporations, deserve and expect respect. Too often, design offices forget that if it were not for the clients there would be no business. After all, clients may not pay their bills unless they are happy and feel they are receiving services for which they contracted. This kind of a situation would obviously have an adverse affect on the cash flow and possibly even the survival of the operation.

Cash flow management is a speciality in itself. Making sure that the bottom-line expenses are met in a timely fashion—with a profit—becomes a daily juggling act. Balancing the fixed costs of operation such as rent, salaries, equipment, and insurance with unexpected and variable costs such as equipment failure, telephone expenses, auto expenses, utilities, and taxes requires planning and attention to detail. Here, without question, the most helpful external ally is the banker. Establishing a good solid banking relationship that includes borrowing possibilities such as lines of credit becomes paramount in times of cash flow problems.

Banks, like designers, are in the service business, and some offer better service than others. Once a bank has been selected, stick with it for a while. Loyalty in banking is essential. Credibility must be established and longevity helps to build loyalty.

Communication

A key word to be remembered is communication—communication to and with employees; communication to and with clients, bankers, and other consultants; and communication to and with manufacturers, vendors, and suppliers. Throughout it all, directness, professionalism, and honesty must be the guide. Be warned, however, not to become so bogged down in communication and paper management that you lose sight of the goals. There are horror stories about firms whose written communications are so complex no one is truly aware of what is going on in the firm.

CONCLUSION

It should never be forgotten that a good interior design business must be ethically irreproachable and must practice sound business procedures. Of course it is exciting and gratifying to develop beautiful spaces in which people live and work, but unless there is proper business management with a profit realized, the vehicle to create these environments is nonexistent. The designer must accept the fact that it is okay to make money while being creative—in fact, it's not only okay, it's essential!

Financial Management

HARRY SIEGEL AND STEVEN L. SACKS

Financial management is the development of short- and long-term financial goals and procedures correlated with actual results. Successful financial management means that a firm functions within its capacity to generate and control the funds necessary to maintain itself by meeting its operating expenses and its obligations to clients, vendors, and employees. In addition to overhead expenses, operating costs include compensation for employees and the establishment of pension and benefits programs. A sound financial management plan integrates the development of a capital goal or "nest egg" for the future.

An effective financial management plan for an interior design firm dictates the monitoring of several key elements. These include:

Capital requirements.
Cash needs and requirements.
Income and operating expense projections, including the fee basis and control of operating expenses.
Direct project costs, including evaluation of the project's budget.
Assets and liabilities management, including cash, clients' deposits, and accounts receivable accounts.
Vendor deposits and accounts payable for establishing lines of credit.
Financial reports.

Let's take a closer look at each of these areas in turn.

CAPITAL REQUIREMENTS

The interior design profession runs the gamut from the one-person firm operating out of the home with low operating expenses to the large firm with many employees, a heavy overhead, and extensive capital requirements. To complicate the matter further, the profession also includes firms that supply furniture and accessories in a retail setting. As a result, it is impossible to present a capital requirement format that is applicable to all segments.

A generic look at the profession suggests that there are two basic factors of concern relative to capital requirements: location and start-up conditions. Possible organizational structures that affect the location of the business are:

The home studio.
The office in a business atmosphere.
The retail establishment (with interior design service).

Start-up conditions affecting a new business include:

No clients or immediate prospects.
Client prospects in hand or follow-up of previous exposure.
Human resource needs.
Product purchases for a retail establishment.

The start-up capital requirements for a home studio are minimal until the business begins to flourish. There should be enough capital to purchase simple office and stationery supplies, retain a professional to guide in the organization's formation, and secure the required governmental registrations.

For other types of business start-ups, like the business office and the retail/design establishment, factors such as these must be considered:

- Cost of organizing the business and its initial outlay of funds.
- Cost of office furnishings, equipment, and capital requirements.
- Negative cash flow. (At what point will the business generate a cash flow to cover operating expenses?)

The elements of overhead must be thoroughly analyzed, and enough funds should be available to cover overhead for at least three to four months of operations. Ordinary overhead involves rent, insurance, utilities, telephone, payroll, professional and office expenses, travel, payroll fringe costs, and a small discretionary fund for minor emergencies.

The retail/design establishment has one additional element to be considered—the cost of purchasing an inventory of furnishings and accessories. These initial purchases are usually paid for immediately and should be considered a permanent capital outlay.

CASH NEEDS AND REQUIREMENTS

Sound financial management calls for sound cash flow—the matching of incoming cash to outgoing cash. To put it simply, a designer must channel incoming cash so that bills can be paid promptly and operating expenses met. "Robbing Peter to pay Paul" is a game that results in dire consequences.

INCOME AND OPERATING EXPENSE PROJECTIONS

Successful financial management demands a correlation between income and overhead expenses. This can be easily observed by reviewing professionally prepared financial statements. (See the examples later in this chapter.)

Interior design firms earn income based upon a fee structure. This may be a mark-up on cost, a retail basis, or a combination of various other fees. The fee basis determines what will be available for salaries and overhead. The following outline serves as an example for projecting expenses and determining a fee base for a typical interior design firm.

Assume that a small design firm projects its annual overhead to be:

Rent	12,000
Insurance	4,000
Utilities	2,000
Telephone	3,000
Advertising	3,000
Printing, postage, and stationery	3,000
Auto expenses and travel	3,000
Dues and subscriptions	1,000
Professional fees	2,000
Entertainment	2,500
Salaries—office	15,000
—designer	35,000
Taxes—payroll and other	10,000
Principal's salary	50,000
Miscellaneous other expenses	5,000
Total projected overhead	$150,500

If a design firm uses a fee basis of 35 percent mark-up on cost, then it must generate approximately $580,000 of billing to meet its projected overhead budget. This computation is arrived at in the following manner:

Purchases made for clients	$430,000
35 percent mark-up	150,500
Total billing	$580,500

If the design firm operates on a retail basis, it must generate approximately $460,000 of gross billings. This amount is arrived at on the basis of the experience factor that the gross profit on the retail basis averages between 30 percent and 35 percent of the sales dollar:

32.5 percent (average) of $460,000 = $149,500

Constant monitoring is required during the operating year to ascertain whether the necessary billing level is being generated. If not, then the firm must reconsider its overhead burden or change its fee structure. If a design firm does not procure products for clients, then fees sufficient to cover the overhead expenses and provide a suitable profit must be established.

DIRECT PROJECT COSTS

An area of management that is often overlooked is the prospective client's budget or the amount available for the execution of a design project. There are many aspects of this, but the most important is the allocation of the budget amount. The designer must recognize that when clients establish a budget amount for their projects, the budget actually consists of three elements: (1) that portion allocated to the direct cost of furnishings, services, and so forth; (2) that portion allocated to the designer's compensation; and (3) that portion allocated to sales tax and other indirect costs.

For example, a client's budget is $50,000 and the designer's compensation is 30 percent mark-up on cost.

Problem: How much of the $50,000 should be allocated to cover the cost of furnishing, services, and so on necessary for the satisfactory completion of the project, and how much must be available for payment of the designer's fee?

Arithmetic: To establish the amount available for costs, divide 130 percent into $50,000. This equals $38,460. To establish the amount to be allocated for the designer's fee, multiply $38,460 by 30 percent, which equals $11,540. $38,460 + $11,540 = $50,000. This calculation is not complete without the sales taxes included. If the above project is in a 7 percent sales tax area and all cost items—including the designer's mark-up—are subject to this tax, the budget amount has to be adjusted.

To establish the estimated sales tax amount, multiply $50,000 by 7 percent. This is $3,500. The net available budget amount is now $50,000 less $3,500, or $46,500. The amount to be allocated for costs is 130 percent divided into $46,500, or $35,770.

Result: Instead of having $38,460 available for costs as first indicated, there is $2,690 less to work with, or $35,770. Even the designer's fee is reduced in this example by $810 to $10,730. It should be noted that there may be other indirect costs, such as freight and delivery charges, that may also affect the base.

The above theory and calculations can be applied in the same fashion when working on the retail basis. The designer must establish the average gross profit percentage as the mark-up base.

The importance of this simple arithmetic calculation is obvious. It should be used as a guide for the designer in controlling the costs of the design project. If the design costs are not established up front and the budget firmly controlled, excessive expenditures may have to come from the designer's pocket.

ASSETS AND LIABILITIES MANAGEMENT

There are three major areas of concern in this area of financial management: (1) available cash funds, (2) client deposits and accounts receivable, and (3) vendor deposits and accounts payable.

Availability of Cash

The availability of cash funds and the proper allocation of the expenditures of these funds is key to the survival of any business. Funds must be apportioned on a continuing basis toward payment to creditors, payment for salaries, payments for overhead expenses, and a contingency fund to meet any dry periods that may occur. Cash funds that accumulate should be carried in interest-bearing depositories which, when handled properly, result in a good source of additional income.

Client Deposits and Accounts Receivable

In a firm that incorporates product sales as part of its fee base, the incoming cash flow is derived from two sources—deposits from clients, and receipts from clients for furnishing and services billed. Most interior design firms adhere to the deposit principle, which requires the client to pay a deposit before furnishings are ordered or before are performed.

A deposit is based either upon a specific item to be purchased or upon a sizable deposit with the signing of a contract. These deposits should be used to meet the deposit or payment requirements of the trade sources. Since many firms do not have sufficient capital, they use these deposits as working capital. This can be a dangerous procedure and should be predicated only on the deposit amount, which is a combination of direct costs and the designer's mark-up. That portion generated by the mark-up should be used for overhead needs, while the direct cost portion should be used for its intended purpose.

A billing to client's program should be developed to suit both the cash flow needs and the office routine. Timely billing and the collection of amounts due from clients in accordance with the firm's credit terms are prime requisites for ensuring that there will be a smooth flow of funds to carry on business.

VENDOR DEPOSITS AND ACCOUNTS PAYABLE

Good management requires that the design firm research the credit standing and the reputation of the vendors to whom it is paying deposits. Deposit requirements vary with individual trade sources. However, designers should always be aware that they, not the clients, are responsible for such advances.

Prompt payment of accounts payable to trade sources and adherence to credit terms are major factors in establishing and maintaining lines of credit. Credit sustains the economy and the flow of goods and services.

Credit is obtained by providing reassuring financial information to a trade source, and by a history of prompt payment of bills. This is especially important for a thinly capitalized firm. The design firm, in most instances, extends credit to its clients, but in order to do so, needs credit from its trade sources. The ability to extend credit is based upon the designer's ability to establish it.

FINANCIAL REPORTS

Financial statements properly prepared—either by an independent accountant, or in the large firms by the comptroller or financial executive—are the key to interpreting and analyzing the financial results of any business operation. They are the guide to the development of future budgetary requirements and possible restructuring of the fee or income basis. These financial statements should be prepared on a periodic basis and most importantly on an annual basis. They indicate the results of operations for a given period and the financial position at the end of each period.

The information and guidance that these financial statements can provide are illustrated in the following example of a financial report for a small firm with one principal whose focus is residential interior design.

Exhibit A

ABC INTERIORS, INC. INCOME STATEMENT
FOR THE YEAR ENDED DECEMBER 31, 1990

		Percent	Notes
Sales	$856,000	100.00	
Cost of Goods Sold			
Inventory—Work in Process			
Beginning	50,000	5.84	
Purchases	580,000	67.76	
Cost of Goods Available	630,000	73.60	
Less: Inventory-W/I/P-Ending	60,000	7.01	
Costs of Goods Sold	570,000	66.59	
Gross Profit on Goods Sold	286,000	33.41	#1
Design Service Fees	70,000	8.18	#2
Total Gross Profit	356,000	41.59	#3
Operating Expenses			
Officer's salary	100,000	11.69	
Design salaries	90,000	10.51	
Office salaries	15,000	1.75	
Rent	18,000	2.10	
Telephone and utilities	6,000	.70	
Stationery and office expenses	6,000	.70	
Travel and entertainment	8,500	1.00	
Advertising and sales promotion	21,000	2.45	
Auto expense	4,500	.52	
Insurance	13,500	1.58	
Payroll taxes	13,000	1.52	
Other taxes	5,500	.64	
Profit sharing plan	25,000	2.92	
Employee benefits	6,000	.70	
Contributions	1,000	.12	
Sundry other expenses	1,300	.15	
Depreciation	7,000	.82	
Total Operating Expenses	341,300	39.87	
Income from Operations	14,700	1.72	#4
Other Income—Interest Earned	10,000	1.17	#5
Net Income	$ 24,700	2.89	

EXHIBIT A—ANNOTATED REFERENCES

Note 1 Gross profit percentage on goods sold of 33.41 percent indicates the firm is working on the retail basis theory. It is an excellent mark-up. If this firm was operating on a mark-up of 30 percent on cost, the resulting gross profit would be:

Cost of Goods	$570,000
30 percent Mark-up	$171,000

The firm could not meet its overhead expenses without doing one of the following:

- Severely cut costs.
- Develop another source of income, perhaps a substantial increase in mark-up combined with a more positive attitude toward design fees.

Note 2 Design service fees of 8 percent are a minor factor in this firm's fee structure; however, it did add $70,000 of additional income that helped the firm meet its operating goals.

Note 3 The gross profit of $356,000 allows this firm to meet its operating expenses of $341,000, which includes four major and important areas:

- The principal's salary of $100,000.
- Design staff salaries—(two designers and one assistant) for a total of $90,000.
- A profit sharing plan with a cost of $25,000.
- An advertising and promotion budget of $21,000.

These four major items total $236,000 or 66.30 percent of the total gross profit ($356,000). All other operating expenses totalled $105,300, which indicates a good control of the overhead burden. The remaining operating profit of $14,700 is not very substantial and reflects the firm's objectives of good remuneration to the principal and employees (see Note 4). The final net profit for the firm in the amount of $24,700 was enhanced by $10,000 of interest earned on idle funds (see Note 5).

Note 4 Net income from operations in the amount of $14,700 or 1.72 percent of the selling dollar is probably a little low and does not add much to the financial stability of the firm. However, the average net profit for most small firms does not exceed 5 percent.

Note 5 Other income $10,000—(Interest Earned). This company maintains a very solid cash position with a good portion maintained in interest bearing instruments or deposits. It is a wise policy to keep money working whenever possible.

Exhibit B

ABC INTERIORS, INC. BALANCE SHEET
DECEMBER 31, 1990

			Notes
Current Assets			
Cash	$160,000		#1
Accounts receivable	62,000		#2
Deposits with vendors	108,000		#3
Inventory	60,000		
Prepaid expenses	11,000		
Total Current Assets		$401,000	#4
Fixed Assets			
Furniture and fixtures	8,000		
Trucks and auto	30,000		
Less: Depreciation	(18,000)		
Total Fixed Assets		16,000	
Other Assets			
Deposits		2,000	
Total Assets		$419,000	
Liabilities and Stockholders' Equity			
Accounts payable—trade	$ 53,000		#5
Customers' deposits	235,000		#6
Accrued taxes and expenses	30,000		
Total Liabilities		318,000	#4
Stockholders' Equity			
Capital stock	20,000		
Retained earnings	81,000		
Total Stockholders' Equity		101,000	#7
Total Liabilities and Stockholders' Equity		$419,000	

EXHIBIT B—ANNOTATED REFERENCES

Note 1 At an average day-to-day expense rate of $28,500 a month, this firm maintains an excellent cash position relative to meeting trade source payments.

Note 2 Accounts Receivable balances of $62,000 is less than the average monthly billing of $77,166. (Sales of $856,000 plus design fees of $70,000 total $926,000, and $926,000 ÷ 12 = $77,166). This shows a solid collection management approach.

Note 3 Deposits with vendors is in line with client deposits (note 6) at slightly under 50 percent of the client deposits received.

Note 4 Total current assets are in excess of total liabilities by $83,000 and gives this firm ample room to meet its financial responsibilities.

Note 5 Accounts payable in the amount of $53,000 show this firm pays its bills on a current basis. The monthly purchases average $48,333. While this is less than the current amount due to creditors, it still indicates that vendors are paid promptly and establishes good credit for the firm.

Note 6 Customers' Deposits. This firm requires a 50 percent deposit from its clients before it processes a purchase order; therefore, the customers' deposit amount of $235,000 indicates a backlog of projects-in-work of approximately $470,000.

This backlog of projects-in-work is perhaps one of the most important indicators for financial management since it guides management budget and expense projections for the future. This firm has already booked more than half of the billing of the previous successful year at the very beginning of its new operating year. Customer deposits are a vital indicator of where the company is going. A decrease in the number of projects-in-work automatically triggers a decrease in cash flow. Such a decrease should alert management to review its overhead burden so that it can weather a dry spell.

Note 7 Stockholders' Equity, which is the difference between Assets and Liabilities of $101,000, is made up of two factors:

1. Initial Capital Investment of $20,000.
2. Retained Earnings of $81,000 that has accumulated during the life of the business. This factor illustrates a conservative financial approach and shows that management does not expend every dollar that it earns, but saves part of each year's profit in the event of a poor business period.

Legal Management

ALAN M. SIEGEL AND JERROLD M. SONET

The practice of interior design has undergone major changes since its evolution in the 1920s from what many thought was an avocation, to its present position as a recognized profession. The registration effort, already successful in many states; the revolutionary changes in interior design education and the availability of such education to aspiring practitioners; as well as the legal and quasi-legal efforts to measure qualifications for practice—all are evidence of the public's acceptance of interior design as a professional activity.

The practice of any profession necessarily involves the operation of a business. In the case of interior design, both design and business elements require careful attention to legal management.

BUSINESS TYPES

As is the case with most professional businesses, interior designers have the opportunity to select from among several business formats within which to operate; among them are the sole proprietorship, the partnership, the corporation, or the professional corporation (the PC) in states that authorize it. This selection should not be left to chance, but should be based upon an analysis of which business format is best suited for the practitioner's operations.

Operating on one's own (a sole proprietorship) or pursuant to agreement in combination with other practitioners (a partnership) can be, at times, a simple and useful methodology for conducting an interior design practice, provided that issues of potential liability are adequately addressed through maintenance of substantial amounts of errors and omissions insurance as well as general forms of liability insurance. Even then, the risk to the practitioner of personal liability is not eliminated, since insurance coverage will not protect against liability arising from every breach of a design contract or failure to comply with a lease or other business arrangements. These risks can be minimized if the practitioner opts to operate through a corporation.

Business operation in corporate form does not present any unusual problems for the practitioner operating either alone or in conjunction with one or more associates. Although careful attention must be paid to detail and statutory compliance, corporate format permits the practitioner to operate, in large part, in the same manner as if he or she were operating as an individual.

What is a corporation? A corporation is a creature of law, endowed with a personality separate and distinct from that of its owners. It is a legal entity that enjoys many privileges and has responsibilities. A corporation may sue and be sued; it may purchase and sell personal and real property; it may enter into contracts and transact legitimate business. It can undertake any of the myriad functions that are required to be performed in the day-to-day practice of interior design. The functions are, in fact, performed by the practicing designer, but they are performed in the name of and on behalf of the corporation, a separate legal entity, rather than in the name of or on behalf of the individual practitioner. The reason for interposing this legal entity between the practitioner and those with whom he or she deals is to limit the scope of the practitioner's personal legal liability.

The business of interior design by its very nature exposes the practitioner to areas of potential legal liability. Practitioners routinely enter into contracts with clients, vendors, and other providers of services. Recognizing the potential for serious legal liability, the privilege of "limited liability" afforded by law to corporations is a key consideration in a practitioner's business planning.

The law permits incorporation of a business for the very purpose of escaping, whenever permitted, personal liability. The law treats a corporation as having an existence separate and apart from that of its shareholders and consequently will not ordinarily impose liability upon its shareholders for the acts of the corporation. Corporate "limited liability" may be all that serves to protect the practitioner's personal assets (other than the practitioner's investment in the corporation) from the claims of judgment creditors.

The corporate privilege of "limited liability" can be lost where the shareholder and/or practitioner either carries on the business on a personal basis or utilizes the corporate format in an effort to mislead or defraud third parties. A common situation is where a practitioner unintentionally executes a contract with either his client or a supplier is his own name rather than on behalf of the corporation, thus giving rise to potential claims for personal liability. This occurs when documents are signed by the practitioner in "personal name" without indicia of corporate capacity. The cardinal rule to be followed is that whenever and wherever a document is entered into between the design corporation and some third party, such document(s)—including correspondence and checks—should be signed by the practitioner in his capacity as an *officer* of the corporation and that capacity should be expressly disclosed in the document.

As is the case with other privileges the law bestows, the privilege of "limited liability" is not absolute. Many laws impose personal liability upon shareholders and/or officers of a corporation in specific instances. For example, the obligation to collect and remit sales tax may well be, depending on the concerned jurisdiction, a personal obligation imposed upon the corporate officers, directors, or employees who are under a duty to act for such corporation in complying with the requirements of the State Sales Tax law. Withholding taxes and, in specific cases, unpaid wages to employees become the personal responsibility of the controlling individuals. The corporate shield of limited liability will not always protect against loss of personal assets, particularly in instances where stockholders seek to utilize the corporate shield through willful and fraudulent guises. Limited liability is available to and is a benefit to stockholders who seek to protect their personal assets against the ordinary claims of corporate creditors who must usually look to satisfy their claims against corporate assets.

One final comment regarding "limited liability": In most states, professionals who are required to be licensed to *practice* their profession (such as doctors, dentists, or lawyers) are prohibited from practicing their profession through the vehicle of an ordinary business corporation. The obvious reason for this is that such a professional should not be allowed to shield himself or herself from personal liability arising out of negligent or wrongful acts committed while rendering such professional services. The concept of Professional Service corporations, commonly known as PC's, came into existence to permit such licensed professionals to utilize the corporate form of business in order to organize their activities more efficiently. Federal tax benefits accorded to executives and employees of ordinary business corporations also become available to these professionals and their employees. In a PC, each shareholder (the licensed professional) remains personally and fully liable and accountable for any negligent acts committed by him or her, or by any person acting under his or her direct supervision and control, while rendering professional services on behalf of the corporation.

Where states have enacted registration statutes governing the profession, the registered practitioner may, depending on the applicable statutory scheme, be able to operate either as a PC or through a business corporation. Whenever a practitioner operates as a PC—or, for that matter, in either a partnership or a sole proprietorship—maintenance of errors and omissions insurance should be a business requisite. In such instances, it constitutes the only method of limiting the practitioner's liability by substituting insurance proceeds for the practitioner's personal assets in the instance of design mistake or professional negligence. Use of the business corporation format is not a reason for dispensing with errors and omissions coverage. The corporation format still requires protection for assets, which are, in effect, the property of the practitioner. Perhaps even more significant is the protection that errors and omissions insurance affords against substantial legal costs that might otherwise be incurred by the practitioner, notwithstanding his or her choice of business format, in defending against unwarranted claims by clients or other third parties.

SUBCHAPTER S

Any design practice is confronted with numerous tax laws, rules, and regulations on the federal, state, and local levels. It is not the purpose of this chapter to address this vast area, but an understanding of the Subchapter S tax concept is useful in the practitioner's selection of business format.

A Subchapter S corporation is a tax concept only, not a corporate law concept. Under federal and many state tax laws, corporations may, if eligible, elect Subchapter S tax treatment. A prerequisite to the election, however, is the existence of a corporation.

The basic purpose of the Subchapter S election is to allow closely held corporations and their shareholders the right to enjoy the benefits afforded to corporations (for example, the privilege of "limited liability") without the accompanying burden of *corporate* taxes. This is particularly crucial in those instances where the individual practitioner's personal income tax rates are less than corporate tax rates. Overly simplified, the Subchapter S election obviates at the corporate level a tax on its income by effectively passing corporate income through to its shareholders, who are taxed at their *individual* rates (whether or not the corporate income has actually been distributed to the shareholders).

This is not to say that practitioners should always seek to elect Subchapter S tax treatment, since existing federal and state corporate tax laws also afford the corporate taxpayer and thus its stockholders flexible and potentially advantageous tax treatment. Planning with professional advisers should be sought before making decisions regarding Subchapter S elections, or for that matter, before taking any material actions that have tax consequences.

PRECONTRACT ACTIVITY

The precontract phase of a project begins when the designer meets with a prospective client and ends when a written design agreement is signed.

No designer should proceed with a project, notwithstanding its type or size, without first reaching and setting forth, in writing, the arrangements worked out with the client. Use of a handshake or other oral agreement should be avoided at all costs, since reliance on such agreements will usually lead to difficulty, disagreement, and dispute. Notwithstanding its critical nature, insufficient time is often devoted to the precontract phase in the understandable effort to sign up the client and proceed with the project. However, the ultimate financial success of any project rests upon a sound working arrangement, which originates from a thorough analysis of the project during the precontract phase. During this period, the designer undertakes the role of a negotiator, a salesperson, an investigator, and an educator.

The last aspect is key in explaining to the prospective client the role of the interior designer and what the client can expect in terms of project services, working arrangements, and the resolution of the project problems that invariably arise during the course of execution. An informed client is less likely to react adversely to the inconveniences and petty annoyances often encountered in a design project.

As a negotiator, the designer is required to reconcile the designer's business methods and fee requirements with the client's concerns about time, performance, and related factors. During the precontract phase, the designer may have a prospective client who is currently interviewing other design firms. The designer then exercises selling skills to persuade the prospective client to select him or her over other candidates. As an investigator, the designer seeks to obtain information from the client in the precontract phase, information that will enable the designer to undertake proper precontract analysis of the design project.

Precontract discussions with the client and project analysis permit the designer to:

- Evaluate the economic validity of the project.
- Identify the design areas and the design services required.
- Ascertain the client's budget and time considerations.
- Determine appropriate arrangements for securing furniture, furnishings and equipment and third-party services.
- Determine the most appropriate design compensation arrangement.
- Focus upon unusual aspects of the project which require special design agreement provisions.
- Be aware of technical concerns of the project and the possible need for the services of other professionals.

Until the designer has sufficient information with regard to such items, the designer is in no position either to accept the project, quote a fee arrangement, prepare a design agreement, or proceed with the project. The process not only educates the designer and the client, but, most importantly, provides an opportunity to develop client trust and confidence, which is essential to any client-professional arrangement and which is one of the essentials of good legal management of an interior design practice.

THE DESIGN AGREEMENT

Most designers are not comfortable with the requirement of having to devise a project design agreement. This dictates the development by the designer, preferably in concert with legal counsel, of the type of design agreement that the designer can use again and again with appropriate modifications, without having to reinvent the wheel for each new project.

The important elements of such an agreement are twofold: (1) that it is tailored to encompass the design and business procedures normally utilized by the designer; and (2) that it is easily retailored to meet the specific requirements of a particular design project.

Development of such a tailored form agreement by the designer can be effected either by modifying one of the design agreements published by ASID to meet the designer's specific requirements, or by creating the designer's particular prototype agreement predicated on the designer's prior experience and methods of operation. In both cases, assistance of legal counsel is essential.

Either method should result in a document that includes, at a minimum, provisions governing the following matters:

- Identity of the parties.
- Identification of each design area.
- Description of design services pertaining to each design area.
- Procedures for securing requisite furniture, furnishings, and equipment.
- Procedures for securing requisite services of third-party contractors.
- Procedures for securing services of other design professionals such as architects, engineers, and lighting consultants.
- Procedures for approval of design submissions and recommended furniture, furnishings, and equipment.
- Compensation arrangements, including designer's charges, reimbursable expenses, and applicable taxes.
- Project cost and limitation of designer's liability therefor.
- Time frame and limitation of designer's liability therefor.
- Limitation of designer's liability for nonperformance by third parties.
- Ownership and use of design documents.
- Termination rights.
- Methods of dispute resolution.
- Rights and limitations with respect to photographing and/or publishing of project.

A form agreement can properly serve legitimate and professional business interests of a designer, provided that the form agreement is used correctly. It is not a straightjacket to which blind adherence is required. With respect to every new project, the form must be reviewed and retailored to ensure that its provisions are in tune with the project's objectives and arrangements, which were worked out between client and designer in the precontract phase.

Proper use of a form agreement by a designer means more than simply filling in the blanks. It requires the designer to:

- Understand the form agreement as written.
- Understand application of the provisions of the form agreement to the particular design project.

- Modify the language of the form contract, wherever required, to ensure compliance with designer/client arrangements and to maximize economic benefits while minimizing legal and financial exposure.

PROJECT DEVELOPMENT AND EXECUTION

It is axiomatic that interior design development will include preparation by the designer of plans, layouts, specifications, and like documents (project documents). While preparation of project documents is entirely within the designer's expertise, it is still necessary to ensure that they conform not only to project requirements, but to the client's expectations. To avoid subsequent problems, each completed project document should be submitted to the client for review and endorsement; the client should give written approval on the face of each concerned project document.

The sign-off procedure is equally applicable to sample materials submitted for client approval. It is really not good enough to leave a piece of fabric or carpet sample with a client, or have a client approve a finish sample by catalog number, since invariably the client will lose his piece of fabric and will not remember having ever looked at the catalog. Good legal management mandates that the designer's file contain direct client approval of samples of all materials that are intended to be utilized. Again, this can be done by simply having the client endorse directly on the sample his or her name or initials to indicate such approval.

This principle is equally applicable to completed materials; particularly, custom-order or built-in items, as well as on-site installations. As the client reviews and approves each such item and each installation aspect, the designer should secure, for its file, a memo signed by the client evidencing such approval. This may sound like an awful lot of paperwork, but the old adage that an ounce of prevention is worth a pound of cure is literally applicable here, and the time expended is minuscule compared to the time that would be devoted to resolving a dispute with a client about any of these matters.

In order to ensure that the design concepts—as originated by the designer and reflected in the project documents—are not improperly used, it is recommended that each such document bear the designer's copyright notice, which is simply a © followed by the year in which the document was prepared, the design firm's name, and then the words "All Rights Reserved."

Proper legal management warrants that the designer has general knowledge and appreciation of a body of law commonly known as "intellectual property rights." Federal copyright law and federal and state trademark law come within this area. The basic tenets of intellectual property rights have direct application to design practice. This is certainly one area where consultation with legal counsel is essential so as to protect the designer's proprietary rights—not only in project documents, but also in any original design concept developed for the project.

Other keys to good legal management during the course of the project are the preparation of accurate purchase specifications for furniture, furnishings, and equipment or other materials, and the preparation of accurate instructions (often in the form of plans and design specifications) to contractors responsible for project installations or the fabrication of project items.

Instructions to contractors should convey to the installer or fabricator the designer's requirements for look and size, as well as the location. The details required to fabricate or install the item, whether created in the form of shop drawings or otherwise, should be left solely to the expertise of the contractor.

The intelligent use of form documents extends not only to the subject matter of agreements between designer and client, but to the transactional documents routinely exchanged between designer and resource. The practitioner routinely sends purchase orders to its resources (that is, its vendors). The resources typically respond by way of confirmations, acknowledgments, or sales agreements. These documents pose serious business and legal hazards when they are exchanged by the parties without a complete understanding of their legal effect.

A typical purchase and sale transaction between designer and resource consists of the following:

1. After selecting the merchandise for purchase (and ultimate resale to the client), the designer prepares a purchase order on designer's preprinted form describing, among other things, the merchandise to be purchased, the price to the designer, the address for shipment, and other purchase order terms prepared by the designer's lawyer to protect the designer's interests.

2. The purchase order, together with the required deposit, is sent to the resource. The resource then confirms the transaction by returning to designer its response usually in the form of a purchase acknowledgment prepared on the resource's own form. The acknowledgment invariably contains its own terms and conditions, carefully crafted by the resource's attorneys with the objective of protecting the resource's interests.

3. The designer receives the acknowledgment, reviews it usually in a cursory manner—noting the typed or handwritten portion pertaining to description of merchandise, price, and delivery date and usually ignoring the printed provisions of the resource's acknowledgment. The designer files away the acknowledgment with no expectation of having to review it again and generally without being concerned about the legal impact of the acknowledgment's printed provisions.

In this typical scenario, neither designer nor resource has signed the other's document and each believes that his document sets forth the purchase agreement. In this typical situation, it is legally difficult to determine the actual terms of the purchase agreement, particularly where there is substantial conflict between the printed provisions of the purchase order and the printed provisions of the acknowledgment.

These conflicts often involve matters that go to the heart of a transaction, such as warranty disclaimer (no guarantee against fading or shrinking), liability limitation (claim must be made before fabric is cut), time limitations (claim must be presented within three months of delivery of merchandise), and the like (arbitration of disputes required).

It is often anyone's guess as to whether a particular provision in either document is a legally enforceable term of the purchase agreement. To resolve such issues, it is necessary to resort to legal decision based upon a court's interpretation of applicable statutes governing commercial transactions.

This does not mean that a designer must become learned in the law of contracts or in those provisions of the Uniform Commercial Code that govern purchase and sale transactions. What it does mean is that a designer must pay real attention to the large number of transactions typically entered into in the ordinary course of practice. Proper legal management requires the designer to understand the legal implications of transaction documents and to seek legal advice when a particular provision goes beyond his prior experience. Proper legal management requires the designer to insist that the same document be signed by both designer and resource and that any unacceptable provision either be modified or excised. Negotiation with resources about their fine print provisions is no less important than negotiations pertaining to price or delivery date. Where a resource insists upon acceptance of an onerous provision, the designer should either obtain the client's approval (in writing, of course) or purchase elsewhere. Proper legal management demands that the agreed-upon provisions of the purchase agreement with the vendor be consistent with arrangements between the designer and client pertaining thereto, as set forth either in the initial design agreement or in confirmation of order approved by the client, in writing.

The foregoing concepts are equally applicable where the designer acts as the client's agent in effecting purchases from resources for the client's direct account. The client must always look to the designer to protect the client against contractual provisions that benefit the vendor as opposed to the client (the purchaser). To avoid eventual legal dispute with the client, proper legal management requires the designer to be equally careful about the enforceable provisions of a purchase contract when acting either for the client or acting on his or her own behalf.

THE ROLE OF THE DESIGNER AS A CONTRACT ADMINISTRATOR

The contract administration phase of projects usually commences with the award of one or more contracts to third parties who provide materials and/or labor to effect the interiors background in accordance with the designer's design intent plans. The responsibility of the designer during the contract administration phase is often misunderstood by designer and client.

During the early years of the design profession, it was common practice for the designer to provide background installations directly to the client. This practice should never be utilized unless (1) the designer is prepared to assume total financial and legal responsibility for the work of others and (2) the designer is in compliance with applicable state and/or local contractors licensing laws (that is, unless the designer has secured, in his or her own name, Home Improvement Contractor's license and the like).

The designer who provides interior installation services directly to a client through the use of the designer's own subcontractors assumes direct legal responsibility for the proper performance of all such work and the financial obligation to pay the subcontractors whether or not the client pays the designer for the services.

Effective legal management and good business sense dictate against the designer undertaking legal responsibility for the performance of work by others. During the installation phase, the designer's obligation should be limited to exercising professional skill and judgment in the interpretation of design concept plans and specifications, alerting the client and the concerned contractor to any observable deficiencies in the interiors work. All interiors contractors should be engaged directly by the client with the designer acting as the client's eyes and ears so as to ensure proper execution of the design plans and specifications, as prepared by the designer and approved by the client.

The design agreement should carefully address this role of the designer as contract administrator. Essentially, the design agreement should specifically provide for the:

- Client's obligation to engage third-party services directly.
- Designer's responsibility as contract administrator to observe the work and point out deficiencies.
- Disclaimer of the designer's legal responsibility with respect to any failure of third-party performance.
- Manner and method of payment of the designer's compensation for contract administration services.

The design agreement should make it clear that these contract administration provisions apply not only to third party installations at the site, but also to materials prepared offsite by third parties in compliance with the designer's plans and specifications, such as draperies, custom-designed rugs, specially designed cabinetry, and the like.

A proper understanding of the designer's role as contract administrator, coupled with an awareness of statutory proscriptions governing contractors, helps minimize the many difficulties otherwise confronting the design professional in sorting out and resolving problems between the client and third-party contractors.

DON'T STEP OVER THE LINE

Sound legal management requires the design practitioner to be fully cognizant of statutory limitations that have an impact upon the design profession. Performance by the designer of statutorily proscribed services typically renders the contract between designer and client unenforceable as a matter of law and may well subject the designer to civil and criminal sanctions.

Laws governing the practice of engineering, architecture, and landscape architecture vary from state to state; particularly with respect to the types of buildings and to the type of design activities that are statutorily exempt from the purview of the licensed practice of such professions. The design practitioner must consult with counsel to ensure that the designer's practices, contract documents, advertisements, and promotional materials are purged of any proposed activity or language that would otherwise place the designer in jeopardy of violating state licensing laws.

Designers often innocently blunder into such violations and can find themselves in very substantial difficulty even though there was no real intent to undertake, or any actual undertaking of, proscribed services. To illustrate, a design agreement that included a category entitled "Architectural Fees" resulted in the inability of the designer to enforce his contract against his client, notwithstanding the fact that the only services described under this category of the design agreement were decorative treatments such as wall and ceiling finishes, floor coverings, window treatments, custom built-ins, closet work, and the like.

Good legal management requires that all documents pertaining to design activities, or advertisement or promotion of the same, be strictly confined to a proper and clearly defined description of permitted interior design services so as to eliminate any possibility of a claim that the designer has stepped over the line.

OTHER PROBLEM AREAS

Disputes between client and designer are often predicated on the client's flat assertion that the designer exceeded the client's budget, resulting not only in a breach of the design agreement but in serious economic damage to the client. Budget limitations are usually explored in the precontract discussions between designer and client with the amount concerned often being voiced by the client as the maximum available for the project. At times the amount is arrived at on the basis of the designer's estimate of project requirements. Unfortunately, too often the amount discussed is not addressed in the design agreement. Where the design agreement is silent in this regard, a client dispute often escalates into a claim that the designer represented by verbal agreement that the project cost would not exceed the budget, or that the budget was an absolute requirement of the contract, which the designer has violated.

This issue should be defused up front by inserting an appropriate disclaimer clause into the design agreement; such a clause, in effect, eliminates any representation or warranty that bids or negotiated prices will not vary from the client's proposed budget or from any cost estimate or evaluation prepared by the designer. It is important that the designer not make inadvertent or unintentional legal representations that the project can be completed for a specific sum. The client's budget concerns can be quieted by reminding the client that merchandise and services will not be ordered for the client's account without first obtaining the client's written consent and that, in consequence, it is the client who has overall control over project costs, not the designer.

Another area often fraught with difficulty is where the client seeks to impose arbitrary deadlines on the designer for the delivery of merchandise, completion of third-party services, and/or complete performance of all project services. Unfortunately, the designer has little or no control over timely performance by third parties, either in the preparation and delivery of merchandise or the completion of work at the site. Specified delivery or completion dates, even if agreed to by a resource or contractor, are usually more honored in the breach than in the performance.

To avoid difficulty, the designer should not agree to any schedule of performance that is dependent upon the actions of anyone outside of the designer's own office. Any completion agreement should be limited solely to matters within the designer's own control, such as plans, specifications, or other work produced to be generated solely by designer's own office. Even here, care should be taken to provide adequate time for realistic completion of such services.

Once again, in order to avoid any misplaced reliance on oral statements or other misunderstandings, a disclaimer should be included in the design agreement setting forth, in effect, that the designer is not to have any responsibility for any neglect or failure of any contractor or resource to meet completion schedules or otherwise to perform his or her respective duties or services in a timely manner.

A third area often glossed over in precontract discussions is the extent to which the designer's presence at the project site is requisite. Clients often anticipate that the designer will be at the job site on a daily basis, observing every aspect of the work being performed. Since this is not usual or within a designer's normal expectation, it is again necessary to avoid misunderstanding and possible dispute by including a disclaimer in the design agreement. Such a disclaimer should state, in effect, that the designer's observation will be conducted from time to time at concerned workrooms and at the site during the course of installation and on completion thereof, in order to determine, in general, that the work is proceeding in accordance with design plans and specifications, but that the designer is not required to make exhaustive or continuous inspections at the site or at workrooms where custom merchandise and materials are being produced.

The design agreement should, as well, make clear that drawings and specifications to be produced by the designer are in the nature of "design intent" drawings providing design scheme, layout, furniture, furnishings and equipment selection, location, color scheme, choice of materials, and the like and are not intended to constitute working drawings for any electrical, mechanical, architectural, or engineering work that the project might require, or as shop drawings pertaining to site construction or preparation of custom-designed merchandise.

Finally, the design agreement should, in every instance, include a termination clause notwithstanding the designer's psychological distaste for such a provision. The design agreement is intended to set forth the respective rights and obligations of each party to the agreement. The existence of a properly prepared design agreement including a termination clause enhances the future relationship by avoiding ambiguities and misunderstandings that may develop at a later date. A properly drafted termination clause should give comfort and security to both parties since it provides a sensible basis for termination of the relationship if the worst comes to pass.

The absence of a termination clause does not prevent the designer or client from terminating the design agreement. Rather, its absence may seriously compound the difficulty in determining how and when to exercise one's common-law right to terminate the agreement. By way of illustration, if in the course of a design project, the designer is owed a design fee and the amount has been outstanding for twenty days after the invoice date, is the designer entitled to terminate the agreement for nonpayment? If the designer does not wish to terminate the agreement, is the designer nevertheless entitled to legally withhold performing further services for the client until he or she is paid?

In the absence of a specific provision governing these issues, there is substantial potential for dispute and eventual resort to litigation.

There are many different types of termination clauses, and no one clause fits every design project. Care should be taken to draft a clause that is tailored to fit the specific design agreement, having particular reference to the scope and nature of the project.

Many termination clauses provide the opportunity on the part of the nondefaulting party to notify the other of the claimed default and that unless the default is remedied within a specified time, the nondefaulting party is entitled to terminate the contract. This kind of termination clause, requiring notice of default, serves a purpose other than just to provide the legal mechanism to terminate the design agreement. The requirement to give written notice of default (that is, default in payment of the design fee) may serve as a catalyst to obtaining payment, since the client would otherwise face contractual termination of the design agreement (perhaps in the midst of the project) and thus be exposed to considerable unnecessary costs and expenses.

In addition to termination clauses that seek to protect the interests of the designer or client against nonperformance of the other, commercial clients often request to have the opportunity to terminate the design agreement after completion of the initial design services. This desire is understandably founded upon the commercial client's reluctance to commit its resources to the entire project without benefit of prior experience with the design firm or drawings that visually demonstrate the design firm's approach to the project. Such a request should be carefully considered, and if agreed to, should be specifically provided for in the design agreement. In any such instance, a minimum design fee should also be specified so as to protect the designer economically for the work performed in completing the initial design services.

A variant often used in multiple-stage agreements permits the client to terminate at any time either at the end of or during a particular stage of performance. Usually, exercise of this right is conditioned upon reasonable notice in writing to the designer, as well as upon payment of a termination fee calculated in accordance with a formula provided for in the agreement. What rights the client may have to use the designer's drawings and specifications in the event of a permitted termination should be specifically provided for within the design agreement. To the extent that use of the designer's drawings and specifications is allowed, appropriate indemnification provisions in favor of the designer should be provided for.

Good legal management requires consideration of these problem areas and appropriate resolution of them by the insertion of design agreement provisions that will protect the designer against unexpected and unintended liability.

DISPUTE RESOLUTION

Disputes will, in fact, arise from time to time, regardless of how professional the designer is. The mechanics of dispute resolution are matters best considered before the project commences and addressed within the written agreements between the parties.

It should come as no surprise that the civil litigation process bears little resemblance to television courtroom drama, where the witness on the stand breaks down and confesses his transgressions. Depending in large part on your locale, the litigation process requires extraordinary time, energy, and expense, even to collect a simple balance due.

Alternatives to the inherent delays and costs associated with the traditional lawsuit approach do exist. Arbitration is a viable alternative for resolution of many types of disputes. Arbitration expects to reach an expeditious and binding result without many of the delays, technical legal formalities, and procedures associated with the traditional lawsuit approach. If arbitration is your preference and that of your counsel, it is important to recognize that the law provides that parties cannot be forced to arbitrate disputes unless an agreement exists between the parties to arbitrate their disputes. Accordingly, if you wish to arbitrate future disputes, an arbitration clause must be included in your design agreements, and in your contracts with resources and others.

The decision to provide for arbitration of disputes should not be taken lightly, but only after consultation with your legal counsel. There are particular drawbacks that might affect your decision whether or not to include an arbitration provision. For example, an arbitrator's decision may be based, in part, on "legally inadmissible" evidence, and the parties have virtually no right to appeal an adverse determination. Third parties involved in the dispute, but who have not previously agreed to arbitrate, may not be able to join in the arbitration, thus preventing a complete determination of all issues.

A program of good legal management necessitates that you be ready for your next dispute by providing appropriate arrangements for resolution of that dispute in advance.

Effective legal management is an ongoing process. Changes in the designer's methods of operation, as well as changes in laws affecting the designer's practice, warrant a periodic review of the designer's legal management program.

Insurance

PATRICIA V. CONLEY

An interior design practice may be a one-person firm, or it may have a number of employees. A designer might work out of the home, travel to clients' homes, or have an office. Regardless, adequate insurance is a necessity. This chapter is a brief insurance guideline for ASID members and their firms.

There are numerous kinds of insurance to consider. Essentially these can be divided into two broad categories: (1) property and liability insurance, and (2) life and health insurance. Property and liability insurance protects the designer's business, while life and health insurance protects the designer's individual needs.

The following is a brief description of some of the types of coverage needed when starting a design business. Of course these should be discussed with a local insurance agent or the ASID insurance administrator to determine specific needs.

PROPERTY AND LIABILITY INSURANCE

All professionals should maintain certain forms of property and liability insurance coverage. However, interior designers are exposed to risks that other businesses may not face, because they are responsible for their own property *and* the property of others.

The designer has a great need for property and liability insurance simply because of the multiple responsibilities that are assumed with each assignment. An interior designer is required to have knowledge of a number of seemingly unrelated areas, such as government rules and regulations, suppliers' merchandise, and business and management.

Also, interior designers are confronted with professional challenges for which they alone must be accountable. Designers are responsible for developing sketches, plans, fabric samples, color charts, and more. They may also have to deal with agreements and contracts, not to mention the supervision of contract work. Naturally, individual designer's needs will vary depending on the size and extent of the operation. There are several types of property and liability insurance that are recommended depending on the need.

Lawsuits can be brought against designers because of advice given to clients for building interiors, office layouts, and dwellings; changes or modifications in design plans; financial loss to a client; errors in materials used; failure to comply with flammability laws, building codes, and fire regulations; and other things that may never have been imagined.

An unexpected lawsuit, valid or not, could result in exorbitant expenses. To avoid this situation, complete insurance coverage is essential for all professionals. In an established firm this type of insurance may already be part of the office business structure. However, when starting a new firm, a designer is more exposed. This means that the designer needs coverage for the business as well as coverage for the acts of the employees. Ideally, a plan should include benefits for legal defense and court costs as a part of the limit of liability.

- *General liability.* This should be purchased on a Comprehensive Form. This form will automatically include bodily injury, property damage, products liability, and many other important features.

- *Protection for real property.* This should include all owned buildings and building service equipment and supplies.

- *Business personal property.* This protects against damage to property owned on the premises and should include such items as desks, chairs, samples, and so on.

- *Umbrella liability.* In addition to comprehensive liability coverage, the purchase of additional limits of protection may be advisable. This would depend on the individual needs, finances, and the size of the firm.

- *Commercial automobile insurance.* If the practice has a vehicle owned and titled by the corporation, this coverage is needed. (Available through your local agent.)

- *Worker's compensation.* Worker's compensation is mandatory coverage that each employer must provide employees. It provides coverage for medical payments and disability income should the employee be injured while working on the job. (Available through your local agent.)

- *Fidelity bond.* A fidelity bond is purchased to protect all assets of the corporation against acts of dishonesty by employees. This should include bank accounts and/or personal property of the corporation.

LIFE AND HEALTH INSURANCE

The following plans briefly describe various kinds of life and health coverage available to designers, whether self-employed or employed by others:

- *Major medical insurance.* It cannot be predicted whether or when illnesses or accidents will strike that will require medical treatment or hospitalization. That's why the broad comprehensive coverage of major medical insurance is essential. Coverage is available to members and their employees through the group insurance plan.

- *Disability insurance.* This insurance protects one of the designer's valuable assets: income. Should a disabling illness or accident prevent the designer from working, this insurance will pay monthly benefits to help replace lost earnings.

- *Business overhead expense insurance.* This is very important coverage if the business or private practice relies heavily on the designer's ability to work. If the owner becomes disabled because of an accident or illness, the business overhead expense insurance will pay for continued business expenses such as rent, electricity, and salaries. Usually benefits are paid for as long as two years.

- *Life insurance.* The more responsibilities and debts a member has, the more life insurance is needed. Financial experts recommend that five times the annual income in life insurance be carried. This coverage is essential to help secure the financial future of the designer's family.

- *Catastrophic major medical insurance.* The cost of a very serious illness or accident is often far beyond the limits of the average hospitalization or major medical insurance policies. Catastrophic medical insurance is designed to pay those extraordinary expenses not covered by a basic major medical policy.

- *Personal accident insurance plan.* This is to protect against the financial disaster that often results from a serious accident. Weeks or even months of medical care could eventually drain personal savings. Personal accident insurance pays various benefits for death, dismemberment, and impairments due to accident.

- *Hospital money program.* This coverage specifically helps meet the rising cost of hospital care. In-hospital insurance provides a daily cash benefit when hospitalized, in addition to other insurance the designer might have.

Plans for the future of the interior design firm should be reviewed with insurance needs in mind. For further information on the group insurance programs officially sponsored for ASID members, write the ASID Insurance Administrator:

Albert H. Wohlers & Co.
ASID Group Insurance Plans
1440 N. Northwest Highway
Park Ridge, Illinois 60068-1400

or call the Customer Service Department toll-free:

1-800-323-2106
Illinois residents: 1-708-803-3100

Information Management: Resources

CATHERINE VON DER HUDE

This chapter provides an outline for setting up a multi-reference resource library. This outline is applicable to any of the specialty design areas in interior design and its related professions. Included are guidelines for organization and maintenance of these resources.

ORGANIZATION GUIDELINES

First establish a resource library unique to the area of design, the clientele, and the company needs. This system should be logical to the area of design, and also logical to the thought processes necessary to achieve the final product. Information and samples are most quickly retrieved for use after they have been edited (reviewed and updated, with obsolete material periodically discarded) and then reorganized. Since each information item or sample category has different needs, a system of organizing like resources together in a similarly formatted style is the most efficient for this kind of library. It is essential to provide adequate space for each category's master set of information and samples, which should never leave the resource library. In addition, adequate space must be set aside for the necessary back-up or lending materials.

Listed below are categories and subcategories specifying the type of format for an efficient reference library for an interior design firm.

I. Interior Design Library

- *Furniture catalogs and furniture cut files*: Arrange alphabetically by manufacturer's name.

- *Accessory catalogs and category cut files*: Arrange accessory catalogs alphabetically. Arrange category cut files alphabetically by subject names used most frequently. These subject names—such as accessories, bathrooms, ceilings, and so on—can serve as cross-references to the numbers and subjects developed by the Construction Specifications Institute and used by Sweet's catalog system for the architecture library. The category cut files also serve as an excellent location to develop cross-reference files, such as furniture, stacking chairs, quick-ship programs, and so on.

- *Carpet*: Arrange manufacturers' master books alphabetically. Arrange extra manufacturer's samples alphabetically or by color.

- *Textiles*: Arrange manufacturers' master books, sample boxes, sample books, or loose samples alphabetically and/or by color or function.

II. Architecture Library

- *Manufacturers' catalogs and cut file*: Manufacturers' catalogs should be arranged by Sweet's subject division numbers 1 through 16. Arrange cut files by the same number system, including all the subdivision numbers. These numbers and subject headings are cross-referenced with the category cut files for the interior design library.

III. Materials Sample Library

Organize master books and loose samples according to this list.

- Paint
- Wood
- Glass
- Metal
- Tiles
- Laminates
- VCT
- Bases
- Vinyl, Rubber Flooring
- Acoustical Tiles/Panels

IV. Reference Book and Reference File Library

This is an area of the library that specifically reflects the specialty design area. Arrange reference books alphabetically by title, subject, or author; or numerically by some system such as the Dewey Decimal System or the Library of Congress System. Similarly, arrange reference files by subject, alphabet, or locale and dates where applicable. The reference book and reference file library provides an opportunity to develop specific information focused on the specialty design of the firm. In addition, it becomes a source of information on related fields.

V. Magazine Library

Arrange magazines per subscription by year. According to needs and space, two to five years' worth of magazines should be retained for reference.

VI. Other Library

This section can reflect the design firm's special focus, such as restoration or European resources. This is an excellent way to incorporate information about past projects of the firm as a central resource for reference. Items such as archives of projects, standard details, or master sets of drawings can be stored and easily retrieved in this area.

MAINTENANCE GUIDELINES

Continued maintenance of the library provides quick, available information and allows for flexibility and future growth. Information management is best achieved with the initial proper setup, in combination with ongoing maintenance. Maintenance includes the following (weekly, monthly, biyearly, or as needed):

Update information and samples.
Replace missing information and samples.
Edit all products frequently.
Maintain organization of information and samples.

A color-code system can be used to identify the resource library's categories. This is useful for cross-referencing information and for coordinating the files, samples, and Rolodex with one another.

Information from the resource library can be adapted to the computer by organizing the manufacturer's product names and addresses within the categories already suggested for setting up the library. These listings serve as a reference for using and maintaining the products. Letters can be issued on a biyearly or yearly basis for updating the resources. A hard copy of the library's manufacturer listing is useful for quick reference. The computer is also an excellent tool for cross-referencing types of resources that are used in various ways.

SUMMARY

By following these simple guidelines and maintenance suggestions, a firm can have an organized and useful resource library. Because of the diversity of products and samples necessary for references in an interior design practice, these can become disorganized and chaotic if they are not properly monitored and maintained. When attention is paid to the care and organization of a resource library, it is invaluable and a cost-saving mechanism.

Information Management: Computers

DAVID H. SWAIN

The most significant impact of the computer on any profession or business is the acceleration of change. The computer, both data base and computer-aided design (CAD), allows decisions and contemplation to be done at a significantly increased rate.

HOW COMPUTERS BENEFIT A BUSINESS

Whether in a one-person practice or a firm of 200 employees, the computer plays a significant role in the business. It permits quicker response, greater detail, the exploration of possibilities, increased accuracy, improved graphics, and improved control.

Quicker Response

CAD systems lend themselves very well to repetition of production documents, which allows quicker response. For example, if a practice is retail and the designer is doing a number of mall stores based on a prototype design, the CAD system allows the preparation of a full set of contract documents for a 3,000 to 4,000 square foot retail store in a matter of days.

Increased Accuracy

The computer gives complete accuracy as long as the input is correct. CAD systems utilize layering of data. This provides a degree of accuracy that is most beneficial, particularly for interior tenant work where a number of different systems such as lighting, electrical, and HVAC must be coordinated. For example, the computer can assist in illustrating conflict points between furniture and electrical outlets so that corrections can be made during the design process instead of having to deal with the problem in the field.

Exploration of Possibilities

"What if's" are always a consideration in any business. How many different ways can a problem be looked at, and how many different solutions are possible? The computer allows a quick exploration of a number of solutions, testing and eliminating possibilities with given criteria until the best solution or solutions are identified. Both personal computers and CAD systems offer the capability to review growth projections for clients as well as stacking and blocking design solutions. The computer encourages change and opens more doors to explore new ideas and methods.

Improved Graphics

Computers, particularly with improved publishing software, have given the practice the ability to produce documents with improved graphics very quickly, professionally, and cost-effectively. A designer can use color, graphics, text, and any number of different options to prepare submittals, reports, and marketing materials.

Enhanced Speed and Quality

Speed is becoming an element of necessity in the practice of interior design. Clients are demanding to know answers quickly. The computer, both data base and CAD, allows the designer to provide answers with confidence in a short period of time.

One of the major benefits of the computer is that it allows more practices to be competitive and turn out good work in less time. The designer can do more with fewer people. With talented, creative, experienced professionals in short supply in the profession, the practice—particularly the small practice—can produce more and better-quality work in a shorter time. Computers allow designers to extend their thinking and creative abilities. Clients benefit by receiving a better product and solution at a more cost-effective rate in a shorter time, while the public at large is provided with aesthetically satisfying, functional interiors at reasonable costs.

APPLICATIONS OF COMPUTERS FOR THE DESIGN FIRM

Many of the benefits of computers just described apply to nearly any type of business. Here are some applications specific to design firms.

Business Development and Marketing

With the competitive nature of interior design, the computer has become a useful marketing tool. Tracking prospects, retaining background data, formatting proposal text and graphics, determining fees and schedules, and tracking historical reference data are just a few examples. The computer can be used to develop a matrix for determining the necessary human resources for a particular project. This can be done by project phase or by calculating personnel hours and costing rates. There are a number of programs on the market for assisting in schedule preparation.

Project Costing
The computer is a useful tool to the project manager. It can assist the manager and cost estimator in projecting costs and budgets. For example, it can assist in managing the fee dollar relative to the budget (projected in the proposal stage) versus actual (as the project progresses). For larger practices, a data base system with accounting software can be used for tracking labor hours and costs for each project. Further, such data base systems can provide project management reports, monthly billing reports, and storage for historical information.

Programming
A combination of data base and CAD software can be used to collate field data to reflect the number of personnel, anticipated growth, space allocations, and space standards. These data become the base for a space planner to use in the development of blocking diagrams and stacking plans. These plans determine how much space is required and the configuration of space for a particular tenant. If adjacencies also are keyed, then the blocking diagrams automatically arrange themselves according to desired adjacencies. This provides the space planner with prioritized options for the placement of departments or people.

Space Planning
The computer allows the space planner to utilize functional data, desired adjacencies, sizes, quantities, and blocking diagram information when developing space plan options quickly for a client's review. Unit costs can be keyed for such things as lineal feet of partition, lineal feet of relites, doors, and so forth. While the space planner is developing a schematic space plan, the computer can provide budget information for the build-out of the space designed. This is particularly important in the fast-paced tenant development space planning practice. Here developers are in a very cost-competitive mode and lean heavily on the space planners to provide a good space at a very cost-effective rate. Developers need to know costs early in the project, and the computer is a helpful tool in this process.

The Design Process
As a project progresses, CAD can be used to refine the budget, refine the space plan, and develop details. These, as well as computer-generated views of interior spaces, can be used to describe the design solutions to the client. Further refinement to CAD systems has provided three-dimensional imaging that allows a designer to walk clients through the space on the computer screen. This enhances the communication of the design intent to the client, allowing for a better understanding of what will happen in the space as the project nears completion.

Preparing Contract Documents
In the contract document phase of a project, the computer can be used to complete floor plans, reflected ceiling plans, elevations, sections, details, electrical plans, mechanical plans, plumbing plans, and furnishings plans. In this phase the initial design documents are expanded. The computer is helpful because it can be used for interiors with repetitive elements.

Templates of standard workstation systems can be loaded into the data bank of a computer. These are often in a plan format and initiated as space standards that have been developed during the programming phase. They can be keyed by elements such as side unit, desk chair, and side chairs. From this, quantity takeoffs for each item can be developed. Unit costs can also be attached, further aiding the design and budgeting process. Particularly for large projects where repetitive items are significant, the computer with a data base connection is a godsend because it provides accurate and timely documentation.

Construction Administration
During the construction process, the computer can be a resource for recording changes based on field conditions, and for tracking submittals and approvals. Required changes for architectural documents and furnishings documents can be recorded easily while maintaining an up-to-date document set. Finally, the computer can assist in the recording and updating of a punch list for the final project closeout.

Systems and Software Applications
All computers, whether micro or mainframe, require software programs that do two things: tell the computer how to operate, and allow the computer to do a specific task. For example, programs such as DOS (Disk Operating System) tell the computer how to use its disk drives to store and retrieve information; meanwhile, specific task software provides the opportunity for a designer to do complicated tasks such as data base analysis.

Software for the microcomputer is available that provides word processing, schedules, fee development and tracking, project costs, graphic and chart development, project budgeting, client personnel and growth projections, specifications, and network capabilities. Mainframe systems provide the same capabilities as the microcomputer with the exception of graphics. However, a mainframe system has the ability to link several types of software, allowing increased capabilities in reporting functions.

CAD programs have various levels of sophistication in graphics and data reporting. Some systems provide software for personnel and growth projections, department adjacency, stacking and blocking, quantity takeoffs, costs, and furnishing reports in addition to graphic capabilities. Useful programs for design professionals are being developed at a phenomenal rate. Some of the most useful include software for spreadsheets and data base creation. Both these programs are indispensable for any firm. Writing letters, notes, and proposals requires a word processing program. There are also numerous billing and accounting programs available, especially for small firms. Larger firms usually use a custom-designed program for their mainframe system.

There are several popular computer-aided design programs available on the market. All programs have similar capabilities and have menus for easy use. All these systems can talk to one another with interpretive devices. Therefore, even if a consultant uses one system and the designer another, files can still be shared. A number of furniture and equipment suppliers are supplying data files on their products to be used for repeated items on drawings. These programs also provide immediate specifications and cost breakdown. Unfortunately, these programs may work only with a specific CAD program. To be valuable to a practice, the CAD program chosen must be compatible with other programs that might be used in the future.

Hardware by Size of Practice

For the small practice, microcomputer capabilities are most typically used for project accounting, word processing, and specific project needs. Larger offices typically utilize more diverse and complex systems. However, as technology advances, systems are becoming smaller and more powerful. While the micro systems seem to be on the increase, a large office will typically utilize a combination of a micro system, mainframe data base system, and a major CAD system. As technology improves, the distinctions among these systems blur.

FUTURE TRENDS

The trend is toward change at an ever-increasing rate. While drawing skills and creativity are the focus in most educational programs, the computer is playing an ever-increasing role in producing graphics. This means the practicing interior designer will not necessarily need sterling graphic skills, but rather the imagination and creativity to utilize the computer as a design tool.

The computer increases the designer's reach. It is an imaginative tool that, coupled with the brain of the designer, gives unlimited possibilities. But it is only a tool. Although its potential is great, its primary function is to increase options, speed, and accuracy. It stimulates the thinking of the designer by allowing more time to investigate alternatives. As time passes, the computer will become faster, cheaper, and smaller. The computer is a tool that is coming to be expected for any interior design practice to compete in the local market, much as the scale, T-square, and triangle were in the past.

Industry Relations

NORMAN POLSKY

The furnishings, furniture, and equipment industries supply designers with the products necessary for completion of their work. Members of these trade industries serve as resources and—when treated as colleagues—are an invaluable part of any design team.

THE DESIGNER'S SOURCES OF INFORMATION AND PRODUCTS

Every interior designer should be aware of the various types of dealers and representatives in the industry, because these are the people who keep the design community up to date and supplied with products. Showrooms and exhibitions also play an important role in the design profession because many new products and ideas are introduced there.

Dealerships

Dealerships vary in size and function. A full-service dealership has the resources to supply a finished facility from concept through the design, purchasing, and installation phases. Many dealerships specialize in such areas as banks, food service, hospitals, or other specific types of interior design projects. Some dealerships bid only projects from specifications, while others do negotiated turnkey projects. A large number of dealerships are independent, family-owned businesses representing many lines of furniture or products. Salespeople from these dealerships usually visit several end users within a geographic location; however, there are instances when salespeople concentrate on only one major corporate account.

In the early 1980s, loft dealerships became common in the New York City area. These dealerships maintain few samples and do not provide a showroom for clients, but perform all the other functions of a traditional dealership. A loft dealership allows for low overhead on the part of the owner/dealer, yet provides the client with the necessary services of a traditional dealership. Around the same time that loft dealerships were developing in New York, the concept of designer/merchants became common in the Los Angeles area. In these types of establishments, the designer/merchant specifies and sells the furniture, while the other services normally provided by a dealership are left as the responsibility of the client.

Sales Representatives

Manufacturer's sales representatives usually represent a single product line or several nonconflicting product lines. Some manufacturers use their own full-time sales personnel, while others combine a manufacturer's representative with their own salespersons in certain territories or regions. Independent representatives usually earn a 5 to 10 percent commission from products sold in their territory. Since the representatives are not employees of the manufacturer, they are usually responsible for their own expenses and benefits. The sales representative's responsibility is to provide service to the design community by updating the catalog library, demonstrating products, providing samples of finishes and fabrics, placing product orders, expediting delivery time, and assisting with installation when necessary.

Consultants

Special industry consultants are available to assist the interior designer and client in complex projects that deal with such things as acoustics, lighting systems, and audiovisual installation. Other industry consultants are available to advise the design firm in specific operations including marketing, sales, and financial organization.

Manufacturers

The manufacturing of furnishings and furniture is a $31 billion industry that supplies products for both commercial and residential installations. The commercial furniture industry represents $8 billion of the gross volume of sales. The big four of commercial manufacturers are: Steelcase with sales of $2 billion; Herman Miller at $700 million; Haworth at $500 million; and Hon at $400 million. Other manufacturers doing over $100 million in sales include American Seating, Kimball, Knoll, Shelby Williams, and Westinghouse.

As with the commercial furniture industry, residential manufacturers are dominated by a few giant corporations. These are Bassett Furniture Company, Broyhill Furniture, Interco, Ladd Furniture, Lazyboy, and Masco. As the profile of the industry changes with mergers and foreign investors, the distribution of products—and the job descriptions of dealerships and sales representatives—will also undergo change.

Showrooms

Permanent showrooms are available throughout the world and provide the design community with access to a manufacturer's newest developments. To promote the sharing of state-of-the-art information with the design community, the concept of trade shows at major marts was developed. The largest trade show in the United States is NEOCON, which originated in 1969 at the Chicago Merchandise Mart. NEOCON attracts 50,000 people working in the residential, commercial, and government furnishings and furniture industry from all over the world. While the Orgatec trade show, held every other even year in Koln, Germany, is larger than NEOCON, the majority of the exhibition spaces are devoted to office machines. It is more common for European manufacturers to rely on factory and dealership showrooms, rather than permanent showrooms or marts as in the United States.

Most major cities have merchandise marts with showrooms and have associated trade shows annually to provide designers with the most current information on manufacturers' product lines. For example, Designer's Saturday Trade Show in New York City includes manufacturers' showrooms in various buildings, with the largest exhibit in the International Design Center New York (IDCNY). Another example is the West Week Trade Show in Los Angeles, sponsored by the Pacific Design Center (PDC), the local merchandise mart for that area. Other important trade show opportunities include the National Restaurant Association at McCormick Place in Chicago; the National Hotel Show in the New York City Exhibition Hall; the International Home Furnishings Market in High Point, North Carolina; and the National Association of Food Equipment Manufacturers (NAFEM) at various cities throughout the country.

The ASID National Conference and Exposition is held annually at various locations and provides for learning opportunities for members and associates through joint sessions and seminars with prominent speakers from industry and education. The exposition portion of the conference includes the display of products from numerous manufacturers. Product exhibitions like these, in conjunction with recognized design conferences, further provide outlets for communication between the design community and the furnishing and furniture industry as new products are developed and perfected.

WHAT DESIGNERS SHOULD CONSIDER WHEN BUYING FROM SUPPLIERS

From the manufacturer's point of view, there are eight essential items that designers should consider when buying furnishings and furniture, for the designers' own benefit and that of their clients. Every feature listed below is essential for a sound investment!

Productivity and Durability

This ensures the client's investment. Advanced design using new materials should provide durability while maintaining a balance with other essential features of the product. Products should be tested under actual conditions of intended use. Product integrity can be assured through testing that meets federal and ANSI-BIFMA standards. A checklist of items that will guarantee customer satisfaction with the product includes (1) consideration of the effect of cigarettes, knives, impact, weather, and stains; (2) evaluation of the strength of connections, glides, casters, moveable parts, hardware, and finish; and (3) examination of upholstery specifications and ease of reupholstery.

Cost

This should include total cost, not just initial cost. When considering total cost, the following must be included: (1) handling cost, (2) labor cost of moving and handling for room setups or cleaning, (3) cost of storage space, 4) maintenance cost of each item, and (5) replacement cost relative to the manufacturer's warranty and reputation.

Comfort

The comfort factor of a product is critical to user satisfaction. It can affect the acceptance of a product, the pleasure associated with an interior space, and individual efficiency and productivity.

Ergonomics

This refers to human factors engineering of products and includes layout, sound, lighting, finishes, and furnishings. Of particular interest relative to ergonomics is the office chair—the most used and personal item in an office. An ergonomic checklist for the manufacturer of office chairs should include an assessment of the following attributes:

- Variety to accommodate different sizes and shapes.
- Active ergonomic controls versus passive noncontrols.
- Free-flowing dynamic motion as opposed to static-posture settings.
- Adjustments that can be easily made while seated.
- Seat front tilt adjustment.
- Seat height adjustment.
- Back tilt adjustment.
- Back height adjustment and full tilt for lumbar support.
- Contoured padded seat and back with waterfall front edge of seat.
- Mechanical reliability and safety.
- Training for the user to ensure optimum results.

Appearance

All furniture and furnishings should enhance and complement the rest of the interior space while at the same time representing a product that will function properly and have a reasonable life span. Consideration should be given to the product's appearance from the back and sides as well as from the front.

Space Savings

Space saved in storage can be used for other purposes. There should be a balance between seating capacity and maximization of comfort in minimum floor space.

Safety

Liability claims are costly and can harm the reputation of the manufacturer, the designer, and the client. "Sick buildings" can affect efficiency and interrupt operations.

Availability

All manufacturers of furnishings and furniture must have a reputation for maintaining delivery promises. This is an essential element for success. Quick Ship programs are usually available, but selection of products in such programs is usually quite limited. Normal delivery from a manufacturer is 8 to 16 weeks for commercial products and 16 to 52 weeks for residential products.

SAFETY AND FUNCTION IN DESIGN

Adherence to and concern for safety standards is critical to a manufacturer's success, especially relative to seating products. An excellent guide for this information is the ANSI-BIFMA X5.1-1985 American National Standard for Office Furnishings. Function and safety go hand in hand. Functional design relates to the facility, the furnishings, and the furniture and cannot be sacrificed for the appearance of the product.

A common feature of most new facilities is multipurpose rooms, and the popularity of such rooms has increased the demand for versatile furniture. Furniture for multipurpose rooms must be made for easy and fast handling, sitting comfort for two hours or more, and easy storage, safety, and durability to withstand continuous folding and stacking. Easy and fast handling means that the product must be light enough for one person to stack, able to be processed for quick ganging into uniform rows, provide unobtrusive table seating, and be stackable on dollies low enough to pass through normal 80-inch doors. In order to provide comfortable seating for two hours or more, the width and contour of the seat and back of a chair are important. A curved, thinly padded seat and back are more comfortable for long-term seating than a flat, heavily padded seat and back. An 18-inch width for seat and back is considerably more comfortable for long-term seating than is a width of 16 inches. However, to maximize on space, many owners desire 16-inch seats to allow ten persons to be seated around a banquet table 72 inches in diameter.

Ultimate comfort and efficiency for employees and clients or end users is a management trade-off for an initial one-time cost. It has been found that an environment designed with sensitivity to ergonomics can increase satisfaction of inhabitants by 27 percent, increase efficiency by 24 percent, and reduce absenteeism. A 24 percent annual savings will rapidly pay back the return on investment for an ergonomically designed environment.

CONCLUSION

From the vast array of products available, designers choose and specify items that best fulfill their vision for interior installations. Manufacturers, working in concert with the design community, provide improved working and living environments for people throughout the world.

III. THE PROJECT

Project Control Book

SHEILA DANKO

As the complexity of evolving a design project from concept to reality increases, so does the challenge to designers of making well-informed, integrated decisions at all levels throughout the design process. With each new research finding linking the interior environment with the health, safety, and well-being of the occupant, the process of creating an interior becomes more difficult—yet more imperative. Expertly managing the metamorphosis from need to idea to physical solution has become the prerequisite for design excellence.

This section of the *ASID Professional Practice Manual* focuses on nurturing design excellence through careful attention to critical issues of the design process. It is an attempt to disentangle some of the complexities inherent in designing interiors by breaking the process down into a series of manageable parts. The goal is to provide day-to-day working tools that will help designers, experienced and inexperienced alike, navigate the process more effectively and efficiently.

The Project Control Book is not intended as a definitive guide to design project management, but rather as an overview framework of issues generic to most contract and residential interiors work. It is intended as a foundation on which more experienced project managers will build, adapt, and customize to fit their special project needs or unique management styles. It is also intended as a training tool for younger design project managers. Most importantly, it is designed as a baseline system of controls and feedback tools to encourage thoughtful analysis, organization, and reflection that will ultimately result in self-improvement and professional advancement.

The Project Control Book is based on the concept of a project job book. It models the design process chronologically from project conception (Phase 1: Initial Client Contact) through occupancy (Phase 10: Evaluation). A straightforward linear process has been used for sake of clarity and organization. Instead of lengthy, theoretical discussions of each phase, there is a "starter kit" of process tools—checklists, worksheets, and record logs that clearly and quickly place the critical issues in the context and time frame of design decisions.

Photocopying any of these materials is encouraged for personal use only. The materials are not to be used for resale or other commercial purposes. No other form or means of reproduction—graphic, electronic, or mechanical, including recording, taping, or information storage and retrieval systems—may be employed without written permission of the publisher.

IMPORTANT ISSUES TO REMEMBER WHEN USING THE PROJECT CONTROL BOOK

- *Use it as a thinking tool.* The Project Control Book is intended to help a designer think through the interior design process more efficiently and expertly, not merely to serve as a record-keeping system. Notice that the forms are coded as either worksheets (W), checklists (C), or record logs (R). All are designed to be used as an active part of day-to-day working.

- *Expand it on the basis of your experience and special project needs.* Remember that the Project Control Book is designed as a "starter kit" of process tools, not an exhaustive set. Incorporate your own strategies and procedures, customizing the Project Control Book to fit your personal management style and concerns. For project types that require specialized information and procedures, the forms and tools will serve as models from which to create a more responsive, customized set of project controls.

- *Use it as a feedback tool.* The majority of tools have been designed to incorporate feedback and learning experiences into the process so that as designers learn, they can share that learning systematically with their colleagues.

- *Make it work for you.* Don't feel locked in to every blank space or subtitle. If you don't need a part of a form, don't use it—or modify it slightly to better fit the way you like to work and think.

- *It doesn't provide the answers; you do.* The Project Control Book is intended as a mechanism for organizing critical, in-process project information in a consistent, easily accessible format for all those who need access to it. Being organized and up to date not only saves time; it takes time. The Project Control Book helps you save time by providing an organizing framework for you. It works only if you are willing to use it.

DISCLAIMER

The information and statements in The Project Control Book are believed to be reliable but are not to be construed as a warranty or representation for which the author or publishers assume legal responsibility. Users should undertake sufficient verification and testing to determine the suitability for their own particular purpose of any information referred to herein. No warranty of fitness for a particular purpose is made.

Acknowledgments

Author

Sheila Danko
Associate Professor, Design & Environmental Analysis
Cornell University

Principal, Sheila Danko Design
Ithaca, New York

Reviewers

Annette Basinger, ASID
Principal, Pearce, Basinger, Bock Ltd.
Rochester, New York

Jeffrey J. Folinus, AIA
Director of Practice, Osgood & Associates, Inc.
Atlanta, Georgia

David Kuckuk, AIA
Director, Fred H. Thomas Associates PC
Architects + Engineers
Ithaca, New York

Hugh Latta, FASID
Principal, Design Continuum, Inc.
Atlanta, Georgia

Research Associates

Thresa M. Gibian
Rhonda Gilmore

Research Assistants

Kathleen Ryan
Meredith Sandman
Virginia Seeley

Computer Graphics

Kathleen Ryan
Carl Shuller

Contents

000C = Checklist

000W = Worksheet

000R = Record/log

Phase 1: Initial Client Contact *114*

100C Critical Issues 114

Phase 2: Proposal Development & Design Contract *116*

200C Critical Issues 116

210W Basic Services Worksheet 117

211C Supplemental Services Checklist 124

260C Risk Management Checklist 126

Phase 3: Project Organization & Start-Up *128*

300C Critical Issues 128

310R Project Directory • Client 129

311R Project Directory • Consultants 130

315R Project Information Sheet 131

325W Project Review Schedule by Phase & Task 132

345W Meeting Agenda Worksheet 134

350R Phone Conversation Log 135

370R Client Sign-Off Sheet 136

Phase 4: Programming *137*

400C Critical Issues 137

430W Activity Profile 139

450W Existing Furniture and Equipment Inventory 141

Phase 5: Schematic Design ... *142*

500C Critical Issues ... 142

510W Code Compliance Worksheet ... 144

520W Product Source Worksheet ... 146

Phase 6: Design Development ... *147*

600C Critical Issues ... 147

610R Vendor Inquiry Log ... 148

620W Cost Estimate Worksheet ... 149

Phase 7: Contract Documents ... *150*

700C Critical Issues ... 150

510W Code Compliance Worksheet (from phase 5) ... 151

720R Project Record • Room Summary ... 153

740R Project Record ... 154

742R Project Record ... 155

745R Project Record ... 156

Phase 8: Bidding, Negotiations & Contract Award ... *157*

800C Critical Issues ... 157

820W Bid Budget Comparison ... 158

Phase 9: Contract Administration ... *159*

900C Critical Issues ... 159

910R Sketch Log • 1/4" ... 161

920R Field Inspection Report Form ... 162

950R Punch List ... 163

Phase 10: Evaluation ... *164*

1000C Critical Issues ... 164

1010W Project Retrospective • Financial ... 165

Initials ______ Date ___/___/___

Phase 1: Initial Client Contact

Project Control Book Form 100C

Operational Definition:

Pre-contract meetings, tasks, and services aimed at securing new design projects. Includes introductory presentations and preliminary research to determine major project parameters for proposal development and design contract.

Critical Issues

☐ **Be Informed**
Become knowledgeable about potential project issues through a review of similar projects (successful and unsuccessful), recent research on user needs and behavior, and past experience with related projects types. In addition to communicating expertise, this information will aid in accurately assessing project scope and in troubleshooting during proposal development.

☐ **Demonstrate an Understanding of Client's Business Arena**
Sensitivity to business issues as they relate to the potential project provide a competitive edge during interviews and throughout the design process. Business issues such as relative market share, growth potential, major competitors, consumer trends and business philosophy can help identify how profitability can be enhanced through design.

☐ **Determine Meeting Agenda and Structure**
Plan the meeting agenda in order of priority. Distribute to all staff who will be expected to participate in presentation to clarify relative roles and timing. Determine visual aids needed and confirm that the meeting room will support those visuals.

☐ **Identify Project Scope**
Discuss client goals, major project parameters, constraints and performance requirements to assess the services required to successfully complete the project. Identify key words, phrases or comparisons that give tangible qualities to the issues and goals.

☐ **Identify Hidden Agendas or Preconceptions**
Determine if the client has preconceived notions about the final design or the design process and evaluate how these may affect perceived scope of services and the potential for success.

☐ **Assess Compatibility**
Analyze the client's expectations relative to your professional goals and standards of performance to determine whether the project is appropriate for your firm.

☐ **Demonstrate Professionalism**
Conduct your presentation in a timely, well-organized, and thorough manner. Anticipate client concerns and address them. Be willing to answer and ask difficult questions thereby communicating a sense of honesty and openness. The meeting should be an equally informative interchange for both parties.

☐ **Emphasize Key Concepts**
When presenting a particular competitive advantage or clarifying a point about project scope, reinforce or clarify ideas through multiple examples or by restating them in different ways.

Initials ______ *Date* ___/___/___

Phase 1: Initial Client Contact

Project Control Book Form 100C

☐ **Identify Project Team**
The client should understand the various levels of expertise, both in-house and through outside consultants, that you will bring to the project. This structure should be made clear at the onset.

☐ **Present Complete Range of Services**
Make the client aware of all the areas in which you practice, even if the potential project focuses on a particular service. This can open new business opportunities.

☐ **Analyze Promotional Materials**
Make sure the image portrayed is consistent across the range of materials used and communicates firm's history, specialities and philosophy. It should be concise, current, and a reflection of the firm's design sensibilities.

☐ **Track Referrals and Potential Client Sources**
Record how the client found out about your firm. Learn to recognize and record profitable sources of new projects.

☐ ____________________

☐ ____________________

☐ ____________________

Initials ______ *Date* ___/___/___

Phase 2:
Proposal Development & Design Contract

Project Control Book Form 200C

Operational Definition:

Pre-contract tasks and services necessary to develop design proposal and receive project award. Also includes those tasks necessary to lay groundwork for contract preparations, negotiations and agreement.

Critical Issues

☐ **Define Scope of Services**
The time and resources needed to fulfill the outlined scope of services comprise the foundation of the design contract. Clear and specific definition of tasks, expected output, and schedule is essential.

☐ **Establish a Mechanism for Revisions to Scope of Services**
Stipulating in advance the procedure and compensation rates for agreed upon changes in the scope of services prevents many future contract disputes.

☐ **Involve Prospective Design Team in Proposal Development**
This "grass roots" level of input provides valuable insight regarding specific tasks, issues of design process and a greater ability to plan in-house workloads. It also serves to heighten the team's sense of commitment to the project and project timeframe.

☐ **Determine Realistic Budget**
Request the budget range from the client and analyze the implications for project quality and performance in terms of finishes, furnishings, custom elements, and design strategy. This will force a priority assessment of project goals in relation to budget.

☐ **Investigate Code Compliance Issues**
This is an essential component in project planning which must be examined during the infancy of a project for impact on project goals, budget, and scheduling.

☐ **Assess Project Feasibility**
Compare major project parameters and constraints against the client's desired goals and performance requirements to determine overall feasibility of project and implications for your scope of services.

☐ **Determine Client's Financial Background**
Establish solid financial capability and credit rating of the client. Investigate their reputation with other businesses and previous designers.

☐ **Determine Client's Knowledge of the Design Process**
Evaluate the client's previous design experience and education in order to tailor future presentations and in-process communication to the appropriate level.

☐ **Consult Legal Counsel When Necessary**
If a contract is nonstandard or covers an area unfamiliar to you, an attorney should review the document.

☐ ____
____
____
____

Project ____________________

Project No. ____________________

Initials ______ Date ___/___/___

Basic Services Worksheet

Project Control Book Form 210W

PROGRAMMING

ASID Contract Reference #		Staff	Hours	Total
1.1.1	**Strategy Session:** Meet with Owner (and other designated parties) to determine project requirements, timetable, and budget.	Principal Project Designer Designer Support Staff		
1.1.2	**Interviews and Activity Analysis:** Interview appropriate staff members and conduct activity analysis to establish client's operating procedures, space requirements, communications relationships, present functional, and future needs.	Principal Project Designer Designer Support Staff		
1.1.3	**Inventory Existing Conditions:** Survey existing site/building/space, as well as existing furniture, fixtures, and equipment. Develop or acquire base drawings and check for accuracy.	Principal Project Designer Designer Support Staff		
1.1.3	**Code Review:** Review code compliance and regulatory agency information to determine building limitations and design parameters. Ascertain project feasibility.	Principal Project Designer Designer Support Staff		
1.1.4	**Analyze/Synthesize Information & Draft Program:** Prepare a written programming document that outlines the project requirements for Owner review and approval.	Principal Project Designer Designer Support Staff		
1.1.4	**Program Document Sign-off:** Revise program draft based on Owner feedback and submit for final approval.	Principal Project Designer Designer Support Staff		
	____________________ ____________________ ____________________ ____________________ ____________________ ____________________	Principal Project Designer Designer Support Staff		

PROGRAMMING ________ Total hours

Project ____________________

Project No. ____________________

Initials ______ Date ___/___/___

Basic Services Worksheet

Project Control Book Form 210W

SCHEMATIC DESIGN

ASID Contract Reference #		Staff	Hours	Total
1.2.1	**Concept Development:** Identify conceptual design approach to project and develop preliminary diagrams of space allotments, traffic flow, furniture, equipment layouts, and other diagrams of functional needs for Owner approval.	Principal	________	
		Project Designer	________	
		Designer	________	
		Support Staff	________	
		....	________	
		....	________	________
1.2.2	**Review Alternative Approaches:** Develop alternative concepts and planning strategies and review with Owner.	Principal	________	
		Project Designer	________	
		Designer	________	
		Support Staff	________	
		....	________	
		....	________	________
	Conceptual Design Sign-off: Revise design and planning strategy based on Owner feedback and re-submit for final approval.	Principal	________	
		Project Designer	________	
		Designer	________	
		Support Staff	________	
		....	________	
		....	________	________
1.2.3	**Space Allocation/Utilization Plans:** Prepare preliminary space plans indicating preliminary locations of partitions, furniture, fixtures, and equipment layouts. Develop proposed concepts for color, materials, finishes, and lighting design.	Principal	________	
		Project Designer	________	
		Designer	________	
		Support Staff	________	
		....	________	
		....	________	________
1.2.4	**Finishes, Furnishings, & Equipment Selections:** Refine selections for finishes, furniture, equipment, etc. in light of design concept and performance requirements. Design and develop custom items.	Principal	________	
		Project Designer	________	
		Designer	________	
		Support Staff	________	
		....	________	
		....	________	________
1.2.5	**Preliminary Costing / Schematic Design Presentation:** Prepare schematic design proposal and preliminary cost estimate for Owner review and approval.	Principal	________	
		Project Designer	________	
		Designer	________	
		Support Staff	________	
		....	________	
		....	________	________
1.2.5	**Refine Plans and Selections:** Revise and refine layouts and selections for furniture, fixtures, equipment, materials, finishes, lighting, window treatments, and custom items based on owner feedback.	Principal	________	
		Project Designer	________	
		Designer	________	
		Support Staff	________	
		....	________	
		....	________	________

Project ______________________

Project No. ______________________

Initials ______ Date ___/___/___

Basic Services Worksheet

Project Control Book Form 210W

SCHEMATIC DESIGN

ASID Contract Reference #

1.2.5

Schematic Design Sign-off:
Revise schematic design proposal and cost estimate based on Owner feedback. Submit for final approval.

Staff	Hours	Total
Principal	______	
Project Designer	______	
Designer	______	
Support Staff	______	
....	______	
....	______	______

Staff	Hours	Total
Principal	______	
Project Designer	______	
Designer	______	
Support Staff	______	
....	______	
....	______	______

Staff	Hours	Total
Principal	______	
Project Designer	______	
Designer	______	
Support Staff	______	
....	______	
....	______	______

Staff	Hours	Total
Principal	______	
Project Designer	______	
Designer	______	
Support Staff	______	
....	______	
....	______	______

Staff	Hours	Total
Principal	______	
Project Designer	______	
Designer	______	
Support Staff	______	
....	______	
....	______	______

Staff	Hours	Total
Principal	______	
Project Designer	______	
Designer	______	
Support Staff	______	
....	______	
....	______	______

SCHEMATIC DESIGN ______ Total hours

Project ______________________

Project No. ______________________

Initials ______ Date ___/___/___

Basic Services Worksheet

Project Control Book Form 210W

DESIGN DEVELOPMENT

ASID Contract Reference #		Staff	Hours	Total
1.3.1	**Design Development Drawings and Documents:** Prepare drawings and documents which fix and describe the size and character of the interior design and proposed work.	Principal	______	
		Project Designer	______	
		Designer	______	
		Support Staff	______	
		....	______	
		....	______	______
1.3.2	**Document Custom Items and Elements:** Prepare data and illustrations for all specially designed finishes, furnishings, and equipment.	Principal	______	
		Project Designer	______	
		Designer	______	
		Support Staff	______	
		....	______	
		....	______	______
1.3.3	**Finishes, Furnishings & Equipment Specifications:** Document recommendations for all finishes, materials, furniture, fixtures, lighting, accessories, and artwork for the project.	Principal	______	
		Project Designer	______	
		Designer	______	
		Support Staff	______	
		....	______	
		....	______	______
1.3.4	**Special Conditions and Supplemental Services:** Prepare design development data, drawings and specifications as may be appropriate for specially contracted services.	Principal	______	
		Project Designer	______	
		Designer	______	
		Support Staff	______	
		....	______	
		....	______	______
1.3.5	**Design Development Presentation:** Provide design development proposal and probable cost for finishes, furnishings and equipment, as well as custom items for Owner review and approval.	Principal	______	
		Project Designer	______	
		Designer	______	
		Support Staff	______	
		....	______	
		....	______	______
1.3.5	**Design Development Sign-off:** Revise design development proposal and cost estimate based on owner feedback. Submit for final approval.	Principal	______	
		Project Designer	______	
		Designer	______	
		Support Staff	______	
		....	______	
		....	______	______
	______________________	Principal	______	
	______________________	Project Designer	______	
	______________________	Designer	______	
	______________________	Support Staff	______	
	______________________	....	______	
	______________________	....	______	______

DESIGN DEVELOPMENT ______ Total hours

Project ______________________

Project No. ______________________

Initials ________ Date ___/___/___

Basic Services Worksheet

Project Control Book Form 210W

CONTRACT DOCUMENTS

ASID Contract Reference #		Staff	Hours	Total
1.4.1	**Working Drawings for Interior Construction/Demolition:** Provide necessary documentation to execute interior design and proposed work.	Principal	______	
		Project Designer	______	
		Designer	______	
		Support Staff	______	
		....	______	
		....	______	______
1.4.2	**Custom Items / Specifications:** Provide specifications, drawings, and other necessary data for procurement and fabrication of finishes, furnishings, equipment, and custom items.	Principal	______	
		Project Designer	______	
		Designer	______	
		Support Staff	______	
		....	______	
		....	______	______
1.4.4	**Preparation of Bid Package:** Assist Owner with the preparation of bid packages for proposed work, and for finishes, furnishings, equipment specifications, and custom items. Preview with Owner for approval.	Principal	______	
		Project Designer	______	
		Designer	______	
		Support Staff	______	
		....	______	
		....	______	______
1.4.4	**Bid Package Sign-off:** Revise bid package based on feedback from Owner and submit for final approval. Process bid addendums as required.	Principal	______	
		Project Designer	______	
		Designer	______	
		Support Staff	______	
		....	______	
		....	______	______
1.4.5	**Governmental Approvals:** Review drawings and specifications to verify compliance with all code and regulatory issues. Assist Owner with the filing of necessary documents.	Principal	______	
		Project Designer	______	
		Designer	______	
		Support Staff	______	
		....	______	
		....	______	______
1.4.6	**Bid Analysis & Contract Award:** Coordinate and assist Owner with bid analysis process. Provide recommendations for contract award.	Principal	______	
		Project Designer	______	
		Designer	______	
		Support Staff	______	
		....	______	
		....	______	______
	______________________	Principal	______	
	______________________	Project Designer	______	
	______________________	Designer	______	
	______________________	Support Staff	______	
	______________________	....	______	
	______________________	....	______	______

CONTRACT DOCUMENTS ______ Total hours

Project ____________

Project No. ____________

Initials ______ Date ___/___/___

Basic Services Worksheet

Project Control Book Form 210W

CONTRACT ADMINISTRATION

ASID Contract Reference #		Staff	Hours	Total
1.5.4	**Contractor Coordination:** Coordinate contractor's instructions and payment schedules acting on behalf of the Owner to the extent provided for in the contract.	Principal	______	
		Project Designer	______	
		Designer	______	
		Support Staff	______	
		....	______	
		....	______	______
1.5.5	**Purchase Order Tracking:** Assist Owner with tracking of finishes, furnishings, equipment, and schedules of delivery and installation.	Principal	______	
		Project Designer	______	
		Designer	______	
		Support Staff	______	
		....	______	
		....	______	______
1.5.6	**Site Visitation:** Conduct site visits to inspect progress and quality of interiors work.	Principal	______	
		Project Designer	______	
		Designer	______	
		Support Staff	______	
		....	______	
		....	______	______
1.5.9	**Authorization of Payment:** Determine the amount owed to the Contractors and issue certificates for payment.	Principal	______	
		Project Designer	______	
		Designer	______	
		Support Staff	______	
		....	______	
		....	______	______
1.5.15	**Finishes, Furnishings & Equipment Inspection:** Survey finishes, furnishings and equipment delivery, installation, and placement for damage, quality of assembly and function.	Principal	______	
		Project Designer	______	
		Designer	______	
		Support Staff	______	
		....	______	
		....	______	______
1.5.17	**Approval of Contractor Submittals:** Check shop drawings, product data and samples for conformance with contract documents.	Principal	______	
		Project Designer	______	
		Designer	______	
		Support Staff	______	
		....	______	
		....	______	______
1.5.18	**Change Orders:** Prepare change orders as needed for Owner review and approval.	Principal	______	
		Project Designer	______	
		Designer	______	
		Support Staff	______	
		....	______	
		....	______	______

Project ______________________

Project No. ______________________

Initials ______ Date ___/___/___

Basic Services Worksheet

Project Control Book Form 210W

ASID Contract Reference #

CONTRACT ADMINISTRATION

Move-In, Punch List & Project Close-out:
Conduct inspections to determine dates of completion. Assist Owner and staff with move-in. Execute punch list and expedite resolution of all items. Coordinate completion of project objectives.

Staff	Hours	Total
Principal	______	
Project Designer	______	
Designer	______	
Support Staff	______	
....	______	
....	______	______

____
____
____
____
____
____

Staff	Hours	Total
Principal	______	
Project Designer	______	
Designer	______	
Support Staff	______	
....	______	
....	______	______

____
____
____
____
____
____

Staff	Hours	Total
Principal	______	
Project Designer	______	
Designer	______	
Support Staff	______	
....	______	
....	______	______

____
____
____
____
____
____

Staff	Hours	Total
Principal	______	
Project Designer	______	
Designer	______	
Support Staff	______	
....	______	
....	______	______

____
____
____
____
____
____

Staff	Hours	Total
Principal	______	
Project Designer	______	
Designer	______	
Support Staff	______	
....	______	
....	______	______

CONTRACT ADMINISTRATION ______ Total hours

Project ______________________

Project No. ______________________

Initials ______ Date ___/___/___

Supplemental Services Checklist

Project Control Book Form 211C

ASID Contract Reference #	Research & Focused Studies	Hours
1.7.1	☐ Feasibility studies	______
1.7.2	☐ Studies for required government or other agency approval(s)	______
1.7.2	☐ Planning surveys, site evaluations or comparisons of prospective sites	______
1.7.3	☐ Future facilities studies	______
1.7.20	☐ Special performance studies such as acoustical, security, communications	______
	☐ Post occupancy evaluation	______
	☐ Healthy building study	______
	☐	______
	☐	______
	☐	______
	Project Documentation	
1.7.4	☐ Verify or generate existing facility documentation	______
1.7.9	☐ Document revisions beyond designer's control	______
1.7.10	☐ Providing data and documentation for change orders resulting in services which exceed the basic compensation	______
1.7.11	☐ Extensive investigations, surveys, evaluations or detailed appraisals of existing facility finishes, furnishings and equipment data	______
1.7.15	☐ Document significant changes in work	______
	☐ Product mock-ups of finishes, furnishings and equipment	______
	☐ Development and documentation of workstation standards	______
	☐ Design and install fire exit diagrams	______
	☐	______
	☐	______
	☐	______
	Project Coordination & Special Services	
1.7.5	☐ "Out-of-sequence" services	______
1.7.6	☐ Services in connection with the work of a construction manager or separate consultant hired by Owner	______
1.7.7	☐ Detailed cost estimates and inventories related to project	______
1.7.8	☐ Planning tenant or rental spaces	______
1.7.12	☐ Finishes, furnishings and equipment delivery/ acceptance for Owner	______
1.7.13	☐ Replacement of fire or other damaged finishes, furnishings and equipment	______
1.7.14	☐ Services from faulty finishes, furnishings and equipment contractor/work	______
1.7.16	☐ Operations & maintenance start-up assistance	______
1.7.17	☐ Services after final payment has been issued to contractor	______
1.7.18	☐ Serving as a witness	______
1.7.19	☐ Providing professional consultants: architectural, mechanical, electrical	______
1.7.21	☐ Purchasing finishes, furnishings and equipment with Owner's fund	______
1.7.23	☐ Procuring artwork for the project	______
	☐ Coordination of move-in	______

Project ______________________

Project No. ______________________

Initials ______ Date ___/___/___

Supplemental Services Checklist

Project Control Book Form 211C

ASID Contract Reference #

	Hours
☐ Artwork installation	______
☐ Coordinate specially commissioned art	______
☐ Coordination of special or custom items	______
☐ Coordination and management of special events	______
☐	______
☐	______
☐	______

Specialized Design Services

☐ Graphic design & signage	______
☐ Interior plantscaping	______
☐ Product design	______
☐ Textile design	______
☐ Photography	______
☐	______
☐	______
☐	______
☐	______
☐	______
☐	______
☐	______
☐	______
☐	______
☐	______
☐	______
☐	______
☐	______
☐	______
☐	______
☐	______
☐	______
☐	______
☐	______

Risk Management Checklist

Project Control Book Form 260C

☐ **Clearly Define Scope of Services**
Outline for the client the basic and supplemental services, the design firm's billing rate, and terms of compensation.

☐ **Obtain Written Approval**
Have both parties sign an agreement/contract before any work begins and if any changes to the contract occur.

☐ **Request a Retainer**
This amount would be deducted from the invoice for final payment.

☐ **Ownership of Design and Contract Documents**
Include a statement in the contract that warns the client against reuse of the design documents and specifications without designer's written permission. Consider including a copyright notice on all design documents. (© Firm/ Individual Name *year*)

☐ **Document all Formal and Informal Communication**
Document all telephone conversations, meetings, site visits, changes and approvals requested by the client. Require that the client "sign off "at the end of each phase and on change orders.

☐ **Termination of the Contract**
Maintain the right to stop work, withhold documents or terminate the contract without penalty if the client does not pay on a timely basis, runs out of money or must end the project due to circumstances beyond the designer's control.

☐ **Arbitration**
Include a clause in the contract stating that any controversy or breach of contract which cannot be resolved between the design firm and the client, shall be settled in accordance with the rules of the American Arbitration Association. Both parties understand that the decision made by the arbitrator is final and binding.

☐ **Maintain Communication with the Client**
Do not avoid client contact. Return all telephone calls as soon as possible. Keep the client informed of any potential problems and issues which require immediate attention or approval.

Risk Management Checklist

Project Control Book Form 260C

- ☐ **Anticipate Delays**
  Make provisions which absolve the designer of responsibility for project delays caused by client, trades people or other circumstances beyond designer's control.

- ☐ **Code Compliance**
  Verify questionable code compliance issues. Contact local building officials or hire a consultant if questionable code issues are present. Improper building/ space classification or failure to comply with state and local codes could result in costly changes once the project is completed and occupied.

- ☐ **Specify Appropriate Materials**
  Specify materials and products which meet or surpass the functional and legal (code) requirements of the project. Absolve the designer of responsibility for product defects or performance due to manufacturer's process or client's inappropriate selection despite designer recommendation, i.e. put a warning in writing.

- ☐ **Construction Observation**
  Clearly state that the designer will not be required to make exhaustive site inspections. Designer is not responsible if the client, consultants or contractor(s) make changes without prior notification. Designer should not be held responsible for the technique or workmanship of any contractor(s).

- ☐ **Purchase Agreements**
  Do not make any purchases for client unless written approval and 50% of the purchase price has been received. The remaining balance of payment is due before delivery and installation.

Initials ______ *Date* ___/___/___

Phase 3: Project Organization & Start-up

Project Control Book Form 300C

Operational Definition:

Post-contract planning and start-up of design project based on scope of services and schedule as agreed upon in design contract. Includes all internal office and filing tasks related to the efficient organization and on-going management of project information, scheduling, documentation and communication.

Critical Issues

☐ **Be Organized**
Take the time to setup a project control book for each job which keeps all relevant data, in-house paperwork, communication and much needed in-process information in one place. Organize in reverse chronological format to keep most recent information at the front of each section. When kept up-to-date, this book reduces managerial time and insures against miscommunication.

☐ **Keep Comprehensive Records**
Maintain complete, accurate, and up-to-date records on every aspect of the project. This includes formal and informal communication, correspondence, drawings, time and expenses. Comprehensive records aid in legal documentation of the design process to protect against litigation and serve as benchmarks for evaluating future projects and office finances.

☐ **Prepare Realistic and Meaningful Schedules**
Schedules should be flexible, allow for normal revisions, and should be agreed upon by all parties involved. Define discreet project tasks based on scope, start and finish dates and the level of effort required to complete each task. Use the schedule to organize meetings, outline responsibilities and choreograph efforts.

☐ **Standardize Project Management**
Within a firm, all project managers should use standardized procedures, and should undergo training to prepare them for this task. Determine how documentation will take place and how information will be distributed. All documentation forms for the firm should be of standard design and include project name, file number and date.

☐ **Assess Project Complexity and Coordination Issues**
Project size, complexity, number of consultants, and client contacts all impact on the time required to proceed from one task to the next. Review the proposed project from a communication/coordination standpoint and factor in adjustments to budget and schedule.

☐ **Retain Records of all Formal and Informal Communication**
Copies of all phone conversations, memos, letters, transmittals, invoices, purchase orders, change orders, sample approvals and other communique must be kept in an organized, easily accessible reference file or project control book.

☐ **Prepare and Distribute Meeting Agenda and Minutes**
Well prepared meeting agendas serve to prioritize topics to be covered and keep meetings focused. Meeting minutes should record actions taken, clearly identify parties responsible for future work, and identify when future work is to be completed.

☐ ____
____
____

Project ______________________

Project No. ______________________

Initials ______ *Date* ___/___/___

Project Directory • Client

Project Control Book Form 310R

page _____ *of* _____

Owner/Firm: ______________________

notes

Primary Client Contact: ______________________ ....

title ______________________ ....

department ______________________ ....

street ______________________ phone ______ / ______________

city.state.zip ______________ ________ fax ______ / ______________

Client Contact: ______________________ ....

title ______________________ ....

department ______________________ ....

street ______________________ phone ______ / ______________

city.state.zip ______________ ________ fax ______ / ______________

Client Contact: ______________________ ....

title ______________________ ....

department ______________________ ....

street ______________________ phone ______ / ______________

city.state.zip ______________ ________ fax ______ / ______________

Client Contact: ______________________ ....

title ______________________ ....

department ______________________ ....

street ______________________ phone ______ / ______________

city.state.zip ______________ ________ fax ______ / ______________

Client Contact: ______________________ ....

title ______________________ ....

department ______________________ ....

street ______________________ phone ______ / ______________

city.state.zip ______________ ________ fax ______ / ______________

Project ______________________

Project No. ______________________

Initials ______ Date ___/___/___

Project Directory • Consultants

Project Control Book Form 311R

page ____ of ____

Project Consultants: ______________________

notes

Architectural: ______________________ ....

Project Contact ______________________ ....

title ______________________ ....

street ______________________ phone ______ / ______________

city.state.zip ______________ ________ fax ______ / ______________

Lighting: ______________________ ....

Project Contact ______________________ ....

title ______________________ ....

street ______________________ phone ______ / ______________

city.state.zip ______________ ________ fax ______ / ______________

HVAC: ______________________ ....

Project Contact ______________________ ....

title ______________________ ....

street ______________________ phone ______ / ______________

city.state.zip ______________ ________ fax ______ / ______________

.... Other ______________________ ....

Project Contact ______________________ ....

title ______________________ ....

street ______________________ phone ______ / ______________

city.state.zip ______________ ________ fax ______ / ______________

.... Other ______________________ ....

Project Contact ______________________ ....

title ______________________ ....

street ______________________ phone ______ / ______________

city.state.zip ______________ ________ fax ______ / ______________

Project ______________________

Project No. ______________________

Initials ________ Date ___/___/___

Project Information

Project Control Book Form 315R

Partner-in-Charge ____________ *Initials*

Associate-in-Charge ____________

Project Designer ____________

Special Problems/Areas of Concern:

- ☐ Code Compliance
- ☐ Regulatory Agency Reviews
- ☐ Severe Time Constraints
- ☐ Unrealistic/Insufficient Budget
- ☐ Asbestos Removal
- ☐ Lack of Problem Focus
- ☐ Move from Closed to Open Plan Office
- ☐ Management/Decision Makers Inaccessible
- ☐ Complex A/V Requirements
- ☐ Computer Workstation & Cabling
- ☐ ______________________ Other

Comments

Account Name: ______________________

Billing Address: ______________________

Project Address: ______________________

Client Contact: ______________________

title: ______________________

phone ________ / ______________

fax ________ / ______________

Project Status: ☐ active ☐ dead ☐ complete (may be billed) ☐ holding

Project Type:

- ☐ Feasibility Study
- ☐ Design/Production
- ☐ Furniture/Finishes only
- ☐ Purchasing only

Proposed Area: ____________ r.s.f. **Proposed Budget** $ ____________

Project Description:

Estimated Project Schedule	Earliest Start	Earliest Finish	Latest Start	Latest Finish
Start-Up complete				
Programming				
Schematic Design				
Design Development				
Contract Documents				
Bids Received				
Construction				
Move-In				
Project Closeout				

Project ____________________

Project No. ____________________

Initials ______ Date ___/___/___

Project Review Schedule by Phase & Task

Project Control Book Form 325W

PHASE AND TASK	Budget Hours	Assign To	Internal Review	Client Review Date Date
PROGRAMMING				
Strategy Session	________	....	___/___/___	
Interviews & Activity Analysis	________	....	___/___/___	
Inventory Existing Conditions	________	....	___/___/___	
Base Drawings	________	....	___/___/___	
Code Review	________	....	___/___/___	
Analyze/Synthesize Information	________	....	___/___/___	
Program Draft	________	....	___/___/___	
Client Review	________	....	___/___/___	___/___/___
Revisions	________	....	___/___/___	
Program Document Sign-off	________	....	___/___/___	___/___/___
SCHEMATIC DESIGN				
Concept Development	________	....	___/___/___	
Review Alternative Approaches	________	....	___/___/___	
Revisions	________	....	___/___/___	
Conceptual Design Sign-off	________	....	___/___/___	___/___/___
Space Allocation/Utilization Plans	________	....	___/___/___	
Refine Materials & Furn Selections	________	....	___/___/___	
Custom Items Development	________	....	___/___/___	
Preliminary Costing	________	....	___/___/___	
Schematic Design Presentation	________	....	___/___/___	___/___/___
Revisions	________	....	___/___/___	
Schematic Design Sign-off	________	....	___/___/___	___/___/___
DESIGN DEVELOPMENT				
Refine Plans & Selections	________	....	___/___/___	
Detailing and Custom Items	________	....	___/___/___	
Verify Code Compliance	________	....	___/___/___	
Cost Estimates	________	....	___/___/___	___/___/___
Design Development Presentation	________	....	___/___/___	___/___/___
Revisions	________	....	___/___/___	
Design Development Sign-off	________	....	___/___/___	___/___/___
CONTRACT DOCUMENTS				
Working Drawings and Documents	________	....	___/___/___	
Specifications	________	....	___/___/___	
Verify Code Compliance	________	....	___/___/___	
Bid Package Sign-off	________	....	___/___/___	___/___/___
Code Review	________	....	___/___/___	
Bid Analysis	________	....	___/___/___	
Contract Award	________	....	___/___/___	___/___/___

Project ____________________

Project No. ____________________

Initials ______ Date ___/___/___

Project Review
Schedule by Phase & Task

Project Control Book Form 325W

	Budget Hours	Assign To	Internal Review Date	Client Review Date
CONTRACT ADMINISTRATION				
Contractor Coordination	________	....	___/___/___	
Purchase Order Tracking	________	....	___/___/___	
Site Visitation	________	....	___/___/___	
Authorization of Payment	________	....	___/___/___	
Code Review	________	....	___/___/___	
FF&E Inspection	________	....	___/___/___	
Approval of Contractor Submittals	________	....	___/___/___	
Change Orders	________	....	___/___/___	
Move-in, Punch List, Project Close-out	________	....	___/___/___	___/___/___
....	________	....	___/___/___	
....	________	....	___/___/___	
....	________	....	___/___/___	___/___/___
....	________	....	___/___/___	
....	________	....	___/___/___	
....	________	....	___/___/___	___/___/___
....	________	....	___/___/___	
....	________	....	___/___/___	
....	________	....	___/___/___	___/___/___

Project ____________________

Project No. ____________________

Initials ______ Date ___/___/___

Meeting Agenda Worksheet

Project Control Book Form 345W

Meeting Date: ____/____/____

Meeting Time: .... am pm

Meeting Location: ....

Attendees: cc√

.... ☐

.... ☐

.... ☐

.... ☐

.... ☐

.... ☐

.... ☐

Agenda:

....

....

....

....

....

....

....

....

....

....

Next Meeting: _____/_____/_____ (*date*) ________________ (*time*) ________________ (*location*)

Responsibility

____

___/___/___ *Deadline* ____________ *Initials*

____

___/___/___ *Deadline* ____________ *Initials*

____

___/___/___ *Deadline* ____________ *Initials*

____

___/___/___ *Deadline* ____________ *Initials*

____

___/___/___ *Deadline* ____________ *Initials*

The following report will be considered correct unless written notice is promptly received.

Meeting Notes/Report:

Name ______________________

Phone Conversation Log

Project Control Book Form 350R

Notes

Date: ___/___/___

Contact: ______________________

____

Project: ______________________

Project #: ______________________

____

____

Date: ___/___/___

Contact: ______________________

____

Project: ______________________

Project #: ______________________

____

____

Date: ___/___/___

Contact: ______________________

____

Project: ______________________

Project #: ______________________

____

____

Date: ___/___/___

Contact: ______________________

____

Project: ______________________

Project #: ______________________

____

____

Project ____________________

Project No. ____________________

Client Sign-Off Sheet

Project Control Book Form 370R

In order for design work to continue in an expedient manner, each phase of work must be approved by an authorized representative of the Owner as satisfactory and complete before work can begin on the subsequent phase.

All services and information contracted for in this phase of the project are hereby approved and authority is granted to proceed to the next phase of work.

Programming Phase

Authorization ____________________ Date ___/___/___

Conceptual Design Phase

Authorization ____________________ Date ___/___/___

Schematic Design Phase

Authorization ____________________ Date ___/___/___

Design Development Phase

Authorization ____________________ Date ___/___/___

Contract Documents & Bid Package Phase

Authorization ____________________ Date ___/___/___

Contract Administration Phase

Authorization ____________________ Date ___/___/___

Project Close Out & Approval for Final Payment

Authorization ____________________ Date ___/___/___

Initials ______ Date ___/___/___

Phase 4: Programming

Project Control Book Form 400C

Operational Definition:

Tasks and services related to developing a hierarchy of information and goals which will guide the evolution of the design. Includes collecting, analyzing, and synthesizing information, clarifying major goals, determining performance requirements and prioritizing design objectives.

Critical Issues

☐ **Gathering Sufficient Information**
The final design quality and success of the project is directly affected by the insight obtained during the programming phase. Inadequate or inaccurate information at this point can put the entire project in jeopardy. Refer back to the client goals and objectives, major project parameters and initial scope of services to assure your information gathering strategy is on track.

☐ **Develop thorough but Concise Tools for Information Gathering**
When researching a project, work to develop systematic methods of gathering and recording crucial information. Standardized interview formats, checklists which help identify present and future needs, behavioral observation tools, and techniques for documenting existing conditions all aid in making the programming process more accurate, and efficient.

☐ **Maintain Objectivity**
Resorting to standard design approaches or stereotyping needs and function based on facility type or personalities can result in misguided design. A questioning attitude is needed for programming which identifies the needs unique to that situation.

☐ **Foster User Participation**
The people who will occupy and use the space on a daily basis are sources of valuable design information. Develop techniques which allow them to contribute to the development of the project in a meaningful way. User participation has been shown to increase satisfaction with the completed project.

☐ **Guide the Client with Your Knowledge and Experience**
Help the client or people being interviewed to distinguish between needs and wants at this stage, to prioritize their objectives, and to be realistic about goals and future projections. Also work to aid the client in understanding the design implications of their decisions.

☐ **Understand Corporate Culture**
Project goals and design objectives must accurately reflect the corporate philosophy and standards of the client.

☐ **Balance Needs**
Individual needs must be balanced with department needs and overall corporate goals and objectives.

☐ **Formally Document Programming Information**
Present all of your findings clearly to the client in order that they may fully understand and approve of the premises on which you plan to proceed.

Initials ______ Date ___/___/___

Phase 4: Programming

Project Control Book Form 400C

- ☐ **Further Verbal to Visual Understanding**
  The program serves as a bridge for the client to move from a verbal to a visual understanding of the project. Whenever possible, findings should be translated to a graphic level and the physical design implications clearly outlined.

- ☐ **Resolve Disagreements**
  All team members and client must come to a mutual understanding and consensus regarding program content. Disagreements and misinterpretations will carry into later design phases.

- ☐ **Establish Justification**
  A program provides justification for the design process. The myriad of information should be simplified, distilled and complete with documentation of the original data or sources of information which lead to your conclusions. It serves as design validation criteria.

- ☐ **Confirm the Scope**
  A program will clarify the scope of the project at hand. This in turn helps define the budget.

- ☐ **Employ the Active Participation of All Parties**
  Designers, architects, management, consultants, and in-house team members must be closely involved in the programming phase.

- ☐ **Finalize Programming**
  Feedback from in-house and client reviews must be incorporated into the program document and presented to the client for approval and sign-off. Be sure that the client representative has the authority to give final approval to proceed to the next phase of work. Approval should be in writing. Avoid the temptation to proceed to the next phase of work without sign-off approval.

- ☐ ____________________

- ☐ ____________________

- ☐ ____________________

Project ________________

Project No. ________________

Initials ______ Date ___/___/___

Activity Profile

Project Control Book Form 430W

JOB DESCRIPTION

Title: ________________

Name: ________________

Primary Responsibility: ________________

____

____

Secondary Responsibility: ________________

____

____

COMMUNICATION/INTERACTION
(in order of importance)

With Whom	Frequency	Nature of	Location
1			
2			
3			
4			
5			
6			
7			
8			
9			
10			

Comments

....

....

....

....

....

MATERIALS FLOW

To: ________________

Nature of: ________________

Frequency: ________________

Project ____________________

Project No. ____________________

Initials ______ Date ___/___/___

Activity Profile

Project Control Book Form 430W

WORK AREA NEEDS

Privacy: ____________________

Equipment: ____________________

Storage: ____________________

Outside Work Area: ____________________

Personal: ____________________

☐ Right Handed ☐ Left Handed

General Comments: ____________________

ANTICIPATED USE

Facility Spaces most frequently used:

Room /Space	Use

Project ______________________

Project No. ______________________

Initials ________ Date ____/____/____

Existing Furniture & Equipment Inventory

Project Control Book Form 450W

page ____ of ____

Room Name ______________________

Room # ______________________

Item/Description	Inventory #	Qty	Dimensions L x W x H	Condition good fair poor	Comments
				☐ ☐ ☐	
				☐ ☐ ☐	
				☐ ☐ ☐	
				☐ ☐ ☐	
				☐ ☐ ☐	
				☐ ☐ ☐	
				☐ ☐ ☐	
				☐ ☐ ☐	
				☐ ☐ ☐	
				☐ ☐ ☐	
				☐ ☐ ☐	
				☐ ☐ ☐	
				☐ ☐ ☐	
				☐ ☐ ☐	
				☐ ☐ ☐	
				☐ ☐ ☐	
				☐ ☐ ☐	
				☐ ☐ ☐	
				☐ ☐ ☐	

Special Conditions

Initials ______ Date ___/___/___

Phase 5: Schematic Design

Project Control Book Form 500C

Operational Definition:

Tasks and services related to idea generation and communication of design solutions including identifying design strategies, formulation of the design concept, studying alternate solutions, evaluation and refinement based on client feedback. Building systems integration, product sourcing, product selection and preliminary cost estimation are also tasks central to this phase.

Critical Issues

☐ **Clarify the Conceptual Framework**
The design concept should be written as a clear statement of purpose which lays the groundwork for future design decisions. It should be articulated both visually and verbally in a concise manner so that the design intent is clearly communicated to in-house design staff as well as to the client. It should evolve with client input.

☐ **Employ all Pertinent Information**
Design studies must consider the full range of factors outlined in the program. Utilize the input of all consultants and code officials. Check evolving solutions against critical project parameters including building systems compatibility and code compliance.

☐ **Verify and Enhance Program**
Design strategies resulting from the programming phase should be verified and elaborated upon during conceptual design. Use the conceptual framework to strengthen and reinforce program. Concepts developed during schematic design must enhance goals and objectives.

☐ **Study Ideas from Various Vantage Points**
Begin developing ideas which address the issues generated by the program. Study the design problem from multiple perspectives generating alternative approaches and solutions.

☐ **Use a Variety of Design Methods**
Study design ideas using a wide range of both 2-dimensional and 3-dimensional modeling tools to ensure accurate representation and communication of ideas. Presentation drawings, renderings, mock-ups and samples are crucial in this phase. They communicate the concepts and enable the client to visualize the design. This helps to alleviate surprises during installation.

☐ **Assess Finishes, Furnishings and Equipment Selections Relative to Performance Criteria**
All items selected for the project must be evaluated in terms of their ability to meet the overall requirements of the project. Selections must reinforce design concept, meet with code compliance and be capable of withstanding the anticipated use and misuse for their particular application.

☐ **Review In-process Design with Client**
Schematics should be presented using direct references to project goals, concrete programming findings and conceptual framework to justify design decisions. Presentations at this stage should be professional, but not overly detailed as to commit to specific design elements prematurely.

Initials ______ Date ___/___/___

Phase 5: Schematic Design

Project Control Book Form 500C

- ☐ **Ensure that Your Message is Understood**
  Determine if your client understands the drawings and/or the jargon you may employ. This should be done tactfully to minimize embarrassment.

- ☐ **Coordinate Communication between Separate Entities**
  When there are a variety of consultants or other groups involved in the design relative responsibilities must be carefully coordinated and constant communication must be maintained.

- ☐ **Know Your Design Sources**
  When a new supplier is being considered, they should be researched by requesting references as well as checking other previous installations and user satisfaction. Retain only relevant and source information. It is a waste of space and money to store catalogues and samples that will never be used.

- ☐ **Include Cost Estimates**
  Make certain the client realizes the preliminary nature of the estimates. Cost estimates should include price increases and availability of products and add contingencies to allow for future cost fluctuations.

- ☐ **Finalize the Schematic Design**
  Feedback from in-house and client reviews must be incorporated into the design solution and presented to the client for approval and sign-off. Be sure that the client representative has the authority to give final approval to proceed to the next phase of work. Approval should be in writing. Avoid the temptation to proceed to the next stage of work without sign-off approval. Deal with problems related to Schematic Design now, so as not to compound their magnitude and ramifications later.

- ☐ ______________________________

- ☐ ______________________________

- ☐ ______________________________

Project ____________________

Project No. ____________________

Initials ________ Date ____/____/____

Code Compliance Worksheet

Project Control Book Form 510W

Classifications

Occupancy ____________________

____

Construction ____________________

____

# of Floors/Stories	____________	max
Height of Bldg.	____________	max ft
Fire Area	____________	max sq ft
Increases (sprinkler, access)	____________	% + sq ft
....	____________	

Fire Resistive Ratings (hours)

Fire Walls	____________	
Bearing/Partitions	____________	
Non Bearing/Partitions	____________	
Partition Enclosures	____________	stair
	____________	corridor
	____________	
Tenant Separation	____________	
Columns, beams, etc.	____________	
Floors	____________	
Roof	____________	
....	____________	
....	____________	

Notes

....

....

....

....

....

....

....

....

....

....

....

....

....

Means of Egress

Exit Requirements:			Code Ref #	Notes
Floor Area	____________	sq ft	________	....
Sq ft/occupant	____________	sq ft	________	....
Occupant Load	____________	# persons	________	....
Persons/Exit units	____________	exit units	________	....
# of Exits	____________	minimum	________	....
Exit Doors				
Width	____________	minimum	________	....
Height	____________	maximum	________	....
Swing Direction	____________		________	....
Hardware	____________		________	....
Emergency Lighting	____________		________	....
Exit Signage	____________		________	....
Corridors				
Width	____________	minimum	________	....
Height	____________	maximum	________	....
Distance of travel	____________		________	....
Deadend	____________		________	....
Aisles	____________		________	....
Stairs				
....	____________		________	....
....	____________		________	....
....	____________		________	....
....	____________		________	....
....	____________		________	....

Space Requirements

	occupied	habitable	non-habitable	
Ceiling Height	________	________	________	....
Ventilation	________	________	________	....
Lighting	________	________	________	....
Plumbing Fixtures	________	________	________	....
....	________	________	________	....
....	________	________	________	....

Project ____________

Project No. ____________

Initials ______ Date ___/___/___

Code Compliance Worksheet

Project Control Book Form 510W

Notes

Prevention of Interior Fire Spread

	Code Ref #	Notes
Finishes		
Fire Suppression Systems		
Detection Systems		
Opening Protectives		
Glazing		

Barrier Free Considerations

	Code Ref #	Notes
Path of Travel		
Ramps		
Vestibule		
Threshold		
Hardware		
Signage		

Doors & Corridors

	Code Ref #	Notes
Width		
Swing Direction		
Clearance		

Facilities

	Code Ref #	Notes
Bathrooms		
Drinking Fountains		
Telephones		

Project ______________________

Project No. ______________________

Initials ______ Date ___/___/___

Product Source Worksheet

Project Control Book Form 520W

Product: ....
....
Location: ....
Selection Criteria:
- ☐ Budget ....
- ☐ Function ....
- ☐ Material ....
- ☐ Finish ....
- ☐ Style ....
- ☐ Delivery ....

Manufacturer	Item (name, #)	Price

Product: ....
....
Location: ....
Selection Criteria:
- ☐ Budget ....
- ☐ Function ....
- ☐ Material ....
- ☐ Finish ....
- ☐ Style ....
- ☐ Delivery ....

Manufacturer	Item (name, #)	Price

Product: ....
....
Location: ....
Selection Criteria:
- ☐ Budget ....
- ☐ Function ....
- ☐ Material ....
- ☐ Finish ....
- ☐ Style ....
- ☐ Delivery ....

Manufacturer	Item (name, #)	Price

Product: ....
....
Location: ....
Selection Criteria:
- ☐ Budget ....
- ☐ Function ....
- ☐ Material ....
- ☐ Finish ....
- ☐ Style ....
- ☐ Delivery ....

Manufacturer	Item (name, #)	Price

Initials ______ *Date* ___/___/___

Phase 6:
Design Development

Project Control Book Form 600C

Operational Definition:

Tasks and services aimed at evolving schematic design ideas into buildable reality. Includes design detailing, development of custom items, product pricing and availability, coordination of design with building systems and cost confirmation.

Critical Issues

☐ **Verify Code Compliance**
Systematically reevaluate the design scheme for compliance with all local, state, and federal building codes, life safety requirements, and health regulations. This includes proper egress, provision of emergency systems and proper specification of all materials, finishes, and furnishings.

☐ **Refine and Test Critical Design Elements**
Focus and finalize all schematic design drawings and information, but remain flexible and open to alternatives. Identify elements of the design that are critical to the success of the project and need further elaboration and testing. Consider producing large scale mock-ups or actual samples of those elements for client review and approval.

☐ **Consider Availability of Finishes, Furnishings, and Equipment**
All items selected for the project must be confirmed for price and availability relative to the project budget and schedule. Alternatives should be selected for those products whose price or delivery is suspect.

☐ **Include Accessory Items**
Art, signage, and accessories (if part of the scope of services outlined) need to be developed and estimated as part of the total design package.

☐ **Price Items Correctly**
When pricing furniture or equipment include all the extras that add to the price, including shipping costs, discounts, sales tax, etc.. Verify that your prices are reliable and be aware of pending price changes.

☐ **Prepare Complete Cost Estimates**
Estimates must be developed to a fairly detailed level. Take the time to do a thorough cost estimate. Hire a consultant if necessary to help estimate fixed building costs, i.e. drywall, HVAC, electrical, etc.. Include contingencies. Remind the client that these are in-house estimates and not final prices.

☐ **Assess Cost/Benefit Trade-offs**
Final evaluation of design elements should include a cost/benefit analysis of their contribution to the success of the project. Take the time to review the priorities and goals. Assess whether the money may be better spent somewhere else.

☐ **Finalize Design Development**
The design must be brought to a satisfying closure and presented to the client for approval and sign-off so that contract documents can begin. Deal with problems related to design development now, so as not to compound their magnitude and ramifications later.

Project ____________________

Project No. ____________________

Initials ______

Vendor Inquiry Log

Project Control Book Form 610R

page ____ of ____

Notes

....

Vendor: ____________________

____

Date: ___/___/___

% Discount: ____________________

Delivery: ____________________

Freight: ____________________

Comments:

....

Action Taken:

....

Vendor: ____________________

____

Date: ___/___/___

% Discount: ____________________

Delivery: ____________________

Freight: ____________________

Comments:

....

Action Taken:

....

Vendor: ____________________

____

Date: ___/___/___

% Discount: ____________________

Delivery: ____________________

Freight: ____________________

Comments:

....

Action Taken:

....

Vendor: ____________________

____

Date: ___/___/___

% Discount: ____________________

Delivery: ____________________

Freight: ____________________

Comments:

....

Action Taken:

....

Project ______________________

Project No. ______________________

Initials ________ *Date* ____/____/____

Cost Estimate •
Finishes, Furnishings & Equipment

Project Control Book Form 620W

page _____ of _____

Location Key	Item	Mfr #	Qty	List $	+/-%	Amount	Tax	Freight	Total $
....	....	....	....	$.........	....	$............	....	....	$...............
....	....	....	....	$.........	....	$............	....	....	$...............
....	....	....	....	$.........	....	$............	....	....	$...............
....	....	....	....	$.........	....	$............	....	....	$...............
....	....	....	....	$.........	....	$............	....	....	$...............
....	....	....	....	$.........	....	$............	....	....	$...............
....	....	....	....	$.........	....	$............	....	....	$...............
....	....	....	....	$.........	....	$............	....	....	$...............
....	....	....	....	$.........	....	$............	....	....	$...............
....	....	....	....	$.........	....	$............	....	....	$...............
....	....	....	....	$.........	....	$............	....	....	$...............
....	....	....	....	$.........	....	$............	....	....	$...............
....	....	....	....	$.........	....	$............	....	....	$...............
....	....	....	....	$.........	....	$............	....	....	$...............
....	....	....	....	$.........	....	$............	....	....	$...............
....	....	....	....	$.........	....	$............	....	....	$...............
....	....	....	....	$.........	....	$............	....	....	$...............
....	....	....	....	$.........	....	$............	....	....	$...............
....	....	....	....	$.........	....	$............	....	....	$...............
....	....	....	....	$.........	....	$............	....	....	$...............
....	....	....	....	$.........	....	$............	....	....	$...............
....	....	....	....	$.........	....	$............	....	....	$...............
....	....	....	....	$.........	....	$............	....	....	$...............
....	....	....	....	$.........	....	$............	....	....	$...............
....	....	....	....	$.........	....	$............	....	....	$...............
....	....	....	....	$.........	....	$............	....	....	$...............

Initials ______ *Date* ___/___/___

Phase 7: Contract Documents

Project Control Book Form 700C

Operational Definition:

Tasks and services which relate to the production of the legal set of documents required for project bidding, installation and construction.

Critical Issues

☐ **Prepare Accurate Documents**
Contract documents are legal documents. The accuracy of information, completeness and consistency of graphics is essential. Develop systematic methods for checking contract documents for errors, ambiguities, and omissions.

☐ **Detail and Specify to Appropriate Levels**
Completeness of documents should not be misconstrued to imply excessive detailing and specification. Concise documents will identify the necessary level of quality and craftsmanship. Overdetailing and specification can result in higher project costs, increased coordination problems between documents and loss of profits due to misplaced efforts.

☐ **Coordinate Plans and Specifications**
All information in the contract documents must work together logically. Duplication and inconsistencies must be avoided. Working drawings are pictorial and show what is involved by detailing important dimensions and locations. Specifications are written and state the materials that are used, their performance specifications, and manufacturers.

☐ **Introduce Production Quality Standards**
Take the time to develop office standards for document production and enforce their use. This may include guidelines for content, formatting, standardized graphic symbols, detailing standards, master specifications, and quality control measures.

☐ **Verify Compliance with Codes**
Contract documents must conform to all applicable codes. Regulatory issues and code compliance notations must be accurate and done in accordance with the prescribed standard.

☐ **Prepare a Production Schedule**
A schedule which phases document production, review, and completion should be set up before work on contract documents is delegated.

☐ **Finalize Contract Documents**
Present the contract documents and bid strategy to the client for approval and sign-off. Ensure that the client representative has the authority to give final approval to proceed to the next phase of work. Deal with problems related to developing a complete set of contract documents before they are sent out for bid, so as not to compound their magnitude and ramifications later.

☐ ____
____
____
____

Project ____________________

Project No. ____________________

Initials ______ Date ___/___/___

Code Compliance Worksheet

Project Control Book Form 510W

Classifications

Occupancy ____________________

____

Construction ____________________

____

# of Floors/Stories	____________	max
Height of Bldg.	____________	max ft
Fire Area	____________	max sq ft
Increases (sprinkler, access)	____________	% + sq ft
....	____________	

Fire Resistive Ratings (hours)

Fire Walls	____________	
Bearing/Partitions	____________	
Non Bearing/Partitions	____________	
Partition Enclosures	____________	stair
	____________	corridor
	____________	
Tenant Separation	____________	
Columns, beams, etc.	____________	
Floors	____________	
Roof	____________	
....	____________	
....	____________	

Notes

....

....

....

....

....

....

....

....

....

....

....

....

....

Means of Egress

Exit Requirements:			**Code Ref #**	Notes
Floor Area	____________	sq ft	______	....
Sq ft/occupant	____________	sq ft	______	....
Occupant Load	____________	# persons	______	....
Persons/Exit units	____________	exit units	______	....
# of Exits	____________	minimum	______	....
Exit Doors				
Width	____________	minimum	______	....
Height	____________	maximum	______	....
Swing Direction	____________		______	....
Hardware	____________		______	....
Emergency Lighting	____________		______	....
Exit Signage	____________		______	....
Corridors				
Width	____________	minimum	______	....
Height	____________	maximum	______	....
Distance of travel	____________		______	....
Deadend	____________		______	....
Aisles	____________		______	....
Stairs				
....	____________		______	....
....	____________		______	....
....	____________		______	....
....	____________		______	....
....	____________		______	....

Space Requirements

	occupied	habitable	non-habitable	
Ceiling Height	______	______	______	....
Ventilation	______	______	______	....
Lighting	______	______	______	....
Plumbing Fixtures	______	______	______	....
....	______	______	______	....
....	______	______	______	....

Project ____________________

Project No. ____________________

Initials ______ Date ___/___/___

Code Compliance Worksheet

Project Control Book Form 510W

Notes

Prevention of Interior Fire Spread

	Code Ref #	Notes
Finishes		
Fire Suppression Systems		
Detection Systems		
Opening Protectives		
Glazing		

Barrier Free Considerations

	Code Ref #	Notes
Path of Travel		
Ramps		
Vestibule		
Threshold		
Hardware		
Signage		

Doors & Corridors

	Code Ref #	Notes
Width		
Swing Direction		
Clearance		

Facilities

	Code Ref #	Notes
Bathrooms		
Drinking Fountains		
Telephones		

Project ______________
Project No. ______________
Initials ______ Date ___/___/___

Project Record • Room Summary

Project Control Book Form 720R

page ____ *of* ____

Room Name ______________
Room # ______________
Square Footage ______________
Ceiling Height ______________

Sheet/Drawing **#**

Sheet/Drawing	#

Door(s)

type	frame	hardware set	glazing

Windows

type	frame	hardware set	glazing

Outlets

	Location/Height	Qty
Elec.		
Phone		
Computer		
Other		

Special Conditions

....
....
....
....
....
....
....
....
....
....

FLOOR

Location Key	Location Key
Mfr	Mfr
Mfr #	Mfr #
Name	Name
Color	Color

BASE

Location Key	Location Key
Mfr	Mfr
Mfr #	Mfr #
Name	Name
Color	Color

TRIM

Location Key	Location Key
Mfr	Mfr
Mfr #	Mfr #
Name	Name
Color	Color

WALLS

Location Key	Location Key
Mfr	Mfr
Mfr #	Mfr #
Name	Name
Color	Color

Location Key	Location Key
Mfr	Mfr
Mfr #	Mfr #
Name	Name
Color	Color

CEILING

Location Key	Location Key
Mfr	Mfr
Mfr #	Mfr #
Name	Name
Color	Color

LIGHTING

Location Key	Location Key
Mfr	Mfr
Mfr #	Mfr #
Name	Name

Project ______________
Project No. ______________
Initials ______ Date ___/___/___
Room No. ______________

Project Record

Project Control Book Form 740R

page ____ of ____

Location Key __________ **Tag #** ______
Mfr ______________
Mfr # ______________
Name ______________
Color ______________
Dimensions ______________ Qty ______

Location Key __________ **Tag #** ______
Mfr ______________
Mfr # ______________
Name ______________
Color ______________
Dimensions ______________ Qty ______

Location Key __________ **Tag #** ______
Mfr ______________
Mfr # ______________
Name ______________
Color ______________
Dimensions ______________ Qty ______

Location Key __________ **Tag #** ______
Mfr ______________
Mfr # ______________
Name ______________
Color ______________
Dimensions ______________ Qty ______

Location Key __________ **Tag #** ______
Mfr ______________
Mfr # ______________
Name ______________
Color ______________
Dimensions ______________ Qty ______

Location Key __________ **Tag #** ______
Mfr ______________
Mfr # ______________
Name ______________
Color ______________
Dimensions ______________ Qty ______

Project ______________
Project No. ______________
Initials ______ Date ____/____/____
Room No. ______________

Project Record

Project Control Book Form 742R

page ____ of ____

Location Key ____________ **Tag #** ______
Mfr ______________
Mfr # ______________
Name ______________
Color ______________

Dimensions ______________ Qty ______

Location Key ____________ **Tag #** ______
Mfr ______________
Mfr # ______________
Name ______________
Color ______________

Dimensions ______________ Qty ______

Project ______________

Project No. ______________

Initials ______ Date ___/___/___

Room No. ______________

Project Record

Project Control Book Form 745R

page ____ of ____

Location Key ____________ Tag # ______
Mfr ______________
Mfr # ______________
Name ______________
Color ______________
Dimensions ______ Qty ______

Location Key ____________ Tag # ______
Mfr ______________
Mfr # ______________
Name ______________
Color ______________
Dimensions ______ Qty ______

Location Key ____________ Tag # ______
Mfr ______________
Mfr # ______________
Name ______________
Color ______________
Dimensions ______ Qty ______

Location Key ____________ Tag # ______
Mfr ______________
Mfr # ______________
Name ______________
Color ______________
Dimensions ______ Qty ______

Location Key ____________ Tag # ______
Mfr ______________
Mfr # ______________
Name ______________
Color ______________
Dimensions ______ Qty ______

Initials ______ Date ____/____/____

Phase 8: Bidding, Negotiations and Contract Award

Project Control Book Form 800C

Operational Definition:

All tasks and services which relate to the preparation and receipt of bids through contract award.

Critical Issues

☐ **Be the Client's Representative**
Remember that the contract is between client and contractor. The designer acts as client's representative only, informing the client of the pros and cons related to major decisions and advising them accordingly. Final decision making authority must remain with the client.

☐ **Keep Budget and Project Scope in Balance**
As soon as a client decides to alter the project's scope the budget should be adjusted accordingly and the client informed of the implications of his/her decision.

☐ **Organize the Bid Process**
Bidding is time-consuming and expensive. It involves extensive preparation time and complicated evaluation of bids. An organized bidding process includes all documentation, drawings, notices, bid submissions, inquiries and communications. Organization increases efficiency, reduces mistakes, and protects against future disputes.

☐ **Uphold the Quality of Design**
Be prepared to wage a polite war to uphold the level of quality you specify in the contract documents.

☐ **Be Fair and Ethical**
Complete confidentiality and fairness is essential in dealing with bidders and vendors.

☐ **Require a Standard Bid Proposal**
In the bidding instructions, spell out how bids should be submitted to insure a standard form to make bid comparison easier. Research clauses required by client's policies such as equal opportunity issues, bid bonds, or standard procedures and properly include them in the package.

☐ **Compare Equivalent Services**
The client must be able to judge any differences in services out to bid. If products or services being compared are not equal, the design may suffer. Verify ambiguities in bid price and substitutions. Clear, careful analysis of all facts and discrepancies during this process makes comparison and awarding the contract objective and fair.

☐ **Check References**
Award contracts only to suppliers who have a verifiable record of successful performance. Check bidders' business solvency and confirm that the bidder carries the proper types and amount of insurance required on the project.

Project ____________________

Project No. ____________________

Initials ______ Date ___/___/___

Bid Budget Comparison

Project Control Book Form 820W

page ____ of ____

Bidder A:

Firm

Contact

Comments

Bidder B:

Firm

Contact

Comments

Bidder C:

Firm

Contact

Comments

Bidder D:

Firm

Contact

Comments

Bid Item/# *denotes alternate	A	B	C	D
	$	$	$	$
	$	$	$	$
	$	$	$	$
	$	$	$	$
	$	$	$	$
	$	$	$	$
	$	$	$	$
	$	$	$	$
	$	$	$	$
	$	$	$	$
	$	$	$	$
	$	$	$	$
	$	$	$	$
	$	$	$	$
	$	$	$	$
	$	$	$	$
	$	$	$	$
	$	$	$	$
	$	$	$	$
	$	$	$	$
	$	$	$	$
	$	$	$	$
	$	$	$	$
	$	$	$	$
	$	$	$	$
	$	$	$	$
	$	$	$	$
	$	$	$	$
	$	$	$	$
	$	$	$	$
	$	$	$	$

Initials ______ Date ___/___/___

Phase 9: Contract Administration

Project Control Book Form 900C

Operational Definition:

All tasks and services required to ensure proper administering of the construction contract through project installation and move-in.

Critical Issues

☐ **Be the Client's Representative**
Act as the agent for the client during contract administration. Remember that the contract is between the client and the contractor. Keep the client abreast of the project progress with regular contact. Set a time for a regularly scheduled update.

☐ **Establish a Team Approach with Contractors**
The overall project should be explained to contractors and crafts people so they know where they fit into the process. Outline critical quality issues and design intent. Approach problems as a team member rather than as "the enemy". This will establish a spirit of cooperation and pride in the work being done.

☐ **Supervise Progress**
Regular site visits should be scheduled, but need not be exhaustive in number. Check work in progress as well as upon completion. Let contractors know that you are available for questions at any time. This will prevent lost time on the project.

☐ **Confirm Permits**
Verify that the proper permits were obtained by the contractor, however, the responsibility of obtaining them should be with the contractor.

☐ **Document all Formal and Informal Communication**
Change orders, addenda, substitutions, and meeting minutes must be completely and accurately documented. Distribute copies of documents to all parties.

☐ **Outline Responsibilities**
Meetings between parties involved in the project should outline action to be taken to remedy problems, who will be responsible for the action, and when it is expected to be completed.

☐ **Inspect Merchandise**
When any merchandise arrives at the warehouse, inspect it thoroughly to verify proper merchandise before it arrives at the site.

☐ **Document Condition upon Arrival**
Note the exact condition of items as they are delivered. This will prevent the designer from being blamed for damage which occurred during delivery.

☐ **Prepare a Maintenance Manual**
Give the client all the materials and information needed to maintain the space properly in an organized manual.

Initials ______ Date ___/___/___

Phase 9:
Contract Administration

Project Control Book Form 900C

- ☐ **Inform Users**
  Users of the space should be oriented to the controllable features of their work place and use of the space. Furniture and equipment features should be explained and demonstrated.

- ☐ ______________________________

- ☐ ______________________________

- ☐ ______________________________

Project ____________________

Project No. ____________________

Initials ______ Date ___/___/___

Sketch Log • 1/4"

Project Control Book Form 910R

page ____ of ____

Sketch No:

Drawn by: *Approved by:* *Date:*

Scale:

Project ______________________

Project No. ______________________

Initials ______ *Date* ___/___/___

Field Inspection Report

Project Control Book Form 920R

page ____ *of* ____

Report No: ______________

Date: ____/____/____

Location: ______________

Floor: ______________

Room No: ______________

Send Copies To: cc√

.... ☐

.... ☐

.... ☐

.... ☐

.... ☐

.... ☐

.... ☐

Contractors present at site:

....

....

....

....

....

....

....

....

....

....

....

....

....

....

....

Item	% Complete	Comments

Project ______________________

Project No. ______________________

Initials ________ *Date* ___/___/___

Punch List

Project Control Book Form 950R

page ____ *of* ____

Report No: ______________

Date: ____/____/____

Prepared by: ______________

Send Copies to: **cc√**

.... ☐

.... ☐

.... ☐

.... ☐

.... ☐

Location	Item	Deficiencies	% Complete	Action

Initials ______ Date ____/____/____

Phase 10: Evaluation

Project Control Book Form 1000C

Operational Definition:

Typically, post-contract tasks and services which help determine the specific successes and failures of both the design process and final design product. This phase represents the learning feedback loop in the design process.

Critical Issues

- ☐ **Determine Occupant Satisfaction**
  Inquire from the users regarding their level of satisfaction with the facility. Dissatisfaction may cause reduced productivity and efficiency. Problems may be alleviated with slight adjustments.

- ☐ **Determine Client Satisfaction**
  Find out if the client's expectations were met on the project. Determine how your service was perceived and if you will receive referrals from this client.

- ☐ **Document the Project Now**
  Photograph the installation as soon as possible after completion to avoid the signs of daily wear and tear. Consider photographing all in-process and developmental work, from conceptual through presentation drawings, to ensure complete documentation for future reference.

- ☐ **Timing is Important**
  Wait to evaluate a minimum of six weeks, and a maximum of six months so that the client has "lived" with the design for some time. Track changes or modifications to the solutions which may reveal new programming insights.

- ☐ **Check Accuracy of Work and Budget Estimates**
  Throughout the project, estimates were made regarding time and budget. After the project is completed, check to see how close the estimates came, and where problems occurred.

- ☐ **Maintain Objectivity During Evaluation**
  A lack of objectivity can prevent you from obtaining valuable feedback which could improve your future practice. Consider developing a systematic format for assessing success. If done regularly and consistently, evaluation can be a powerful marketing tool.

- ☐ **Evaluate both Process and Product**
  Assess the project comprehensively, including issues of design process as well as quality of final product. Evaluate how well personal and professional goals were achieved in addition to the client's goals for the project.

- ☐ **Determine Future Marketing Directions**
  After a new project type is undertaken, and the overall success evaluated, determine what new marketing strategies can be employed as a result of this project.

- ☐ ____
  ____
  ____
  ____

Project ______________________

Project No. ______________________

Initials ________ Date ____/____/____

Project Retrospective • Financial

Project Control Book Form 1010W

	Hours Budgeted	Actual	Variance +/-	$ Labor Budgeted	Actual	Variance +/-
PROGRAMMING						
Strategy Session	................./	________	________hrs	................./	________	$________
Interviews & Activity Analysis	................./	________	________hrs	................./	________	$________
Inventory Existing Conditions	................./	________	________hrs	................./	________	$________
Base Drawings	................./	________	________hrs	................./	________	$________
Code Review	................./	________	________hrs	................./	________	$________
Analyze/Synthesize Information	................./	________	________hrs	................./	________	$________
Program Draft	................./	________	________hrs	................./	________	$________
Client Review	................./	________	________hrs	................./	________	$________
Revisions	................./	________	________hrs	................./	________	$________
Program Document Sign-off	................./	________	________hrs	................./	________	$________
		Subtotal =	________**hrs**		**Subtotal =**	**$**________
SCHEMATIC DESIGN						
Concept Development	................./	________	________hrs	................./	________	$________
Review Alternative Approaches	................./	________	________hrs	................./	________	$________
Revisions	................./	________	________hrs	................./	________	$________
Conceptual Design Sign-off	................./	________	________hrs	................./	________	$________
Space Allocation/Utilization Plans	................./	________	________hrs	................./	________	$________
Refine FF&E Selections	................./	________	________hrs	................./	________	$________
Custom Items Development	................./	________	________hrs	................./	________	$________
Preliminary Costing	................./	________	________hrs	................./	________	$________
Schematic Design Presentation	................./	________	________hrs	................./	________	$________
Revisions	................./	________	________hrs	................./	________	$________
Schematic Design Sign-off	................./	________	________hrs	................./	________	$________
		Subtotal =	________**hrs**		**Subtotal =**	**$**________
DESIGN DEVELOPMENT						
Refine Plans and Selections	................./	________	________hrs	................./	________	$________
Detailing and Custom Items	................./	________	________hrs	................./	________	$________
Verify Code Compliance	................./	________	________hrs	................./	________	$________
Cost Estimates	................./	________	________hrs	................./	________	$________
Design Development Presentation	................./	________	________hrs	................./	________	$________
Revisions	................./	________	________hrs	................./	________	$________
Design Development Sign-off	................./	________	________hrs	................./	________	$________
		Subtotal =	________**hrs**		**Subtotal =**	**$**________
CONTRACT DOCUMENTS						
Working Drawings & Documents	................./	________	________hrs	................./	________	$________
Specifications	................./	________	________hrs	................./	________	$________
Verify Code Compliance	................./	________	________hrs	................./	________	$________
Bid Package Sign-off	................./	________	________hrs	................./	________	$________
Code Review	................./	________	________hrs	................./	________	$________
Bid Analysis	................./	________	________hrs	................./	________	$________
Contract Award	................./	________	________hrs	................./	________	$________
		Subtotal =	________**hrs**		**Subtotal =**	**$**________

Project ____________

Project No. ____________

Initials ______ Date ___/___/___

Project Retrospective • Financial

Project Control Book Form 1010W

CONTRACT ADMINISTRATION	Hours Budgeted / Actual	Variance +/-	$ Labor Budgeted / Actual	Variance +/-
Contractor Coordination	........../____	____hrs	........../____	$____
Purchase Order Tracking	........../____	____hrs	........../____	$____
Site Visitation	........../____	____hrs	........../____	$____
Authorization of Payment	........../____	____hrs	........../____	$____
Code Review	........../____	____hrs	........../____	$____
FF&E Inspection	........../____	____hrs	........../____	$____
Approval of Contractor Submittals	........../____	____hrs	........../____	$____
Change Orders	........../____	____hrs	........../____	$____
Move-In, Punch List, Close-out	........../____	____hrs	........../____	$____
	Subtotal =	____hrs	Subtotal =	$____

EVALUATION	Hours Budgeted / Actual	Variance +/-	$ Labor Budgeted / Actual	Variance +/-
....	........../____	____hrs	........../____	$____
....	........../____	____hrs	........../____	$____
....	........../____	____hrs	........../____	$____
....	........../____	____hrs	........../____	$____
....	........../____	____hrs	........../____	$____
....	........../____	____hrs	........../____	$____
....	........../____	____hrs	........../____	$____
	Subtotal =	____hrs	Subtotal =	$____
	Total =	____hrs	Total =	$____

IV. SPECIALTY DESIGN AREAS

Residential Design

JACK LOWERY

Residential design deals, in almost every instance, with that most sacrosanct of environments: the home. Solutions for the arrangement of, and appointments for, a person's dwelling are governed by many factors. Some of these factors may not necessarily have to do with good design or suitable function. Joan Kron in her book *Home-Psych: The Social Psychology of Home and Decoration* calls the word home "four economical letters that combine to form one of our most enduring symbols, signifying safety and familiarity and love."[1] Witold Rybezynski in *Home, A Short History of an Idea* states, "Domestic well being is a fundamental human need that is deeply rooted in us, and that must be satisfied."[2]

Residential design is just that, the design of spaces for living, eating, sleeping, relaxing, obtaining privacy, and performing other desirable activities. The interior designer who embarks on the shaping of interior space to meet the needs of other human beings must perform several duties at once, including those of a social observer, a psychologist, a cultural arbiter, a sympathetic observer, an artist, a historian, a space and function analyst, and perhaps a fortune teller. At the same time this person must be an organizer, a bookkeeper, and a general factotum who provides creative solutions for residential environments.

DISTINCTIVE CHARACTERISTICS OF RESIDENTIAL DESIGN

What makes residential design distinctive from other interior design specialty areas? When this question was posed to practicing residential designers,[3] the following comments were offered:

> *. . . the residential interior designer works directly with the client. . . . in a unique one-on-one situation, . . . playing a great role in changing the client's life for better or worse. The project must be taken in hand and thought about intellectually first and emotionally second. . . . Indecision is the most destructive word associated with residential interior design; it destroys the clients, and finally the designer's ability to make it all work.*
>
> Mario Buatta, ASID

> *A designer must be able to listen carefully to his clients' requests and then be able to provide a space that captures the clients' needs in a functional, as well as aesthetic, manner. In many cases, this means helping a couple or family communicate with one another.*
>
> Charles D. Gandy, FASID

> *One needs to be able to interpret what the client doesn't know he or she wants.*
>
> Barbara Jacobs, ASID

> *The interior designer must know how to probe without prying.*
>
> Penny Bonda, ASID

One distinctive characteristic of residential design is that many specifications are contingent upon the desires of the client. There is an intimate participation in the project that is absent from most other design projects. This is not a detrimental factor, but it demands that the designer pay close attention to the client's desires. Testimony to this distinct characteristic of residential design is given in the following comments from professional residential designers.

> *Residential design . . . is a highly personal process where the client often makes decisions based on feelings rather than fact. . . .*
>
> Barbara Jacobs, ASID

> *Clients invest more of themselves—of their hearts, minds, and souls—in the design of their residences.*
>
> Penny Bonda, ASID

> *Probably the most distinctive skill a residential designer needs is the ability to listen . . . to sometimes act the part of psychologist.*
>
> Michael de Santis, ASID

TYPES OF PROJECTS

Residential projects include the design of single and attached houses, apartments, lofts, vacation homes, guest quarters, mobile homes, houseboats, yachts, hotel suites, dormitories, hospices, retirement dwellings, camps, barracks, and even prisons.

Clients today range from married couples with children to single persons, unmarried partners, couples of the same or opposite sex, single parents with children, couples with children from more than one marriage, and multigenerational families—to name only a few.

Residential environments mean different things to different people—from citadels that provide privacy and a haven from an often hostile, complex, and competitive world, to a showcase for a lifestyle that is to be shared with outsiders. Whatever the desired function and attributes, a residence should sustain its occupants and inspire them in the pursuit of their lives.

CREATING A RESIDENTIAL DESIGN

To begin the process of creating a residential design, the designer must first establish communication with those who will occupy the residence and attempt to assess the expectations of those occupants. This means a determination of their real and perceived needs and their resources. This includes the money they have to spend, their possessions, experiences, social aspirations, cultural heritage, and lifestyle orientations.

How does a residential designer establish open communication and interchange with clients? According to the following residential designers, confidence, trust, and tact are key factors in this process.

> *I have always thought that residential designers must be part philosopher, part psychologist, part personal planner, and part practical advisor. Tact in projecting design elements, consideration of budget limitations, and planning to meet clients' schedules play a large part in bringing a project to successful conclusion.*
>
> James Merrick Smith, FASID

> *Your clients must be very confident and trusting. This is the most important element for you to achieve if you are to create a wonderful interior for someone else to live in."*
>
> George Constant, ASID

RESIDENTIAL PLAN DEVELOPMENT

Stanley Abercrombie in *A Philosophy of Interior Design*[4] notes that a designer's plan must be based upon two considerations: 1) the determination of limits and 2) the function.

Determination of Limits

The limits are established by the building shell, the character of its structure, and the time and funds with which the designer must work. Accurate plans must precede space and traffic planning and must include indications of structural columns, mechanical systems, and plumbing lines that may or may not be diverted. The site, the approach, and possible entrances and exits must be determined and analyzed.

Function

The determination of function depends on the ability of the designer and the client working together to identify the uses and characteristics of the spaces to be included in the design package. The designer must utilize experience, insight, and technical skill in the translation of these into spaces defined by interior architecture, furnishings, and accoutrements that physically and psychologically support the lifestyle of the inhabitants.

Because of these very personal requisites, and the extreme diversity of people and their individual needs, the residential designer must have a design repertoire of impressive range. Abilities in human relations and communications, a strong foundation in human engineering, and an extensive knowledge of available furniture, fabrics, and accessories is essential.

NECESSARY SKILLS FOR RESIDENTIAL DESIGNERS

Specific skills are required to practice residential design. Professional residential designers responding to the question, "What are the necessary skills needed to practice residential design?" offered the following observations:

> *Probably the most important skill is clairvoyance. How often clients are completely dishonest about what they really want or need! How often they cannot express themselves! By dishonest I mean by saying they want this year's fad or trend when in reality they cannot stand it, but only want it as a status symbol.*
>
> Rubén de Saavedra, ASID

> *. . . the residential designer has to address the personal and perhaps very peculiar needs and preferences of clients. After all, you get into their bedrooms, their bathrooms, their refrigerators, and their closets. When the relationship is a good one, such familiarity breeds trust.*
>
> Joan Lerner, ASID

> *Clients have a very hard time turning their lives over to you . . . to allow you to really do the job.*
>
> George Constant, ASID

> *Unique problems run the gamut from dealing with household staffs who resent the intrusion into "their world," to coping with sensitive clients whose personal lives are so intermingled with their interiors that they cannot "let go" and let their designer assist them.*
>
> Charles D. Gandy, FASID

A residence today incorporates mechanical systems of considerable complexity, including systems for air conditioning, communication, entertainment, heating, maintenance, and security. Bathrooms and kitchens must incorporate state-of-the-art components. The designer of these spaces must have the same full spectrum of skills required for any of the various specialities of the design profession, plus a number of additional ones that are particular to the residential environment.

The skills required to design and implement a home environment are equal to those required of other types of interior spaces. The difference is that these skills are observed and evaluated within the intimate confines of the residence by the occupant—who is usually also the client.

The designer must know and recognize excellence and be able to guide and inspire the craftspeople and workers doing the work. This is an essential component of a successful residential practice.

Attention to Detail

A residential designer must be extremely sensitive to detail. This sensitivity manifests itself in several different ways. When interviewed, residential designers offered the following observations relative to the importance of attention to detail.

> *. . . in regard to the execution of the job, the designer must have an eagle eye for detail and accuracy. The workmanship must be the best and done in the authentic style.*
>
> Rubén de Saavedra, ASID

> *. . . A sense of scale that is appropriate not only to the room and its architecture, but also to the client [is essential].*
>
> Sharon Chatham, ASID

Specific areas where attention to detail are extremely important include the following:

- *Painting and finishing.* A residential designer must have a working knowledge of finishes, surface characteristics, glazes, textures, and "effects" for ceilings, walls, floors, furniture, and cabinetry.

- *Use of materials.* A residential designer needs to understand the appropriate details to use with materials like marble, glass and mirrors, aluminum, wrought iron, wood, laminates, cork, leather, and fabrics on walls, ceilings, and floors.

- *Upholstery and fabrics.* Knowledge of upholstery and fabric selection appropriate to the piece or application, and an understanding of its maintenance and care, are critical for the residential designer. Color, pattern, texture, and character must be considered before selections are made.

- *Cabinetry.* A residential designer must understand how to design furniture and enclosure features so that they satisfy the needs of the client and the character of the interior environment. In residential design these can become very specific and very complex.

- *Furniture and accessories.* A working knowledge of furniture and accessories in order to satisfy a wide spectrum of styles, historic periods, contemporary classics, and specialty items is essential for a residential designer. Quality of construction; means of maintenance; and appropriateness of scale, form, and design are all important considerations. The residential designer needs a far greater understanding of furniture and accessory possibilities than any other design specialist and must know sources, values, and correct characteristics of all items.

- *Knowledge of history.* The residential designer should possess an understanding of historic furniture styles, details, and characteristics. This is important to guarantee that selections and specifications deal with the appropriate historical antecedents. Since the residential designer often advises the client, the more extensive his or her knowledge of the accoutrements of a residence, the more substantive will be the designer's role as provocateur in the assemblage of the appointments of a home.

It is impossible to be expert in all subjects. For this reason the residential designer must have reliable sources and outside specialists who provide consultation to best meet the client's diversified needs. Additionally, the residential designer must be flexible and willing to work with the client. The importance of reliable services, outside specialists, and a designer's ability to be flexible is reinforced by the following statements from residential designers.

> *A successful residential interior designer should be versatile. The designer might not want to live with every style, but should be able to work and be conversant with all the styles.*
>
> Rubén de Saavedra, ASID

> *[The designer needs] contact with special sources to do unusual custom work, as well as good knowledge of lighting design and of special materials and cabinetwork detail. A well-designed residence can be more fun and more satisfying than the routine contract job.*
>
> Eve Frankl, ASID

Other Necessary Skills

In other designed spaces one makes decisions based on general use, reasonable maintenance, flexibility, accessibility, and durability of the products specified. In a residence, the client sets the criteria. It behooves the designer to inform the client of these basic design considerations; however, it is very possible that the residential client will want fabrics that are vulnerable, will request cabinetry that is highly individual, use materials that may have very personal appeal, or ask for interior details that will not have future market appeal. This is the client's prerogative and a specific characteristic of residential design.

Specific things that may appeal to a residential client include craft items, artwork, and unusual lighting treatments.

- *Craft items and commissioned artwork.* Inclusion of one-of-a-kind decorative pieces and custom-designed features by artists and artisans enlarges the decorative interest in a home and ensures individuality and originality. Murals, carpets, wall hangings, dividers, furnishings, accessories, lighting fixtures, and architectural features such as railings, grilles, and insets are all concerns of the residential designer.

- *Lighting.* The ability to design for the most appropriate lighting solutions in a home environment calls upon the residential designer's knowledge and skill. Clients should have dimming capabilities and switching control in locations most appropriate to their needs. The lighting itself can be as specific and eccentric as the client's expectations.

EDUCATION

As noted earlier, the residential interior designer is greatly aided by a thorough knowledge of period and contemporary design, of craft skills, and of appropriate details for residential components. Educational curricula provide this foundation upon which the designer builds. A young designer specializing in residential interior design should work in a residential design office. This provides an environment for learning, where a young designer can be closely involved in every aspect of the process—including shopping, specifying, working with suppliers, detailing, installing, bookkeeping, quality control, correcting mistakes, and so on. The school of real-life experience is the most instructive mechanism for advancement in the field of residential design.

Because the success of residential projects is often the result of the bond and camaraderie between the designer and the client, it is essential that a designer develop a facility for human relations. This includes the ability to listen, empathize, inspire, and provide leadership. This human interchange and sense of mutual understanding and trust is essential to all designer/client relationships. For the residential designer, it is the most intense and most direct. There is no school for this. The rapport—the symbiosis—must be genuine and sincere. The following comments by residential designers reinforce this concept and delineate the educational requirements seen as necessary to successful practice in the field.

> *Comfort, individual taste, personal habits, a place for family relationships, and a retreat from public pressures are factors in establishing residential harmony and practical functioning.*
>
> James Merrick Smith, FASID

> *I would recommend studies in sociology and psychology. Tact and a perceptive intuition are very important also.*
>
> Sharon Chatham, ASID

> *A sense of humor!! Very important. Also . . . schooling at an accredited design school, and at least five years of internship with a designer whose work you really admire.*
>
> Mario Buatta, ASID

> *[A designer should be] passionate about designing, and full of innovative ideas, always reading and researching the market, responsible, available, curious, convincing, a good listener, patient, detail-oriented, truthful, and wise.*
>
> Joan Lerner, ASID

BUSINESS AND PROJECT MANAGEMENT IN RESIDENTIAL DESIGN

By its very nature, the relationship between the client and the residential designer makes it imperative that business matters and the day-to-day progress of the residential project be very clear. It is the designer's responsibility to act as interpreter and liaison between the client and the various trade sources and business practices that are encountered on a residential assignment.

From the outset, the client must fully understand the costs, necessary deposits, terms of payment, delivery times, factors that may cause delays, and the designer's method of charging. These factors should be conscientiously delineated in writing as well as carefully explained. The relationship between the client and residential designer can be a very strong and satisfying one because of the intimate nature of designing a home; however, nothing is more fragile when misunderstandings result because of careless concern for the business and the financial side of the project.

The designer must keep in touch with the trade sources and contractors with regard to the project's progress. These contacts should be well documented, and the client should be constantly apprised of the project's status. It is important to make personal contact with the client regarding urgent or possibly disappointing matters, such as delays or the unavailability of items ordered. The communication should be done in writing accompanied by a verbal explanation. The client will respect the responsible attitude of a designer who is alert to problems and willing to share them with the client.

Documentation and recordkeeping are essentials in any design practice. These provide valuable reference material for future projects as well as a legal documentation of the processes used throughout the project's duration.

CONCLUSION

Residential design is an exciting and unique specialty area of the interior design profession. It challenges the designer to creatively fulfill clients' needs for their most personal environment—their living space.

Office Design

PETER B. BRANDT

Times have changed since the days when Bob Cratchit sat on his tall clerk's stool in the offices of Scrooge and Marley. Today most people spend more time in an office than in any other location outside the home. The white-collar office workforce includes more than 50 percent of all workers, and the numbers are increasing dramatically. Instead of a quill pen and inkwell, office workers use computers, and instead of a lump of coal for heat and a half-day holiday at Christmas, office workers expect a wide range of benefits, including a well-designed, comfortable, and safe office environment.

The field of office design deals with some of the most basic problems of human life and offers significant challenges to the interior designer. At issue is the nature of work, communication, privacy, flexibility, and comfort. Much has already been done. The modern office is one of the extraordinary accomplishments of this century. Chief elements of this accomplishment include:

- Lightweight interior construction systems that are high in quality, flexible, relatively inexpensive, and quick to build.
- Workstation systems that provide privacy, the use of vertical space, usage flexibility, and configuration variety.
- Heating, ventilating, and air conditioning systems that provide a high level of comfort for office workers.
- Expanded capacity to process information through computer technology.
- The high-rise office building itself, which has become the single most prominent symbol of modern urban life.

The office exists to process information. Information is generated, received, computed, analyzed, communicated, and stored. Decisions are then made on the basis of this information, decisions that affect all aspects of life. The purpose of office design is to provide an atmosphere conducive to maximum productivity, worker satisfaction, and morale—that is, to maximize the quality and amount of information being processed.

INTERIOR VERSUS EXTERIOR OFFICE DESIGN

From a design and construction standpoint, an office is composed of a base building and an interior. The base building/core and shell are designed by an architect for a developer or corporate owner. This consists of the structure, exterior walls, windows, roof, basic mechanical and electrical systems, and a core of elevators, stairs, and toilet rooms.

The office interior, sometimes referred to as tenant improvements or tenant work, includes the interior partitions and doors, ceilings, lighting, mechanical and electrical distribution, finishes, furnishings, and equipment. While the base building is expected to have a useful life of 50 to 100 years or more, office interiors often last no more than ten years. This is not because of physical deterioration but because organizational and technological change makes the facilities obsolete.

DESIGN SERVICES

There are many types of professional services and many ways to structure a contract for office projects. Three of the most common are office planning and design services, tenant development services, and facility management services.

Office Planning and Design Services

The client for traditional office planning and design services is the organization that will occupy the new office space. Projects generally follow the sequence of programming, schematic design, design development, contract documentation, and contract administration.

Tenant Development Services

Building owners often retain the services of a design firm to assist the leasing effort by providing tenant development services. These include preliminary space planning for prospective tenants, preparation of standards for public areas, development of building standard construction details, preparation of building standard construction documents for tenants, and assisting the tenant with the implementation of the construction and move-in process.

Tenant development work requires a design professional with marketing talent, space planning ability, and good management skills. Time is of the essence in tenant development work. Fees are paid by the building owner, generally on a square foot or hourly basis. Some design professionals believe that tenant development work opens the door to prospective clients for full-service office design work. Others believe that the association with the building owner creates a conflict of interest.

Facilities Management Services

These services involve an ongoing relationship with a client for implementing office space changes. The work may begin with a full-service design project or with a contract to develop corporate design and furnishings standards. The work may involve long- and short-term projections of space needs; the inventory of space and furnishings; and the space planning, documentation; and administration of remodeling projects.

Facilities management services require a logical, systematic approach and the ability to manage many different and overlapping activities at once. The interior designer must be able to maintain the quality of design and furnishings while being responsive to a myriad of challenges. Fees for facility management work are paid in a variety of ways, including an hourly basis, an hourly basis with a maximum, and a fixed-fee basis for a specific scope of work.

NECESSARY SKILLS AND EDUCATION

Success in office design requires extensive knowledge and skill in interior planning and design. Additional skills that may be useful for the practitioner of office design include knowledge of business, finance, and management; a background in sociology; and computer expertise.

Business, Finance, and Management

Education in business, finance, and management provides the design professional with a better understanding of the client's goals and operation, fosters communication on the client's own terms, and assists in dealing with leasing agents, landlords, and contractors.

Sociology Background

Studies in sociology provide the design professional with a background in human needs, motivation, and behavior, which are useful tools for dealing with the questions of productivity, satisfaction, and morale.

Computer Expertise

Computer expertise has two levels for the design professional. The first level deals with an understanding of the best technical environment for a client's computers and a knowledge of the necessary supportive environment for the workforce of the office. The second level is an understanding and knowledge of computer-aided design (CAD), increased productivity, and efficiency in the designer's own studio.

BUSINESS AND PROJECT MANAGEMENT IN OFFICE DESIGN

Besides residential design, office design is probably the most common interior design project undertaken by a design professional. Interior design methods and procedures used in other project types are equally applicable to office design. However, special considerations in office design include client organization, lease implications, corporate standards programs, and base building design.

Client Organization

There is considerable variety in the ways clients organize for an office design project. Generally, however, the three functional groups (or constituencies) that must be satisfied are senior management, facility management, and end users.

Senior management consists of the chief executive officer or a responsible committee of executives. This person or group establishes the overall project goals, approves design, and has ultimate decision-making and cost responsibility.

Facility management includes the client's project manager, who may be the facility manager or office manager, and the other in-house technical personnel who carry responsibility for the project. In large organizations these may include a purchasing agent, a telecommunications expert, and a construction head. These people have day-to-day responsibility for the project including scheduling, budgeting, and administration.

The personnel who will actually occupy the new offices are the end users. They provide the designer with program requirements and functional review of space plans.

Lease Implications

Most office space is in leased facilities. A developer or institutional owner constructs the base building as an investment and leases floors or portions of floors to tenants. The tenant then retains the services of a design professional to plan and design the office space. The design professional is expected to assist the tenant in fulfilling the conditions of the lease workletter. Lease conditions are often strict and may include:

- Dates for submittal of preliminary drawings, submittal of construction documents, and move-in with penalties when dates are missed.
- Restrictions on materials and construction systems.
- Lists of acceptable consultants and contractors.
- Policies and procedures for implementation.

As an inducement to lease, building owners may offer dollar allowances to be applied toward the construction of the new office space or offer to construct building standard improvements at no cost to the tenant. Building standard construction may be defined as the minimum required for the tenant to occupy the space. Typical building standard construction includes:

- Full-height partitions of 2½" metal studs, 5/8" gypsum wall board each side, painted, with resilient base.
- 3'0" x 1¾" x full height (or 7'0") solid-core wood doors, stained veneer (or painted), with hardware.
- Concealed spline (or lay-in) acoustical tile ceiling, typically 8'6" above finished floor.

- Recessed fluorescent fixtures.
- Standard electrical and telephone outlets.
- Heating, ventilating, and air conditioning (HVAC) system.
- Standard draperies (or blinds) at exterior windows. (Because of the exterior appearance of the building, there is usually no option on this item.)
- Allowance for carpeting and resilient flooring.

If the tenant chooses to use other than the building standard for certain items, an additional cost is usually charged. The building standard provides the benchmark against which different materials and systems are evaluated and costed out. Building standard construction does not include decorative or discretionary items such as special ceilings, incandescent lighting, plumbing or computer room HVAC, acoustical partitioning, wallcoverings, cabinetwork, or furnishings.

CORPORATE STANDARDS PROGRAMS

Most large corporate clients have standardized many aspects of office layout and furnishings, such as:

- The allowable square footage for each level of office or open workstation.
- The manufacturer, model numbers, and finish of furnishings items.
- The size and selection of workstation components.
- Cost allowances for construction and furnishings items.

Interior designers may be retained to assist in the development of corporate standards either in the context of a planning and design project or as an independent study. Once these standards have been established, designers are generally required to work within them in the planning and design of office space, although there may be flexibility in modifying or improving the standards.

A formal standards program is appropriate for an organization with a large office facility, many facilities, or facilities in different locations. For such an organization a standards program has many advantages. These include:

- Assured equality of offices and workstations for personnel with similar functions or titles in different departments or locations.
- Minimal inventory and simplified purchasing procedures for frequent changes in layout.
- Predictable cost and square foot data to assist in long-range planning.
- Savings through volume purchasing.
- A standard corporate image in various locations.
- Lower design fees.

Disadvantages of corporate standards programs include:

- Difficulty in implementing, and unsatisfactory results from, poorly organized and incomplete programs.
- Uninteresting standards that produce office space that is boring, bland, and unproductive.
- Bureaucratic rigidity that is resistant to change.

The process used in the establishment of corporate standards is similar to that used in the sizing and selection of furnishings for a specific project. Existing conditions are examined, work flow and functional requirements are determined, costs and availability are analyzed, and the aesthetic possibilities are developed. Because of the potential for a great quantity of items to be purchased over time, however, proportionately greater time and detail are spent on the selection of each item. Universal rather than project-specific solutions are emphasized, and flexibility and long-term maintenance have increased importance.

Base Building Design

Over the years the office building as a building type has developed certain typical design features. Speculative office buildings are designed to appeal to a wide variety of potential office space users and include those features that experience has shown are flexible, cost-effective, and most acceptable to the marketplace. Even buildings designed to be used by their owners, such as corporate headquarters, are generally designed with an eye to possible future sale or lease to other tenants.

Design professionals are often asked by clients to assist in site selection by analyzing competing office buildings for suitability with the client's needs. This work is generally performed as an additional service. Some of the factors to be evaluated include the building module, the core-to-window dimension, the ceiling height, and the building systems and materials.

- *The building module* affects the sizes of offices and corridors and the configuration of ceilings and lighting. The module is defined by the spacing of columns and window mullions. A 4'0" window mullion spacing encourages corridors of 4'0" and room dimensions of 8'0", 12'0", and 16'0". A 5'0" module is more generous, favoring 5'0" corridors and rooms of 10'0", 15'0", and 20'0". A 30'0" column spacing with a 5'0" module would allow for three offices 10'0" wide or two offices 15'0" wide within each bay.
- *Core-to-window dimension*: The desirability of various core-to-window dimensions depends on the client's program. A shallow building with a core-to-window dimension of 25'0" to 40'0" provides a high ratio of exterior window to total floor area and is conducive to executive or professional service office space where private offices at the perimeter are required. A deep building with a core-to-window dimension of 40'0" and higher allows large open work areas and large interior spaces for computer rooms or meeting rooms.
- *Standard ceiling height*: The standard ceiling height from floor slab to finished ceiling affects the appearance of the office space and becomes critical if raised floors are to be part of a design concept. A height of 8'0" is considered minimum. A height of 8'6" is common in first-class high-rise

office buildings, and 9' or higher may be desirable if a raised floor is to be installed by the tenant.

- *Building systems and materials*: Since the cost of base building systems and materials is ultimately passed on to the tenant in rental rates, the highest quality may not be the most cost-effective for the tenant. Items to be evaluated include exterior appearance and detailing, ground floor lobby and elevator graphics and finishes, capacity and quality of mechanical and electrical systems, quality of tenant standard construction, and quality of maintenance.

CHALLENGES FOR THE FUTURE OF OFFICE DESIGN

There are significant opportunities still ahead. Questions to be addressed by the interior design profession in the immediate future include:

- What can be done to make office work more challenging, interesting, and satisfying to the workers?
- How can environments be created that will make computer work more conducive to human comfort and satisfaction—more user-friendly in the broadest sense?
- What steps can be taken to avoid the "sick building" syndrome, to make the office more accessible to the handicapped, to minimize energy use, and to be ecologically sensitive?

The last few decades have seen the office evolve into a sophisticated technical machine for working. The next few decades must deal with human factors that make the office more responsive to human needs.

ORGANIZATIONS FOR OFFICE DESIGNERS

Many office designers find membership in the following organizations helpful in building up a strong practice:

Business and Institutional Furniture
Manufacturers Association (BIFMA)
2335 Burton S.E.
Grand Rapids, MI 49506
616-243-1681

Building Owners and Managers Association (BOMA)
1201 New York Avenue,N.W.
Washington, DC 20005
202-408-2662

International Facility Management Association (IFMA)
1 Greenway Plaza East, 11th Floor
Houston, TX 77046
713-623-4362

Health Care Design

JAIN MALKIN

Twenty years ago, the words "medical" and "design" were rarely used in the same sentence. Today, however, the design of health care facilities represents one of the largest market segments, offering architects and designers a broad spectrum of projects requiring highly developed skills and specialized experience.

KEY ISSUES FOR THE FUTURE

The design of health care facilities for the future will be shaped by a number of key issues such as infection control, reimbursement policies, new technologies, the graying of America, and an attempt to design therapeutic environments that enhance healing. There will be an increased need for highly specialized structures, with an emphasis on ambulatory care.

In the future only critically ill patients will be treated in hospitals; others will be treated in various types of ambulatory care facilities. This change is expected to result in lower health care costs. In order to keep pace with this trend, hospitals are currently constructing large ambulatory services buildings as well as increasing their critical care beds. Expansion of both rehabilitation and mental health services is also prevalent.

COMPETITION FORCES CONCERN FOR IMAGE

Forecasters predict that the future will see the closure of many small community hospitals. Fierce competition with multihospital systems and for-profit chains will result in health care delivery being dominated by a number of large providers. In order to compete effectively for a larger share of the pie, hospitals have become increasingly concerned about the image of their facilities, often spending large sums on interior design and improvements.

These improvements often have a hospitality ambiance. There are a number of parallels between a hospital and a hotel. Both offer lodging, maid service, and meals for guests, who pay for the service. The difference is that people choose to be in a hotel, but they don't choose to be in a hospital. Hospitals are by their very nature associated with pain, sadness, and enforced confinement. This means that designers must use the tools of color and texture to comfort and reassure. While materials such as granite, wood, and etched glass help to create a nonclinical environment, the hospitality approach to health care is largely an attitude about patient care. The focus is placed on patient convenience and satisfaction; the patient is thought of as a guest because guests make choices about where and how to spend their money.

A REDEFINITION OF HOSPITAL/ PATIENT RELATIONSHIP

For years hospitals were run like military ships with considerable emphasis on maintenance and efficiency. Patients had to fit in with the system. Wall surfaces were stripped of embellishment to make them easy to clean. This philosophy went unchallenged until the market-driven 1980s, when hospitals found themselves competing for patients. The legacy of the 1980s for health care delivery is a redefinition of the relationship between hospitals and their patrons.

No longer viewed as a captive market, patients now benefit from hospital staff trained in guest relations and from facilities designed to look like a hotel. This is by no means an attempt to minimize the importance of clinical care or the hospital's investment in high-technology equipment. But in reality few patients are able to assess the quality of the clinical care they receive; they judge a hospital stay by their interactions with staff and by the appearance of the interior environment.

This redefinition of the hospital/patient relationship has created a large market for interior design services. Few hospitals embark upon renovation or new construction without engaging a designer. In fact most hospitals are under construction year-round, renovating one area or another. Many hospitals employ teams of staff architects and construction inspectors to work with outside consultants (architects, engineers, contractors, interior designers) to coordinate their work.

CHALLENGES AND FRUSTRATIONS

The challenges and frustrations of health care design are many, but the rewards are high. Codes with respect to sanitation and fire are very strict, limiting types of allowable materials. Budgets are often slim. New construction requires anywhere from three to five years from schematic design to occupancy, requiring thoroughness and an ability to manage a highly complex project over an extensive period of time. The payoff—seeing the project completed—seems as if it will never arrive.

A major factor in the design of health care facilities is the review and approval of plans by various regulatory agencies. This is partially responsible for the long lead time to complete these projects. No building type is as complex as a hospital; therefore plans and specifications must be highly detailed. Often the work is broken into phases so that construction can take place without interrupting hospital operations. To gain access to certain areas, patients have to be transferred to another location, making the logistics of a major renovation a project manager's nightmare.

It takes many years to gain sufficient experience to understand how to meet the needs of each specific patient population. Designing for hospitalized children is different from designing for psychiatric patients, or for the elderly. This is what makes health care design fascinating and challenging. One must constantly study to understand the design approach needed for new treatment modalities and to incorporate new technology.

TEAMWORK IS IMPORTANT

Health care design requires the ability to work with large groups of people. The interior designer is part of a team of consultants who work closely for a number of years with each other and with a committee of hospital staff representing the owner. Added to that are individual user groups within the hospital whose needs must be met. Last, but certainly not least, are the patients.

MEETING PATIENTS' NEEDS REQUIRES IMAGINATION

Despite the frustrations and challenges of trying to create a noninstitutional environment within code guidelines, the rewards of this type of work are many. Designers have the satisfaction of knowing that many people will benefit from their work. Anyone who has experienced serious illness, faced major surgery, or been challenged by a difficult recuperation can understand the totally devastating psychological effect. A person is rendered suddenly helpless, dependent upon others to meet the most basic needs, perhaps nauseous and dizzy with blurred vision due to medications, and worried about loved ones at home or a lengthy absence from work; individually or together these setbacks create a stunning vulnerability. Add to that unfamiliar surroundings, the loss of privacy when sharing a room with a total stranger, puzzling medical jargon, probing in intimate places by strangers and cold instruments, terrible food, and the isolation of being cut off from everyone and everything you love.

A designer cannot change those conditions, but a harmonious environment in which color, texture, and lighting act to comfort and embrace the patient can be created. It's a fact that color and lighting influence feelings of well-being. Visually stimulating environments reduce feelings of isolation and boredom. Artwork can do much to alleviate stark corridors and can provoke memories of pleasant experiences shared with family and friends. Attractive furniture designed for rehabilitation can restore some of the patient's independence. The patient's room can be designed to preserve privacy and dignity. Carpeting, wood detailing, residential-type lighting, comfortable furnishings can all contribute to a therapeutic environment that supports healing.

In no other field can an interior designer play such a vital and ultimately rewarding role in having a positive effect on people's lives when they are at their most vulnerable. This is a great challenge for the health care designer, but the rewards are well worth the effort.

Health Care Design

JIM SEEKS

What must be included in the interior design of a hospital? To help understand the complexity of a hospital design project, a clear definition is necessary. The American Hospital Association defines hospital as a health care institution with an organized medical and professional staff and with inpatient beds available round-the-clock, whose primary function is to provide inpatient medical, nursing, and other health-related services to patients for both surgical and nonsurgical conditions, and that usually provides some outpatient services, particularly emergency care. For licensure purposes, each state has its own definition of hospital. This broad-based definition includes facilities that treat mental health, physical health, and substance abuse, as well as facilities for the elderly.

What will be the future of health care design? Hospitals of the future will continue to be built as the population increases. For the interior designer, the majority of work will consist of minor to major renovations of existing facilities and projects that combine new construction with renovation. There will be a continuing need for acute-care inpatient services; in addition, the ancillary and ambulatory services offered by hospitals will continue to change to keep pace with medical and technological advances.

CHALLENGES AND CONSTRAINTS TO ANTICIPATE IN HOSPITAL DESIGN

Certain aspects of hospital design are unique to this area of the design field. The designer should be well aware of the following types of challenges.

Minimizing Visual Clutter

A confusing array of medical and nonmedical paraphernalia such as instruments, equipment, corner guards, handrails, and bumper guards clutter almost every patient care area in a health care institution. This jumble creates visual chaos in an environment already laden with anxiety for the patient. One of the interior designer's most significant challenges is to provide a soothing patient environment by conquering the clutter. Some of the most successful projects are those in which the finishes and colors of door frames, corner and bumper guards, armor plating, grilles and diffusers, pass-thru cabinets, fire hose cabinets, medical cabinetry, and signage elements are successfully blended with the surrounding surfaces.

Taking the time to organize wall-mounted mechanical/electrical cover plates and medical valve and gauge plates pays dividends in reducing the cluttered look. In renovation work, the demolition plans should include the removal of all such abandoned items. If time is spent in minimizing such negative elements, the interior architectural finishes chosen by the designer stand a better chance of gaining the desired visual impact.

Designing in the Fourth Dimension

Interior designers and sculptors have in common the fact that the medium they work in is three-dimensional and possesses a static quality. As with a sculpture, interior space remains in a dormant state until there is some interaction with the viewer or occupant/user. When designers or sculptors move from the third to the fourth dimension, they add sensory elements to the assemblage of inanimate objects and materials.

Health care interiors can also be elevated to a fourth dimension. This change in attitude concerning the designer's role requires that the designer and client approach the planning and design of projects in an expansive, open-minded way.

Take for example, a burn center facility. Many severely burned patients lie in their beds and are able to move only their fingers and toes without experiencing excruciating pain. As a result of a designer's concern and empathy for patients in a recent design project for this type of center, patients' televisions were mounted on a moveable track to allow omnidirectional positioning. The patients could then see the screen from appropriate angles depending on their immobile positions in bed. A small remote control device that could be manipulated by hands or feet was developed, allowing the patients to determine which movies they wanted to watch, or which video games to play with other patients, or to compose messages which could be printed. This concept created a space with a higher level of design consciousness, or the fourth dimension. It provided an integrated environment to assist patients in interacting with their surroundings, thereby allowing them to focus on something other than their painful conditions.

Lighting Design

As hospitals increasingly demand the hotel look in their public and patient care areas, the demand for creative lighting solutions will increase. It is important for designers to develop design solutions that move beyond the common use of the decorative wall sconce or coved ambient lighting effects.

Although such lighting solutions can achieve important residential ambiance, designers should provide creative solutions to the quality of lighting in the patient rooms and treatment areas. Moving beyond the public areas to impact the patient areas directly should be a designer's goal.

Incorporation of Art

The designer is in a position to offer many opportunities for art to be incorporated into hospital facilities. Many times overall project budgets are not sufficient, or artwork is cut to meet a more pressing need for hospital equipment. An art program should be treated by the designer and the hospital administration as a stand-alone program, not tied to specific renovation or new construction projects. The designer can be hired on a consultant basis to establish a plan of action for a continuing art program maintained by a staff person and/or volunteers. This approach takes time but, in many cases, will allow more opportunities for art to be incorporated.

Functional Space Planning

There are several important functional considerations in health care design. Among these are the following:

- *Waiting and lounge areas*: Furnishing arrangements in waiting and lounge areas need to be thoughtfully considered by the designer. For example, inclusion of open locations where people in wheelchairs can be comfortably moved and situated is an important consideration.

- *Patient rooms*: In patient rooms (especially in maternity units), there should be ample space for display of flower arrangements. This may seem like a minor point; however, if plants and flowers clutter every surface, the medical staff's ability to perform in an emergency situation may be hampered.

- *Entries*: In hospital entry lobbies, there is typically a need to design in a holding area for wheelchairs to assist people at the front door as they enter or leave the facility.

- *Trash areas*: It is important to provide ample space for trash receptacles in all lounge and waiting areas. Trash should be sensitively treated and unobstructive to those waiting.

- *Areas for children*: Children are many times confined to the lounge and waiting areas in health care facilities. Their needs and interests should be accommodated.

- *Overnight accommodations*: Especially in hospitals serving rural areas, relatives of patients may refuse to leave the facility and insist on remaining overnight. If the needs of such visitors are not addressed, individuals may be found sleeping in very inappropriate areas.

THE INTERIOR DESIGN MASTER PLAN

When working with a master plan, designers and administrators should proceed slowly and address specific concerns early in the design process. When an owner decides to embark on the development of a master plan, it should be clear that this will serve as a guide for a specific time frame.

Determining a master plan for a stand-alone building is a simpler process than developing a master plan for a complex campus situation where common denominators and acceptable variations must be established between buildings of different vintages. Regardless of the situation, it is essential that a master plan determine the type of area and identify which departments fit and which do not. If the plan is intended to have a working life beyond five years, then the plan should specify alternate product selections for the life of the program. Owners need to be told by the designer—up front—that product changes will be inevitable. The designer should suggest a plan to include updated patterns, textures, and colors that can be successfully integrated with the currently specified ones.

The designer and administrator should develop a common neutral palette of materials to serve as the building standards. Sometimes it may be worth suggesting that a client consider stockpiling materials if ongoing small renovations occur frequently, and if the designer knows that a product or color will be dropped from a manufacturer's standard line. Owners should be cautioned that future renovations may require the assistance of a full-time interior designer to police the system and to make judgment calls from a design perspective.

RESEARCH, REFERENCES, AND CONTINUING EDUCATION

Designers of health care facilities need to update their knowledge of the field on a continual basis. There are several good ways to achieve this.

Discovery Trips to Similar Facilities

An effective way to understand the planning and design concerns and desires of owners is for the designer to arrange to visit those facilities that the owner considers to be the best. In most cases, the host facility is generous in discussing what works and what doesn't work.

References and Continuing Education

Several good reference sources exist for health care design. These include state medical schools or medical science libraries, the American Hospital Association, and trade magazines such as *Hospitals* and *Modern Healthcare*. There are numerous opportunities for continuing education through various professional organizations such as ASID, IBD, and the AIA. Local, regional, and national conferences frequently conduct seminars and workshops on health care design, and universities sponsor continuing education programs for professionals. Additionally, national health care symposiums and trade shows by state health care associations are available.

GLOSSARY OF TERMINOLOGY

Even designers who have specialized in the field of medical design and who have worked in this specialty for a number of years often find it difficult and confusing to keep up with terminology. Medical technology changes at an increasingly rapid pace; however, the departments within a medical facility and the various types of facilities change at a slower rate. For that reason, the following glossary of terms is provided as a reference guide for facilities terminology rather than technological advances.[1]

Acute Care: Short-term health care.

Acute Hospital: See Hospital, Short-Term.

Alcoholism Rehabilitation Center: Facility with an organized professional and trained staff that provides treatment and rehabilitative services to alcoholic patients.

Ambulatory Care: Health services rendered to patients who are not confined to an institutional bed as inpatients during the time services are rendered.

Ambulatory Care Center, Freestanding: Facility with an organized professional staff that provides various medical treatments on an outpatient basis only and that may be one of three types of center, depending on the level of care it is equipped to provide: freestanding emergency center, freestanding urgent care center, or primary care center.

Ambulatory Care Center, Hospital-Based: Organized hospital facility providing nonemergency medical and/or dental services to patients who are not assigned to a bed as inpatients during the time services are rendered; services provided to nonemergency patients in the emergency department do not constitute an organized ambulatory care program.

Ancillary Services: Those services other than room, board, and medical and nursing services, such as laboratory, radiology, pharmacy, and therapy services, that are provided to hospital patients in the course of care. See also Environmental Services Department; Support Services.

Auxiliary, Hospital: Self-governing membership organization founded by persons from the community to assist the hospital in promoting the health and welfare of the community.

Buildings and Grounds, Director of: Engineer, administrative.

Burn Care Unit: Intensive care unit for treatment of inpatients with severe burns.

Cardiac Care Unit: Intensive care unit for treatment and continuous monitoring of inpatients with acute or impending cardiac disorders.

Cardiology Services: Service providing diagnosis and treatment of patients with cardiovascular disorders.

Central Processing: Receiving, decontaminating, cleaning, preparing, disinfecting, and sterilizing of reusable items.

Central Service Department: Department providing for sterilization, storage, and distribution of sterile equipment and supplies.

Certificate of Need: Certificate of approval issued usually by a state health planning agency to health care facilities that propose to construct or modify a health care facility, incur a major capital expenditure, or offer a new or different health service.

Chaplaincy Service: Service administering religious activities and providing pastoral counseling to patients and their families and to hospital staff.

Chemical-Dependency Service: Service providing diagnosis and treatment of drug-dependent patients.

Chief Executive Officer: Person usually qualified by a master's degree in an accredited educational program in health services or business administration who is appointed by the hospital governing body and who directs the overall management of the hospital.

Chief of Service: Member of a hospital medical staff who is elected or appointed to serve as the medical and administrative head of a clinical department.

Chief of Staff: Member of a hospital medical staff who is elected, appointed, or employed by the hospital and who serves as the medical and administrative head of the medical staff.

Clinical Engineering Department: Department providing management, maintenance, service, and, in some cases, design and development for the hospital's medical equipment and instrumentation.

Clinical Laboratory: Laboratory for examination of material derived from the human body by means of bacteriological, biochemical, cytologic, hematologic, histologic, and serologic tests.

Clinical Psychology Service: Service providing counseling of and psychometric services to patients with mental or emotional problems.

Cobalt Therapy Service: Service providing radioactive cobalt therapy for patients with malignancies.

Community Health Center: Organization capable of delivering both health care and related social services, generally in a geographic area with scarce or nonexistent health services.

Comprehensive Health Care Delivery System: Health care facilities and professionals organized and coordinated to provide comprehensive health care to a defined population group.

Computed Tomography Service: Service providing diagnosis of disease through visualization of internal body structures by means of computer synthesis of x-ray particles.

Consolidation: Formal combination of two or more hospitals into a single new legal entity that has an identity separate from any of the pre-existing hospitals.

Controller: Person who directs a hospital's day-to-day financial administration, accounting, business services, financial and statistical reporting, and related activities and who may serve as the chief financial officer.

Coronary Care Unit: See Cardiac Care Unit.

Critical Care: Health care provided to critically ill patients during a medical crisis, usually within a critical care area such as an intensive care unit to coronary care unit.

Delivery Room: Unit for obstetric delivery and infant resuscitation.

Detoxification Service: Service providing treatment to diminish or remove from the body the poisonous effects of chemical substances such as alcohol or drugs, usually as the first step in the treatment of chemical-dependent patients. See also Alcohol Rehabilitation Center; Chemical Dependency Service.

Development, Director of: Person who plans and directs a hospital's fund-raising activities.

Diagnostic Services: Services related to diagnosis performed by physicians, nurses, and other professional and technical personnel under the direction of a physician.

Dietary Development: See Food Service Department.

Education Department: Department providing staff educational programs, including orientation, on-the-job training, continuing education, and, in some instances, patient and community education programs.

EKG: See Electrocardiography.

Electrocardiography: Diagnosis of heart disease through video or graphic recording of the variations in electrical potential caused by electrical activity of the heart muscle, detected by means of electrodes placed at the body surface.

Emergency Center, Freestanding: Facility that is designed, organized, equipped, and staffed to provide medical care on a 24-hour-per-day basis for injuries and illnesses, including life-threatening ones; that provides laboratory and radiographic services and has established arrangements for transporting critical patients or patients requiring hospitalization once stabilized; and that does not provide continuity of care but treats episodic, emergency, and primary care cases.

Emergency Service, Hospital: Service providing immediate initial evaluation and treatment of acutely ill or injured patients on a 24-hour basis.

Emergicenter: See Urgent Care Center, Freestanding.

Engineer, Administrative: Hospital engineer who has overall administrative responsibility for planning, managing, and maintaining a hospital's physical environment, equipment, and systems.

Engineering and Maintenance Department: Department providing for maintenance of the hospital's physical plant, including heating, ventilating, and air conditioning systems; utilities; telecommunications; and clinical engineering equipment.

Environmental Services Department: Department providing for maintenance of a safe and sanitary hospital through such means as control of solid and liquid wastes, radiation exposure, and pathogenic organisms. See also Housekeeping Department.

Epidemiology Department: See Infection Control.

Family-Centered Maternity/Newborn Center: Delivery of safe, high-quality health care while recognizing, focusing on, and adapting to both the physical and psychosocial needs of the client-patient, the family, and the newly born.

Family Practice Service: Service providing general medical care to members of family groups, regardless of age.

Food Service Department: Department providing for food preparation and services to patients and hospital personnel and also providing nutritional care to patients.

For-Profit Hospital: See Hospital, Investor-Owned.

Group Practice: Combined practice of three or more physicians and/or dentists who share office space, equipment, records, office personnel, expenses, or income.

Health Care: Provision by professional and paraprofessional personnel of services for the maintenance of health, prevention of illness, and treatment of illness or injury.

Health Care Delivery: See Comprehensive Health Care Delivery System.

Health Care Institution: Health facility with organized staff that provides medical and/or health-related services.

Health Facility: Facility whose primary function is to provide health care, such as a hospital, nursing home, or ambulatory care center, having an organized medical or professional staff and providing either ambulatory or inpatient services or both.

Health Facility Licensing Agency, State: Unit of state government legally empowered to set standards for and grant permission to operate health care institutions.

Health Maintenance Organization: Organization that has management responsibility for providing comprehensive health care services on a prepayment basis to voluntarily enrolled persons within a designated population.

Health Systems Agency: Not-for-profit organization or unit of local government designated under the Health Planning and Resources Development Act of 1974 (Public Law 93-641) to perform various health planning functions within a defined geographic area, develop the area wide health systems plan, conduct certificate-of-need reviews, and review the proposed use of some federal health funds.

Hemodialysis Unit: Unit for treatment of patients with renal insufficiency by means of hemodialysis.

Hospice Care: Care that addresses the physical, spiritual, emotional, psychological, social, and financial needs of the dying patient and his or her family; that is provided by an interdisciplinary team of professionals and volunteers in a variety of settings, both inpatient and at home; and that includes bereavement care for the family.

Hospital: Health care institution with an organized medical and professional staff and with inpatient beds available round-the-clock; whose primary function is to provide inpatient medical, nursing, and other health-related services to patients for both surgical and nonsurgical conditions; and that usually provides some outpatient services, particularly emergency care. For licensure purposes, each state has its own definition of Hospital.

Hospital, Accredited: Hospital recognized upon inspection by the Joint Commission on Accreditation of Hospitals as meeting its standards for quality of care, for the safety and maintenance of the physical plant, and for organization, administration, and governance.

Hospital, Acute: Hospital that treats patients in an acute phase of illness or injury.

Hospital, Affiliated: Hospital that is associated in some degree with another institution or program, for example, a medical school, a shared services organization, a multihospital system, or a religious organization.

Hospital, Certified: Hospital recognized by the U.S. Department of Health and Human Services as meeting its standards for participation as a provider in the Medicare program.

Hospital, Chronic Disease: Hospital that provides medical and skilled nursing services to patients with long-term illnesses who are not in an acute phase but who require an intensity of services not available in nursing homes.

Hospital, Community: Hospital–usually short-term, general, and nonfederal–whose services are used primarily by residents of the community in which it is located.

Hospital, County: Hospital that is controlled by an agency of county government.

Hospital, District: Hospital that is controlled by a political subdivision of a state, which subdivision is created solely for the purpose of establishing and maintaining health care institutions.

Hospital, Federal Government: Hospital that is managed by an agency or department of the federal government.

Hospital, General: Hospital that provides diagnostic and therapeutic services to patients for a variety of medical conditions, both surgical and nonsurgical.

Hospital, Investor-Owned: Hospital that is owned and operated by a corporation or an individual and that operates on a for-profit basis.

Hospital, Licensed: Hospital granted by an appropriate state agency the legal right to operate in accordance with the requirements of the state.

Hospital, Long-Term: Hospital that treats patients who are not in an acute phase of illness.

Hospital, Municipal: Hospital that is controlled by an agency of municipal government.

Hospital, Not-For-Profit: Hospital that operates on a not-for-profit basis under the ownership and control of a private corporation.

Hospital, Private: Investor-owned or not-for-profit hospital that is controlled by a legal entity other than a government agency.

Hospital, Psychiatric: Hospital that provides diagnostic and treatment services to patients with mental or emotional disorders.

Hospital, Registered: Hospital recognized by the American Hospital Association as having the essential specific characteristics of a hospital.

Hospital, Satellite: Part of a hospital that is geographically separated from the hospital and that offers limited services to persons in its vicinity.

Hospital, Security: Hospital controlled by, physically located within or attached to, and servicing the inmates of a penal institution.

Hospital, Short-Term: Hospital in which the average length of stay for all patients is less than 30 days or in which more than 50 percent of all patients are admitted to units where the average length of stay is less than 30 days.

Hospital, Teaching: Hospital with accredited programs in medical, allied health, and/or nursing education.

Housekeeping Department: Department providing for cleaning of hospital premises and furnishings, including control of pathogenic organisms.

Infection Control: Policies and procedures followed by a hospital to minimize the risk of infection to patients and staff.

Inpatient: Person who receives medical, dental, or other health-related services while lodged in a hospital or other health care institution for at least one night.

Inpatient, Ambulatory: Inpatient who is able to walk about and does not require confinement to bed.

Inpatient Care Unit: Unit for treatment of inpatients, often grouped according to diagnosis or other common characteristics.

Intensive Care Unit: Unit for treatment and continuous monitoring of inpatients with life-threatening conditions. See also Step-Down Unit.

Joint Commission on Accreditation of Hospitals: Private, not-for-profit organization composed for representatives of the American College of Surgeons, American College of Physicians, American Hospital Association, American Medical Association, and American Dental Association whose purpose is to establish standards for the operation of health facilities and services, conduct surveys, and award accreditation.

Labor Room: Hospital room regularly maintained for maternity patients who are in active labor.

Life Safety Code: Standard developed and updated regularly by the National Fire Protection Association that specifies construction and operational conditions to minimize fire hazards and provide a system of safety in case of fire.

Materials Management Department: Department providing centralized management and control of supplies and equipment from acquisition to disposition and, in many hospitals, with responsibility for central services, laundry, and print shop.

Medical Center: Hospital usually affiliated with a medical school, or group of hospitals located within a limited geographic area and usually affiliated with a medical school, that provides a broad range of medical and health-related services to patients.

Medical Center, Academic: Medical complex consisting of medical school, university and teaching hospitals, clinics, libraries, and administrative facilities.

Medical Director: Physician, usually employed by a hospital, who serves in a medical and administrative capacity as head of the organized medical staff and who also may serve as liaison for the medical staff with the administration and governing board. See also Chief of Staff.

Medical Engineer: Person who applies the principles of biomedical engineering and technological concepts to developing equipment and instruments required in health care delivery.

Medical Office Building: Office facilities constructed for the use of physicians and other health care personnel.

Medical Record Department: Department providing systems and services for filing, maintenance, security, and retrieval of primary and secondary medical records; for collecting, coding, and indexing health care data; for processing authorized disclosure of medical record information; for quantitative analysis of medical records; and for preparation of administrative and clinical statistical reports.

Medical Staff: Organized body of fully licensed physicians and other licensed individuals permitted by law and by the hospital to provide patient care services independently in the hospital, all of whose members have delineated clinical privileges that allow them to provide patient care services independently within the scope of their clinical privileges. All members of the medical staff are subject to medical staff and departmental bylaws, rules, and regulations, and subject to review as part of the hospital quality assurance program. As a staff, they have overall responsibility for the quality of the professional services provided by individuals with clinical privileges and are accountable for this to the governing board.

MRI: Magnetic Resonance Imaging. Service providing diagnosis of disease typically through visualization of cross-sectional images of body tissue, using strong static, magnetic, and radio-frequency fields to monitor body chemistry noninvasively, unimpeded by bone, and using no ionizing radiation or contrast agents.

Nurse, Head: Registered nurse who, as an ongoing responsibility, directs and manages the nursing care activities of one patient care unit.

Nurse Coordinator: Registered nurse who coordinates and manages the activities of nursing personnel engaged in specific nursing services, such as obstetrics or surgery, for two or more patient care units.

Nursing Service Administrator: Registered nurse responsible for the overall administration and management of nursing services provided in a hospital.

Obstetrics and Gynecology Service: Service providing care, examination, treatment, and other services to women during pregnancy, labor, and the puerperium, or with diseases peculiar to women, involving such areas as the female genital tract, female endocrinology, pelvic disease and/or dysfunction, and reproductive physiology.

Occupational Therapy Department: Service providing assistance to patients in restoring, developing, or maintaining skills necessary to permit them to perform daily living tasks.

Oncology Service: Service providing treatment to patients with cancer.

Operating Room: Unit for the performance of surgery.

Outpatient: Person who receives medical, dental, or other health-related services in a hospital or other health care institution but who is not lodged there.

Outpatient Service: Service providing treatment to patients who do not require admission as inpatients.

Pathology Service: Service providing for the study and diagnosis of disease through laboratory examination of body tissues and fluids.

Patient Care Coordinator: Registered nurse who manages and directs a specific nursing service such as obstetrics, pediatrics, or surgery, for two or more patient care units. See also Nurse Coordinator.

Patient Education Department: Department providing patients and their families with instruction related to health maintenance and the management of illness and disability. See also Education Department.

Patient Isolation: Segregation of patients with communicable diseases, or the seclusion of patients in a near pathogen-free environment in order to protect them from cross-infection.

Patient Representative: Person who investigates and mediates patient's problems and complaints in relation to a hospital's services and who may also be called patient advocate or ombudsman.

Pediatrics Service: Service providing diagnosis and treatment of patients usually under the age of 14.

Pharmacy Department: Department controlling the preparation, dispensing, storage, and use of drugs.

Physical Therapy Department: Service providing for treatment of disease and injury by physical means such as massage, exercise, heat, cold, water, electricity, light, and ultrasound.

Planning Agency: See Health Systems Agency; State Health Planning and Development Agency.

Postoperative Care: Provision of medical, nursing, and other health-related services to patients following surgery.

Postpartum Care: Provision of medical, nursing, and other health-related services to patients following childbirth.

Preferred Provider Organization: Term applied to a variety of direct contractual relationships between hospitals, physicians, insurers, employers, or third-party administrators in which providers negotiate with group purchasers to provide health services for a defined population, and which typically share three characteristics: (1) a negotiated system of payment for services that may include discounts from usual charges or ceilings imposed on a charge, per diem, or per discharge basis; (2) financial incentives for individual subscribers (insureds) to use contracting providers, usually in the form of reduced copayments and deductibles, broader coverage of services, or simplified claims processing; and (3) an extensive utilization review program.

President of Medical Staff: Member of hospital medical staff who is elected or appointed by the medical staff to serve as its administrative head for a designated time. See also Chief of Staff.

Primary Care: Provision of basic or general health care by a primary care physician, emphasizing those medical services required to maintain health, to treat simpler and more common diseases, usually at the point when patient first seeks assistance from medical care system.

Primary Care Center: Facility that provides primary care on a scheduled basis and is open approximately eight hours per day, that is staffed by a physician, that is supported by a basic laboratory and sometimes radiology services, and that provides continuity of care.

Private Room: Hospital room designed and equipped to house one inpatient.

Provider: Health care professional or hospital or group of health care professionals or hospitals that provide health care services to patients.

Psychiatric Care: Provision by or under the direction of a psychiatrist of services related to the diagnosis and treatment of mental illness.

Public Relations Department: Department responsible for news media relations, special events, reports, publications, and promotional materials.

Purchasing Department: Department providing for purchasing of equipment and supplies. See also Materials Management Department.

Radiology Service: Service providing diagnosis and treatment through the use of x-rays and other forms of radiant energy.

Recovery Room: Room for monitoring and treatment of postoperative patients.

Renal Dialysis Unit: See Hemodialysis Unit.

Respiratory Therapy Service: Service providing ventilatory support and associated services to patients, such as pulmonary function studies and blood gas analysis, administration of oxygen and certain potent drugs through inhalation or positive pressure, and the teaching of breathing exercises.

Security Department: Department providing for the security and safety of patients, employees, medical staff, visitors, and their property while in the hospital or on its grounds.

Skilled Nursing Facility: Facility with an organized professional staff that provides medical care, continuous nursing, and various other health and social services to patients who are not in an acute phase of illness but who require primarily restorative or skilled nursing care on an inpatient basis.

State Health Planning and Development Agency: Unit of state government organized in accordance with the Health Planning and Resources Development Act of 1974 (Public Law 93-641) to perform various health planning and development functions, including administration of the state's certificate-of-need programs and preparation of a state health plan. See also Health Systems Agency.

Step-Down Unit: Specialized intensive nursing unit that accommodates the same monitoring and patient support equipment as an intensive care unit, but with a higher ratio of patients to nurses, use being determined by establishing threshold values for the volume of care required.

Strategic Planning: Long-range, comprehensive, and structured decision process that ensures logical steps within a time frame in reaching a desired goal by weighing each decision step against alternative choices.

Support Services: Those services other than medical, nursing, and ancillary services that provide support in the delivery of clinical services for patient care, including laundry service, housekeeping, food service, purchasing, maintenance, central supply, materials management, and security.

Surgery Department: Department providing diagnosis and treatment through surgical procedures.

Surgical Suite: One or more operating rooms plus necessary adjunct facilities, such as scrub room(s), recovery room(s), and sterile storage areas. See also Operating Room.

Surgicenter: Independent surgical facility that provides services on an outpatient basis to patients who do not require hospitalization, but whose treatment exceeds the capabilities of the physician's office.

Terminal Care: Medical and nursing care of dying patients in the final stages of an illness.

Tertiary Care: Provision by a large medical center, usually serving a region or state and having sophisticated technological and support facilities, of highly specialized medical and surgical care for unusual and complex medical problems.

Trauma Center: Service providing emergency and specialized intensive care to critically ill and injured patients. See also Emergency Service, Hospital.

Triage: Sorting or classification of patients according to the nature or degree of their injury or illness.

Ultrasonic Diagnosis Service: Service providing diagnosis of disease through visualization of internal body structures by means of recording reflected acoustic waves above the range of human hearing.

Unit: Area of hospital that is staffed and equipped for treatment of patients with a specific condition or with other common characteristics.

Urgent Care Center, Freestanding: Facility that provides primary and urgent care treatment on a less than 24-hour-per-day basis and that is supported by laboratory and radiology services but does not receive patients transported by ambulance, is not equipped to treat true medical emergencies such as heart or stroke victims, and does not provide continuity of care.

Urology Service: Service providing study, diagnosis, care and treatment of diseases and dysfunctions of the urinary tract in females and genitourinary tract in males.

Volunteer Services Department: Department of hospital responsible for coordination of the volunteer services provided in the institution and in institution-based programs.

Ward: Hospital room designed and equipped to house more than four inpatients.

Hospitality Design

TRISHA WILSON

The hospitality industry can trace its roots to earliest recorded times. The Roman government established the first organized system for lodging with mansiones, or temporary shelters, along roads to serve government officials traveling in the expanding empire. Spas constructed by Roman engineers in England and other colonies were the first resort hotels. In the Middle Ages, abbeys and monasteries offered lodging to travelers. In fact, the word hospice is derived from an abbey in the Swiss Alps operated by the monks of St. Bernard, who offered not only shelter and hospitality but also bred and trained dogs to rescue lost travelers. Country inns began in England in the 1200s, and 200 years later, the British government established the first regulations for the lodging industry. In colonial America, Massachusetts law reportedly required that every town provide an inn to serve travelers.

Today, lodging facilities offer guests a variety of specialized services. In addition to traditional hotels, motor inns, and resorts, travelers can stay at convention hotels, casino hotels, conference centers, or suite hotels. In every type of facility, from budget motor inns to luxurious and expensive resort hotels, a wide range of costs and services is available.

Hospitality means satisfying guests' needs and ensuring that every stay is a pleasant experience. According to *Design for Hospitality* by Thomas Davis, Jr. and Kim A. Beasley, successful hospitality design results from an understanding and concern for the needs of guests. This is reflected in the personal services from staff and the design of the physical environment.

NECESSARY SKILLS AND EDUCATION

A basic prerequisite to hospitality design is an education, preferably from a four- or five-year FIDER-accredited program with an architectural component. Additional coursework in public relations, business management and marketing, CAD, graphic design, furniture construction, speech, and fiber/carpet construction is also recommended.

Other helpful skills include the ability to sketch quickly for concept meetings, to communicate well verbally and in writing, and to be computer-literate, especially for specification writing and finish schedules.

A TYPICAL HOSPITALITY DESIGN PROJECT

The usual steps in the acquisition of a typical hospitality project are:

Request for proposal
Interview process
Contract negotiations/fee determination
Presentation

The areas for interior design consideration in a typical hospitality project include:

- Tower/guestrooms: typical guest room, typical guest room bath, suite, suite bath, elevator lobby, typical guestroom corridor, concierge area.
- Lobby area: registration desk, public rest room, lobby, administration area, grand stair.
- Elevator cab.
- Food and beverage area: cafe, lobby lounge, specialty restaurant, entertainment lounge.
- Conference areas: meeting room, boardroom, ballroom, junior ballroom, prefunction room (lobby), public rest rooms.
- Business center.
- Pool/health club.

BUSINESS AND PROJECT MANAGEMENT FOR HOSPITALITY DESIGN

It is important that the project management to be used in a hospitality project be well developed and established prior to the commencement of the job. A critical component of this is the development of a project organizational chart. This will clearly establish the lines of communication and responsibility for the project. See Figure 1 for an example of a typical hospitality project management chart.

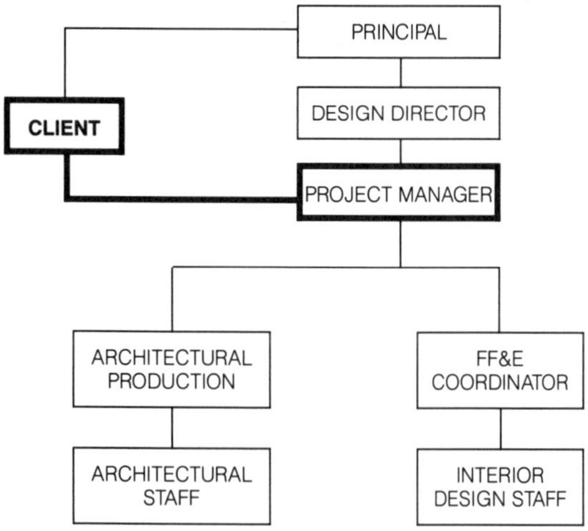

Figure 1. Project management chart. The relationship between client and project manager is crucial.

PHASES OF A HOSPITALITY PROJECT

Once a hospitality project has been acquired by the steps mentioned earlier, it will go through the following phases:

- *Programming*: This phase defines the parameters of the project and scope of services of the designer and establishes a contractual agreement.

- *Schematic design*: This phase is a broad-brush overview of all aspects of the project, including space planning, budget analysis, preliminary floor plans, furniture plans, elevations, schematic elevations, reflected ceiling plans, fabric and furnishing selections, and lighting. A formal presentation is held at this phase to obtain client input.

- *Design development*: On the basis of the approved conceptual design and budget, the designer develops floor plans with furniture, furnishings and equipment (FF&E) layout, elevations, and some detail drawings for all project areas. These drawings describe design intent and are suitable for preliminary pricing. The designer may provide full-color renderings during this phase. Documentation for model rooms are supplied at this stage, and the designer coordinates with the architect and operator to ensure that the model room represents the finished product. The designer coordinates with the lighting designer to further refine reflected ceiling plans and fixture layouts.

- *Construction documents*: All documentation of the design is included in this phase. Drawings, details, and elevations are coordinated with the documentation of various consultants on the project to generate accurate bidding and ease of construction. The furnishings, furniture, and equipment are documented in a specification format, and items are let out for bid by the purchasing agent for the proper purchase and installation of the project. The designer prepares a color finish schedule and finish notebook, including samples of all applied finishes and materials. Specially designed furnishings should be fully specified and detailed.

- *Construction administration*: The final step in the execution of the design of the project is the construction administration phase. This includes the actual construction and installation of the project elements. The designer reviews the special finishes and final placement of furnishings for food and beverage areas, conference/meeting rooms, public lobbies and corridors, and one prototypical suite and guest room of each configuration in order to determine the furniture, furnishings, and equipment are installed in accordance with the contract documents. The designer reviews and processes contractors' submittals such as shop drawings, product data, and samples to the submittals that relate to the items within the scope of the designer's services. The designer also provides a punch list to the owner showing all interior finish items as well as furniture, furnishings, and equipment items. In many ways this is the most important phase of the project, because the designer is ultimately judged on the product that is built, *not* the job that was designed.

In order to ensure that each phase of the project is executed in a systematic and timely manner, the project manager is responsible for the supervision and coordination of many different areas of expertise. A sample list of the types of responsibilities of the project manager include:

Facilitation of communication between owner, architect, purchasing agent, outside consultants, operators, and in-house staff.
Contractual agreement negotiations.
Delegation of design team responsibilities.
Schedule review.
Review and management of the entire project.
Maintenance of morale for the design team and clients.
Monitoring of profitability of the project.
Monitoring of work in progress.
Final decisions.

Note that a successful hospitality designer must be not only an excellent designer, but an excellent project manager. There are important characteristics a project manager must possess to accomplish the complex responsibilities outlined. According to *Strong PM Systems*, a project manager must have the following abilities and characteristics:

- Be a leader—that is, have the ability to take charge, make decisions, and implement them.

- Have a thorough knowledge of the firm and what can be done within the firm's perimeters.

- Have a personality and approach geared to client relations.

- Be able to conceptualize and identify tasks.

- Be a team player, willing to organize and work through others.

- Be aware of how to apply pressure calmly without upsetting the team.

- Be calm under pressure and know when to speak and when to listen.

- Be able to create a stimulating, motivating environment.
- Have the courage to take an issue to supervisors for resolution.
- Be dogged for detail.
- Have experience in all phases of work and familiarity with all staff abilities.

UNIQUE PROBLEMS IN HOSPITALITY DESIGN

Hospitality projects must integrate the skills and knowledge of more consultants than nearly any other type of design project. An average hotel may have twenty or more consultants. The need to integrate as a team is both necessary and difficult.

A designer must stay current because the codes vary from state to state and country to country. As a specifier, the designer must specify the correct product or treatment. This means that an ongoing process of staying abreast of code requirements is a necessity.

In a hotel, a designers' main charge is the creation of an environment that is beautiful and functional. To be functional, spaces must be accessible to the physically impaired. This consideration must be addressed for all public spaces and a percentage of the guest rooms.

As with all types of design projects, it is paramount to design within a budget. It is a wise idea to be familiar with the hotel's consultants who can provide important cost information. A general knowledge of construction costs, kitchen costs, and electrical and mechanical costs is also helpful. Additionally, a working knowledge of the best-quality products at the least cost and familiarity with the manufacturers of specialized products is important for the hospitality designer to have as a resource to draw upon throughout the project.

The designer must always keep in mind that time is money. Budgeting time against a given fee for a project that could last over five years is difficult to do. Design time versus bottom-line numbers is a continuing issue in hospitality design.

In general, most hospitality clients want their project to look different from others on the market. The interior designer in the hospitality field must always be sensitive to this issue. Many hotels have set standards that must be followed by the design team. It is sometimes difficult to adhere to the standards, yet at the same time create an individual and unique environment. The identification of a hotel by region or location is often used to address this issue.

IMPORTANT CONSULTANTS FOR HOSPITALITY DESIGN

Some of the key consultants necessary for a successful hospitality installation include the following:

- *Lighting experts*: Lighting consultants are integral to the creation of dramatic interior design. The furnishings and finishes can be superb, but without the proper lighting, these will appear flat and uninteresting. Proper lighting can make or break a hospitality project.
- *Artists*: Artists and art consultants are helpful in organizing the artwork program on the basis of the direction established by the interior designer. These consultants serve as valuable resources for identifying particular artists who are capable of working on demanding commercial projects, often within moderate budgets.
- *Graphics/signage experts*: Experts in graphics and signage provide interior directional signage as well as collateral items such as menus, matches, and stir sticks for the food and beverage outlets. In addition, they are often responsible for the guest amenities in the guest rooms.
- *Kitchen/food service consultants*: Kitchen consultants lay out and specify equipment as well as coordinate with the designer for support cooking areas such as bars or display cooking areas.
- *Acoustical experts*: Acoustical consultants help with the design of areas such as ballrooms, meeting rooms, and restaurants where noise can be a problem for the proper function of the space. These consultants recommend materials and finishes that may be incorporated into the design.
- *Security consultants*: Security is a primary concern in a hotel or hospitality project. Consultants who are familiar with security systems provide a necessary expertise to the interior design team.
- *Audiovisual consultants and telecommunications experts*: In today's world the clientele who stay in hotels expect sophisticated audiovisual and telecommunications access. Consultants in these areas provide the design team with the necessary information to provide state-of-the-art audiovisual and telecommunications for the project.
- *Purchasing agents*: Purchasing agents facilitate the project, purchase all the furniture, fixtures and equipment, and organize installation.

NETWORKING OPPORTUNITIES FOR HOSPITALITY DESIGNERS

Specific professional organizations for hotel interior designers are not readily available. However, by joining other professional design organizations, designers can establish networks with others working in the area. Important organizations for exploring these opportunities include the following:

American Hotel & Motel Association
International Hotel Association
Caribbean Hotel Association
Trade shows such as the International Hotel/Motel and Restaurant Show are another source of information for hotel specifiers. Publications are also an excellent source of information. The following list, although not inclusive, provides insight into published sources available for the designer's reference.

Hotel and Motel Management
Lodging Hospitality
Restaurant/Hotel Design International
Restaurants and Institutions
Hotels
Restaurant Hospitality
Lodging

Along with these publications, the generic trade journals such as *Interior Design* and *Interiors* regularly feature innovative hospitality design projects.

CONCLUSION

Hospitality design is an exciting and challenging specialty area for the interior designer. More than many other interior design specialty areas, hospitality design provides the opportunity to create spaces that are visually stimulating while at the same time functionally appropriate and safe for the occupants.

Historic Preservation and Rehabilitation

JOSETTE RABUN AND ROBERT MEDEN

During the past two decades, the level of consciousness regarding the preservation and rehabilitation of buildings and their interiors has increased dramatically. Society has come to realize the lasting value of saving a historic structure—a value that transcends not only aesthetic improvements, but also economic and social gains. This realization has spawned various approaches toward the preservation and rehabilitation of a structure.

To rejuvenate older or historic buildings to accommodate contemporary occupants and user demands, it is essential to look at a structure in the context of its existence in time. Prior to the current historic preservation and rehabilitation movements, a structure was altered or adapted in a manner that was necessary or in vogue. The bicentennial and roots movements have provided a sense of heritage and a new perspective for examining our built environment. The past is no longer considered in terms of one particular time, place, or event; rather, it is examined as a continuum of social, economic, and political currents through which the people and their buildings have transpired.

DEFINITIONS

Since historic preservation and rehabilitation projects normally rely on interdisciplinary teams of specialists (interior designers, architects, planners, historians, archaeologists, craftsmen, contractors, lawyers, and so on), it is absolutely necessary that all involved be able to comprehend and communicate with basic terminology. A lack of understanding of these or other terms associated with a preservation or rehabilitation project adds confusion to an already complicated and challenging situation. Some of the more significant terms, as defined by various publications of the National Park Service and the National Trust for Historic Preservation, are:

- *Preservation*: The act or process of applying measures to sustain the existing form, integrity, and material of a building or structure and the existing form and vegetative cover of the site. It may include initial stabilization work, where necessary, as well as ongoing maintenance of the historic building materials and vegetation.

- *Rehabilitation*: The process of returning a property to a state of utility, through repair or alteration, which makes possible an efficient contemporary use while preserving those portions and features of the property that are significant to its historic, architectural, and cultural values.

- *Adaptive use*: The process of converting a building to a use other than that for which it was designed, such as changing a factory into housing. Such a conversion is accomplished with varying alterations to the building.

- *Restoration*: The act or process of accurately recovering the form and details of a property and its setting as it appeared at a particular period of time by means of the removal of later work or by the replacement of missing earlier work.

- *Renovation*: Questionable modernization of a historic building in which inappropriate alterations are made and important features and details eliminated.

- *Reconstruction*: The act or process of reproducing by new construction the exact form and detail of a vanished building, structure, or object or a part thereof, as it appeared at a specific period of time.[1]

THE PRESERVATION AND REHABILITATION MOVEMENT IN THE UNITED STATES

Concern for preserving New England houses, southern plantations, battlefields, Indian relics, and the like, represented the early development of the American preservation movement. The first instance of a significant documented effort for preservation in the United States seems to have occurred in 1816, when Independence Hall was purchased by the city of Philadelphia from the state of Pennsylvania. By that time, unfortunately, two wings of the building had already been torn down and the woodwork stripped from the Assembly Room where the Declaration of Independence had been signed.

During the middle of the nineteenth century, there were several private efforts to preserve structures of prominence, including the Touro Synagogue in Newport, Rhode Island; Andrew Jackson's home, the Hermitage, in Nashville, Tennessee; Carpenter's Hall in Philadelphia, Pennsylvania; a house that withstood an Indian massacre in Deerfield, Massachusetts; and Thomas Jefferson's home, Monticello, in Charlottesville, Virginia. There does not appear to have been any significant preservation efforts by any branch of government until the late 1840s, when the state of New York purchased the Hasbrouck House in Newburgh, New York, one of Washington's headquarters. By doing so, New York created our country's first historic house museum.

Ann Pamela Cunningham and the Mount Vernon Ladies' Association of the Union organized the attempt to save Mount Vernon, George Washington's estate, and this is considered to be the first real nationwide preservation effort. In 1853, Miss Cunningham appealed to the women of the South to do something to prevent the commercial exploitation of Mount Vernon. Six years later, their efforts were rewarded with the purchase of the estate.

Over the ensuing years, special legislation has been passed in support of the historic preservation and rehabilitation movements. A summary of the significant legislation follows:

The Antiquities Act of 1906 (P.L. 59-209)

The federal government, for the first time, identified a concern about preservation policies. This act authorized the President to set aside historic landmarks, structures, and objects located on lands controlled by the United States as national monuments and required permits for archaeological activities on federal lands while establishing criminal and civil penalties for violations of the act.[2]

The National Park System Organic Act of 1916

The National Park Service was established, as part of the United States Department of the Interior, and took over the administration of nine existing national monuments.[3]

The National Historic Sites Act of 1935 (P.L. 74-292)

This act required that all historic sites owned by the federal government be placed under the jurisdiction of the National Park Service. It also created the Historic Sites Survey, now known as the National Register of Historic Places, the government's list of the nation's cultural resources that are worthy of preservation. Today, the National Register includes National Historic Landmarks, an elite group of properties with national significance; properties with national, state, or local significance; and all of the historic areas in the National Park system.[4]

An Act providing for a National Trust for Historic Preservation, 1949

Created by Congress, the National Council for Historic Sites and Buildings, now known as the National Trust for Historic Preservation, became the only national, nonprofit organization chartered by Congress dedicated to stimulating and leading public involvement in historic preservation. The National Trust provides technical and financial assistance to groups and individuals and also serves as an advocate and lobby for preservation policies.[5]

The National Historic Preservation Act of 1966 (P.L. 89-665)

This act authorized the Secretary of the Interior to expand and maintain the National Register of Historic Places, a list that has met the criteria established to determine the significance of a property. Being listed on the National Register then qualified a property for federal assistance in the form of matching grants. Secondly, the act encouraged the establishment of state and local preservation programs and designation of a State Historic Preservation Officer (SHPO). The act then required each SHPO to identify and inventory historic properties in the state; nominate eligible properties to the National Register; prepare and implement a statewide historic preservation plan; serve as a liaison with federal agencies on preservation matters; and provide public information, education, and technical assistance. Thirdly, the act authorized a grant program that provided funds to the states for the preservation of properties listed in the National Register. The grants were to be used for purposes of surveying, planning and/or acquiring historic properties, and for their restoration or rehabilitation. Finally, the statute established the Advisory Council on Historic Preservation as an independent federal agency. The Council's purpose was to advise the President, Congress, and other federal agencies on historic preservation matters, to conduct training and other educational programs, and to encourage public interest in preservation.[6]

Executive Order #11593 for the "Protection and Enhancement of the Cultural Environment," 1971

This executive order required federal agencies to administer cultural properties under their control and direct their policies, plans, and programs in such a way that federally owned sites, structures, and objects of historical, architectural, or archaeological significance are preserved, restored, and maintained. In order to achieve this, federal agencies were required to locate, inventory, and nominate to the National Register of Historic Places all properties under their jurisdiction or control. It also directed agencies to reconsider any plans to transfer, sell, demolish, or substantially alter any property determined to be eligible for the Register.[7]

Tax Reform Act of 1976 (P.L. 94-455)

This act represented a breakthrough for the preservation movement because it established important tax incentives for the preservation and rehabilitation of income-producing historic structures. The act included tax penalties for the demolition of historic buildings and also encouraged the charitable donation of partial property interest, such as facade easements, for historic preservation purposes. Commercial or business-related structures that qualified as "certified historic structures," those that were listed in the National Register or located within a registered historic district, were entitled to tax advantages under the new law. The owner was then allowed to amortize the rehabilitation expenditures which were part of a certified rehabilitation of the property over a 60-month period. This was attractive because the taxpayer could now deduct all rehabilitation costs in five years rather than over the life of the property, a substantial tax savings in shorter period of time. The burden of responsibility for certification of properties and review of preservation projects fell on the SHPO, thus generating more visibility and credibility for state and local preservation agencies.[8]

Revenue Act of 1978 (P.L. 95-600)

This act provided an investment tax credit for the rehabilitation of older buildings used for commercial and industrial purposes.[9]

1980 Amendments to the National Historic Preservation Act (P.L. 96-515)

These amendments required consent of owners before listing a property in the National Register of Historic Places; made the Advisory Council on Historic Preservation an independent federal agency and changed its membership; directed federal agencies to nominate and protect properties; and provided for a National Museum of the Building Arts.[10]

Economic Recovery Tax Act of 1981 (P.L. 97-34)

The Internal Revenue Code was revised to add an accelerated cost recovery system, to repeal previously existing incentives (60-month amortization and accelerated depreciation) for rehabilitation of older buildings. The act also substituted a new three-tiered investment tax credit (15 percent for 30-year-old structures, 20 percent for 40-year-old structures, and 25 percent for Certified Historic Structures). Except for Certified Historic Structures, residential rental properties did not qualify for the tax credit. A Certified Historic Structure was any building listed on the National Register of Historic Places or located in a Registered Historic District and certified by the Secretary of the Interior as being of historic significance to the District.[11]

Tax Equity and Fiscal Responsibility Act of 1982 (P.L. 97-248)

This act reduced somewhat the financial incentives created by the Economic Recovery Tax Act of 1981 by requiring that the depreciable basis of historic buildings be reduced by 50 percent of the tax credit provided.[12]

Tax Reform Act of 1986

This act made comprehensive changes to the Internal Revenue Code with respect to preservation. Two of those changes directly affect the rehabilitation of historic buildings:

(a) A 20 percent tax credit was established for the substantial rehabilitation of historic buildings for commercial, industrial, and rental residential purposes, and a 10 percent tax credit was established for the substantial rehabilitation for nonresidential purposes of buildings built before 1936.

(b) A straight-line depreciation period of 27.5 years was established for residential property, and 31.5 years for nonresidential properties, for the depreciable basis of the rehabilitated building reduced by the amount of the tax credit claimed.[13]

(It is important to note that the 10 percent tax credit is not available for rehabilitations of Certified Historic Structures, and owners who have properties within registered historic districts who wish to elect this credit must obtain certification that their building is not historic.)

BEGINNING A HISTORIC PROJECT

Several questions are raised when conserving old buildings, whether it is a preservation or a rehabilitation project. To paraphrase James Fitch, author of *Historic Preservation: Curatorial Management of the Built World*, there are these important questions to consider:

- Should there be respect for the deceased craftsperson and designer?
- Is there a willingness to investigate and respect the historical development?
- Is there a willingness to subordinate one's own preferences and prejudices to that of a historic builder?
- Is there a willingness to collaborate with other specialists?

A designer working with historic structures or old buildings must have a keen design ability and technical skills. In addition, the designer should be trained in preservation skills in order to deal with the uniqueness of restoring or adapting an old building. The interior designer involved in a preservation or rehabilitation project needs to be historically literate and able to interpret the building in time and place. The designer must be interested in research because it is essential that one become as familiar as possible with the life, manners, background, taste, and aspirations of the various generations who have inhabited or been associated with the building or space, in order to reach accurate conclusions. Care must be taken not to read into the building what is not there. Some designers find working with an old building too restrictive. If so, the project should be referred to someone who respects and understands the value and integrity of the building.

The team concept is important to historic projects. The design professional must rely heavily upon other consultants. A structural engineer who understands the technology of a historic structure is critical to the success of the project. A mechanical/electrical engineer who respects the historic interior must be identified. Other professionals such as historians play an important role in the preservation process. Most important to the success of a historic project is the relationship between the interior designer and the architect. It is critical to the project's outcome to have an architect who is sympathetic to the significance of the interiors of the building, its fabric and its character, and who understands the importance of the special expertise an interior designer brings to the project.

According to Orin M. Bullock. Jr., author of *The Restoration Manual,*

> *. . . the designer fortunate enough to be awarded a commission to restore a historic building should be one who has a careful and inquiring mind. One must be able to subordinate one's own design ideas to the taste of past generations; one must resist at all costs the natural tendency to become enamored of any one particular period, style, or architectural idiom; one must leave no stone unturned in finding out all there is to know about the building and its interior, and in restoring exactly what existed in it during the period selected for preservation. Every part should, if possible, be provably authentic; facilities and services necessary to present-day use, such as plumbing, climate control, electrical work, fire protection or alarm devices, should be unobtrusive.*[14]

PREDESIGN

Since there is no particular formula that provides an instant solution to the overall procedure for preserving or rehabilitating a historic building or space, it is necessary to investigate, research, and analyze each structure individually. Without a doubt, a restoration will normally be more time-consuming than most new construction or new alteration projects.

Historic preservation work requires an enormous amount of preliminary work. Before the design process begins, preliminary surveys and investigations are a must. Many offices that specialize in historic preservation projects strive to provide personnel continuity throughout the job to prevent errors and/or omissions. Contrary to new construction design projects where the design team may change depending on the phase, with a historic project it is important that the same team follow the project through to completion.

Preservationists such as William J. Murtagh feel that integrity is at the heart of a historic project. A successful project develops the integrity of the building. W. Brown Morton, professor of historic preservation, defined integrity as "those qualities in a building and its site that give it meaning and value." Once the designer understands this, the goal is to formulate a course of action. Of particular concern is an effort to maintain and preserve all original historic elements or features of the structure, including fabrics, wall coverings, and other interior finishes. If historic elements or features are lost during a rehabilitation project, they are lost forever.

RESEARCHING AND DOCUMENTING THE HISTORY OF A STRUCTURE

Since character-defining features in a building must be protected, the professional designer must understand the step-by-step process of saving an old building. First, an inventory of historic features must be compiled using a systematic examination and analysis process. Often referred to as a survey, this inventory serves to identify what is not important. This information often provides the groundwork for the National Register nomination if the structure has not been certified as a historic structure.

In addition to the examination of the building's physical remains, a written documentation of the historic building provides even greater understanding. Often the written documentation is done by a historian and the measured drawings by an architect or a designer. The books *Recording Historic Structures/Historic American Building Survey (HABS)* and *Historic American Engineering Record (HAER)* give specific information and outline a general methodology for producing written historic documentation. Included are guidelines on how to document the historic features.

Photographs complement the historical documentation of a structure and often convey information not found in other areas. Spatial qualities, texture, building context, and current conditions are conveyed through photographs. In addition, good photographs provide insight on the integrity of the building. Specialized equipment techniques such as X-ray photography, radiography, infrared photographs or even computer enhancements of photographs are often necessary. Interior designers may have a need to use these specialized techniques to avoid damaging original materials and finishes. For example, it may be necessary to uncover what's inside a wall or to uncover the type of nails used to construct a stair in order to date the structure. Guidelines for designers inexperienced in photographing old structures are available through several sources such as *Recording Historic Structures, HABS/HAER,* and also in *Photographing Historic Buildings.*

Measured drawings are necessary to support the survey, historical research, and photographic work done. This is one of the most expensive processes, but one of the most valuable. Measured drawings are used:

- As a basis for planning restoration or rehabilitation work.
- To record a historic structure that possibility will be demolished .
- To aid in maintaining a historic structure.
- To protect against catastrophic loss.
- As scholarly study and documentation.

It is mandatory that these drawings be to scale and that figured dimensions agree with scaled dimensions. These drawings differ from those done for a new construction project because on a preservation or rehabilitation project they are a historical record of the building. As such, they indicate the original source of each design detail, profile of molding, and architectural feature.

Before expending resources and time on measured drawings of the interiors of the historic building, it is wise to check the HABS archival collection. Since its birth, HABS has developed an extensive archival collection, which is deposited in the Division of Prints and Photographs of the Library of Congress and contains documentation of thousands of buildings recorded on sheets of drawings with photographs and data pages.

In the historic research process it is important to distinguish between primary sources and secondary sources. Primary sources carry more credibility because they are original documents such as legal records, deeds, probate records, tax records, or things such as city directories, newspapers, letters, diaries, real estate insurance maps of the period, and old photographs. On the other hand, secondary sources often provide a starting point, particularly if a well-documented bibliography is provided in the secondary source.

The primary focus of the research that must be done on historic preservation or rehabilitation projects is to determine whether the structure is historically significant. Properties listed in the National Register of Historic Places possess historic significance and integrity. One registration form is completed for each entry in the National Register. The entry may be a single property, such as a historic house or bridge, or it may be a historic district containing many buildings, structures, sites, and objects. Registration forms may be submitted separately or may be grouped within multiple property submissions. The information on the National Register form has several purposes; it:

Identifies and locates the historic property.
Explains how it meets one or more of the National Register criteria.
Makes the case for historic significance and integrity.

Preparation of a nomination for a building to the National Register requires a thorough knowledge of the property. Facts can be gathered about the structure by physically inspecting the property and conducting historical research. Claims for historic significance and integrity are supported by these facts and link the property to one or more of the National Register criteria.

The three key criteria used by the National Register program to decide whether a property qualifies for listing are historic significance, historic integrity, and historic context. These are defined in *National Register Bulletin 16: Guidelines for Completing National Register Forms*, in the following way:

- *Historic significance is the importance of the property to the history, architecture, archaeology, engineering, or culture of a community, a state, or the nation. It is achieved through: (1) association with events; (2) association with important persons; (3) distinctive physical characteristics of design, construction, or form; or (4) potential to yield important information.*

- *Historic integrity is the authenticity of a property's historic identity, evidenced by the survival of physical characteristics that existed during the property's historic or prehistoric period. Historic integrity is the composite of seven qualities: location, design, setting, materials, workmanship, association, and feeling. Historic integrity enables a property to illustrate significant aspects of its past. For this reason, it is an important qualification for National Register listing. Not only must a property resemble its historic appearance, but it must also retain physical materials, design features, and aspects of construction dating from the period when it attained significance. All seven qualities do not need to be present for eligibility. Some of the qualities are more important than others depending on the property's significance.*

- *Historic context is information about historic trends and properties based on an important theme, trend, or pattern in the history of a community, a state, or the nation during a particular period of time. Because historic contexts are organized by theme, time, and place, they link historic properties to important historic trends. In this way, they help determine whether the property has historic associations, physical characteristics, or information potential that qualifies it for the National Register listing. Historic contexts also make it possible to compare the character of a place today to that of the past to access the property's integrity.*[15]

Facts such as date of construction, early owners or occupants, and functions and activities not only verify the property's history, but also place the property in a particular time, place, and course of events. With this information, applicants can relate the property to patterns of history that extend beyond the doorstep or immediate neighborhood. From this perspective, applicants can begin to sort out the facts that give the property its historic identity and significance. Certain events, associations, or physical characteristics of the property will take on greater or lesser importance. Properties of the same time and place can be compared to determine whether their character and associations are unique, representative, or pivotal in illustrating the history of a community, a state, or the nation. It is easier to make the case for significance when a property is associated with historic themes or trends that have been widely recognized and fully studied, such as textbook examples of an architectural style.

Applicants are ready to complete the registration form for the National Register when they can answer the following list of questions:

- What was the property called at the time it was associated with the important events or persons, or took on its important physical character that gave it importance?
- How many buildings, structures, and other resources make up the property?
- When was the property constructed and when did it attain its current form?
- What are the property's historic characteristics?
- What changes have been made over time and when? How have these affected its historic integrity?
- What is the current condition of the property, including the exterior, grounds, setting, and interior?
- How was the property used historically, and how is it used today?
- Who occupied or used the property historically? Did its occupants individually, or as a group, make any important contributions to history? Who is the current owner?

- During what period of history was the property associated with important events, activities, or persons?
- Which of the National Register criteria apply to the property? In what areas of history or prehistory is the property significant?
- How does the property relate to the history of the community where it is located?
- How does the property illustrate any themes or trends important to the history of its community, its state, or the nation?
- How large is the property, where is it located, and what are its boundaries?

Once a property has been listed in the National Register, documentation in the form of written records and a computerized data base called the National Register Information System (NRIS) becomes part of a national archive of information about significant historic properties in the United States. Any person or organization may prepare a National Register nomination in the form of a completed registration form. Applicants submit completed forms to the State Historic Preservation Officer (SHPO) in the state where the property is located. An affidavit by the owner consenting to inclusion of the building on the National Register of Historic Places must accompany the application form. Forms for properties owned by the federal government are submitted to the Federal Preservation Officer (FPO) of the agency responsible for the property.

Since the 1970s, historic preservation and rehabilitation projects in the United States have been numerous, and many leading design periodicals and trade journals have published articles on this type of project. Before a historic preservation or rehabilitation project is begun, a review of case studies is advisable. Even though each old building is unique with its own solution, case studies open possibilities. In addition, case studies offer suggestions for important steps to take to ensure the success of historic projects.

FEASIBILITY STUDY

Following the initial historical research, the designer should do a detailed feasibility study before the design process begins. According to the book *All About Buildings: The Whole Preservation Catalog*, there are four key areas to address in a feasibility study:

Market support and economic evaluation
Site and location characteristics
Structural considerations
Architectural and historical aspects[16]

A key determinant in a feasibility study is the net to gross square footage cost. According to William C. Shopsin, author of *Restoring Old Buildings for Contemporary Use*,

> *The feasibility study is an ongoing process in which you begin to consider a wide variety of alternatives for your project and gradually narrow them down to a few. The feasibility study tests possibilities against the limitations imposed by the programmatic needs, zoning and building codes, construction costs, financing, and other special considerations.*[17]

A vital part of a feasibility study is the market survey. It helps to determine the most profitable use of the historic building. Lending institutions and other funding sources want to know that the building will be occupied after rehabilitation and that the loan will be repaid.

GUIDELINES FOR HISTORIC PROJECTS

The National Trust defines adaptive use as "the process of converting a building to a use other than that for which it was designed, e.g., changing a factory into housing. Such conversions are accomplished with varying alterations to the building." Buildings that have little important historical value, yet have exceptional architectural value, cannot all be saved as museums. However, many owners of old buildings save the buildings by adapting them for a new use for today's society. Studies show that adaptive use is an economical way for many old buildings to be saved.

James Marston Fitch, author of *Historic Preservation*, explains that "compared with new construction, adaptive use offers many advantages."[18] Further he notes that adaptive use usually requires less capital to start and less time to complete, with the additional advantage that less money will be tied up before income from the building can be generated. Even though it is a labor-intensive project, adaptive use relies less on expensive machinery and costly structural materials. In addition, the reuse of old buildings produces social benefits by conserving resources and employing more workers.

The tax laws provide incentives to stimulate capital investment in income-producing historic buildings and the revitalization of historic communities. The United States Department of the Interior is responsible for approving a certified rehabilitation, thus qualifying the project for preservation tax benefits. Therefore, rehabilitation and adaptive use projects using Tax Act incentives are one of the more important means of adapting old buildings for new uses.

From October 1, 1976, through September 30, 1987, there were 18,736 certified rehabilitation investment tax credit projects (RITC) approved by the Park Service. The investment that resulted from these projects totals $12 billion. The National Park Service estimates that without the tax benefits, 75 percent of these projects would not have been done. William J. Murtagh in his book *Keeping Time* discusses the Tax Reform Act of 1986 and states that it "limits annual tax credits to an amount equal to tax liability on passive income from rental properties and limited partnerships."[19] This has created a great reduction in private investors utilizing older buildings for income-producing properties. In the year 1990, only 994 projects chose to use the tax credits.

Currently many investors are adapting older buildings for new usage without using the tax credit, in an attempt to avoid following the Standards for Rehabilitation that protect both the interior and exterior historic integrity of the building. As a result, many historic buildings are being cosmetically damaged and the original fabric of the building is being destroyed. Reinstatement of the tax incentives for rehabilitating historic buildings would help preserve our architectural heritage. Interior designers should be educated and be aware of the importance of historic buildings; they should encourage investors and developers to save historic structures through rehabilitation and adaptive use projects that utilize the tax credits and follow the Secretary of the Interior's Standards for Rehabilitation.

THE ROLES OF SHPO, NPS, AND IRS

The state historic preservation officer, the National Park Service, and the Internal Revenue Service all play specific roles, which are clearly spelled out in various publications from the U.S. Department of Interiors and summarized below:[20]

The State Historic Preservation Officer (SHPO)

Property owners interested in obtaining federal tax incentives should contact their SHPO to obtain the necessary application forms and for information on the procedural requirements for certification. Each SHPO has complete records of buildings and districts listed in the National Register of Historic Places, including state and local historic districts, and can provide both technical assistance and literature on selecting appropriate rehabilitation treatments and techniques.

All applications submitted to the SHPO receive a thorough review for completeness of documentation and appropriateness of rehabilitation work before being forwarded to the appropriate NPS regional office. Owners seeking certifications must provide sufficient information in the application to permit the review and evaluation required prior to a decision on certification. The recommendation of a SHPO receives careful attention at the federal level. Early consultation with the SHPO can help avoid problems and delays in obtaining the necessary certifications.

The National Park Service (NPS)

The NPS reviews all certification requests for conformance to legal standards and issues the certifications and approvals in writing directly to the property owner or applicant for certification. Owners denied certification of significance or rehabilitation may appeal under Department of the Interior regulations governing certifications for preservation tax incentives.

The designer needs to explain to the owner that certain standards and guidelines have been developed by the Secretary of the Interior. The building cannot be changed without addressing these requirements. Even if it is necessary to rearrange the interior of a building for the new use, the NPS evaluates the appropriateness of a new plan as it relates to the original one. The NPS, with the recommendation of the state office, has the final word.

The Internal Revenue Service (IRS)

The IRS is responsible for all procedures and other legal matters concerning the tax consequences of certifications, including determining which rehabilitation expenditures qualify for the tax credit. The IRS regulations governing the tax credits for rehabilitation expenditures are contained in Title 26 of the Code of Federal Regulation, Part 1.

STANDARDS FOR HISTORIC BUILDINGS

The following guidelines have been extracted from the Federal Register, Volume 55, No. 38, Feb. 1990, and outline how to do a historic project consistent with the intent of the Secretary of the Interior's "Standards for Rehabilitation." These guidelines pertain to buildings of all occupancy and construction types, sizes, and materials.

1. *Every reasonable effort shall be made to provide a compatible use for a property which requires minimal alteration of the building, structure, or site and its environment, or to use the property for its originally intended purpose.*

2. *The distinguishing original qualities or character of a building, structure, or site and its environment shall not be destroyed. The removal or alteration of any historic material or distinctive architectural features should be avoided when possible.*

3. *All buildings, structures, and sites shall be recognized as products of their own time. Alterations that have no historical basis and which seek to create an earlier appearance shall be discouraged.*

4. *Changes which may have taken place in the course of time are evidence of the history and development of a building, structure, or site and its environment. These changes may have acquired significance in their own right, and this significance shall be recognized and respected.*

5. *Distinctive stylistic features or examples of skilled craftsmanship which characterize a building, structure, or site shall be treated with sensitivity.*

6. *Deteriorated architectural features shall be repaired rather than replaced, wherever possible. In the event replacement is necessary, the new material should match the material being replaced in composition, design, color, texture, and other visual qualities. Repair or replacement of missing architectural features should be based on accurate duplications of features, substantiated by historic, physical, or pictorial evidence rather than on conjectural designs or the availability of different architectural elements from other buildings or structures.*

7. *The surface cleaning of structures shall be undertaken with the gentlest means possible. Sandblasting and other cleaning methods that will damage the historic building materials shall not be undertaken.*

8. *Every reasonable effort shall be made to protect and*

preserve archaeological resources affected by, or adjacent to, any project.

9. Contemporary design for alterations and additions to existing properties shall not be discouraged when such alterations and additions do not destroy significant historical, architectural, or cultural material, and such design is compatible with the size, scale, color, material, and character of the property, neighborhood, or environment.

10. Whenever possible, new additions or alterations to structures shall be done in such a manner that if such additions or alterations were to be removed in the future, the essential form and integrity of the structure would be unimpaired.

In addition to the Secretary of the Interior's Standards for Rehabilitation, additional information on technical preservation and rehabilitation techniques is available. The National Park Service, Preservation Assistance Division, publishes Preservation Briefs, Technical Reports, and Preservation Case Studies. A complete set including the cost and the Government Printing Office stock numbers can be obtained from: Preservation Assistance Division, National Park Service, Washington, DC 20240.

QUALIFICATIONS FOR TAX INCENTIVES

To qualify for tax incentives, the property owner must apply for the certification form from the Secretary of the Interior. Two very important aspects of the review will be the historic character of the structure and the quality of the rehabilitation work performed on the structure. The National Park Service provides an application, Part 3: "Request for Certification of Completed Work," with detailed instructions. A set of guidelines and a checklist for filling out the Historic Preservation Certification Application (request for final certification of completed work) gives the applicant assurance that all is complete.

Certified rehabilitation will be issued only after the project is done and Part 3 of the application has been completed. It is quite possible that a designated person from the SHPO and/or the National Park Service will inspect the completed project to see if the work meets the "Standards for Rehabilitation" before final approval is received.

PROBLEMS UNIQUE TO HISTORIC PROJECTS

The designer is more likely to encounter certain types of problems in historic preservation and rehabilitation than in any other type of project.

Historic Preservation

Techniques used in earlier construction must be carefully evaluated and understood before any restoration effort is to be successful. Materials and construction methods of today's contractors may not replicate the work of the original builders and must, therefore, be carefully orchestrated and specified. On the site, the potential for hazardous conditions to exist is an important concern. According to F. Neale Quenzel in his paper, "Assessing the Condition of Historic Interiors Prior to Work," the most common are:

- *Asbestos:* The majority of asbestos or asbestos-related products were installed in buildings between 1940 and 1970. If remodeling was carried out between these dates, there is a high probability that some form of asbestos exists. Most commonly, asbestos was used as a fireproof binder in insulation products, particularly on piping. To the naked eye, asbestos look fibrous and hairy; however, positive identification requires the aid of a high-powered microscope and a trained analyst. Asbestos is commonly found in sprayed-on acoustical ceilings and decorative plaster where it was used for its rigidity as a binder. Many fire-rated metal door and window assemblies are filled with asbestos. Vinyl asbestos tiles cannot be removed with introducing this carcinogen into the air.

- *Structural conditions:* Conditions overhead and underfoot can be dangerous to more than the building. Key locations to check include areas where extensive water leaks are evident.

- *Bats, pigeons, and rodents:* Bats and rodents are sometimes found to be carriers of rabies. Buildings where they are present should be treated by professional exterminators before the designer commences with conditional assessment. Several dangerous diseases can be contracted from pigeon guano, including cryptococcosis and histoplasmosis, diseases that affect the central nervous system of humans. A respirator fitted with the proper filters should be worn when inspecting buildings with these problems.

- *Exterior conditions:* Deterioration of interior building fabric is often caused by deficiencies in the exterior envelope, so it is usually advantageous to make a brief inspection of exterior conditions prior to inspecting the interior. Familiarity with problems in the weather barriers and structural systems will help to prevent a misdiagnosis when evaluating interior conditions. By quickly checking the exterior elevations, changes and modifications to the building will become apparent. Chimneys that have been abandoned, skylights that have been covered over, and windows and doors that have been infilled are some of the alterations to the exterior that usually have a direct effect on the interior design. An overall assessment of the conditions of the water protection systems will usually have a direct correlation to problems that may exist on the interior. Old, deteriorated, or missing roofing components—such as roof shingles, metal pans and gutters, and downspouts—are common indications of potential water problems. Isolated areas of extreme peeling paint and isolated or overall masonry deterioration are warning signs that moisture penetration into the interior is very likely.

- *Interior structural assessment:* The evaluation of structural deficiencies in a building interior should be resolved by an appropriately trained and licensed individual. Under normal conditions, if finish materials have failed because of structural deficiencies, they will fail again following rehabilitation if the structural problems are not corrected. Sloping or spongy, sagging floors may indicate beam or joist failure. Badly cracked ceilings or loss of plaster may give indications of vibration or impact loading on floors above. Misaligned window and door heads are signs of settlement problems. Springy or shaky stairs warn of damage to the undercarriage.

Secondary rehabilitation structural members that have been added to a building are indications of previous failure or insufficient sizing or spacing of the original framing. Conditional assessment of a structure should include observations to locate potential deterioration resulting from outside aging. Examples of such agents include insect infestation, bacteriological decay, and fire damage. For example, the presence of termites can be noted visually by observing the mud tubes or tunnels that they build on the interior and exterior surfaces of masonry walls, particularly foundations. Small accumulations of sawdustlike material may also be noted on horizontal floors. In extreme cases, the chewing activities of termites becomes audible to the human ear. Because tunneling of termites may be extensive, the structural integrity of wood members cannot be evaluated by visual inspection alone, evaluation requires probing with a sharp instrument. Powder post beetles may be detected from the presence of tiny pinholes on the surface of a beam or joist. Unlike termites, the beetles bore into the wood only to lay their eggs; they do not consume it as a food source.

The presence of molds, mildew, and fungus can be detected visually and often by smell as well. In general, they depend on the same environmental conditions as people. The primary problem in evaluating the extent of damage caused by them is that normally, the extent of deterioration inside a wood member is often several times greater than the evidence exhibited on the outside. Fire damage to structural members should be evaluated by a structural engineer. The residual cross section of a charred member may or may not be adequate to permit the continued dependency on its structural capabilities.[21]

Rehabilitation and Adaptive Use

In rehabilitation and adaptive use projects, most problems result from the alterations that must be addressed in adapting an old building, while preserving the historic integrity of the building. Until recently the tendency has been to concentrate on the exterior and gut the interior. Today there is a move to preserve the distinctive historic interiors and to minimize the alterations done to the plan of the building. This can be a difficult task. Charles E. Fisher, editor of the National Park Service's Preservation Tech Notes, states,

> *Certainly, interior preservation is the most complex, least understood aspect of historic preservation, and very little has been written on the technical issues designers often encounter. The greatest damage to historic interiors, however, results from poor planning.*[22]

Fisher further emphasizes the extreme importance of early project planning identifying the qualities in the interior that give the building its historic character; this often determines the success of the project. Space planning in a historic building seems to be the most difficult problem that a designer encounters in meeting the Standards. Frequently problems occur when the new plan is not compatible with the existing historic plan.

According to the NPS, a successful rehabilitation must meet *The Secretary of the Interior's Standards for Rehabilitation and Guidelines for Rehabilitating Historic Buildings.* Complying with the Standards creates problems for designers as they strive to receive rehabilitation certification. The inability to comply with the Standards creates major problems for the tenant/client who is denied certification. The National Park Service, Technical Assistance Division, releases bulletins on "Interpreting the Secretary of the Interior's Standards for Rehabilitation." By utilizing case studies, the NPS bulletins highlight certain standards that may create difficulties for designers.

If a building is already completely divested of its original interiors and walls, there is no need for concern for saving interior historic fabric. The designer merely approaches the job as new construction. The designer is free to use either contemporary or historical interior treatment and plan. However, it would be a mistake to recreate a period interior that is not representative of the historical style of the building. A clearly contemporary style or a reconstructed correct historical interior is more acceptable and is known as respectful rehabilitation.

It is the designer's responsibility to protect the historic interior features during construction and to include this in the contract. In his article on the importance of historic interiors in preservation, Charles E. Fisher warns the designer that inadequately protected architectural features and finishes during rehabilitation incur costly and often irreversible damage.

As noted earlier, the Secretary of the Interior defines restoration as "the act or process of accurately recovering the form and details of a property and its setting as it appeared at a particular period of time by means of the removal of later work or by the replacement of missing earlier work."

Difficulty arises when changes have taken place in the course of the history and development of the historic building. The designer often is unsure as to the proper historical period to which to restore the building.

As Fischer explains in his article on rehabilitating the interiors of historic buildings, it is important that the designer do his or her homework prior to the project construction. Planning early is a vital part of the rehabilitation design process.

> *Evaluating the individual and collective significance of a building interior's architectural features is invaluable in planning its rehabilitation needs. All interior architectural elements original to the structure need to be considered as to condition, whether these elements should be retained and possibly repaired, or whether they could be replaced.*[23]

EDUCATIONAL REQUIREMENTS FOR HISTORIC PROJECTS

In the late 1970s the National Trust for Historic Preservation sponsored a national assessment of higher education in historic preservation. In 1978 the formation of a Higher Education Study Group, sponsored by the Trust, recommended the formation of a national association of preservation educators. In 1979, the National Council for Preservation Education (NCPE) began to work on outlining pertinent goals and objectives. At the 1980 annual meeting in New York City, the newly formed Council pinpointed improved training standards as one of its national priorities.

In 1989, during the National Trust's Annual Conference in Philadelphia, the NCPE recommended that a five-year plan be implemented to encourage member institutions to begin internal planning and development efforts to bring their programs into compliance by 1994 for initial accreditation. The new guidelines deal not only with students and faculty, but an increased concern for improved facilities, equipment, and financial support.

CONCLUSION

Although the complexities of working with a historic structure are many, so are the rewards a designer can gain from the experience. Examples of preservation projects, respectful restorations, rehabilitation, and adaptive use projects are important to the interior design community at large and preserve our sense of heritage.

Retail Store Design

CHARLENE NELSON-PENSKI

The one thing that sets retail design apart from all other types of interior design is that sales are the primary motivation for every design decision. And, while there is no single element that results in a successful retail store, many subliminal factors contribute to high-volume sales.

Just as a restaurant must achieve a balance between quality food, level of service, and ambience, a retail store must strive for a balance between innovative merchandising, responsive service, and an exciting environment that stimulates the senses.

TYPES OF SHOPPERS

There are two primary types of buying behaviors: impulse buying as a form of entertainment, and preplanned purchases such as food, drink, clothing, and gifts.

Items and services purchased on impulse must continually be exposed to potential customers, while goods and services that customers seek on a preplanned basis do not require the same degree of exposure. The shopper with preplanned objectives may be in a hurry. Therefore, it is paramount to provide easy, efficient circulation, clear graphic identification, and effective display concepts for this type of shopper. The impulse shopper, on the other hand, responds to the shopping experience as much as to products to be purchased. Shopping for the impulse buyer should be a multisensory experience that appeals to a variety of the senses.

While visual displays are the obvious answer to wooing customers into buying, and customers are attracted to a dramatic theatrical environment, an appropriately placed perfume counter or soft background music can play an equally powerful role in enhancing sales opportunities.

CATEGORIES OF RETAIL DESIGN

There are four primary categories of retail design: shopping centers, large department stores, specialty shops, and off-price retail outlets.

Shopping Centers

During periods of positive economic times, shopping becomes a pastime of the American people. Parents, children, teenagers, and young professionals come to shopping centers for entertainment, as well as to purchase goods. Thus, the interior design of shopping malls—either a new center or a renovation—should create visual excitement, focal points such as garden courts and clock towers, or a central stage area that draws shoppers into and through the center. Many malls incorporate child-care services, theaters, hotels, and entertainment parks to provide increasing appeal and encourage shoppers to spend more time at the mall.

A careful balance must be struck between dramatic common area elements and colors, and the visual presence and excitement of the individual storefront designs. A drab monochromatic center adds nothing to the shops' presence, while complicated and overly bold common areas can overpower the designs of the stores and shift the center's focus away from its primary purpose—maximizing sales.

Large Department Stores

Circulation and individual department identity are the predominant challenges in the design of a large retail store. Circulation must be conducive to shoppers moving easily to and from departments, while also encouraging browsing and spontaneous impulse purchasing.

Hard-surface aisles can be utilized as primary circulation paths to encourage easy movement, while carpeting or other floor treatments can be implemented in the individual departments to slow a shopper's pace and create a more relaxed shopping environment.

Large stores also require that the design team create continuity throughout the store, as well as distinctive identities for each of the individual departments. Many department stores treat each department as a boutique. Each has its own distinctive identity, while at the same time complementing the other departments and the overall store architecture. Custom-designed carpets, wall coverings, furnishings, fixtures, and interior detailing are frequently used to create the various boutique themes.

Specialty Retail Shops

Specialty shops are often designed on a tight budget and are, by definition, restricted to a relatively confined space. With the intense competition between specialty shops, getting the potential customer to cross the threshold is a paramount goal. This is typically achieved in the following ways:

- Creating a cohesive design statement that instantly transmits the store image: high-end or discount, modern or traditional, conservative or radical, warm or cool.
- Developing a store sign and/or logo that is memorable, identifiable, and at the same time related to the kind of goods being offered.
- Presenting the store merchandise to the passing shopper in an eye-catching and unique manner in the storefront windows.
- Merchandising the store as a whole with easy traffic flow, multiple points of interest, organized departments, and a focused point-of-sale counter with carefully placed impulse sales items. Two special locations are especially critical: displays at the store entrance to entice the shopper in, and a strong focal point at the rear of the store to pull the shopper back to the deeper merchandise.
- Designing a lighting system that is appropriate to the style and design of the store and that complements the merchandising systems and areas of focus.

Another consideration in the design of specialty stores is the ability—and the need—to maintain an extremely current design image. Specialty stores are redesigned an average of every five to seven years, so the design approach can be more dramatic and avant-garde than with a large department store.

Off-Price Retail Outlets

Functional space that provides the ability to handle high volumes of merchandise is the major criterion for off-price store design. These stores generally require a cost-effective design solution that is suitable for high-volume traffic and requires relatively low maintenance.

Careful choice of materials and an understanding of their cost and performance is especially critical. The design must also be built around a concept and display method that requires little maintenance and provides for the large volume of goods that move from truck to storeroom to showroom floor.

DESIGN CONSIDERATIONS FOR RETAIL SPACES

Several design considerations are of extreme importance when creating a retail space. These are display, lighting, and interior finishes.

Display

Technical advances have affected a variety of display techniques. For example, a recent issue of *Visual Merchandising & Store Design* discussed an eye-tracking device that measures the eye movement of the customer. This device has helped retailers understand the behavior of the shopper and monitoring the manner in which the shopper views items, and for what length of time.

Lighting

A dramatic change has taken place in lighting during the last few years. Energy codes have become more restrictive, so designers have had to become much more creative in their use of lighting and their specification of efficient lamps and fixtures.

Even traditional forms of lighting, such as fluorescent and incandescent, have undergone radical changes. The development of tri-phosphor coatings for fluorescent tubes has created a group of lamps with exceptional color rendering capabilities, such as G.E.'s SPX series. Miniaturization of fluorescent lamps, such as the T-4 double twin tube lamps, has improved efficiency, increased lumens per watt output, and allowed new and varied fixtures to be developed to house these fluorescent lamps.

The development of a variety of low-voltage halogen lamps has provided the retail designer with excellent sources of narrow-focus, high-quality light (high CRI) for merchandise spotting. The advent of line-voltage halogen in both large and small PAR lamps—PAR 38 to PAR 16—has allowed the use of halogen lighting as a retrofit element in stores and also as a less expensive alternative to low-voltage fixtures.

General Electric has announced the introduction of a 60-watt PAR 38 halogen lamp with the same lumen output as a 150-watt regular PAR 38. This is a revolutionary advancement in incandescent efficiency and will become a workhorse lamp for the retail design field, where quality light from an energy-efficient source is critical.

Improvements such as these are occurring almost daily in the lighting field. To provide the highest-quality and most efficient designs, retail designers must be well versed in lighting design and must stay abreast of this constantly changing field.

Interior Finishes

An interesting array of man-made materials surfaced in the marketplace in the late 1980s and early 1990s. Because of ever-increasing concerns about cost, designers are replacing costly natural materials such as wood and marble with less costly man-made materials. For example:

- Plastic laminates have evolved from flat, solid colors to a multitude of patterns, textures, and color statements.
- Synthetic stones have emerged that offer designers the character of expensive materials at a reasonable price.
- Carpets are being perfected for durability and appearance through the technical advancement of fibers in the marketplace. An impressive selection of colors, patterns, and textures is available, and the advancement of printed carpet techniques is offering an alternative to woven products.

NECESSARY SKILLS OF A RETAIL DESIGNER

The success of any retail interior design project depends on how well the design team has addressed four key issues:

- *Market*: Who are the end users, and how will they respond to the retail environment?

- *Function*: How does the owner want the store to operate and be maintained?
- *Design*: How can the designer create the proper balance between image, aesthetics, costs, function, maintenance, and schedule?
- *Value*: Does the project make economic sense?

The successful designer is committed to providing design solutions that maximize value to the client. This means attaining the appropriate image, function, and return on investment. The goal of successful retail design is to combine function, design impact, and cost-effective visual merchandising to create the most profitable selling environment.

To achieve this end, retail designers must have a thorough understanding of how merchandise is marketed and displayed. They must be able to manipulate and control the lighting for maximum visual impact, while conforming to energy code restrictions.

The effective retail designer understands the psychological effect of color on human behavior; the use of visual clues to indicate the location of certain types of merchandise; the performance of various materials as they relate to the retailer's maintenance program; and effective fixturing design, layout, and space planning that results in maximized circulation and sales. Most importantly, the designer must understand the retailer's business. For the designer to understand these things, an education is essential—preferably from a FIDER-accredited institution with an emphasis on interior architecture, furniture design, and detailing. This, coupled with an apprenticeship program, provides a sound foundation for someone wishing to specialize in retail design.

BUSINESS AND PROJECT MANAGEMENT

Good design requires good management. Active project management is required during all phases of design to ensure that the final product meets or exceeds the fiscal and scheduling objectives established by the project pro forma.

To provide a comprehensive design service, the project manager is responsible for the coordination and management of all aspects of the project—from initial studies to design and production of contract documents. To complete a project, the team must be supplemented with specialized consultants who have been chosen for their specific expertise and experience.

As in any project, it is critical that the designer understand the scope of work:

- What is the nature, size, and location of the project?
- What is the design concept, image, and clientele?
- What relationships exist between the designer, owner, contractors, and consultants?
- What is the project schedule and time frame?
- What is the budget, and how will the purchasing be accomplished?
- What is the merchandise mix?

A qualified designer can offer a wide range of services, depending on the size and qualifications of the staff. It is very important to clarify which services can be provided at the onset of the project. A few services that are typically provided include code research, block planning, interior design, casework design, fixture design, graphics, display layouts, material selections, lighting design, and electrical coordination.

Once the scope of work is determined, the organization and management of the project can be developed. The management of retail projects is not unlike other interior design projects. The typical stages of schematic design, design development, contract documents, construction administration, and project closeout are followed in each retail design project.

CRITICAL DESIGN PATH OUTLINE

Following are the critical design paths necessary for a successful retail design project.

Predesign

Establish proper channels of communication:

Within the designer's in-house team.
With the client's project manager and other key personnel.
Among owner, architect, designer, consultants, and contractor.

Establish design and program criteria:

Meet with individuals—managers, operational staff, merchandise buyers, security personnel, visual merchandising personnel, marketing representatives, and members of the customer base—who are responsible for the facility's design.
Identify image.
Identify merchandising goals and future direction.
Identify consumer target and product needs.

Define criteria:

Merchandise categories to be included.
Services to be included.
Display requirements.
Necessary operational equipment.
Analysis of proposed project sales.
Special limitations and considerations such as lease considerations, landlord requirements, and applicable building codes.

Define project schedule.

Design

Concept design:

Prepare visual representations of program options.
With owner, evaluate and choose direction.

Design development:

Develop initial scheme for client review. Studies include plan and elevation, entrance and facade design, special features (display areas, signage, show windows), color and material finish, casework and fixture designs, and preliminary lighting layout.

Prepare budget estimates.
Obtain client's approval or revisions.
Have proposal reviewed by Building Department officials, as required.
Have contractors review building materials and construction methods to ensure cost control.
Review and update project schedule.
Present materials for landlord approval.

Construction documents:
Organize construction document package and establish CAD involvement as necessary.
Coordinate with design/build mechanical and electrical consultants.
Prepare construction documents.
Assemble necessary product data and specification.
Provide necessary documentation for the purchase of furnishings, fixtures, and equipment.
Assemble graphics and signage bid package.
Submit construction documents to bidders.

Bid phase:
Collect, analyze, and award contract.
Submit construction documents to Building Department for necessary permits.
Ensure that contractor reviews and updates construction costs.

Administration/construction observation:
Hold preconstruction meeting.
Prepare orders for contractor.
Follow contractor's progress and adhere to schedule.
Visit site and approve of subcontractor work, as required.
Review shop drawings, samples, and alternative product submittals and schedules.
Do punch list.
Verify contractor billing.
Follow up on owner's comments.

UNIQUE PROBLEMS IN RETAIL DESIGN

Retail design requires the coordination of numerous experts to produce the project. For example, there may be a general contractor, millwork contractor, casework contractor, fixture contractor, and furniture supplier working on a typical project, at the same time as acoustical, graphics and signage, lighting, mechanical, and electrical consultants.

The coordination of finishes alone can become quite involved. Clear contract documents and a well-defined scope of work will help construction proceed smoothly while minimizing cost and budget overruns.

Other unique problems specific to retail design include:

- *Maximum utilization of space.* This means with no "dead corners."

- *Security optimization.* Because shoplifting and shrinkage are major problems for retailers, designers must work with the owner to minimize the opportunities for shoplifting and aid security personnel in the protection of the store.

- *An efficient, responsive process for updating the store.* Retailers must remain up to date on trends and fashions. This results in many changes during design and construction.

- *Minimizing risks.* Retailers are prime targets for slip-and-fall claims. Designers must be sensitive to risk management when selecting materials and designing retail space.

USEFUL PUBLICATIONS, ORGANIZATIONS, AND CONSULTANTS

The following list of resources, organizations, and consultants is provided for designers entering the retail design field.

- Publications:
  Visual Merchandising & Store Design
  Lighting Dimensions
  Stores of the Year
  Best of Store Design
  MONITOR

- Organizations:
  Institute of Store Planners (ISP)
  American Society of Interior Designers (ASID)
  Institute of Business Designers (IBD)
  International Council of Shopping Centers (ICSC)

- Consultants:
  Graphics
  Acoustical
  Mechanical
  Electrical
  Structural
  Display
  Fixturing
  Security
  Fire protection

CONCLUSION

Interior designers must be prepared to play many roles during a retail project. Throughout the project they must serve in the role of engineer, planner, statistician, market researcher, economist, manager, psychologist, sociologist, artist, and visionary. Qualified designers with a degree in interior design—and the expertise to offer quality retail space that meets the needs of store owners—play an important role in this exciting and challenging market.

Retail Store Design

BARBARA EBSTEIN

Retail store design is a specialty area practiced by a growing number of individuals with various backgrounds and experiences. The largest groups include interior designers and architects. The term "store planner" includes these professionals, as well as designers and planners with backgrounds in visual merchandising, the trades, and store construction. Some have a design education, while others bring a background of experience in store design to the specialty area. As a group, these are knowledgeable professionals, respected by landlords and clients alike.

THE CLIENTS

The successful store designer understands that the retail client may change marketing direction quickly on the basis of economic influences and consumer habits. In the past, the life span of a store design was about ten years. This was approximately the amount of time before finishes needed replacing, lighting needed upgrading, and customer preferences required a new look. Today changes may occur faster.

Savvy shopping center developers and retailers are placing their facilities close to the living and working locations of the customers to whom they sell. A more market-driven approach to leasing of space with centers is becoming common. In general, centers cater either to the upper-income customer or to the off-price customer. The strategy of the developer is to increase traffic and sales by having all the stores in a shopping center aimed at the targeted group.

Location and market position are prime considerations for the retail store designer. Store design cannot be a monument to the retailer or the designer. To be successful, a store must attract the targeted segment of the buying population, fit their design comfort level, and encourage them to purchase. Take, for example, the off-price retailer selling to the 15- to 25-year-old female group, who decided to upgrade the store by using marble flooring at the storefront. It was a disaster. Customers were confused and felt that they were no longer wanted. Older, more sophisticated women were drawn to the store, but upon entering discovered that the product was not for them, and sales dropped.

In another instance, a well-known lighting designer was hired by a discount department chain to suggest energy-efficient lighting changes. One suggestion was to replace the glaring ceiling lighting with high-output, low-surface brightness fixtures. The retailer refused because the existing lighting contributed to his discount look, and he felt that his customers would immediately perceive the suggested changes as a departure from low discount prices.

STORE DESIGN AS RETAIL THEATRE

The designer's job is to create an attractive functional space that promotes sales. The basics of good store design are that the design is functional, serves the needs of the owner and customer, enhances the product, and captures the interest of the market. Retail design is theatre. The designer incorporates illusion, history, and humor into the shopping experience. Stores should be fun with a dominant theme element.

One way to achieve a theatrical appearance is through product dominance. For this strategy to be successful, the product should have some inherent drama of its own. The store should be treated as a neutral scene with a strong lighting statement supportive of, and never in competition with, the product.

Another approach to the design of retail as theatre is to integrate the designer image with the product. Product is still the focal point, but the style and feel of the product's designer is clear in the store design. Examples of this kind of store would be the Disney store, Ralph Lauren stores, Abercrombie and Fitch, and Banana Republic.

A third approach in the creation of retail theatre is to establish designer dominance. Although one might think this is contrary to some of the concepts of retail store design, it can work and be successful. The shopper is transported beyond time or place, and the product is secondary. Victoria's Secret and Laura Ashley are two stores fitting this category.

Mood is also a part of retail theatre. Tone sets mood. The interior can be playful or serious; active or passive; exciting or subdued. The way a store is designed and the way merchandise is displayed tell the shopper more about the store than the merchandise alone reveals. Visualize a jewelry store with an awe-inspiring solid front and jewelry displays locked within cases. The authority figure, the salesperson, is behind the cases. Customers must be helped. Immediately the customer clearly perceives that the items sold here are exclusive and expensive. On the other hand, an adult toy store selling gadgets, funky telephones, and gifts with an open, informal, nonthreatening, fun facade invites the customer to pick up the product. The tone of each is different but clear to the consumer.

Visual clues are also used by store designers to help create an image in retail theatre. Visual clues include the quality and choice of materials, the type and quantity of lighting, the extent of the storefront closure, the type of display fixtures, and the signage and graphics. Of course, of primary importance as a visual clue is the product itself.

A well-designed and well-merchandised storefront is the single most important area to create retail theatre. As noted store designer Ken Walker once said, "You never get a second chance to make a first impression." Statistics show that it takes three seconds for a shopper to decide whether to enter a store. Presentation and threshold resistance are factors affecting that decision. Once a commitment to enter is made, people automatically are convinced that they made the right choice.

Storefronts are of three basic types in today's shopping malls and downtown areas. There are (1) closed storefronts with small distinctive show windows displaying a few expensive items and a small entry, (2) a combination of closed and open storefronts, with small show windows or a large display window with a wide entry, and (3) the open storefront.

Most popular today is the combination front. It allows visibility into the store while affording interesting product display in view of the entrance. Additionally, shoppers are attracted by other people shopping within and by the color, light, and motion of the combination front.

The open storefront was popular in the 1950s and 1960s, when shopping malls were perceived as retail stores and specialty stores were perceived as departments within the retail environment. This type of storefront lacks image and requires no commitment to enter.

FUNCTION AS A KEY TO RETAIL DESIGN

Functional retail design provides for focal display areas, merchandising, product evaluation, consummation of sale, and backup stock areas available for retailers and customers. Focal display includes window display and special displays throughout the store. These are separate from mass merchandise display and are accented by lighting or other design techniques. Areas of product evaluation are places where customers can view themselves and the product, such as mirrors and fitting rooms. Sale consummation areas are at cash desks.

With retail rents increasing rapidly, the design focus is to provide as much space as possible for the sales area. To avoid jamming products in, a simple circulation pattern can be designed that prevents the consumer from bumping into things. If displayed merchandise and/or fixtures are too close together, shoppers become uncomfortable. There should be an unconfused, clear exit from the store for customers.

THE RETAIL DESIGNER'S RESPONSIBILITIES

The designer is responsible for designing the store to meet the retailer's criteria and to prepare the design drawings necessary for bid and construction. These include:

- Storefront design and signage
- Interior construction plan with fixed walls, exits, lavatories, and stockroom
- Electrical plan
- Reflective ceiling plan and lighting
- Color and decor plan
- Construction/color/decor elevations
- Fixture plan
- Custom construction and fixture details
- Items not usually included as the designer's responsibility include:
- Structural engineering
- Mechanical engineering
- Electrical wiring and load calculations
- Plumbing diagrams

In general, the scope of a retail store project is similar to that required in other design specialties. Often the designer will put the job out to bid, review the bids with the owner, answer contractors' questions, and prepare a punch list for the final installation of the store. The designer is responsible for the safety of the design, but not its execution or the performance of the contractors. The normal method of financial compensation is based on either a fee per square foot, or an hourly billing not to exceed a predetermined dollar amount. Normal out-of-pocket expenses are billed separately.

CONCLUSION

Creating a retail space is a challenging experience for the interior designer. When done effectively, retail design combines theatre and visual merchandising to create an environment that stimulates a shopper's senses and promotes the sale of products.

Government Design

MARY KNOPF

The three main areas of government design are space planning for government agencies, interior design for the various arms of the Department of Defense, and term or individual private-sector interior design contracts.

GOVERNMENT AGENCIES

There are several agencies that require residential space planners or designers. The best known is the General Services Administration (GSA). GSA is the property manager for most space leased and owned by the government. However, several other agencies have authority to manage their own space, including the ability to hire staff designers. These agencies include the administrative office of the Courts, the Federal Aviation Administration (FAA), the Internal Revenue Service (IRS), the National Aeronautics and Space Administration (NASA), the National Park Service (NPS), and the National Oceanic and Atmospheric Administration (NOAA). Available design positions are at the regional or national level. For example, Region 10 GSA covers the West Coast states, while the other agencies listed generally house their design staffs at a national level.

Department of Defense (DOD)

Divisions of the Department of Defense that include interior design staff include the Army Corps of Engineers (C.O.E.), Naval Facilities Engineering Commands (NAVFACENGCOM), the Air Force Civil Engineering Squadrons (CES), and the Air Force Division of Engineering & Housing (DEH). The operations of these military divisions are broken down into regional and local offices. For example, WESTDIVNAVFAC is the Western Division of the Naval Facilities Engineering Command located in San Bruno, California, and it covers the Western states' naval facilities. At the base level there is the CES/DEEEA division or Civil Engineering Squadron Department of Engineering, Engineering and Environmental Planning, the Architectural Section.

A local base may have authority over a project—or, depending on size, the regional or national military offices may control the project. Interior designers are most likely to be found at the regional or the national level. However, because the size of each installation may vary, the hiring policies of each military base and regional command in the area may differ.

Term or Individual Design Contracts

Various government agencies and local Department of Defense offices have the authority to award design contracts up to a certain dollar or delivery amount. Some of these contracts cover individual projects, such as a new dormitory; others cover a term of one to three years to produce various projects. Term contracts may include planning general office space, a new officers' club, or a base chapel.

Each project under a term contract is negotiated separately. Contracts will vary in scope and delivery amounts. The government advertises for these contracts through requests for proposals (RFPs), which are generally advertised in the *Commerce Business Daily* and/or in local newspapers under the invitation-to-bid section of the classifieds. These RFPs are most often requesting information on a firm's experience—not a bid amount for a project.

NECESSARY SKILLS AND EDUCATION IN GOVERNMENT DESIGN

The required degree of skill and education necessary to secure a design project in government design will vary according to the requirements of each firm, agency, or position.

Government Agencies and the Department of Defense

Positions offered regionally by government agencies are most often those of space planners. Some local DOD positions and national agency offices also include interior design work, specifications, procurement/acquisition, and project management. The degree of education required varies from a two-year drafting program to a college degree or even a graduate degree.

Government agencies offer numerous on-the-job training programs, enabling a person with a two-year drafting certificate to specialize in space planning. An individual with a four-year college degree, or more, will enter at a higher level and have the opportunity for accelerated advancement. Government positions generally start at a slightly lower pay level than equal positions in private industry.

However, there are more fringe benefits, and advancement is faster from entry-level positions. For self-motivated designers, the government provides valuable presentation and time-management training along with the sharpening of such design skills as space planning, client relations, and public relations. All positions offer the possibility of continuing within the government hierarchy into project or people management positions.

Project size varies according to the position in the organizational flow of each agency. Obviously, the national headquarters of an agency is going to offer the largest and most in-depth projects. However, at a regional or local level, an agency or military office may have in-house architectural and engineering staffs of varying sizes that will support larger projects.

Individual and Term Contracts

The education and skills necessary depend upon the requirements of the private firm that receives a contract. Proposals as requested by the government consist of Standard Forms SF-254 and SF-255, both several pages long. These forms provide a record of past experience relating to the particular project, or of general government experience, including staff resumes on each member of the proposed design team. (See Figures 1 and 2.) Form SF-255 provides a small amount of flexibility for expressing the firm's experience, whereas form SF-254 is a cut-and-dried, fill-in-the-blanks format.

Term and individual project contracts allow for various levels of expertise from drafting to interior design and project management, with the pay levels varying accordingly. These contracts generally require a minimum of two designers who have successfully completed the NCIDQ examination. Beyond contract staffing specifications, it is up to each individual firm to determine its own staffing requirements. Under a term contract, specific projects may be further supplemented through in-house expansion or through subcontracts with other individuals or firms.

Many of the proposal invitations require the prime contractor to be an architectural and/or engineering (A/E) firm, to which an interior design firm then becomes a subcontractor. For design firms wishing to break into government design, this is the type of contract offering the most opportunity. As a subcontractor or part of a joint venture, the design firm may not need previous government experience. Government work obtained through a subcontract or joint venture can be used as experience for future RFPs.

BUSINESS AND PROJECT MANAGEMENT IN GOVERNMENT DESIGN

The field of government design includes many business and project management positions, which vary from one area of government to another.

Government Agencies

The design staff support for an agency in the business of property management is fairly small. Design positions are associated with the agency's real estate division. Offices offering these positions are at the regional level or above, and the positions cover at least a multistate area. A staff of three or four space planners or designers may be individually appointed to a state or area, or an office may have each planner available for projects in any regional state or area. The positions require travel and individual responsibility. The small number of design staff rarely allows for a team approach to design. The division may assign a manager over the design staff who assigns projects and follows up with periodic time frame checks. Other than this, each staff member manages his or her own project time frames and design style. This translates into a necessity for management skills and self-starters.

An individual designer in the field may work alone or travel and work with counterparts from other branches or divisions. Although this is not a team approach, the designer does work closely with counterparts and with a representative from the agency, office, or building affected. This requires training in various positions and job responsibilities within an agency to accomplish interdivisional working efficiency and growth potential. Refer to the sample GSA organization chart shown in Figure 3 to understand the workings of most real estate divisions.

Government designers, both those within individual agencies and those working for GSA, must have both political and public relations skills. Whether the designer is assisting a local office supervisor for an agency or working for GSA with a district court judge, there is a fear of territorial interference. Government designers often find themselves participating in client education and justification of services.

The primary publication for the various agencies is the Federal Property Management Regulation, Temporary Regulation D-73 (FPMR Temp. Reg. D-73) which is published by GSA. Here is an excerpt from it:

January 8, 1987

To: Heads of Federal Agencies

Subject: Quality Workplace Environment

1. Philosophy. These regulations establish a program through which the quality of Federal office space is improved and productivity is enhanced, while the total amount of space is reduced. The ultimate goal of the program is to accomplish cost-effective space reductions which will result in long-term monetary savings to the Federal Government. However, the regulations recognize that space costs for most agencies represent less than 2 percent of their operational costs and GSA's efforts must focus primarily on the quality of the work environment. In fact, recent experiences have shown that well designed space using modern technologies can both substantially increase productivity and reduce total space costs. These goals will be accomplished by placing greater emphasis on modernizing existing space; making health and safety improvements; consolidating agencies; purchasing and leasing high quality, efficient buildings; and encouraging the use

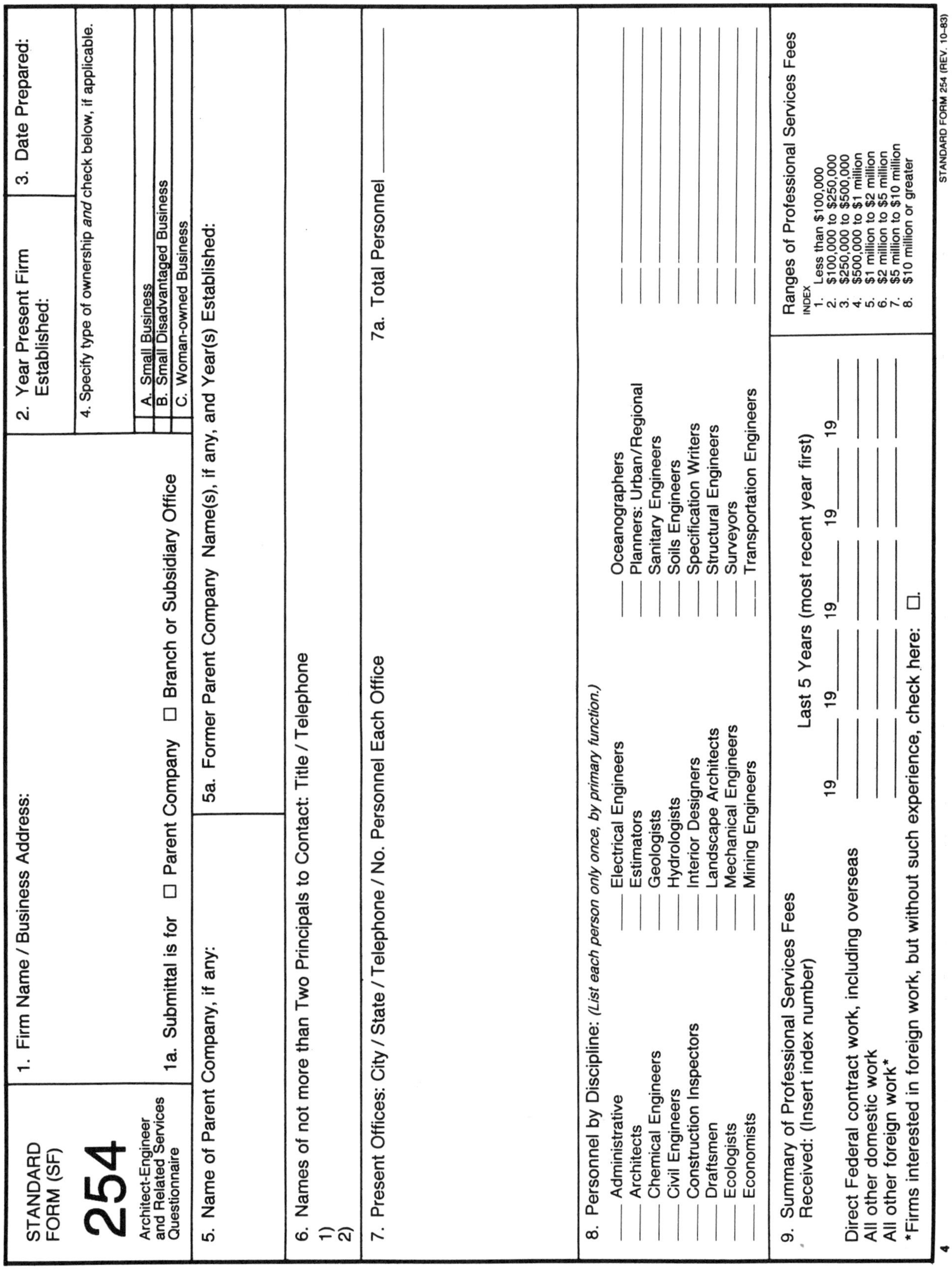

STANDARD FORM (SF)

254

Architect-Engineer and Related Services Questionnaire

1. Firm Name / Business Address:

2. Year Present Firm Established:

3. Date Prepared:

1a. Submittal is for ☐ Parent Company ☐ Branch or Subsidiary Office

4. Specify type of ownership *and* check below, if applicable.

A. Small Business

B. Small Disadvantaged Business

C. Woman-owned Business

5. Name of Parent Company, if any:

5a. Former Parent Company Name(s), if any, and Year(s) Established:

6. Names of not more than Two Principals to Contact: Title / Telephone

1)

2)

7. Present Offices: City / State / Telephone / No. Personnel Each Office

7a. Total Personnel ______

8. Personnel by Discipline: *(List each person only once, by primary function.)*

___ Administrative	___ Electrical Engineers	___ Oceanographers
___ Architects	___ Estimators	___ Planners: Urban/Regional
___ Chemical Engineers	___ Geologists	___ Sanitary Engineers
___ Civil Engineers	___ Hydrologists	___ Soils Engineers
___ Construction Inspectors	___ Interior Designers	___ Specification Writers
___ Draftsmen	___ Landscape Architects	___ Structural Engineers
___ Ecologists	___ Mechanical Engineers	___ Surveyors
___ Economists	___ Mining Engineers	___ Transportation Engineers

9. Summary of Professional Services Fees Received: (Insert index number)

	Last 5 Years (most recent year first)				
	19___	19___	19___	19___	19___
Direct Federal contract work, including overseas	___	___	___	___	___
All other domestic work	___	___	___	___	___
All other foreign work*	___	___	___	___	___

*Firms interested in foreign work, but without such experience, check here: ☐

Ranges of Professional Services Fees

INDEX

1. Less than $100,000
2. $100,000 to $250,000
3. $250,000 to $500,000
4. $500,000 to $1 million
5. $1 million to $2 million
6. $2 million to $5 million
7. $5 million to $10 million
8. $10 million or greater

STANDARD FORM 254 (REV. 10–83)

4

Figure 1. The first page of Standard Form SF-254 to be filled out by the applicant.

OMB Approval No. **3090–0029**

STANDARD FORM (SF) 255 Architect-Engineer Related Services for Specific Project	1. Project Name / Location for which Firm is Filing:	2a. ***Commerce Business Daily*** Announcement Date, if any:	2b. Agency Identification Number, if any:

3. Firm (or Joint-Venture) Name & Address	3a. Name, Title & Telephone Number of Principal to Contact 3b. Address of office to perform work, if different from Item 3

4. Personnel by Discipline: (List each person only once, by primary function.)

___ Administrative	___ Electrical Engineers	___ Oceanographers	___ ________
___ Architects	___ Estimators	___ Planners: Urban/Regional	___ ________
___ Chemical Engineers	___ Geologists	___ Sanitary Engineers	___ ________
___ Civil Engineers	___ Hydrologists	___ Soils Engineers	___ ________
___ Construction Inspectors	___ Interior Designers	___ Specification Writers	___ ________
___ Draftsmen	___ Landscape Architects	___ Structural Engineers	___ ________
___ Ecologists	___ Mechanical Engineers	___ Surveyors	___ ________
___ Economists	___ Mining Engineers	___ Transportation Engineers	___ Total Personnel

5. If submittal is by JOINT-VENTURE list participating firms and outline specific areas of responsibility (including administrative, technical and financial) for each firm: (Attach SF 254 for each if not on file with Procuring Office.)

5a. Has this Joint-Venture previously worked together? ☐ yes ☐ no

3

STANDARD FORM 255 (Rev. 10–83)

Figure 2. The first page of Standard Form SF-255 to be filled out by the applicant.

of furniture systems where cost effective. These regulations are an important part of the total effort. Through this program, GSA will help make the Federal Government operate more efficiently and economically, and make it a better place to work for its employees.

Every position in a real estate division makes use of this publication. The form is available through GSA, National Forms and Publications Center, Box 17550, 819 Taylor Street, Fort Worth, TX 76102-0550.

Beyond having its own regulations for various applications of design, the federal government operates under a slightly different set of building codes. The application of government codes may exceed or fall short of local codes. The federal requirements supersede those of local governments for federally owned facilities.

Department of Defense

The various branches of the Department of Defense operate under different requirements. An interior designer will work either under a Civil Engineering Squadron (CES), a Department of Engineering & Housing (DEH) division, a Corps of Engineers (C.O.E.) A/E division, or a Naval Facilities Engineering Command (NAVFACENGCOM). The size of the projects completed depends upon the type of staff within a division. Some base installations may not include on-staff architects, whereas a regional office will. A base interior designer may wear many hats because of the lack of a complete design team. Designers working with fully staffed CES, DEH, C.O.E., or NAVFAC divisions interact with a team of architects and engineers, possibly as the only designer on a base facility or with a group of two to four designers in a regional office. The base offices that lack a full design staff work the majority of the time on base rehabilitation projects, rather than on new construction.

All positions require knowledge or on-the-job-training in government design and government purchasing practices. The Department of Defense has created its own set of regulations and guidelines. The most prevalent for interior design is the "Department of Defense Construction Criteria," Department of the Army Circular #415-84-1. Exact design criteria need to be verified with each branch of the armed services to determine discrepancies between branches.

Term or Individual Contracts

A new firm working in government design may be startled by the paperwork. Not only is the amount of paperwork larger for government projects, but the firm's books must be kept ready for an audit before, during, or following a project. Additionally, the prime contractor must submit to procurement integrity regulations, agreeing not to utilize employees of the government in the future as firm employees.

When a design firm contracts directly with the government, the fee structure is determined by a firm's employee pay scale plus a percentage for the firm's overhead. Calcu-

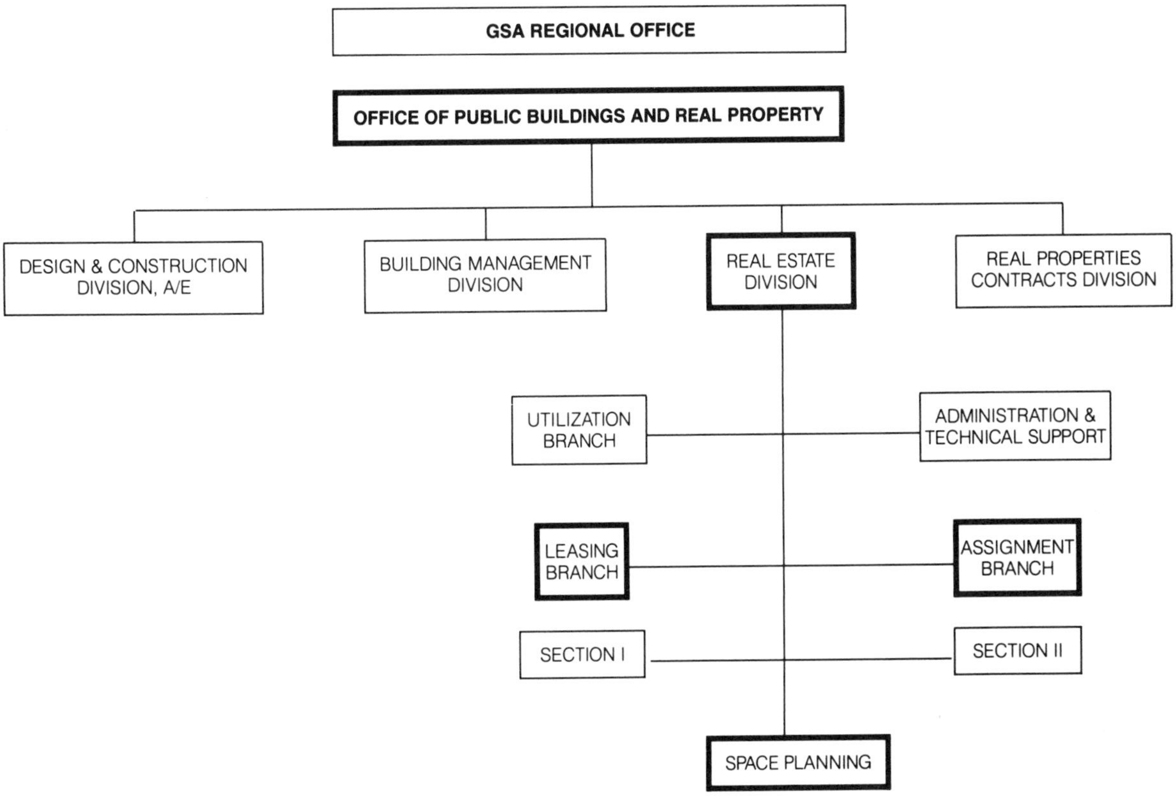

Figure 3. GSA organization chart.

lation of these figures requires a history of good job-costing practices. Whatever the standard hourly fees are, the firm should be prepared to accept less from the government. The advantage to government work is a steady workload and guaranteed payments for services rendered—not the fee schedules.

Whether a contract is with the government or an A/E prime, one or two representatives from a design firm will become the contacts. This requires a high degree of in-house review and interaction for projects with a large design team. Government contract projects operate within percentage completion stages similar to the design phases of other projects: programming/schematic (35 percent), design development (65 percent), construction documents (95 percent), and construction administration (100 percent). The main deviance from a private-sector project is in the schematic or 35 percent stage, where initial furniture specifications and cost estimates may be required in finished form. Because this information is provided so early in the process, computerizing the information for ease of change is imperative to stay within the time allotments in future phases.

UNIQUE AREAS OF CONCERN IN GOVERNMENT DESIGN

Problems faced by staff designers and those on contract to the government vary; however, many of the key areas of concern overlap.

Government Agencies and the Department of Defense

The biggest concern within the government design community is control over the implementation of a project. Because of the heavy departmentalization within the government, once a design has been approved, it is turned over to others for implementation. These documents may be changed without consulting the designer. Further, if a project site requires travel, the completed project may never be seen by the designer. For those facilities leased by the government, the staff designer is not able to provide input on building elements such as building colors and materials or lighting layout. The responsibility for these items lies with the lessor. Specific acceptability factors of schemes and lighting levels are included within the lease.

Rules and Guidelines

The federal government has reams and volumes of rules and regulations and information sources. Included in this vast store of resources are guidelines on design, including drafting requirements, general office space allotment, classroom sizes for educational facilities, square footages for courtrooms, and design layout.

Under a private contract this information may appear impossible to locate, but persistence and experience generally provide the necessary publication for any project. Never assume that a guideline or publication is not in existence for a project. Also, never assume the guidelines for one agency are the same as those of another. For example, each branch of the military has its own publication for dormitory guidelines—and they do differ!

Term or individual contracts will state that the contracting agency will provide all guidelines or publications required. This does not guarantee that a local office knows where to find the information. Obviously, it is in a firm's best interest to start to obtain the necessary documents even while still in the negotiation stage of a contract, before days are lost during the finite time frame for contract completion.

Keeping a government library can be a monumental task. Furniture purchased by government agencies must be specified through manufacturers with a current GSA contract. The most common duration for furnishings contracts is two years. At the end of that contract the companies supplying manufacturer's literature do not automatically update a firm's library. Unless a firm is continually requesting information for government specifications, designers will find the library out of date very quickly. This means that the design firm may have to research and rebuild a government library every two years.

The short duration of these furniture contracts has another ramification directly affecting a project. If a project has a completion date one and a half to two years down the road, the specifications written now may be obsolete at the time the procurement orders are placed. For example, during a typical project time frame, here's what may occur:

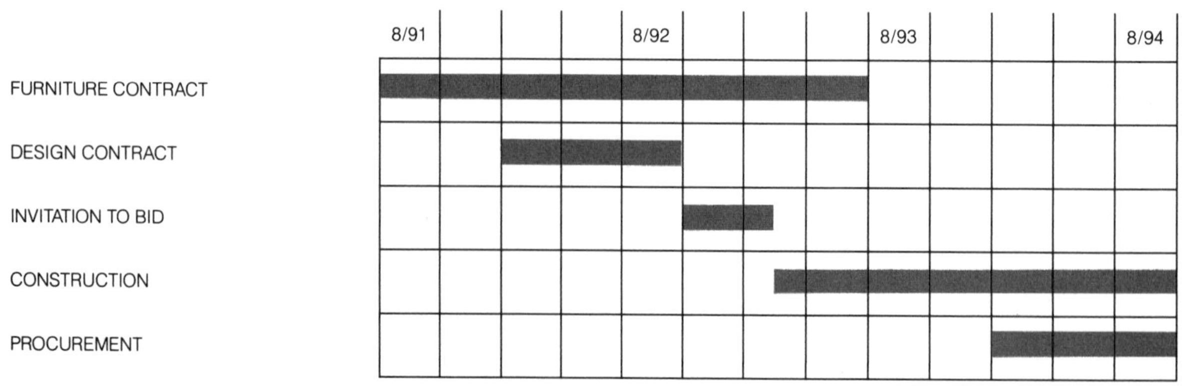

Figure 4. Bar chart illustrating how specifications can become obsolete before procurement.

A conference table has a contract schedule valid from 8/1/91 through 7/31/93. The table is selected during the 35 percent phase of the project on 2/1/92, six months into the contract. The design contract for the building is completed 11/30/92. The construction contract is let 3/1/93 for completion 9/30/94. Obviously the procurement of furniture specified during the design contract will not take place until six to eight months prior to completion of the building, or starting 1/1/94. Figure 4 shows how the furniture contract for the conference table expired prior to the start of procurement for that item. The design contract was completed, leaving the procurement officer with no direction for a comparable substitute. Generally furniture contracts are renewed, but some specialty items may change with each contract schedule.

RESOURCES AND ORGANIZATIONS IN GOVERNMENT DESIGN

There are a number of resources available to the design firm trying to establish itself in the field of government design.

Resources

One of the most valuable tools for anyone specifying government furniture is the GSA *Source One Master*. This publication has several ways of researching supply contracts: by contract number, by contractor name, by schedule index number, and by subject index. Identification of the item determines which section is used. The contractor name index is the most useful for checking a manufacturer for a known contract's expiration date, or for contractors' addresses. When attempting to locate all contracts for a specific item, it is best to start in the subject index. For example, when looking for classroom chairs with table arms, the first step is to look under chairs in the subject index. Using the schedule group number found there, look in the numerical schedule index to find all contracts that may contain classroom chairs with table arms.

Once the designer has learned how to utilize this publication, the literature needed to complete a project must still be secured. Because contracts are expiring and being renewed all year long, each issue of *Source One Master* is incomplete the minute it rolls off the presses. However, this is still the best available resource for specifying government furnishing and is extremely helpful. The current *Source One Master* is available through IHS/VSMF Sales Office, 15 Inverness Way East, Englewood, CO, 80150; phone (303) 790-0600 or (800) 525-7052.

Organizations

The Council of Federal Interior Designers (CFID), a new professional organization, has been created specifically to identify and deal with problems in the design field that are uniquely government. CFID suggests FIDER and NCIDQ to assist in the professional development of the field. This organization is open only to designers who are currently employed by the federal government. For information, write to the Council of Federal Interior Designers, P.O. Box 27565, Washington D.C. 20038.

Another organization that applies to government interior designers is the Building Owners and Managers Association (BOMA). BOMA offers educational courses that, when completed, provide an RPA designation. These courses are used as part of GSA's training program within the Real Estate Division for Assignment and Leasing staff (refer to the GSA organizational chart). BOMA courses are part of an important link between government coworkers.

CONCLUSION

Government design offers many opportunities for the design professional. Although the paperwork associated with government design may be somewhat daunting, this provides excellent project management and control experience for a design firm's personnel. Government design provides attractive security and excellent opportunities for advancement, making it a worthwhile and exciting option for a designer to explore.

GLOSSARY OF GOVERNMENT TERMS

AAC: Alaskan Air Command
AAFC: Army, Air Force, Exchange System
ACC: Army Communications Command
ADC: Aerospace Defense Command
ADP: Automatic Data Processing
AFCC: Air Force Communications Command
AFCS: Air Force Communications Service
AFLC: Air Force Logistics Command
AFOSR: Air Force Office of Scientific Research
AFSC: Air Force Systems Command
AGE: Aerospace Ground Equipment
AHSC: Army Health Services Command
AMA: Air Material Area
ANSI: American National Standards Institute
APO: Army/Air Force Overseas Post Office
ARO: After Receipt of Order
ARRADCOM: Army Armament Research and Development Command
ARRCOM: Army Armament Materials Readiness Command
ASL: Atmospheric Sciences Laboratory
ASPR: Armed Service Procurement Regulation
ATC: Air Training Command
AV/ATVN: Military Phone System (Autovon)
AVRADCOM: Army Aviation Research & Development Command
BAQ: Bachelor Airmen Quarters
Billeting: Transient or Hotel Quarters
BEQ: Bachelor Enlisted Quarters
BMD: Ballistic Missile Defense
BMEWS: Ballistic Missle Early Warning System
BOD: Beneficial Occupancy Data
BOQ: Bachelor Officers Quarters
CBD: Commerce Business Daily
CECOM: Army Communications Electronics Command
CID: Commercial Item Description
CID: Comprehensive Interior Design
CNO: Chief of Naval Operations
CONAD: Continental Air Defense Command

CO: Contracting Officer
COR: Contracting Officer Representative
CSTAL: Combat Surveillance & Target Acquisition
DAR: Defense Acquisition Regulation
DARCOM: Army Material Development & Readiness Command
DARS: Defense Acquisition Regulation System
DCAS: Defense Contract Administration Services
DCASMA: Defense Contract Administrations Services–Management Area
DCASR: Defense Contract Administratino Services–Region
DEEE: Refers to Division Engineering, Engineering & Environment
DEH: Division–Engineering & Housing
DIDS: Defense Integrated Data System
DLA: Defense Logistics Agency
DOD: Department of Defense
DQ: Definite Quantity
DVQ: Distinguished Visitors Quarters
EAM: Electric Accounting Machine
ECM: Electronic Countermeasures
EA: Environmental Assessment
EIS: Environmental Impact Statement
ERADCOM: Army Electronics Research & Development Command
ETDL: Electronics Technology and Devices Laboratory
EWL: Electronics Warfare Laboratory
FAMCAMP: Air Force Travel Camp
FAR: Federal Acquisition Regulations
FBM: Fleet Ballistic Missle
FORSCOM: Armed Forces Command
FPO: Federal Protective Officer (GSA)
FPO: Fleet Post Office (DOD)
FPR: Federal Procurement Regulation
FSC: Federal Supply Classification
GEM: Ground Effect Machine
GFAE: Government-Furnished Aerospace Equipment
GFE: Government-Furnished Equipment
GOQ: General Officers Quarters
GSA: General Services Administration
HDL: Harry Diamon Laboratories
IFB: Invitation for Bid
ITT: Information Ticket or Tour & Travel
JP-4: Jet Fuel (USAF Aircraft)
JP-5: Jet Fuel (Navy Aircraft)
MAC: Military Aircraft Command
MAJCOM: Furnishing Management Officers
MAP: Military Assistance Program
MERADCOM: Army Mobility Equipment Research and Development Command
MICOM: Army Missile Material Readiness Command
MOL: Maximum Order Limitation
MOU: Memorandum of Understanding
MSA: Morale Support Activities
MSC: Military Sealift Command
MTMC: Military Traffic Management Command
MWR: Morale, Warfare, Recreation
NADC: Naval Air Development Center
NASA: National Aeronautics Space Administration
NAVAIR: Naval Air Systems Command
NAVELEX: Naval Electronics Systems Command
NAVFAC: Naval Facilities Engineering
NAVSEA: Naval Sea Systems
NGB: National Guard Bureau
NICP: National Inventory Control Point
NLABS: Army Natick Research & Development Laboratories
NMP: National Maintenance Point
NSFO: Navy Special Fuel Oil
NUSC: Naval Underwater Systems Center
NVEDL: Night Vision & Electro-Optics Laboratories
O & M: Operation and Maintenance (Manuals)
OCE: Office Chief of Engineers
ONR: Office of Naval Research
OSD: Office of Secretary of Defense
PACAF: Pacific Air Forces
PAO: Public Affairs Office
PCS: Permanent Change of Station
QPL: Qualified Product List
RDTE: Research, Development, Test & Evaluation
RFP: Request for Proposal
RFQ: Request for Quotation
SAC: Strategic Air Command
SADBUS: Small & Disadvantaged Business Utilization Specialist
SBA: Small Business Administration
SF- : Standard Form, as in Standard Form-81 (SF-81)
SFO: Solicitation for Offers
SLUC: Standard Level User Charge (Rent)
SOQ: Senior Officers Quarters
SWL: Signals Warfare Laboratory
TAC: Tactical Air Command
TDY: Temporary Duty
TECOM: Army Test & Evaluation Command
TLF: Transient Lodging Facility
TLQ: Temporary Living Quarters
TRADOC: Army Training & Doctrine Command
TSA: Army Troop Support Agency
TSARCOM: Army Troop Support & Aviation Materials Readiness Command
TSG: Army, the Surgeon General
UPEH: Unaccompanied Enlisted Personnel Housing
UOPH: Unaccompanied Officer Personnel Housing
VAQ: Visiting Airmens Quarters
VIP: Very Important Persons
VOQ: Visiting Officers Quarters
WESTCOM: Army Western Command

Military Grades

0-1 to 0-10: Officer Pay Grades (i.e. 0-6-Colonel)
E-1 to E-9: Enlisted Pay Grades

Federal Agency Grades

GS-1 to GS-11: Non-supervisory Grades
GS-11 to GS-13: Supervisory
GS-13 to GS-16: Management
GS-16 & up: Political Appointee

Facilities Management

ROBERT LEE WOLF

Facilities management is multifaceted and embraces many areas of specialization for the planning of maximum flexibility and efficiency in the workplace. The overriding goal of an organization in the coordination of physical components is to make the interior environment cost-effective, efficient, productive, aesthetically pleasing, physically safe, and ergonomically sound. At the same time, these concerns must address the profitability of the organization and the well-being of the employees.

EDUCATIONAL BACKGROUND FOR FACILITIES MANAGEMENT

A bachelor's degree in facilities management is the preferred professional prerequisite, although to date, individuals working in facilities management have come from various professional fields, including interior design, architecture, industrial design, construction, and business. It is anticipated that in the near future, formal undergraduate education will become mandatory and possibly regulated in consort with the International Facilities Management Association. Most of the existing educational programs are interdisciplinary and require a formal internship experience.

A number of graduate-level programs developing across the United States offer master's degrees to students after they have studied in residence and completed a research-based thesis or thesis project focused on some aspect of facilities management. A number of these advanced programs require a bachelor's degree in a program related either to design or to business.

Whether someone is involved with facilities management as an offshoot of another field or has obtained formal education in the profession, the educational and training emphasis must enhance that person's basic expertise in facilities management by developing the professional skills necessary to work in consort with an interdisciplinary team. It is important to obtain an education in facilities management at an institution that provides an interdisciplinary experience. Programs associated with a design studio discipline usually address these interdisciplinary concerns and provide a working knowledge of the allied professions.

When selecting an institution, look for:

- A major in facilities management and the department affiliation.
- The breadth and depth of the facilities program and/or associated design program.
- If a major is not available, a minor in facilities management through an associated program.
- If a minor does not exist, at least 24 credit hours of free electives focused on facilities management.
- The national visibility of the program and its faculty.
- Whether or not the courses are taught by instructors with appropriate professional training and experience.
- The length of the internship program or other field experiences with industry groups.
- The facilities and their amenities.

Undergraduate requirements for degrees in facilities management may be met in either the professional or liberal arts areas. Regardless of the degree, a four-year undergraduate curriculum should include at least 25 to 35 percent (approximately 40 semester credit hours) of the total program in facilities management. The remainder of the course work should be devoted to studies directly related to the major, including working methods; evaluation criteria; vocabulary; financial significance; fundamental planning and design; and visual, verbal, and written skills.

PROFESSIONAL SKILLS AND AREAS OF KNOWLEDGE

The educational experience should develop an awareness and comprehensive understanding of the interdisciplinary functions of various facilities management roles. This includes the total facilities management team, the application of special areas of expertise in the overall team concept, and allied areas of expertise.

The educational experience must address the complexities of:

- Real estate acquisition for site selection, building lease or purchase, and property disposal.

- Facilities planning and development relative to tactical planning and policy development.
- Facilities financial forecasting and budgeting relative to capital, operating expenses, and furniture and fixtures.
- Long-range facilities planning covering a period of three to ten years.
- Programming for interior space planning, workstation specifications, installation, and space management.
- Architectural and engineering planning and design services, including interior and system design, code compliance, and construction management.
- Evaluation of estimates for new construction and/or renovation; maintenance and operations management of the physical plant.
- Telecommunications integration, security, and general administrative services.

The primary educational requirement for facilities management is a solid and accurate working knowledge of these areas within the constraints of the existing structure and system. Without a sound base of information and a current network of resources, the practitioner will be handicapped. Each of these help the designer/facilities manager create and maintain cost-efficient spaces for high productivity as well as a pleasant working environment.

BUSINESS AND PROJECT MANAGEMENT IN FACILITIES MANAGEMENT

As a business function, facilities management involves two levels of managerial/administrative activity. The first is the use of the organization's facilities to achieve its organizational objectives, both long- and short-term. The second is the effective management of the departments or units within the organization. Of particular importance are the following:

- *Maintenance/operations* includes furniture/finish maintenance, housekeeping, breakdown, and security landscape.
- *Space management* includes inventory, furniture standards, allocations, and forecasting.
- *Master interior planning* emphasizes plan development and furniture specifications.
- *Interior installations* includes major moves, postoccupancy evaluation, furniture inventory, and user surveys.
- *Architecture/engineering services* includes construction management and code compliance.
- *Real estate* covers building lease, site selection, site acquisitions, property disposal, and appraisals.
- *Long-range facilities planning* focuses on emergency planning, energy planning, and strategic planning.
- *Financing/budgeting* covers operations and capital budgets, furniture budgets, and major financing.

UNIQUE DESIGN PROBLEMS IN FACILITIES MANAGEMENT

Because facilities management focuses on the coordination of the workplace, unique design problems center on interdisciplinary and interdepartmental issues. Problems related to telecommunications, energy conservation, automation, growth rate, lease negotiations, property disposal, data collection, and measurement are among the most often cited by professionals in this field. Without proper understanding and experience, the uninformed facility manager runs the risk of mounting costs associated with unforeseen problems such as toxic substances, delays in the building process, inefficient space allocations and considerations for department expansion, redesign and construction associated with rebuilding, and expenses related to unanticipated multiple relocation of personnel.

RESOURCES, CONSULTANTS, AND PROFESSIONAL ORGANIZATIONS IN FACILITIES MANAGEMENT

The network of resources one develops in the profession is vital to a smooth, well-organized operation. Every professional/manager has a personal list that forms the basis of his or her operation. Resources are identified by referral and/or quality of past performance. The selection of talented, reliable consultants is not to be taken lightly: It is the most important aspect in the management of a facility. It is imperative that consultants be active team players. The selection of an experienced consultant who represents the designer's interest in the facilities management process means that the firm and client are provided with the maximum design value for the investment.

Important networks for facility planners are architects, interior designers, lighting designers, engineers, performance and productivity analysts, life/fire safety and barrier-free specialists, product representatives or manufacturers, audio and video systems specialists, computer-aided design/software management system installers, and inventory management specialists.

Professional organizations are of prime importance to any practicing professional. These organizations not only help in the networking process but support the practitioner with continuing education course work, and involvement with local and regional professionals and legislative endeavors. The most notable organizations that support facilities management are the International Facilities Management Association, the Design Management Institute, the European Facilities Management Network, the Institute of Administrative Management, the Construction Industry Computing Association, and the International Association of Corporate Real Estate Executives.

Sports Facility Design

DOUG STEAD

In general there are two types of sports facilities, and both use designers. One type is private because it is used primarily to support major league sports activities. The second type is public, open to the general public for the purpose of fitness and exercise. A more accurate name for this type of facility is an exercise club. Because the demand for these facilities has increased with the public's sensitivity to health and fitness, this article focuses on exercise clubs.

ESTABLISHING IDENTITY

Because they are open to the general public, exercise clubs must appeal to diverse groups. These clubs tend to proliferate in urban and suburban areas, so they are very competitive with one another. This means that the fees must be kept within a suitable market range, while at the same time the club must be attractive and equipped with the latest in fitness equipment. It is a challenge for the interior designer to accomplish this—particularly with a limited budget, which is often the case.

One of the first design considerations is identity. In instances where a building has been designed distinctively as an exercise club, identity is not as big a problem. However, in many cases a club is located in a high-traffic area, such as a shopping mall or converted corner building. In all cases, signage is extremely important in establishing the club's identity.

In addition to signage, identity for the facility can be established by utilizing windows effectively. A view of a high-activity area—such as exercise bicycles or stair machines—will catch people's interest from the outside and clearly identify the facility. The view of activities acts like a display window for the facility.

Exercise clubs rely on a high traffic flow—in particular, on traffic generated because of a promotion or solicitation. In order to stay in business, exercise clubs need a constant turnover of new members. It is common for a new client to be someone who has never—or rarely—exercised at a club and suddenly decides to get in shape. Typically, this person will look for a club in a highly traveled area and join. After about two weeks to a month, the interest wanes, and eventually the person stops going. In most cases, these individuals continue to pay dues, and the club continues to promote new memberships. This is the profile of clientele with the exception of the regulars who are committed to fitness and utilize the club routinely.

MARKETING THE EXERCISE CLUB

The exercise club can be thought of as a selling environment. Most clubs employ an active sales staff who solicit and greet prospective new members, show them around, and entice them to join. From a designer's perspective, this means that the club has to look up to date, inviting, and bright, and it must provide a certain comfort level. The interior cannot be threatening or imposing .

In the old days of gymnasiums, the environment was male-dominated with boxing and weight-lifting as the main forms of workout. The high-tech fitness apparatus of today was not available. In today's exercise clubs and with the focus on aerobics, at least 50 percent of the exercise club's members are women. Colors used must be generic enough to be unisex in their appeal. Because of the high turnover in members, exercise clubs should use materials that are highly resistant to vandalism, of lasting quality, and easy to maintain.

SPACE PLANNING

Of primary importance is the entrance and an adequate reception area. The reception area serves several different functions. First, it provides an area for the identification of members as they enter the club. For convenience, members should not wait but pass through. Therefore, a seating or waiting area is normally discouraged.

A second important function of the reception area is to allow members to make appointments for racquetball courts, tanning beds, trainers, and so forth. In some cases, where these items are not included in the membership fee, cash is obtained for such services. To accommodate these activities, a 42-inch stand-up counter is required. In a small club it should accommodate from two to six people. This enables one person the freedom to deal with the constant flow of members, and others behind the counter the freedom to deal with new prospects, inquiries, and phones.

A third function of the reception area is greeting prospective new members. Adjacent to the main reception counter should be a waiting area where prospective new members can sit, fill out any required paperwork, read, or just wait for an available salesperson. Reasonably close to the reception area should be the sales area. This should contain six to eight desks with two side chairs at each desk. Depending on the client's wishes and the space available, privacy walls can be provided around each desk area. These walls should maintain a high degree of visibility, either open or glazed. If possible, the sales area should have a view of the reception area, and an entrance should be provided from the sales area into the club. This allows the salesperson to sit at his or her desk while talking to a prospect before taking the prospect on a club tour.

SHOWER AND LOCKER ROOMS

Shower and locker facilities should be located close to the reception area, or with a direct access route to it. Adequate lockers, toilets, lavatories, and showers should be provided. In larger facilities these areas may also contain saunas, steam rooms, and whirlpool baths. Specific design requirements for these facilities should be cleared with local health officials. Most people prefer individual shower stalls as opposed to gang showers. Although men do not mind gang showers, women will avoid clubs that do not have private shower facilities.

Maintenance is a big issue in shower and locker room areas. For this reason the use of ceramic tile is recommended on the floors and exposed wall surfaces in the locker area. Tile is not necessary behind lockers. A floor tile color of mid-gray with a mottled texture works best in the shower and locker rooms. This color hides hair and powders that fall on it during the day and prevent it from looking soiled. To guarantee cleanliness, there should be plenty of floor drains with a proper slope for drainage.

Floor tile should always be mudset and not thinset. Thinset tile comes loose very easily and mudset does not. Mudset tile also allows the floor to be properly sloped. Floor drains should be self-primed to avoid drying out and allowing sewer gas into the locker room. Using the approach of placing tile from the floor up the face of the locker bench to a wainscot height on the walls creates a bathtub effect throughout the locker room. This allows the maintenance staff to hose the entire floor down at the end of each day. If the locker room is located above the ground floor, a waterproof membrane under the entire floor area is necessary. If there is a lot of wetness, you need the membrane regardless.

Benches for people to place their belongings on or sit on while dressing are an important feature of showers and locker rooms. Because loose benches or benches in front of lockers get in the way of traffic flow, the creation of a locker base that extends to form a bench is a functional design solution to this problem. Maple wood is preferred because it is warm to sit on and will not splinter. A couple of coats of stain and six or more coats of polyurethane on the maple wood creates a very hard surface that can always be refinished. Tile benches are not advised because they are cold to sit on and will chip if heavy items such as padlocks are dropped on them.

The layout of the locker area is important and should be discussed carefully with the club owner. In certain clubs, theft is a big problem. Despite warnings to members about liability for valuables left in locker rooms, club owners can still be sued. It is not a wise solution to fill the space with lockers, because only 30 to 50 percent of a club's members use lockers; the rest arrive ready to work out. Filling the locker rooms with as many lockers as possible creates corners and pockets where someone could break in with out being seen. One solution to this is to provide an open locker area with lockers around the perimeter only. In addition, by alternating half lockers with full lockers, the number of lockers can be maintained while providing an open space in the middle of the room. This makes access to lockers easier and creates a more comfortable, less tense environment. If the lockers are not ceiling height, then a soffit is important to include so that these areas do not become a collection point for dust and trash. A workable sequence of spaces in locker rooms is to provide lockers upon entering, then lavatory counter area, toilets, and finally showers. This keeps the steamy wet areas furthest away from the dry areas.

A major concern in the locker area is the deterioration of the facility because of rust and corrosion caused by airborne water vapor. One of the biggest contributors to this problem is air conditioning. When cold air is introduced into a warm environment such as a shower room, the amount of steam and condensation increases dramatically. This problem can be solved by the removal of doors between the locker area and the main exercise rooms and strategically placing exhaust ducts that draw cool air from the exercise area through the locker room. Privacy is created by the juxtaposition of privacy walls that allow people to enter and exit the space without opening doors. This is especially convenient when they are carrying workout bags and other associated equipment. This approach drastically reduces the moisture in locker areas, thus preventing rust and corrosion, while the air passing through keeps the room cool. At least five air changes per hour in a low-activity club to ten air changes per hour in a high-activity club are recommended .

Hard lid ceilings in locker areas are the best solutions, but use of a suspended ceiling in some areas may be necessary. Painted aluminum grid systems and vinyl faced gypsum lay-in ceiling tiles take more abuse and last longer. Careful attention should also be paid to light fixtures and ceiling grilles. The use of aluminum or plastic materials wherever possible to avoid rust or corrosion is highly recommended. Other considerations in locker areas include:

- *Self-metering faucets*: This is critical in areas where water shortages are a concern.
- *Pressure-balanced shower controls:* These prevent showers from scalding or freezing people when toilets are flushed.
- *Flush-valve toilet fixtures instead of tanks*: These fixtures take more abuse and do not clog as easily.
- *Electric wall-mounted hand and hair dryers*: These are cleaner and produce less trash than paper towels.

● *Sealed mirrors*: Unsealed mirrors corrode on the back over time.

● *Ceiling-mounted toilet partitions made of solid-core plastic laminate or plywood:* Ceiling-mounted toilet partitions are easier to clean around, especially if the club's maintenance staff uses a hose. (These partitions should be heavily braced because members will do chin-ups on them.) Plastic laminated partitions will not rust or corrode.

● *Properly secured accessories:* Such accessories include grab bars for handicap toilets and counter tops. Because these areas can be subject to a lot of misuse and abuse, it is important that items cannot be easily pulled away from the walls.

CHILD-CARE AREA

Many clubs provide a child-care area where a nominal fee is charged for this service. Depending on the size of the club, an area of 100 to 300 square feet is appropriate. If possible, a child-size toilet should be provided so the care taker doesn't have to leave the area while attending a child who has to use the bathroom. Placement of a sink in the play area where it can be observed is important. Other things to consider in the child-care area include a playpen for very small children; storage for toys; small tables and chairs; and bright, stimulating colors and lighting.

EXERCISE WORKOUT AREA

Although this area represents at least 75 percent of the facility, from a design standpoint it is the least technical. There is great opportunity for creativity in this area because it is generally an open space.

The aerobics area should allow for approximately 30 to 50 square feet per person. Most clubs need to accommodate about 100 people, so 3,000 to 5,000 square feet meet these requirements. A strategically placed stage, no more than seven inches in height, is required for the instructor. Close at hand for the instructor should be music equipment, such as an amplifier and cassette deck. Most instructors have custom-made aerobic tapes tailored to suit their particular program. Having the equipment close at hand allows them to adjust volume or make selections as they deem appropriate during the routine. The stereo equipment is usually placed in a lockable cabinet mounted on the wall. This prevents theft or unauthorized use when the aerobics area is not being used.

Speakers for the sound system are best placed at the four corners of the aerobics area and preferably below the suspended ceiling. The speakers should be angled downward toward the floor at a 45-degree angle and pointed toward the center of the aerobics area. This gives the best dispersion of sound and prevents the loud noise from disturbing neighbors. Soundproofing around this area may be necessary.

In addition to adequate air conditioning, some powerful commercial fans, mounted high, blowing down on the exercisers may be needed. These should be the oscillating type to ensure coverage across the entire area and, like the sound speaker, located in each corner of the room.

Careful attention must be paid to the floor covering, since miscalculation can result in injury to the exerciser. Too thin a material could result in sore joints, back injuries, or shin splints. Too thick a material can result in a loss of stability, causing ankle injuries and sprains. A good quality cut pile carpet between 3/8 and 1/2 inch in thickness is recommended. Underneath the carpet, a pad of 1/2-inch sodium silicate rubber closed-cell foam or similar pad should be used. This will give an overall thickness of one inch of material that is not too soft but will absorb the energy impact that might otherwise cause injuries. This combination also wears extremely well.

The carpet fiber should be man-made and static-free. Do not use a carpet made from wool or with a jute backing. The sweat from the exercisers will rot a jute-back carpet, and wool produces offensive odors. A carpet with an antimicrobial agent is best. This helps to protect the carpet from the growth of fungus, bacteria, and mold and keeps it fresh and odor-free. Acoustically, carpet keeps the noise of exercisers down so that the music and the instructor can be heard clearly. The foam pad should be directly glued to the existing floor if possible. Do not glue it over existing carpet. The new carpet should then be directly glued to the foam pad, creating a monobond installation. This will prevent the carpet from moving and rippling during use.

Mirrors play an important part in aerobics, enabling people to evaluate their exercise form. Mirrors should be placed behind the instructor, who is facing the class. They should be 8 feet high and cover the entire area. Side mirrors can also be advantageous. Mirrors placed opposite each other should be avoided as this creates an infinity effect and can cause dizziness or nausea. It is important that mirrors be installed correctly because any distortion can cause unpleasant effects.

A designer can let imagination and creativity rule the rest of the aerobics space. Ideas such as unusual color, graphics, and even neon lights have been used effectively in these spaces. Don't forget the ceiling when planning the aerobics space. Because many exercises are done lying on the floor looking at the ceiling, it can become an important design element.

WORKOUT EQUIPMENT

In today's modern high-tech health and exercise club, the workout equipment provides computerized readouts. Good electrical distribution is essential to accommodate this equipment. If outlets can be buried in the floor in areas where the machines are placed in the open, this eliminates safety hazards and creates a better design.

Machines and equipment are normally laid out with the help of the owner, trainers, and equipment supplier. In some instances the location of machines is based upon muscle groups such as leg machines together, abdominal machines together, and so forth. In other cases they are laid out according to the trainer's circuit training program.

Some clubs integrate free weights such as barbells and dumbbells among their machines, but most separate them into their own area. This separation allows for a different floor finish from the machine area, which should be carpeted. It also allows the serious body builders to maximize the weights on the machines. When the areas are separated, the free-weight area should have rubber tile flooring made especially for this type of use. It is easy to maintain and doesn't get damaged when weights are dropped. It also saves the weights from getting damaged. In both areas, good placement of mirrors is important so that the people working out can see themselves as they exercise. Other considerations in the workout and exercise area include:

- *Water coolers*: People exercising need easy access to water coolers.
- *Clocks:* Many people work out to a specific deadline, and others want to time their workouts. Locker room clocks are also important so that people can keep track of other appointments.
- *Juice or snack bar:* This provides additional income to the club. Clubs that don't have bars of some kind may want an area set aside for vending machines.
- *Sports shop:* A captive audience will often use an in-house shop for items they use all the time such as racquetballs, gloves, and shampoo. There is also a market for clothing that they might buy on impulse or that replaces clothing damaged during exercising.
- *Pay telephones:* Some clubs buy their own pay phones to provide an additional income source.

CONCLUSION

Designing any type of exercise club or other sports facility is an intriguing challenge. Many of the design concerns that must be addressed are the same regardless of whether it is a public or private facility. The challenge to the designer is to create a space that provides adequate and functional support for the sports activities that go on, while at the same time creating an attractive and appropriate atmosphere.

Notes and Bibliography

Numbered entries are notes and unnumbered entries are bibliography. They are listed one chapter at a time.

Philosophical Framework
Kerwin Kettler

Abbott, Andrew. *The System of Professions: An Essay on the Division of Expert Labor.* University of Chicago Press, 1988.
Ben-David, Joseph. "Professions in the Class System of Present Day Societies." *Current Sociology,* 1964, pp. 247-330.
Bledstein, Burton. *The Culture of Professionalism: The Middle Class and the Development of Higher Education in America.* New York: W.W. Norton, 1978.
Bucher, Rue, and Joan G. Stelling. *Becoming Professional.* Beverly Hills, Calif.: Sage, 1977.
Carr-Saunders, A.M., and P.A. Wilson. *The Professions,* London: Frank Cass & Company, Ltd., 1964.
Cullen, John B. *The Structure of Professionalism.* New York: Petrocelli, 1978.
Derber, Charles. *Professionals as Workers: Mental Labor in Advanced Capitalism.* Boston: G.K. Hall, 1982.
Dingwall, Robert, and Philip Lewis. *The Sociology of the Professions: Lawyers, Doctors and Others.* New York: St. Martin's, 1983.
Freidson, Eliot. *Professional Powers: A Study of the Institutionalization of Formal Knowledge.* University of Chicago Press, 1986.
Hughes, Everett C. "Professions." *Daedalus,* Vol. 92, pp. 655-668, 1963.
Larson, Magali Sarfatti. *The Rise of Professionalism, A Sociological Analysis.* Berkeley: University of California Press, 1979.
Levy, Richard Michael. *The Professionalization of American Architects and Civil Engineers, 1865-1917,* Ph.D. Dissertation, University of California, Berkeley, 1980.
Lynn, Kenneth S., ed. *The Professions in America.* Boston: Houghton Mifflin, 1965.
Moore, Wilbert Ellis. *The Professions: Roles and Rules.* New York, Russell Sage Foundation, 1970.

Philosophical Framework
Norman Dehaan

1. William Duff, *An Essay on Original Genius and its Various Modes of Exertion in Philosophy and the Fine Arts* (Delmar, N.Y.: Scholars' Facsimilies and Reprints, 1978). Reprint of 1767 edition.

Design and Human Ecology
Ronald Beckman

1. From a speech by Joseph Esherick at a Gold Medal Honors and Awards Luncheon for the American Institute of Architects, St. Louis Art Museum, 1989.

Space, Memory, and Visualization
Catherine Bicknell

1. Frances A. Yates, *The Art of Memory* (University of Chicago Press, 1974).
2. Merleau Ponty, *Phenomenology of Perception,* trans. Corin Smith (New York: Humanity Press, 1962).

Education
Ronald M. Veitch

Appointment, Tenure and Promotion: A Position Paper on Criteria for Evaluation of Interior Design Faculty in Post-Secondary Institutions. IDEC, Richmond, Va., January 1985.
Covington, D. *A Review of the Role of the Liberal Arts in the First Professional Degree.* FIDER, 1985.
Definition of an Interior Designer. New York: NCIDQ, 1989.
Dohr, J., et al. *A Study of Two Year Para-Professional Interior Design Programs.* FIDER, 1987.
FIDERFORM 401: *FIDER Standards and Guidelines for the Accreditation of the Pre-Professional Assistant Level Program in Interior Design.* FIDER, 1989.
FIDERFORM 402: *FIDER Standards and Guidelines for the Accreditation of First Professional Degree Level Programs in Interior Design.* FIDER, 1989.
FIDERFORM 403: *FIDER Standards and Guidelines for the Accreditation of Post-Professional Masters Degree Programs in Interior Design.* FIDER, 1989.
Friedmann, A. *A Critical Study of Interior Design Education.* IDEC, Amherst, Mass., 1969.
Hardy, D., et al. *The Interior Design Practice: Qualifying Factors of Competent Practice.* NCIDQ, 1984.
Jackman, D., and D. James. "A Study of Recommendations Based on Evaluations of Student Work in Selected Baccalaureate and Professional School Programs." *Journal of Interior Design Education Research,* Vol. 11, No. 2, Fall 1985.
Rogers, Kate E. *From Your Point of View.* FIDER, 1979.
——, et al. *The Study of Two-Three-and Four-Year Interior Design Programs in the United States and Canada - Phase II.* FIDER, 1982.
Smith, Ray C. *Interior Design in 20th Century America: A History.* New York: Harper & Row, 1987.
Veitch, R.M. *NCIDQ Qualifying Factors of Competent Practice Related to FIDER Categories and Content Units.* FIDER, 1984.
——. *The History and Philosophy of the FIDER Standards and Guidelines.* FIDER, 1989.

Design Research
Jo Ann Asher Thompson

1. John Zeisel, *Inquiry by Design* (New York: Cambridge University Press, 1984), p. 18.
2. Stanley Abercrombie, *A Philosophy of Interior Design* (New York: Harper & Row), p. 165.
3. John Zeisel, op. cit., p. 32.
4. John Zeisel, op. cit., pp. 3, 5, and 18.

Professional Practice Choices: Overview of the Profession
Joyce Burke-Jones

Larson, Magili Sarfatti, George Leon, and Jay Bolick. "The Professional Supply of Design: A Descriptive Study of Architectural Firms," in *Professionals and Urban Form,* ed. Judith R. Blau, Mark E. LaGory, and John S. Pipkin. Albany: State University of New York Press, 1983.
The Coxe Group, Inc. *Success Strategies for Design Professionals.* New York: McGraw-Hill, 1987.
Coxe, Weld. *Managing Architectural & Engineering Practice.* New York: Wiley, 1980.

Guidelines for Starting a Practice
Diane B. Worth

1. Harry Siegel, *A Guide to Business Principles and Practices for Interior Designers,* rev. ed. (New York: Watson-Guptill, 1982), p. 19.
2. Magili Sarfatti Larson is a well-known sociologist who has written several books.
3. Andrew Loebelson, *How to Profit in Contract Design* (New York: Interior Design Books, Van Nostrand Reinhold, 1983), p. 137.
4. John Myer, *Accounting for Non-Accountants* (American Research Council, Inc., Grayson Russell, Inc., 1967), p. 1.

Getz, Lowell. *Business Management in the Smaller Design Firm.* Newton, Mass.: Practice Management Associates, Ltd., 1986.
Justis, Robert R. *Managing Your Small Business.* Englewood Cliffs, N.J.: Prentice Hall, 1981.
Loebelson, Andrew. *How to Profit in Contract Design.* New York: Interior Design Books, division of Whitney Communications Corp., 1983.
Myer, John B. *Accounting for Non-Accountants.* American Research Council, Inc., Grayson Russell, Inc., 1967.
Petrowski, Christine. *Professional Practice for Interior Designers.* New York: Van Nostrand Reinhold, 1989.
Siegel, Harry. *A Guide to Business Principles and Practices for Interior Designers.* New York: Whitney Library of Design, 1982.
Stasiowski, Frank, and Lowell Getz. *Financial Management for the Design Professional.* New York: Whitney Library of Design, 1984.
Worth, Diane B. *Designers Reference Handbook: Management and Cost Accounting for Interior Designers.* Scottsdale, Ariz.: Interior Consultants Inc., 1989.

Strategic Planning and Management
Martha G. Rayle and Sandra H. Sober

1. From a presentation made to ASID leaders by Harrison Coerver and Associates, Management Consultants, Affiliate of Lawrence-Lelter and Co., Kansas City, Mo.

The Project Control Book
Sheila Danko

Abercrombie, S. *A Philosophy of Interior Design.* New York: Harper & Row, 1990.
Becker, F. *The Total Workspace.* New York: Van Nostrand Rheinhold, 1990.
Broom, H.N., and Justin Longenecker. *Small Business Management.* Cincinnati: South-Western Publishing Co., 1975.
Burden, E. *Design Presentations.* New York: McGraw-Hill, 1984.
——. *Design Communication.* New York: McGraw-Hill, 1987.

Burstein, D., and F. Stasiowski. *Project Management for the Design Professional.* New York: Whitney Library of Design, 1982.
Coxe, W., et al. *Success Strategies for Design Professionals.* New York: McGraw-Hill, 1987.
——. *Marketing Architectural and Engineering Services.* New York: Van Nostrand Reinhold, 1971.
Epstein, L. *Legal Forms for the Designer.* New York: Design Publications, 1977.
Flaugher, R. *Report of the Job Analysis of Interior Design.* New York: National Council for Interior Design Qualification, 1988.
Getz, L. and Frank Stasiowski. *Financial Management for the Design Professional: A Handbook for Architects, Engineers, and Interior Designers.* New York: Whitney Library of Design, 1984.
Jones, G. *How to Market Professional Design Services.* New York: McGraw-Hill, 1983.
Kleeman, W. *The Challenge of Interior Design.* Boston: CBI, 1981.
Kliment, Stephen. *Creative Communications for a Successful Design Practice.* New York: Whitney Library of Design, 1977.
Lawson, B. *How Designers Think.* London: Butterworth Architecture, 1988.
Loebelson, A. *How to Profit in Contract Design.* New York: Interior Design Books, 1983.
Merrifield, D. Bruce. *Guide to Innovation Resources and Planning for the Smaller Business.* Springfield, Va.: U.S. Dept. of Commerce National Technical Information Service, 1984.
Morgan, J. *Marketing for the Small Design Firm.* New York: Whitney Library of Design, 1984.
NCIDQ Examination Guide. New York: National Council for Interior Design Qualification, 1989.
Pile, J. *Interior Design.* Englewood Cliffs, N.J.: Prentice-Hall, Inc, 1988.
Piotrowski, Christine. *Professional Practice for Interior Designers.* New York: Van Nostrand Reinhold, 1989.
Reznikoff, S. C. *Specifications for Commercial Interiors.* New York: Whitney Library of Design, 1989.
Rose, Stuart. *Achieving Excellence in Your Design Practice.* New York: Whitney Library of Design. 1987.
Rossman, W. *The Effective Architect.* Englewood Cliffs, N.J.: Prentice Hall, Inc., 1972.
Shoshkes, E. *The Design Process.* New York: Whitney Library of Design, 1989.
Siegel, H. *This Business of Interior Design.* New York: Whitney Library of Design, 1976.
—— and Siegel, A. *A Guide to Business Principles and Practices for Interior Designers*, rev. ed. New York: Whitney Library of Design, 1982.
Stasiowski, F. *Negotiating Higher Design Fees.* New York: Whitney Library of Design, 1985.
Stin, Fred. *Design Office Management Handbook.* Santa Monica, Calif.: Arts and Architecture Press, 1986.
Tropman, J., and M. Gersh. *Meetings--How to Make Them Work for You.* New York: Van Nostrand Reinhold, 1985.
Wade, John W. *Architecture, Problems and Purposes.* New York: John Wiley and Sons, 1977.

Residential Design
Jack Lowery

1. Joan Kron, *Home-Psych: The Social Psychology of Home and Decoration* (New York: Clarkson N. Potter, 1983).
2. Witold Ribezynski, *Home, A Short History of an Idea.*
3. The designers quoted in this chapter shared their opinions and experiences by filling out a questionnaire and returning it to Jack Lowery. Their contributions are much appreciated.
4. Stanley Abercrombie, *A Philosophy of Interior Design* (New York, Harper & Row, 1990), p. 11-15.

Office Design
Peter B. Brandt

Bailey, Stephen. *Offices.* London: Butterworth Architecture, 1990.
Becker, Franklin. *The Total Workplace.* New York: Van Nostrand Reinhold, 1990.
Binder, Stephen. *Corporate Facility Planning.* New York: McGraw-Hill, 1989.
Brill, Michael with Stephen T. Margulis, Ellen Konar, and the Buffalo Organization for Social and Technological Innovation (BOSTI). *Using Office Design to Increase Productivity* (2 vols.). Buffalo: Workplace Design and Productivity, Inc., 1984.
Harris, David, et al. *Planning and Designing the Office Environment.* New York: Van Nostrand Reinhold, 1981.
Klein, Judy Graf. *The Office Book.* New York: Facts on File, 1982.
Pile, John. *Open Office Planning.* New York: Whitney Library of Design, 1978.
Probst, Robert. *The Office—A Facility Based on Change.* Zeeland, Mich.: Herman Miller, Inc., 1968.
Pulgram, William L., and Richard E. Stonis. *Designing the Automated Office.* New York: Whitney Library of Design, 1984.
Saphier, Michael. *Office Planning and Design.* New York: McGraw-Hill, 1968.
——. *Planning the New Office.* New York: McGraw-Hill, 1978.
Shoshkes, Lila. *Space Planning.* New York: Architectural Record Books, 1976.

Health Care Design
Jim Seeks

1. *Hospital Administration Terminology*, 2nd ed. (American Hospital Association, 1987).

Historic Preservation and Rehabilitation
Josette Rabun and Robert Meden

1. William J. Murtagh, *Keeping Time: The History and Theory of Preservation in America* (Pittstown, N.J.: The Main Street Press, 1988), pp. 213 and 216-217.
2. Meden, Robert Paul, *Historic Preservation: The Compatibility of Contemporary Lighting Techniques* (Ann Arbor, Mich.: University Microfilms International, 1989), p. 68.
3. Murtagh, William J., op. cit., p. 206.
4. Hosmer, Charles B., Jr., *Preservation Comes of Age, Vol. 1* (Charlottesville: University Press of Virginia, 1981), pp. 562-577.
5. Mulloy, Elizabeth D., *The History of the National Trust for Historic Preservation* (Washington, D.C.: The Preservation Press, 1984), pp. 11-13.
6. Keune, Russell V., *The Historic Preservation Yearbook* (Bethesda, Md.: Adler & Adler, 1984), pp. 7-19.
7. Meden, Robert Paul, op. cit, pp. 73-74.
8. Ibid., pp. 74-75.
9. Maddex, Diane, ed., *The Brown Book: A Directory of Preservation Information* (Washington, D.C.: National Park Service, Preservation Press, 1983), p. 66.
10. Ibid., p. 67.
11. Keune, Russell V., *The Historic Preservation Yearbook* (Bethesda, MD: Adler & Adler, 1984), pp. 314-317.
12. Ibid., p. 370.
13. U.S. Department of the Interior, *Preservation: Tax Incentives for Historic Buildings* (Washington, D.C.: National Park Service and National Conference of State Historic Preservation Officers, 1987), p. 2.
14. Orin M. Bullock, Jr., *The Restoration Manual* (Norfolk, Conn.: Silvermine Publishers, 1966), p. 2.
15. National Register of Historic Places, *National Register Bulletin 16: Guidelines for Completing National Register Forms, Part B* (Washington, D.C.: National Park Service, 1990), p. iii.
16. Diane Maddex, ed., *All About Old Buildings: The Whole Preservation Catalog* (Washington, D.C.: Preservation Press, 1983), p. 324.
17. William C. Shopsin, *Restoring Old Buildings for Contemporary Uses* (New York: Whitney Library of Design, 1989), p. 54.
18. James Marston Fitch, *Historic Preservation: Curatorial Management of the Built World* (New York: McGraw-Hill, 1982), p. 179.
19. William J. Murtagh, op. cit., p. 75.
20. For example, see *Interpreting the Secretary of the Interior's Standards for Rehabilitation: Nos. 81-017, 82-024, 87-082, 88-099, and 88-100* (Washington, D.C.: Preservation Assistance Division, National Park Service, U.S. Department of the Interior).
21. F. Neale Quenzel, "Assessing the Condition of Historic Interiors Prior to Work," in *The Interiors Handbook for Historic Buildings* (Washington, D.C.: Historic Preservation Education Foundation, 1988), pp. 126-128.
22. Charles E. Fisher, ed., *Rehabilitating the Interiors of Historic Buildings*, Preservation Tech Notes series (Washington, D.C.: Preservation Press), pp. 1-162.
23. Ibid, pp. 1-166.

Blumensen, John J. G. *Identifying American Architecture: A Pictorial Guide to Styles and Terms, 1600-1945.* Nashville, Tenn.: American Association for State and Local History, 1981.
Bullock, Orin M. *The Restoration Manual: An Illustrated Guide to the Preservation and Restoration of Old Buildings.* New York: Van Nostrand Reinhold, 1983.
Burns, John A., ed. *Recording Historic Structures.* Historic American Building Survey/Historic American Engineering Record, U.S. Department of the Interior. Washington, D.C.: The American Institute of Architects Press, 1989.
Chambers, J. Henry. *Cyclical Maintenance for Historic Buildings.* Washington, D.C.: Technical Preservation Services, U.S. Department of the Interior, 1976.
Coleman, Lawrence Vail. *Historic House Museums.* Detroit: Gale Research, 1973.
Coughlin, Thomas, III. *Easements and Other Legal Techniques to Protect Historic Houses in Private Ownership.* Washington, D.C.: Historic House Program, 1981.
Dean, Jeff. *Architectural Photography: Techniques for Architects, Preservationists, Historians, Photographers and Urban Planners.* Nashville, Tenn.: American Association for State and Local History, 1982.
Deetz, James. *In Small Things Forgotten: The Archaeology of Early American Life.* Garden City, N.Y.: Anchor Press, 1977.
Diamonstein, Barbaralee. *Buildings Reborn: New Uses, Old Places.* New York: Harper & Row, 1978.
Ellsworth, Linda. *The History of a House: How to Trace It.* Nashville, Tenn.: American Association for State and Local History, 1976.
Feilden, Bernard M. *Conservation of Historic Buildings.* Woburn, Mass.: Buttersworths, 1982.
Fitch, James Marston. *Historic Preservation: Curatorial Management of the Built World.* New York: McGraw-Hill, 1982.
Gayle, Margot, David W. Look, and John G. Waite. *Metals in America's Historic Buildings: Uses and Preservation Treatments.* Washington, D.C.: Technical Preservation Services, U.S. Department of the Interior, 1980.
Gowans, Alan. *Images of American Living: Four Centuries of Architecture and Furniture as Cultural Expression.* New York: Harper & Row, 1976.
Grow, Lawrence. *The Sixth Old House Catalogue.* Pittstown, N.J.: The Main Street Press, 1988.

Harris, Cyril M. ed. *Historic Architecture Sourcebook*. New York: Dover, 1983.
Herbers, Jill. *Great Adaptations: New Residential Uses for Older Buildings*. New York: Whitney Library of Design, 1990.
Hosmer, Charles B., Jr. *Presence of the Past: A History of the Preservation Movement in the United States Before Williamsburg*. New York: Putnam, 1965.
——. *Preservation Comes of Age: From Williamsburg to the National Trust, 1926-1946*. Charlottesville: University Press of Virginia, 1981.
Hume, Gary L., and Kay D. Weeks. *The Secretary of the Interior's Standards for Rehabilitation and Guidelines for Rehabilitating Historic Buildings*. Washington, D.C.: Preservation Assistance Division, National Park Service, 1983.
Jacobs, Jane. *The Death and Life of Great American Cities*. New York: Random House, 1961.
Keune, Russell V., ed. *The Historic Preservation Yearbook*. Bethesda, Md.: Adler and Adler, 1984.
Kidney, Walter. *Working Places: The Adaptive Use of Industrial Buildings*. Pittsburgh: Ober Park Associates, 1976.
Lauziere, Kenneth E. "Fire Protection and Building Codes: Systems and Solutions," in *The Interiors Handbook for Historic Buildings*. Washington, D.C.: Historic Preservation Education Foundation, 1988.
Maddex, Diane, ed. *The Brown Book: A Directory of Preservation Information*. Washington, D.C.: National Park Service, Preservation Press, 1983.
——. *All About Old Buildings: The Whole Preservation Catalog*. Washington, D.C.: Preservation Press, 1983.
Markowitz, Arnold L., ed. *Historic Preservation: A Guide to Information Sources*. Detroit: Gale Research, 1980.
McAlester, Virginia, and Lee McAlester. *A Field Guide to American Houses*. New York: Alfred A. Knopf, 1984.
McNulty, Robert H., and Stephen A. Kliment, eds. *Neighborhood Conservation: A Handbook of Methods and Techniques*. New York: Whitney Library of Design, 1979.
Meden, Robert Paul. *Historic Preservation: The Compatibility of Contemporary Lighting Techniques*. Ann Arbor, Mich.: University Microfilms International, 1989.
Moore, Charles W., Kathryn Smith, and Peter Becker, eds. *Home Sweet Home: American Domestic Vernacular Architecture*. New York: Rizzoli, 1983.
Moss, Roger W. *Lighting for Historic Buildings*. Washington, D.C.: Preservation Press, 1988.
Mulloy, Elizabeth D. *The History of the National Trust for Historic Preservation*. Washington, D.C.: Preservation Press, 1976.
Munsell, Kenneth, and Anne Smith Denman. *Historic Preservation Resource Book for Small Communities*. Ellensburg, Wash.: Small Towns Institute, 1983.
Murtagh, William J. *Keeping Time: The History and Theory of Preservation in America*. Pittstown, N.J.: The Main Street Press, 1988.
Naeve, Milo M. *Identifying American Furniture: A Pictorial Guide to Styles and Terms*. Nashville, Tenn.: American Association for State and Local History, 1982.
National Park Service. *Preservation Briefs* (series published periodically). Washington, D.C.: The Government Printing Office.
——. *Respectful Rehabilitation: Answers to Your Questions About Old Buildings*. Technical Preservation Services, U.S. Department of the Interior. Washington, D.C.: Preservation Press, 1982.
National Register of Historic Places. *National Register Bulletin 16: Guidelines for Completing National Register Forms, Part A*. Washington, D.C.: National Park Service, 1990.
National Trust for Historic Preservation. *Basic Preservation Procedures*. Washington, D.C.: Preservation Press, 1983.
——. *Information: A Preservation Sourcebook*. Washington, D.C.: Preservation Press, 1979-1985.
——. *New Energy from Old Buildings*. Washington, D.C.: Preservation Press, 1981.
——. *Old & New Architecture: Design Relationship*. Washington D.C.: Preservation Press, 1980.
——. *Preservation and Conservation: Principles and Practices*. International Centre for the Study of the Preservation and Restoration of Cultural Property. Washington, D.C.: Preservation Press, 1976.
Nielson, Sally E., ed. *Insulating the Old House: A Handbook for the Owner*. Portland, Me.: Greater Portland Landmarks, 1979.
Nylander, Jane C. *Fabrics for Historic Buildings*, rev. ed. Washington, D.C.: Preservation Press, 1990.
Nylander, Richard C. *Wallpapers for Historic Buildings*. Washington, D.C.: Preservation Press, 1983.
Peterson, Charles., ed. *Building Early America*. Philadelphia, Pa.: Chilton, 1976.
Poppeliers, John S., Allen Chambers, and Nancy B. Schwartz. *What Style Is It? A Guide to American Architecture*, rev. ed. Washington, D.C.: Preservation Press, 1984.
Quenzel, F. Neale. *Assessing the Condition of Historic Interiors Prior to Work: The Interiors Handbook for Historic Buildings*. Washington, D.C.: Historic Preservation Education Foundation, 1988.
Roth, Leland M. *America Builds: Source Documents in American Architecture and Planning*. New York: Harper & Row, 1983.
Schmertz, Mildred F., ed. *New Life for Old Buildings*. New York: McGraw-Hill, 1982.
Seale, William. *Recreating the Historic House Interior*. Nashville, Tenn.: American Association for State and Local History, 1979.
——. *The Tasteful Interlude: American Interiors Through the Camera's Eye, 1860-1917*, rev. ed. Nashville, Tenn.: American Association for State and Local History, 1980.
Shopsin, William C. *Restoring Old Buildings for Contemporary Uses*. New York: Whitney Library of Design, 1989.
Tomas Vonier Associates. *Energy Conservation and Solar Energy for Historic Buildings: Guidelines for Appropriate Designs*. Washington, D.C.: Technical Preservation Services, U.S. Department of the Interior. National Center for Architecture and Urbanism, 1981.
U.S. Department of the Interior. *Preservation: Tax Incentives for Historic Buildings*. Washington, D.C.: National Park Service and National Conference of State Historic Preservation Officers, 1987.
Von Rosenstiel, Helene, and Winkler, Gail Caskey. *Floor Coverings for Historic Buildings*. Washington, D.C.: Preservation Press, 1988.
Weinburg, Nathan. *Preservation in American Towns and Cities*. Boulder, Colo: Westview Press, 1979.
Whiffen, Marcus, and Frederick Koeper. *American Architecture, 1607-1976*. Cambridge, Mass.: MIT Press, 1981.
Williams, Norman, Jr., Edmund Kellogg, and Frank Gilbert, eds. *Readings in Historic Preservation: Why? What? How?* New Brunswick, N.J.: Center for Urban Policy Research, Rutgers University, 1983.
Winkler, Gail Caskey, and Moss, Roger. *Victorian Interior Decoration*. New York: Henny Holt, 1987.

Periodicals:
APT Bulletin and *Communique*. Association for Preservation Technology, P.O. Box 8178, Fredericksburg, VA 22404.
Architectural Record. McGraw-Hill, Inc., 1221 Avenue of the Americas, New York, NY 10020.
Architecture: The AIA Journal. American Institute of Architects, 1735 New York Avenue NW, Washington, DC 20006.
Commercial Remodeling. 8 South Michigan Avenue, Chicago, IL 60603.
Historic Houses. Historic House Association of America, 1600 H Street NW, Washington, DC 20036.
Historic Preservation and *Preservation News*. The National Trust for Historic Preservation, 1785 Massachusetts Avenue NW, Washington, DC 20036.
History News. American Association for State and Local History, 172 Second Avenue North, Suite 102, Nashville, TN 37021.
Museum News. American Association of Museums, 1055 Thomas Jefferson Street NW, Suite 428, Washington, DC 20007.
Nineteenth Century and *The Victorian*. The Victorian Society in America, 219 East Sixth Street, Philadelphia, PA 19106.
Old-House Journal. Old House Journal Corporation, 435 Ninth Street, Brooklyn, NY 11215.
Progressive Architecture. 600 Summer Street, P.O. Box 1361, Stamford, CT 06904.
SAH Journal, *Forum*, and *Newsletter*. Society of Architectural Historians, 1700 Walnut Street, Philadelphia, PA 19103.
Technology and Conservation, One Emerson Place, Boston, MA 02114.

Facilities Management
Robert Lee Wolf

Journals:
A & D Business
Architecture and Planning Research
Facilities Management
Human Factors Bulletin
Safety Research
The Office

Books:
Binder, Stephenz. *Corporate Facility Planning*. McGraw-Hill, 1989.
Brill, M., Margulis, S., Konar, El, and BOSTI. *Using Office Design to Increase Productivity*. Buffalo, N.Y.: Workplace Design and Productivity, Vol. 1, 1984; Vol. 2, 1985.
Harris, Palmer, Lewis, Gerdes, Musnon & Meckler. *Planning and Designing the Office Environment*. New York: Van Nostrand Reinhold, 1981.
King, William R., and David I. Cleland. *Strategic Planning and Management Handbook*. New York: Van Nostrand Reinhold, 1987.
Lueder, Rani. "Designing the Electronic Office," in *The Ergonomics Payoff*. New York: Nichols, 1986.
Propst, Robert L. *The Office—A Facility Based on Change*. Ann Arbor, Mich.: Herman Miller Research Corporation, 1968.
Pulgram, William, and Richard Stonis. *Designing the Automated Office*. New York: Watson-Guptill, 1984.
Reznikoff, S.C. *Specifications for Commercial Interiors*. New York: Watson-Guptill, 1989.
Stitt, Fred. *Designing Buildings That Work*. New York: McGraw-Hill, 1985.

Authors' Biographical Sketches

ABERCROMBIE, Stanley: FAIA. Chief editor of *Interior Design Magazine*, New York, New York.

BECKMAN, Ronald: Associate professor, Department of Design and Environmental Analysis, College of Human Ecology, Cornell University.

BICKNELL, Catherine: Associate professor, Department of Apparel, Merchandising, and Interior Design, Washington State University. Holds doctor of philosophy degree from the School of Environmental Design at The Royal College of Art, London, England.

BRANDT, Peter B.: AIA, IDEC. Has private practice and teaches at the New York School of Interior Design. Registered architect in six states. Holds bachelor of architecture degree from Massachusetts Institute of Technology.

BURKE-JONES, Joyce: ASID. Director of development and associate in charge of interiors for Buckminster Fuller, Sadao & Zung Architects, Cleveland, Ohio. Holds bachelor of arts in fine arts–design from University of Michigan and master of business administration from Case Western Reserve University in Cleveland, Ohio.

CASTLEMAN, Elizabeth: ASID. Owner of Castleman Interiors, Friendswood, Texas. Holds bachelor's degree in interior design from the University of Texas at Austin.

CLARK, Carl E.: ASID. Principal of Carl Clark Interiors, Flagstaff, Arizona. Guest lecturer and instructor of interior design at Citrus College, California Polytechnic State University, and West Virginia University.

CONLEY, Patricia V.: Senior account analyst, Property and Casualty Sales, Albert H. Wohlers and Co., Park Ridge, Illinois. Member of American Business Women's Association.

DANKO, Sheila: IDEC. Associate professor, Department of Design and Environmental Analysis, College of Human Ecology, Cornell University. Principal, Sheila Danko Design, Ithaca, New York. Holds bachelor of architecture degree.

DEHAAN, Norman (deceased): AIA, FASID. Prior to death was president of Norman DeHaan Associates, Chicago, Illinois. Studied with Meis van der Rohe and served as a leader for ASID and the interior design profession throughout his lifetime.

EBSTEIN, Barbara: FASID. President of Vinick Associates, Inc., Hartford, Connecticut. Holds interior design degree from Paier College of Art in Hamden, Connecticut.

FRIEDMANN, Arnold: Ph.D., FIDEC, ASID (honorary). Professor emeritus at the University of Massachusetts at Amherst. Author of several articles and books on the interior design profession.

GANDY, Charles: FASID. President of Gandy/Peace, Inc. in Atlanta, Georgia. 1988 ASID National President. Former adjunct professor at Auburn University in the School of Architecture. Author of two books on interior design.

GREENLAW, Roger L.: ASID. Principal of Greenlaw Design Associates, Inc., in Montrose, California. Holds bachelor's degree from Syracuse University. Has served in several leadership roles for ASID, including regional vice president for Southern California.

GUEFT, Olga: Honorary Fellow of ASID and holder of the first and only AID/NSID Joint Press Award. Retired editor of *Interiors* magazine and critic-at-large.

JACKMAN, Dianne R.: FIDC, FIDEC, FPIDIM. Professor in the Department of Interior Design, Faculty of Architecture, University of Manitoba, Canada. Past chairperson of the Board of Trustees for the Foundation for Interior Design Educational Research (FIDER). Author of two textbooks on interior design.

KETTLER, Kerwin: Former dean at New York School of Interior Design, New York, New York.

KNOPF, Mary: IBD. Associate in firm of Interior Space Design, Anchorage, Alaska. Holds bachelor's degree in interior design from Washington State University.

LOWERY, Jack: IDEC, FASID. Owner of Jack Lowery and Associates, Inc., in New York, New York. Past ASID National President.

LUECK, Odette: FASID. Owner of Odette Lueck Interiors in Bowie, Maryland. Holds bachelor of fine arts from Ohio University.

MALKIN, Jain: ASID. President of Jain Malkin, Inc., in San Diego, California. A specialist in the health care field, Malkin has taught medical space planning at Harvard University and is on the Board of Directors of the National Symposium for Health Care Design. Author of several books on health care design and contributor to numerous other publications.

MEDEN, Robert: ASID, AIA, IDEC. Program chair and professor of interior design at Marymount University in Arlington, Virginia. Holds bachelor of architecture and master of architecture degrees from Kent State University and doctorate of architecture from the Catholic University of America.

NELSON-PENSKI, Charlene: IBD. Principal, The Callison Partnership, Ltd., Seattle, Washington. Holds degree in interior design from Cornish School of Allied Arts in Seattle, Washington.

POLSKY, Norman: IF member. ASID Industry Foundation member. Chairman of Fixtures Furniture, which he founded in 1947 in Kansas City, Missouri. Fixtures Furniture manufactures commercial furniture and employs more than 300 people.

RABUN, Josette: Ph.D., IDEC, Allied Member of ASID. Associate professor of interior design at the University of Tennessee–Knoxville. Holds Ph.D. in interior design from the University of Tennessee and is an expert in the area of historic preservation.

RAYLE, Martha G.: FASID. Senior associate and project manager for Stetson-Harza Architects, Engineers, Construction Managers, and Planners in Utica, New York. ASID National President in 1992. Holds interior design degree from Purdue University.

SACKS, Steven L.: CPA. President of Siegel, Sacks, & Co., P.C., in New York, New York. Holds bachelor's and master of business administration degrees from Pace University.

SEEKS, Jim: ASID, IBD. Director of design, FORMA, Seattle, Washington.

SIEGEL, Alan M.: Partner in legal firm of Levy, Sonet & Siegel. Legal counsel for ASID.

SIEGEL, Harry: CPA. Author of *A Guide to Business Principles and Practices for Interior Designers*.

SOBER, Sandra H.: ASID. Affiliated with BSW Group, Inc., Tulsa, Oklahoma.

SONET, Jerrold M.: Honorary Fellow of ASID. Partner in legal firm of Levy, Sonet & Siegel.

STEAD, Doug: ASID, IBD. Affiliated with Designtech, San Diego, California. Specialist in sports facility design.

SWAIN, David H.: AIA. Principal-in-charge at NBBJ Interiors, Seattle, Washington. Holds bachelor of architecture degree from Washington State University.

THOMPSON, Jo Ann Asher: Ph.D., ASID, IBD, IDEC. Vice provost and former chair of the Department of Apparel, Merchandising, and Interior Design at Washington State University, Pullman, Washington. Holds Ph.D. in interior design from the University of Missouri–Columbia and bachelor of science and master of arts in interior design from Iowa State University.

TREGRE, Louis (deceased): FASID. Prior to death was owner of Louis Tregre Associates, Inc., New York, New York. Was instrumental in the development of the NCIDQ exam and served as NCIDQ President until 1981.

VEITCH, Ronald M.: BID, M. Arch., FIDC, FIDEC, FPIDIM. Professor in the Department of Interior Design, Faculty of Architecture, University of Manitoba, Manitoba, Canada. Past president of Interior Designers of Canada and of Interior Design Educators Council.

VON DER HUDE, Catherine: Resource specialist with Swanke, Hayden, Connell Architects in New York, New York. Graduate of Green Mountain College and the New York School of Interior Design.

WEBSTER, Daniel: ASID. Founder and president of Webster-Kirby Design Associates, Ltd., in Bowie, Maryland. Graduate of certificate program in interior design from Philadelphia College of Art.

WILSON, Trisha: ASID. Founder and president of Wilson and Associates in Dallas, Texas. Specialist in hospitality projects.

WOLF, Robert Lee: IFMA, Allied Member of ASID. Professor and director, School of Design, College of Architecture and Environmental Design, Arizona State University, Tempe, Arizona. Received training from Southern Illinois University and the University of Missouri–Columbia.

WORTH, Diane B.: ASID. President of Interior Consultants in Scottsdale, Arizona. Associate faculty member at Arizona State University, Tempe, Arizona. Graduate of Stephens College in Columbia, Missouri.

Index

Abercrombie, Stanley, 26, 48, 169
Accounting, 66-68
Accounting for Non-Accountants (Myer), 66
Accounts payable/receivable, 89
Accreditation standards, 28-29
Activity profile, 139-40
Adaptive use projects, 197
Adler, Mortimer, 12
Advertising, 52, 53
Aesthetics, in design theory, 16
Affluent Society, The (Galbraith), 17
All About Buildings: The Whole Preservation Catalog, 194
American Institute of Design (AID), 23, 24, 27, 35, 37, 38, 43
American Institute of Interior Decorators (AIID), 23
American Society of Interior Designers, (ASID), 11, 23, 25, 37, 38, 52,82, 84, 94, 100
  continuing education, 45, 46
  ethics code, 52, 75, 80-81
  exposition, 107
  licensing, 44
Antiquities Act of 1906, 190
Arbitration, 98
Architecture, 10, 26
Architectural/design representatives, 70
Art of Memory, The (Yates), 19
Artwork, 170, 179
Asbestos, 196
Assets/liabilities management, 88-89
Associates, 60, 65
Associations, 65
Ateliers, 22

Bach, Richard F., 23
Baker, Hollis S., 22
Balance sheet, 67
Banking relationships, 66, 83, 86
Beasley, Kim A., 185
Beckman, Ronald, 17-18
Bell, Lloyd, 24
Bicknell, Catherine, 19-20
Bidding, 157-58
Bonda, Penny, 168
Bookkeeper, 68
Brandt, Peter, 172-75
Brewer, Joseph H., 22
Buatta, Mario, 168, 171
Building design, 174-75
Building Owners and Managers Association (BOMA), 211
Bullock, Orin M., Jr., 192
Burke-Jones, Joyce, 55-58
Business management, 33-34, 85-86

Capital, 66, 87
Caplan, Ralph, 12
Cash flow management, 86, 87-88, 89
Castleman, Elizabeth, 44
Chance and Symbol (Hertz), 12
Chatham, Sharon, 170, 171
Clark, Carl E., 52-54
Client
  budget, 88, 97
  deposit, 89
  directory, 129
  sign-off sheet, 136
Client relationship
  areas of dispute, 97-98
  initial contact, 114-15
  ethical guidelines, 52-53
  legal management, 34, 98
  in office design, 173
  precontract phase, 93-94
  professionalism, 86
  in residential design, 169, 171
  traditions/beliefs, 75
Code compliance, 52, 144-45, 151-52
Coerver, Harrison, 73
Community relations, 75
Computer-aided design (CAD), 103, 104, 173
Computers, 103-5, 173
Confidentiality, 53, 75
Congor, Cornelia, 13
Conley, Patricia V., 99
Constant, George, 169
Consultants, 53, 68, 71-72, 86, 130, 187
Continuing education, 45-46, 179
Contract administration, 33, 96, 104, 122-23, 159-63, 166, 186, 202
Contract documents, 32-33, 104, 121, 150-56, 165, 186, 202
Contractors, 95, 96
Corbett, Harvey Wiley, 23
Corporate standards programs, 174
Corporations, 64, 65-66, 92-93
Cost estimates, 149
Cost-plus purchase plan, 59
Council of Federal Interior Designers (CFID), 38, 211
Council on the Continuing Education Unit (CCEU), 45
Critical exposures, 83
Criticism, in design theory, 15-16
Cunningham, Ann Pamela, 190

Dahl, Eric W., 22, 23
Danko, Sheila, 110-66
Davis, Thomas, Jr., 185
Davis & Mewes, 22
Deadlines, 97
Dealerships, 70, 106
Debt financing, 65
DeHaan, Norman, 12-13, 24
Demographic analysis, 69, 82
Department of Defense, 205, 209, 210
Department stores, 199
De Saavedria, Rubén, 169, 170
De Sanis, Michael, 168
Design agreement, 34, 94-95, 96, 97-98, 116
Design centers, 59, 71, 107
Design development, 31-32, 120, 147-49, 165, 186, 201-2
Designers Forum on Continuing Education, 46
Design for Hospitality (Davis and Beasley), 185
Design research, 47-50
Design services, 172-73
Design theory, 14-15
De Wolfe, Elsie, 22
Disclaimer clause, 97
Discount stores, 200, 203
Display techniques, 200
Duff, W., 13

Ebstein, Barbara, 203-4
Economic analysis, 82
Economic Recovery Tax Act of 1981, 191
Education, professional, 10
See also Interior design, education
Educational Testing Services, 35, 36
Employees
  evaluation, 74-75, 76-79
  management, 85-86
  sources for, 71
  in start-up practice, 68
Engineering, 10
Environment/behavior, in design theory, 15
Equity financing, 65-66
Ergonomics, 107
Esherick, Joseph, 17
Essay on Original Genius and Its Various Modes of Exertion in Philosophy and the Fine Art, An (Duff), 13
Ethics, professional, 11, 52-54, 75, 80-81
Evaluation, post-occupancy, 33, 164-66
Executive order #11593, 190
Exercise club, 215-18

Facilities management, 213-14
Facilities management services, 173
Feasibility study, 194
Federal preservation officer (FPO), 194
Fee structure, 88
Field inspection report, 162
Financial management, 33-34, 87-91
Financial statements, 88, 89, 90-91
Financing, equity and debt, 65-66
Finishes, interior, 170, 200
Fisher, Charles E., 197
Fitch, James Marston, 191, 194
Foundation for Interior Design Education Research (FIDER), 23-24, 27, 28, 31, 43, 44, 185
Frankl, Eve, 170
Freelance employees, 85
Friedmann, Arnold, 14-16, 23
From the Other Shore (Herzen), 12
Function, in design theory, 15
Furniture/furnishings
  cost estimates, 149
  government contracts and, 210-11
  inventory, 141
  purchase methods, 59-60
  in residential design, 170
  safety/function of, 108
  selection criteria, 107-8
  sources for, 70-71, 106-7, 146
  See also Suppliers
Furniture industry, 22-23, 59, 106

Galbraith, John Kenneth, 17
Galle, Emil, 22
Gandy, Charles D., 85-86, 168, 169
General Services Administration, 205
Gibson, J.J., 19
Government design, 205-12
Grand Rapids, Michigan, 22-23
Great Ideas of Western Man, The, 12
Greenlaw, Roger L., 52-54
Gueft, Olga, 21-25

Hale Associates, 35
Hardware, computer, 105
Hayakawa, S.I., 12
Health care design, 176-84
Health insurance, 100
Helsel, Marjorie, 24
Hertz, Richard, 12
Herzen, Alexander, 12
Historical research, 192-94
Historic American Engineering Record (HAER), 192
Historic context, 193
Historic integrity, 193
Historic preservation and rehabilitation, 189-98
Historic Preservation: Curatorial Management of the Built World (Fitch), 191, 194
Historic significance, 193
History, in design theory, 15
History of Western Philosophy, A (Russell), 12
Hoffstatter, 22
Home, A Short History of an Idea (Rybezynski), 168
Home-Psych: The Social Psychology of Home and Decoration (Kron), 168
Hospitality design, 185-88
How to Profit in Contract Design (Loebelson), 60
Human ecology, design and, 17-18
Human resources. *See* Employees

Illinois Institute of Technology (ITT), 12

Independent contractors, 60, 65, 85
Industrial Designers Society of America (IDSA), 35
Information sources
for business start-up, 71
computers, 103-5
on government specifications, 210, 211
from industry, 106-7
library, 101-2, 210
project, 131
Inquiry by Design (Zeisel), 47
Institute of Business Designers (IBD), 38, 44, 46
Institute of Store Planners (ISP), 35, 38
Insurance, 71, 99-100
Intellectual property rights, 95
Interest rates, 82
Interior architecture, 21
Interior decoration, 21
Interior design
and allied professions, 26
certification, 35-36, 38-43
design research, 47-50
education
accreditation, 27-29
common body of knowledge, 28, 31
continuing, 45-46, 179
historic preservation, 198
hospitality design, 185
internships, 30, 68
office design, 173
residential design, 171
and facilities management, 213-14
future of, 16
government, 205-12
health care, 176-84
and historic preservation/rehabilitation, 189-98
hospitality, 185-88
as industry, 21-22
internship programs, 30-34
licensing in, 24-25, 44, 45
office, 172-75
philosophical framework, 11-16
Interior design practice
business management, 33-34, 85-86
business structure, 60-65, 92-93
contract administration, 33, 96, 104, 122-23, 159-63, 166, 186, 202
contract documents, 32-33, 95, 104, 150-56, 165, 186, 202
design development, 31-32, 120, 147-49, 165
ethical principles in, 52-54, 75, 80-81
evaluation, postoccupancy, 33, 164-66
financial management, 33-34, 87-91
firm size and, 55-58
insurance for, 71, 99-100
legal management, 71, 83, 92-98, 116, 126-27
programming, 31, 117, 137-41, 165, 186
project organization, 128-36
proposal development, 116-27
schematic design, 31, 118-19, 142-46, 165, 186
starting up, 65-72
strategic planning, 73-84
professionalism in, 16
as profession, 11, 21-22
residential, 168-71
retail store, 199-204
social responsibility and, 17-18
space/memory/visualization in, 19-20
specializations within, 26
sports facility, 215-18
Interior Design Certification Law, 24
Interior Design Educators Council (IDEC), 23, 27-28, 35, 38, 46
Interior Designers for Licensing in New York State (IDLNY), 24
Interior Designers of Canada (IDC), 38, 46
Internal Revenue Service (IRS), 195
International Association for Continuing Education and Training, 45
International Society of Interior Designers (ISID), 38, 44
Internship programs, 30-34, 68

Jackman, Dianne R., 30-34
Jacobs, Barbara, 168
Job description, 68
Joint Commission on Interior Design Accreditation, 27, 35
Joint ventures, 65

Kettler, Kerwin, 10-11
Khan, Louis, 19
Kimbel (A.) & Sons, 22
Knopf, Mary, 205-12
Kron, Joan, 168

Language in Action (Hayakawa),12
Larson, Margil, 60
Lease conditions, office design and, 173-74
Legal management, 71, 83, 92-98, 116, 126-27
Legal recognition, 10, 11, 24
Lerner, Joan, 169
Lewis, Russell, 12
Liability insurance, 99
Library, 101-2
Licensing, 44, 45
Life insurance, 100
Limited liability, corporate, 65, 92-93
Limited partnership, 63
Loebelson, Andrew, 60
Lowery, Jack, 168-70
Lighting, 170, 179, 187, 200, 203
Lueck, Odette, 45-46
Lynford, Ruth, 24

McClelland, Nancy V., 23
Malkin, Jain, 176-77
Man on a Rock (Hertz), 12
Manufacturer's representative, 70
Market analysis, 82-83
Marketing, 34, 53, 103-4
Meden, Robert, 189-98
Meeting agenda, 134
Membership restriction, 10
Memory, visual, 19-20
Merchandise marts, 107
Mies van der Rohe, 12
Moore, William R., 21, 22, 23
Morton, W. Brown, 192
Mueller, Frank W., 22
Murtagh, William J., 192, 194
Myer, John, 66

National Council for Interior Design Qualification (NCIDQ), 24-25, 28, 31, 34, 35-36, 37, 38-43, 44, 82
National Council for Preservation Education (NCPE), 198
National Historic Preservation Act of 1966, 190, 191
National Home Fashion League (NHFL), 35, 46
National Park Service (NPS), 195, 197
National Park System Organic Act of 1916, 190
National Register of Historic Places, 190, 193, 194
National Society of Interior Designers (NSID), 23, 24, 27, 35, 37, 38, 43
National Trust for Historic Preservation, 190, 194
Nelson-Penski, Charlene, 199-202
NEOCON, 107

Office design, 172-75
Office planning and design services, 172
Office/studio, 69-70, 85
Operating statement, 67

Partnership, 62, 92
Percentage-off-retail purchase plan, 59
Performance schedule, 97
Perspective method of visualization, 20
Phenomenology of Perception (Merleau Ponty), 20
Philosophy of Interior Design, A (Abercrombie), 48, 169
Phone conversation log, 135
Polsky, Norman, 106-8
Ponty, Merleau 20
Postwar America Design and Its Cultural Ramifications (Caplan), 12
Professional corporation (PC), 92, 93
Professionalism, 16, 86
Professional organizations, 10, 22-23, 175, 187-88, 202, 214
See also specific names
Professions, 10-11
Programming, 31, 117, 137-38, 165, 186
Project control book, 110-66
Project organization, 128-36
Project record, 153-56
Project review schedule, 132-33
Property insurance, 99-100
Proposal development, 116-27
Public relations, 34
Punch list, 163
Purchase orders, 95

Rambusch Company, 22
Rabun, Josette, 189-98
Rayle, Martha G., 73-84
Receptionist/switchboard operator, 68
Recording Historic Structures/Historic American Building Survey (HABS), 192
Residential design, 168-71
Restoration Manual, The (Bullock), 192
Restoring Old Buildings for Contemporary Use (Shopsin), 194
Retail store design, 199-204
Revenue Act of 1978, 191
Richardson, Frank W., 23
Risk management, 126-27
Rorimer, Louis, 23
Russell, Bertrand, 12
Rybezynski, Witold, 168

Sacks, Steven L., 87-89
St. Clair, Rita, 24
Sales representatives, 70, 83, 106
Schematic design, 31, 118-19, 142-46, 165, 186
Schwartz, Irving D., 24
Secretary, 68
Seeks, Jim, 178-84
Shopping centers, 199
Shopsin, William C., 194
Shower/locker rooms, 216-17
Showrooms, 59, 70-71, 107
Siegel, Alan M., 92-98
Siegel, Harry, 24, 59, 87-89
Sketch log, 161
Small Business Investment Companies (SBICs), 66
Smith, James Merrick, 169, 171
Sober, Sandra H., 73-84
Social analysis, 69, 82
Software, computer, 104-5
Sole proprietorship, 61, 92
Sonet, Jerrold M., 92-98
Source One Master, 211
Space, experiencing, 19-20
Space planning, 104, 179, 215-16
Specialty shops, 199-200
Specification writing, 32
Sports facility design, 215-18
State Businesses and Industrial Development Corporations (SBIDC's), 66
State historic preservation officer (SHPO), 194, 195
Stead, Doug, 215-18
Stetson-Harza Architects, Engineers, and Planners, 75
Storefront, 204
Strategic planning and management, 73-84
Subchapter S corporation, 93
Suppliers, 70-71, 75, 83, 95, 106-7, 146
Swain, David H., 103-5

Tax Equity and Fiscal Responsibility Act of 1982, 191
Tax incentives, 190-91, 194-95, 196
Tax Reform Act of 1976, 190-91
Tax Reform Act of 1986, 191
Tenant development services, 172-73
Termination clause, 97-98
Thompson, Jo Ann Asher, 47-50
Tiffany, Louis Comfort, 22
Trade shows, 107
Tregre, Louis Severin, 24, 35-36, 37

Uniform Commercial Code (UCC), 60, 70, 96

Veitch, Ronald M., 27-29
Vendor inquiry log, 148
Visual orientation, 20
Von der Hude, Catherine, 101-2

Walker, Ken, 204
Webster, Daniel, 45-46
Wilson, Trisha, 185-88
Wolf, Robert Lee, 213-14
Worth, Diane B., 59-72
Wright, Frank Lloyd, 23
Wright, Richardson, 23

Yates, Frances, 19

Zeisel, John, 47, 48